LONER AT THE BALL

Also by Fred Lawrence Guiles

NORMA JEAN
NORMA JEAN: The Life and Death of
Marilyn Monroe (revised and expanded)
MARION DAVIES
TYRONE POWER: The Last Idol
STAN: The Life of Stan Laurel
HANGING ON IN PARADISE
JANE FONDA: The Actress in Her Time

LONER AT THE BALL

THE LIFE OF
ANDY WARHOL

FRED LAWRENCE GUILES

BANTAM PRESS

LONDON · NEW YORK · TORONTO · SYDNEY · AUCKLAND

TRANSWORLD PUBLISHERS LTD
61-63 Uxbridge Road, London W5 5SA
TRANSWORLD PUBLISHERS (AUSTRALIA) PTY LTD
15-23 Helles Avenue, Moorebank, NSW 2170
TRANSWORLD PUBLISHERS (NZ) LTD
Cnr Moselle and Waipareira Aves,
Henderson, Auckland

Published 1989 by Bantam Press
a division of Transworld Publishers Ltd
Copyright © Fred Lawrence Guiles 1989
British Library Cataloguing in Publication Data

Guiles, Fred Lawrence
    Loner at the ball: the life of Andy Warhol
    1. American arts. Warhol, Andy, 1928–1987
    I. Title
    700'.92'4

ISBN 0-593-01540-1

Printed in Great Britain
by Mackays of Chatham Plc, Chatham, Kent.

take it from me kiddo
believe me
my country, 'tis of

you, land of the Cluett
Shirt Boston Garter and Spearmint
Girl with the Wrigley Eyes (of you
land of the Arrow Ide
and Earl &
Wilson
Collars) of you i
sing: land of Abraham Lincoln and Lydia E. Pinkham,
land above all of Just Add Hot Water and Serve —
from every B. V. D.
let freedom ring
amen.

e. e. cummings

To the memory of my grandparents,
Mahala and Richard, and my Aunt Florence;
and Kenneth W. Clifford (1927–87)
and Federico MacMaster (1926–87)

CONTENTS

A NOTE OF ACKNOWLEDGMENT

I have been helped by many people who knew, worked with or for, or were related to Andy Warhol. But some have gone to considerable trouble to keep the project going – sending me to people, giving me encouraging words, helping to sustain my morale. The book is, in large part, a collection of memories. Some of those who shared their recollections of Andy with me, and kept a close eye on its progress were Warhol friends met during the project. I especially want to express my gratitude to Dorothy Berenson Blau, Emile de Antonio, Tina Fredericks, Alan Groh, David Herbert, George Klauber, Paige Powell and Charles Rydell. I saw all of them several times, and they helped to establish a kind of Warhol network leading to other people. Special thanks to my publisher, Mark Barty-King, who took on the book at the very beginning and, as it turned out, kept the author emotionally intact through an inspired belief in the project until the very end. This was an Anglo-American project out of London, where the editorial process was handled by Georgina Morley, who took special care. There was strong support, too, from my agent, Jeffrey Simmons. Thanks to both of them, and to Roslyn Targ, who handled the American end with her usual style and persuasion.

I must make special mention of the crucial cooperation of the late Rupert Jasen Smith. Others whose help was essential were Stanley Amos, David Bourdon, Andreas Brown, Leo Castelli, Ronnie Cutrone, Donna De Salvo, Ronald Feldman, Henry Geldzahler, Nathan Gluck, Halston, Stephen Koch, Professor Bob Lepper, Roy Lichtenstein, Gerard Malanga, Paul Morrissey, Amy Passarelli, James Rosenquist, and not least, John Warhola. Philip Pearlstein was particularly generous with his time and his collection of photos of Andy and his college classmates. Amei

Wallach, art critic of *Newsday* and the PBS network, was helpful beyond measure in assessing Warhol's place in art history, and Hilton Kramer, editor of *The New Criterion*, contributed a contrary view.

Beyond these were the often surprising interviews with Raymond Andersen, Gerald Ayres, Richard Banks, Stanley Bard of the Chelsea Hotel, Billy Boy, Irving Blum, Stephen Bruce of Serendipity, Beverly Chalfen, Arthur Elias, Lois Elias, Gene Feist, Cornelia Guest, Michael Kahn, Ivan Karp, Benjamin Liu, David Mann, Taylor Mead, Sylvia Miles, Buzz Miller, Stuart Pivar, Ed Plunkett, Irving Sherman, Sorietta Silverman, Leila Davies Singeles, Bill Targ, Denis Vaughan, and Ultra Violet. Vreg Baghoomian furnished stories on Jean-Michel Basquiat. Avrom Blumberg was a most articulate source for Eleanor Simon Blumberg and helped with Andy's early work and other contacts. I am grateful to all of them.

Carlos MacMaster was the first to read any of this, and his criticism was valuable. My profound thanks to my artist friends and close companions, Hiram Williams and Leonard Kesl, for their enthusiasm and their generosity in sharing with me their vast collections of archival material and books, and the library staff at Alachua County Library in Gainesville, Florida.

Fred Lawrence Guiles
Gainesville, Florida

1 May 1989

INTRODUCTION

It was to be expected that Andy Warhol would survive death better than most of us. This comment is not meant irreverently, but there was a machine running when the artist died suddenly, a machine carefully put together over a period of several years. His silkscreens were made from polaroid photographs taken by him, but another photographer, his own art director, for example, was so close to the process he could have done it as well. The silkscreens were made by a brilliant technician, who had worked for Warhol for nearly ten years. There was nothing to prevent this smooth machinery from going on indefinitely, nothing but the cold vital statistic. Andy Warhol was dead. The machinery had to stop, whether it turned out Warhol portraits in twos and threes and fours and sixes or not.

Andy Warhol had put everything in place so carefully, even those closest to him found it hard to believe that he had not simply slipped out to a flea market somewhere and would not come back with lots of things in boxes that never would be opened – carded and put in storage because, in addition to being a master of machine-age art, he was also a collector who liked to own things, lots of things.

His legacy is his spirit. He left that behind and it hovers in and around the Warhol headquarters, in the films when they are screened, in the books that he dictated to a tape recorder, and in the tapes themselves, thousands of hours. The truth seems to be that he had prepared to leave us by tiptoeing away from us all the time he was here. He was always on the edges of our lives, never in the middle. He was where we occasionally look for someone quickly gone, who might be coming back.

PROLOGUE

Monday, 3 June 1968, was a balmy, smog-free day in Manhattan. Decent weather usually turns New Yorkers into congenial strangers and there were lots of smiles on the pedestrians that day. The sidewalk entrepreneurs on the 14th Street end of Union Square were doing a brisk business.

Andy Warhol arrived in a taxi from the East 50s where he had run some errands. Before hailing it, he had rung the bell at the apartment of Miles White, a costume designer and an old friend, but White was not at home. He was not yet used to working downtown – his latest Factory at 33 Union Square West had been acquired only seven months earlier. As he left his taxi, he glanced up and recognized a young, blond man coming towards him. Jed Johnson had shown up as a Western Union boy one day soon after Andy's move from East 47th Street, and everyone at the Factory agreed that he was too good-looking to lose. Fred Hughes, Andy's office manager, had hired him, and since then he had done just about everything. Today, Jed was carting a bagful of odds and ends from the hardware store that Andy had wanted. It was just after four o'clock in the afternoon.

Neither Andy nor Jed noticed the woman in the raincoat leaning against the wall of the building as they went inside to ring for the elevator. But then Andy saw who it was as she stepped into the large, all-purpose elevator beside them. It was Valerie Solanis, a thirty-two-year-old woman whom Andy had employed late the previous year in a parody film, *I, a Man*. She was on the screen for several minutes and she was extremely good. But she never thought of herself as an actress, only as a writer, and as a writer she was not only dreadful, but a pest as well. Somewhere in the disorganized files of the Factory lay the pages of the Solanis script, which Andy had been drawn to read because he liked the title, *Up Your Ass.* But, as he later told an interviewer for *Cahiers du Cinéma*, 'It was so dirty I think she must have been a lady cop.' In Solanis's mind, according to one person who had listened to her complaints, the fact that the script had not been returned meant only one thing – Andy was either planning to buy it from her or steal it from her and make a movie. All of her relationships with others, tenuous though they might be, were certain to be freighted with conspiratorial plots against her.

The phone was ringing as Andy and Jed left the elevator. Paul Morrissey, Andy's film director and, with Fred Hughes, part of the triumvirate running the Warhol enterprises, did not see Solanis's arrival. He had gone to the back of the loft for something. Several hours earlier, he had thrown Solanis out of the premises, telling her that Andy had gone for the day.

Viva, one of the most famous of the Warhol 'Superstars', was on the other end of a phone call to Andy, telling him about the filming of John Schlesinger's *Midnight Cowboy*, in which she had a supporting role as hostess of an 'underground movie' crowd party. Viva was a gaunt and angular brunette with frizzy hair, Garbo's mouth and cheekbones, and a whiny voice that was often reciting a litany of mishaps, and her complaints began when she woke up in the morning. Warhol deservedly felt some reflected glory from the commercial Hollywood movie now being shot on location in New York, since the theme of *Midnight Cowboy* was Warholian – the sad-funny experiences of a two-bit Texas hustler, who is so naive he heads for tawdry West 42nd Street to ply his new trade. The outspoken quality of the Schlesinger film, dealing with street pick-ups and random homosexual encounters in Times Square movie-houses, Warhol believed, was due mainly to his tradition-shattering films, such as *Lonesome Cowboys* and *My Hustler*, both of which had surfaced briefly in major cities, and *The Chelsea Girls*, which had gone 'mainstream' and made some real money for Warhol and Morrissey.

Also waiting to say hello to Andy was an art journalist and critic, Mario Amaya, who often socialized with Andy in art circles. Amaya, who dressed in Savile Row suits, was the most elegant-looking person on the premises, although Solanis, strangely, was wearing a dress under her raincoat, and Morrissey earlier had thought that odd indeed, since so far as he knew she wore nothing but slacks.

Shots rang out. Solanis had whipped out a pistol and was firing point-blank at Andy, and he slumped in shock to the floor, dropping the phone. Then two more shots were fired towards Andy, who was crying 'No! No!' This was murder; there was no question about it. Fred Hughes crawled under a desk. Paul Morrissey peeked through a little window that was used by the projectionist when showing Andy's movies. He saw Andy lying on the floor and he thought he must be dead. Jed Johnson had fled into a small sideroom when the first shot was fired and now held onto the doorknob because he could not make it lock. Amaya headed towards the back of the loft, but Solanis winged him with a shot to the buttocks. Then she turned, saw Fred Hughes crouched under the desk and walked straight over to him and pressed the pistol to his forehead. 'Don't shoot me, Valerie,' Fred said, as though there were some reason left in this madwoman. Then suddenly the doors to the elevator mysteriously opened. There was no one inside.

'There's the elevator, Valerie,' Fred said. 'Just take it and leave.' She thought about it for several seconds, which seemed hours to those present, turned on her heel, stepped onto the elevator and disappeared.

The moment the elevator doors closed, all attention was focused on Andy, who lay in a spreading pool of blood, oozing and pumping through the bullet holes in his body. Billy Name stood over him weeping uncontrollably, but Andy thought he was laughing and joined in a macabre sort of chuckle, then abruptly stopped and said: 'Oh, please, stop it, Billy. Don't make me laugh. It hurts too much.' Then he lapsed into a coma and Fred Hughes kneeled over him and began giving him mouth-to-mouth resuscitation. Paul had phoned for an ambulance and it would not arrive for twenty agonizingly long minutes. But the police were there almost at once and one of them helped Mario Amaya, bleeding from a hip wound, downstairs and into a squad car to take him to the hospital.

The reality of what had happened did not register on Fred's consciousness as the shots were being fired. Later, he told Andy that he thought someone was bombing the Communist Party headquarters, which was also in their building.

Fred and Jed Johnson were detained by the police and taken to the Precinct House as material witnesses, as indeed they were. They were not released until nine o'clock that evening. Fred thought that they were being held as 'suspects', but this seems improbable in light of other eye-witnesses such as Mario Amaya and Paul Morrissey. Apparently they were held until Valerie was formally arrested after surrendering and being booked. She had gone up to a policeman in Times Square and told him: 'I think they're looking for me.'

Paul and Billy caught a taxi to Columbus Hospital, where the ambulance was taking Andy. It was only blocks away. But no one had much hope except an absurd one – Valerie had struck just about every vital organ except the heart, which was clearly her target.

PART ONE

THE
MAKING
OF AN
OUTSIDER

ONE

The road between that ambulance racing through the streets of Manhattan and the working-class section of Pittsburgh where it began its eastward probe was an extraordinary one. It was peculiarly American in its outward, Horatio Alger aspects and perhaps even in its John Dillinger-like denouement, but it was pitted with Spenglerian pot-holes which only the man on the litter could define.

For Andy Warhol, the terror of that June day in New York could be matched only by a similar terror he felt when he was five years old. Kindergarten is for most children the first tender step away from mother and family, a testing time when small sons and daughters first connect with the world and their peers. But for the odd-looking, white-haired boy at Soho Elementary School that September morning in 1933, this was an outrage totally unexpected. Always alone with his family before – with his mother and his older brothers or a few cousins – here he was surrounded by nervous little strangers, some of whom burst into frightened tears at the sight of him. He was described by some of their perplexed neighbors as looking 'unborn', an infelicitous way of referring to the little boy down the block. Little Andy began screaming his head off, and the other children stirred still more fretfully. The noise in the Soho kindergarten approached bedlam, and his mother, Julia Warhola, was sent for. There was a brief conference between the small, peasant woman in the babushka and the principal. The latter saw no way such a child could be accommodated by them.

Julia took Andy home, but she did not resign herself to keeping him there. She was a tough-spirited Czech, born in the old country, already used to improvising to fit herself and her sons into the American scheme of things. Meanwhile, she felt the bond between herself and her youngest boy grow stronger than ever before. She knew he was a little different, and she did spoil him a little. Her husband, Ondrej, indulged her. A big, hard-working Czech with a strong back and an even stronger accent, he could not help but see that she was making their young Andy into a momma's boy, but he must have seen, too, that whatever they tried to do to change that, it would not have mattered.

Andy was born during a summer heat-wave that killed dozens of Americans, most of them elderly, in those distant days of no air conditioning and few electric fans. Thunderstorms rocked the Monongahela Valley, turning Pittsburgh into a steam bath. The newspaper headline that day told of three Pittsburghers drowning while trying to beat the heat. In the Warholas' Orr Street home in the working-class section of Soho, Julia went into labor in the evening. The neighborhood midwife, Katrena Elachko, was summoned. Her middle son, John, four years older than his baby brother, remembered when his brother was born. The date was 6 August 1928.★

When Andy Warhol was a commercial artist working in New York, he moved many times, always to a better apartment. Likewise, the Warholas in his infancy and early years moved several times, always to a slightly better house but never too far from their Czech neighbors or Ondrej's brother John and his family. When Andy was two years old, they moved to Beelen Street just north of the Jones and Laughlin Steel Mill along the Monongahela River. Before Andy was six, and with a new school year looming just beyond his birthday, the family moved to their final house, a red-brick home at 3252 Dawson Street in South Oakland. Years later, Andy would 'move' this home where he grew up to nearby McKeesport, a town celebrated for its steel mills and blue-collar values not unlike the steel town

★ An entirely erroneous date, 28 October 1930, taken from a birth certificate belonging to quite a different Andrew Warhola (living in Eastern Pennsylvania), appeared in the book *Edie* (1982), and was picked up by various journalists and biographers. The Warhola family, school records, and Andy's tombstone all confirm the 1928 date. Andy's birth certificate was filed very late, as such matters go, 3 May 1945, created from an affidavit notarized by Julia and the midwife, Katrena Elachko. It was required by Carnegie Tech when processing his application for college.

featured in the movie *The Deerhunter*, which was set in nearby Clairton and dealt with the impact of the Vietnam war on a group of Rusyn American soldiers and their families. Andy never commented publicly on this film released in 1978, but it accurately reflected the super-macho values of the community in which he was raised and with which he would collide in childhood, and it foretold the macho character of the movement in contemporary art – abstract expressionism – against which he would rebel in the future. All of the Warhola family's moves were within the *Ruska dolina* (Rusyn Valley), where most of their neighbors had Carpatho-Rusyn backgrounds, and both of Andy's parents were from the Rusyn village of Mikova in the Presov Region of north-eastern Czechoslovakia.

In Andy's pursuit of a suitable past, Oakland would not do. Besides the working-class section of South Oakland, there was cosmopolitan Oakland itself, with its row houses and, a few blocks away, handsome detached ones of fake Tudor and Victorian design. This was the living heart of Pittsburgh, with a busy shopping district, several movie houses, and two campuses – the skyscraper towers of the University of Pittsburgh and the more conventional Carnegie Institute of Technology. The natural contours of the terrain shaped Oakland. Most of it was on a bluff above the river with rows of houses spilling down the sides. It was a kind of total habitat with everything man needed from birth to death, including a hearth, education, funeral parlors and entertainment. It was an island surrounded by smoking steel mills, a snake-like river, and the snobbish upper middle-class neighborhoods of Squirrel Hill, North and South, and, dividing it from the actual chimneys, foundries and rail yards of the Jones and Laughlin Works – blue-collar Polish Hill. Right next to it was the Rusyn Valley of the Czech immigrants and their families.

Andy had an easy time adjusting to the brisk pace of Manhattan when he moved there as a young man because it was similar to that of Pittsburgh. As for culture, rather than resembling New York, which everyone conceded was the cultural heart of America, Pittsburgh was closer to the Newcastle upon Tyne industrial region of England, where the arts were the more treasured because they were not especially visible.

Andy's two older brothers were enrolled in the Holmes Grammar

School near the Dawson Street house. Paul was just finishing the seventh grade and John was in the fifth when Julia decided to get Andy into the school system. It was 1934, and America and much of the world were in the midst of the Great Depression. Ondrej was off working or looking for work nearly all of the time. For part of those years he worked for the Eichleay Corporation in heavy construction, and when he was laid off he roamed over the entire State of Pennsylvania, parts of Ohio and West Virginia seeking similar work. His son John later said that their father never would have taken charity like the Works Progress Administration, although the WPA, responsible for the construction of countless post offices, roads and public buildings across the nation, was of course not a charitable body but an arm of the government which dispensed real jobs and, not least, paid real money for them.

With Ondrej gone much of the time, the boys lived in a matriarchy. Paul was given strict instruction from Julia about the protection Andy would need. If her Andy was a special child, no one was allowed to notice as Paul gripped his hand and escorted him to the Holmes School. There, that first morning, he was given a kind of intelligence test to determine if he was ready for the first grade, having missed kindergarten. He did so well on that he was put in the second grade. Of course, this greatly pleased Julia and she was proud of her son's native intelligence, which she had never doubted. However, this situation would work to Andy's disadvantage, since he skipped the fifth grade as well, and he was ill-prepared when he arrived in Schenley High. He was usually the youngest person in his class and he was expected to be precocious, but he was not. Except for his art classes, school bored him so utterly, exams were always taken in a climate of crisis and he needed help to get through.

Because of Ondrej's frequent absences, Julia stayed close to her own family. She was a short, stocky peasant woman, altogether belying her quick wit and her sensitive, creative instincts, both qualities inherited by Andy. During those Depression years, she was scrappily resourceful. She cleaned old tin cans, covered them with crepe paper, filled them with paper flowers of her own design, and sold them from door to door. Whenever there was a school holiday or a weekend and she had the money for their fares, she would take the boys up to Lyndora, another mill town forty miles north of Pittsburgh adjoining the town of Butler, which was equally industrial. The tall chimneys of the mills were a familiar part of the Warhola boys' childhood – at home or on holiday, they were always there, pouring out their smoke. Second son John remembered:

> 'We were close to my mother's relatives, and her two brothers lived in Lyndora and one she was real close to, who would be [cousin] Amy's dad, John. He was a successful businessman. He had a store. He had the same nature as my mother. Just an easy-going guy. He was the type that would really want to give you good advice . . . when you'd grow up, you'd really remember it.'

There were several Zawackys settled in Butler and Lyndora. As often as she could, Julia would take the brown interurban trolley up to stay with her brother John (born Janos) Zawacky, who had come to America in 1902 at the age of eighteen.

In 1928, when Julia was pregnant with Andy, Ondrej was again away on a long construction job and it was summer vacation for the boys, so she took them up to their uncle's place and she and John's wife, who was also pregnant, went to the same doctor for check-ups.

Butler figures strongly in Warhol's prehistory. The town had attracted dozens of Czech families to emigrate from the foothills of the Carpathian Mountains in an eastern province of Czechoslovakia near the Polish border. The Standard Car Works (later known as the Pullman Company), where the railway passenger cars were manufactured, was the attraction. When the Pullman Company was hurt by the economic slump during the 1930s, the company switched to putting together a cheap, small car, the Austin, with modest success.

Andy was a timid-seeming boy, who kept to himself and had few playmates. But his timidity or shyness was paradoxically a device he used in dealing with the world. He really wanted to be noticed by others. Once he slipped on some steps at school and came down hard on his bottom, and everybody laughed, and he could not have been more delighted, because he was seen. One of his Lyndora cousins, Amy Zawacky Passarelli, remembered him:

> 'peeking around the corner in the house to see what was going on. My sister went to talk to him, and she found him so interesting because he was showing her all the things that he was collecting. He was already collecting movie stars and pictures like that.'

With cause, Julia may have transferred much of her affection from her husband to her youngest boy. She described Ondrej as coming from her native town, Mikova, Czechoslovakia:

> 'I meet him when I'm seventeen, he's twenty. My husband, Andy, he got to America a year before and then come back to town. He was good-looking. Blond. My husband had curly hair. Oh! He came back to village and every girl want him. Fathers would give lots of money, lots of land to marry daughter. He no want. He want me.'

When Ondrej returned from America, he saw Julia.

> ' "Who's this little girl?" he says. My momma laughs. "She's gonna be your wife," she says. My mother, she jokes, for fun.'

> 'I was seventeen. I know nothing. He wants me, but I no want him. I no think of no man. I was seventeen. My mother and father say, "Like him, like him." I scared. My Daddy beat me, beat me to marry him. What do I know? The priest – oh, a nice priest – come. "This Andy," he says, "a very nice boy. Marry him." I cry. I no know. Andy visit again. He brings me candy. I no have candy. He brings me candy, wonderful candy. And for this candy, I marry him.'

Julia was being perfectly serious. Both she and her small son developed a passion for candy. Later Andy spelled out his fondness for Hershey chocolate kisses and candy bars, telling a reporter that he worked so hard as a commercial artist to achieve success so he could buy all the chocolate he wanted, and 'Now I have a room full of Hershey kisses and candy bars and I don't think about it any more.'

Julia married Ondrej in 1909, and three years later, in 1912, he left again for America. This time it was to avoid conscription, since rumors of war were everywhere. Under cover of darkness, Ondrej ran the one-mile distance from their Czech village of Mikova into Poland. From a Polish port, he caught a boat to America while Julia stayed in Europe with her baby daughter, making her home with her in-laws. Sadly, she remembered that time:

> 'My husband leaves and then everything bad. My hus-
> band leaves and my little daughter dies. I have daughter,
> she dies after six weeks. She catch cold. No doctor. We
> need doctor, but no doctor in town. Oh, I cry, oh, I go
> crazy when baby died. I open window and yell, "My
> baby dies." [She begins weeping.] "My baby dead. My
> little girl." '

Julia was not coddled by the Warholas because of her loss. She said she worked 'like a horse' in her husband's absence, which was to last an incredible nine years, but she was strong and young, and she did not mind. Then in 1921 Ondrej sent her a steamship ticket and money to get to Pittsburgh.

Julia Warhola never was 'Americanized'. She remained loyal to her Czech roots all her life. She attended the Byzantine Ruthenian Catholic Church, the faith of her ancestors, oftener than just for Sunday mass. She spoke Czech in the home and taught it to her sons. The older boys, Paul and John, tried to speak it on occasion to please her, but Andy always rejected it, and if she ever spoke to him in her native tongue, he answered her in English. This was the earliest evidence of Andy's commitment to all things American. But when Paul and John were small, very little was spoken around them but Czech, and their efforts to speak it left them with 'funny accents', causing other children to mock them, and their speech had to be ironed out into flat American during their school years.

Julia had a genuine talent for drawing, and soon all of her sons were able to imitate her rather primitive style. 'We all drew,' John said, pointing out that Paul's son Jaimie was now a painter, too. 'It was inherited from our mother,' he explained. Andy was a natural when he first started to draw. Julia was pleased. His drawing ability helped her define his oddness to others who might be unsettled by his fondness for paper dolls. Within a few years he was making portrait sketches of neighbors up and down their block and selling them for pocket money.

He needed the money to buy movie magazines and admission money for those matinees when his mother did not accompany him to the movies. Even more than drawing, the movies had become as necessary to him as breathing. He later said that at an early age, life began to seem to him 'half television' – not quite real. His reality was framed up there on the silver screen.

Andy had begun cutting out photos of movie queens from newspapers and magazines before he ever started to school. If he was not precocious academically, certainly he was unusually advanced in his attraction to the glamor of Hollywood. By the time he began his school career, he had dozens of favorites and many pages of their likenesses in scrap-books tied with string – Joan Crawford, Bette Davis and, not least, Greta Garbo. He also had been writing off to Hollywood for autographed photos, and his collection included Freddy Bartholomew, Mickey Rooney and Shirley Temple. Julia never worried about his lack of playmates because she knew that he had this host of film stars to relate to. Mother and son shared their adventures on the screen nearly every Saturday, and after school Andy played with his scrap-books, pasting in newspaper photos with a mixture of flour and water.

He seldom drew casually or just 'for fun'. He drew the neighbor portraits for money, and he drew well in school because he liked art better than anything else, except perhaps history, in which he also got decent grades.

It was while he was at Holmes School that he was chosen for free attendance at a Saturday school session in drawing set up in the music hall of the Carnegie Museum. It was called the Tam O'Shanter series (after the beret that artists sometimes wore), and only the most gifted youngsters from the fifth through tenth grade were eligible. The series lasted through several decades and produced, besides Andy Warhol, the painters Philip Pearlstein

and Harry Schwalb, industrial designer Irene Pasinski and sculptor
Henry Bursztynomwicz. Several hundred students attended the
sessions. Joseph Fitzpatrick, who taught the classes, said: 'We
demanded a lot from them and we got it. . . . You could hear
a pin drop.' Fitzpatrick customarily described their assignment
for the morning and then the students picked up their crayons
and masonite panels and went to work. Of Andy, Fitzpatrick
recalled: 'I distinctly remember how individual and unique his
style was. . . . From the very start, he was quite original.' The
best students were singled out to come to the front of the class
and show their drawing for that Saturday to the others. Andy had
that honor often.

Like many adolescents, Andy arrived at Schenley High School
with a feeling of being out of his depth. His skin problems
were no minor thing when he first came among a group of
students who were mostly strangers. The boys from Holmes
Grammar School who moved over to Schenley when he did
still called him 'Spotty'. His face was bleached white except
for a large beige area from his cheek up to his forehead. It
looked like an oversized birthmark and was taken for such.
His baby-fine hair was whitish-blond and added to his albino-
like appearance. But almost at once he met another freshman,
Eleanor Simon, who was not as fearful of her peers as he was.
She was the first to spot his peculiar charisma. He had an
air of helpless innocence about him that his later friend Philip
Pearlstein would call an 'angel' quality. He would have it all his
life. Those who befriended him thought he needed help, and he
did. It was an attribute he shared with his future icon, Marilyn
Monroe. Because of her physical beauty, Marilyn attracted many
samaritans. At this point in Andy's life, he was lucky to have
found Eleanor.

With Eleanor Simon's encouragement, he ventured to shed
some of the invisible layers of protective wrappings in which
Julia had enfolded him. Their art teacher, Mary A. McKibbin,
continued the process of bringing him out, though she later said
that she never got to know him well.

His shyness was a defense. He truly believed that because of
his pallor and the strange discoloration on his face, he was a
freak. He viewed all friendly overtures such as the ones he was
now receiving from Eleanor with mistrust. The real world, that

world where teasing boys called him names, had become a battle zone for Andy. He tried to shut it out with fantasies of movie stars and of becoming famous himself. Yes, that was the strategy he had mapped for himself as early as that – September 1941. Eleanor Simon and then Miss McKibbin made him realize that his best defense was drawing what was before him. Reality could be tamed by sketching it on paper. Years later, he could shout victory when he had tamed everything, from dollar bills to skulls and electric chairs.

Art teacher Mary McKibbin considered Andy a loner who had very little social contact with the other students. She did not know then of his friendship with Eleanor, and her contacts with Andy were largely impersonal; but she could not fail to see his gift for drawing, and she urged him to enter the *Scholastic Magazine* competitions. He won, and Miss McKibbin was not surprised. There was something else she later remembered: 'He had a gift for line drawing, but he very rarely used color.' At that early stage in his life he was still pinning down reality, not attempting to recreate it.

Eleanor Simon was a year and a half older than Andy, since he had skipped the first grade. She was the second child of Morris and Frances Levy Simon; her older brother, Sidney, was to become a successful painter and art historian, eventually becoming curator of the Walker Art Museum and a member of the University of Minnesota art faculty.

Her family was borderline poor with a slippery foothold in the middle class. Her mother's family, the Levys, were better off than the Simons. Her maternal grandmother looked after three unmarried uncles, and it seems likely that Eleanor inherited her maternal streak from Grandmother Levy, since she began looking after Andy as though he were a small, helpless child, seeing that he was passably presentable, well fed, and in reasonably good health.

Eleanor quickly made herself indispensable to Andy. It soon became clear to her that he was faltering in math and science. She began a pattern of going over his assignments each weekday evening after school. In many cases, she did his actual homework herself. She wrote most of his English essays and he copied them in his own handwriting. With Ellie Simon's help, Andy managed to graduate in the top third of his class.

Eleanor's mothering of Andy could be seen as a criticism of Julia's ability to look after her family. What is clear is that Julia saw him as more of a companion than a son. Husband Ondrej was seldom around and her older boys were always off somewhere with their friends, but Andy was by her side or nearby all of the time he was not in school. Some of this mother-son complicity came from her canny sense that outsiders might reject him because of his strangeness, but much of it came from simple affection. She loved her Andy and intuitively knew what he liked best. If she had a dollar to spend on him and it was a choice of buying him a new shirt or a movie matinee and a chocolate sundae, she would invariably opt for the latter.

With Andy's new friendship with Ellie Simon, for the first time he became a person in his own right and not his mother's constant companion. At fourteen Ellie already had defined who she was. Now she set about helping Andy determine the face he wanted to present to the world. This was not easy. As a child, he had cut himself off from other children. Now at high school, he was among civilized peers who allowed him to be himself. It did not necessarily follow that he was a sissy because he hung out chiefly with girls. Much of the taunting by other schoolboys stopped at Schenley High.

Before his freshman year at Schenley was over, he had found the face of Andy (no longer 'Spot' or 'Spotty'). He slipped into the persona of a pale elf. He was slight; he could blend with the woodwork if he so chose, but he could make people aware of his presence when necessary. No one called attention to his strangeness anymore. He came very close to fitting in.

Although Andy and his father had been virtual strangers in life, Ondrej's death in 1941 opened the door to a life and career for his son he never could have comprehended. During the rare times when father and son were together, Andy was a worry to him. It seems probable that he had persuaded himself that they would one day lose Andy to some childhood illness before he became a man. As a child, Andy suffered three breakdowns, which he referred to as 'St Vitus Dance' (Sydenham's chorea), but the episodes all occurred, with astonishing regularity, on the day following the boy's release from school for summer vacation. This made them seem less of a threat to the boy's survival, since they seemed to a degree calculated. These recurring bouts of tremors of the face, legs and arms were frightening nevertheless, and they ensured that he would remain indoors throughout the summer and not have to go outside, which to Andy was hostile territory with all his taunting classmates free on the streets. He explained that the attacks were

> 'spaced a year apart. One when I was eight, one at nine, and one at ten . . . always started on the first day of summer vacation. I don't know what this meant. I would spend all summer listening to the radio and lying in bed with my Charlie McCarthy doll and my un-cut-out cut-out paper dolls all over the spread and under the pillow.'

During Andy's first year at Schenley High, his father was stricken with a lingering illness that was to last nearly a year. According to Andy's brother John, it came from drinking contaminated well water at a construction site in West Virginia. 'When our father died,' he said, 'Andy was not quite thirteen.' It was the boy's first acquaintance with death, and it terrified him. When his father was laid out for viewing, Andy hid under his bed and would not come out until it was over.

   Death can be, and often is, a financial boon to a poor family. And so it was with Ondrej's departure. With some of the insurance money, Andy was able to complete his freshman and sophomore years at Carnegie Tech. His friend Philip Pearlstein (who was not his classmate at Schenley but rather went to Allerdice High) remembered that the tuition at Carnegie was three or four hundred dollars a term. Julia kept most of the inheritance a long time. She later said it came to eleven thousand dollars. John Warhola was proud of his father's achievement as a bread-winner, and said:

> 'He was a good provider. He left enough for Andy's first two years of college. The house was paid for and he had money in the bank. For somebody just being a construction work laborer, to save that money and raise a family. . . . You take even now, there's people make two or three times as much and they can't handle it.

They don't know how to take care of it.'

Andy took from his mother an obsession with money, its acqui-
sition and preservation. In the 1950s in New York when he was
pulling together a stake of his own, he got a reputation for
being tight. One friend said, 'He never ever bought you a coke.
You bought your own.' He exploited his friends and somehow
coerced nearly all of them into helping him complete his little
book publications with 'coloring parties'. But when confronted
with total have-nots, all those unpublished poets and creative
types who surrounded him in the early 1960s, he loosened up
and spent large sums on keeping his succession of Factories going,
on paying the tab for the Factory crowd at a nearby saloon called
Max's Kansas City where painters, poets and underground film
people congregated, and on buying things for himself, often in
multiples.

Early in his college years, Andy got a reputation for being
one of the school's poor boys. His professors were convinced
that he had to struggle all through school, and time and again
they made allowances for him because of that view. Perhaps
it was this perception that allowed him to graduate, because
he was in constant peril of being flunked out. Eleanor Simon
could help him with his non-art subjects, but naturally only
he could handle his art assignments, and very often he was
late in turning them in or else he misinterpreted what was
called for.

Certainly he needed money beyond his tuition fees for his art
supplies (good drawing paper, inks and paints). He took whatever
jobs he could find, and John recalled:

> 'He worked for thirty-five cents an hour. He worked
> in a dairy store for a couple of months. I don't know
> what he earned at Joseph Horne [decorating depart-
> ment store windows]. I remember he used to wash
> dishes, too. He sold fruit off a truck with our older
> brother during the summer months in 1947. I had an
> ice cream truck. I went to [housing] projects. Sort of
> like a Good Humor Man. The kids don't appreciate
> it now because their parents are buying gallons of ice
> cream. Then, when you pulled up and you played a

musical horn or a tune, you had about ten or fifteen kids
around you. They were all orderly and they respected
you.'

Andy's work at Joseph Horne's Department Store expanded his
knowledge of commercial design in a way that was to be pivotal.
He worked for a Mr Vollmer for fifty cents an hour, doing many
of the fashion windows and looking for 'ideas' in back issues of
Vogue and *Harper's Bazaar*. Vollmer thrilled him with stories of
his former life in New York, which seemed to Andy about the
most exciting place on earth.

There were two significant artists working as professors in the
Art School at Carnegie Tech, and from each of them Andy drew
something valuable. The strongest influence on his future painting
was the painter Sam Rosenberg, but the man who channeled
Andy's interest in the direction of consumer icons was Professor
Robert Lepper.

Bob Lepper was a gifted painter in his own right. His focus in
art was on the industrial age. Four years before Andy sat down
in his class in autumn of 1945, Lepper was painting a study of
a bottling machine, just one facet of a huge mural he was then
creating at the campus of West Virginia University. He magnified
the details of factory parts in a way that had the bold look of the
much later work of Roy Lichtenstein. Industrial machinery and
Pittsburgh were natural partners, but Lepper was the most gifted
painter in his era of gears, crank shafts, and the nuts and bolts of
the workplace.

After the traditional European sojourn of the young American
artist Lepper returned to Pittsburgh and, soon, to his alma mater,
Carnegie Tech, as a teacher of industrial design. In 1938 he
created a chart of 'The Elements of Visual Perception' for a
textbook on design. In its particularized way, this chart did for
the student designer what Darwin did in his *Origin of Species*.
Lepper's canvases for exhibition resembled the work of Fernand
Léger. They were shown as recently as 1987 in a traveling show,
The Machine Age in America, 1918–1941.

Lepper was a man of few pretensions and a teacher nearly all
the students admired. He said: 'I was raised on the *American Boy*
and the *Saturday Evening Post*. One half of my class wanted to be
"serious" artists and were regarded as snobs by those like Andy

who wanted to do commercial design. It was my job to make them lie down together.'

Because of Lepper's simplicity and accessibility, it was to be expected that Andy would make some effort to get to know him. Andy had blossomed socially in college. Through Eleanor Simon and his new friend Philip Pearlstein, he had met nearly a dozen classmates who had accepted him. He had come to see himself as someone who needed the friendship of others and had put aside, at least for his college years, his loner status. But he never approached Lepper away from class, and Lepper said that he never really got to know Andy the way he did a number of other students. Later, when fame overtook him, it became Andy's custom to dismiss or minimize influences that might have contributed to his elevation to being 'the Prince of Pop Art'. Lepper was a victim of this practice. When asked about Lepper by a biographer in 1978, Andy said: 'Oh, yeah. He was nice . . . I don't think he ever taught me. I'm not sure. Maybe he did. I don't remember.' Ivan Karp, a savvy art dealer who had befriended Andy and was present at that interview, interjected that Andy's being Lepper's student was the latter's 'only claim to fame'. Karp may have been unaware of Lepper's high rank among painters of icons of the American industrial scene and of the crucial link between this school of art and Andy's Pop Art. Such dismissals became part of the Warhol process of 'myth-making', but they could be cruel, if not offensive, to his benefactors. It was the reverse side of Andy's nature. He had a generally pacific attitude towards everything and everyone, but this seemed to come from a policy of never making waves and not wanting his own passage through life to be 'blighted' by obligations.

Lepper sensed what Andy was about long before Andy's disclaimer. He retorted many years later: 'I make no claim to having touched Andy. [Philip] Pearlstein said I was hard to understand [the content of his lectures, not his speech], and he interpreted Lepper to Andy.' Pearlstein, whose realistic figure paintings and portraits have made him one of the most influential artists of the twentieth century, but whose private self is largely unknown, got close to Lepper during his years as a student at Carnegie Tech. They frequently lunched together, and Pearlstein helped out summers at Lepper's workshop. Lepper believed that Andy missed a lot of his classes because 'he was down at Horne's

Department Store earning some money', but Pearlstein disputes this, saying that Andy missed very few classes.

Lepper remembered that most of Andy's class was composed of veterans returned from the Second World War, and

> 'Andy was the lonesome, skinny little kid who was in that sense out of it. I did say he was not particularly attractive to women, which I need not have said. The women looked after him and, apropos of the context, the women were in no sense intimidated by the veterans. It was a lively and argumentative and very active place. They even had the audacity to quarrel with their teachers. But everybody got along fine and it was a wonderful, wonderful time.'

Still, Andy's college years were marked by uncertainty. In fulfilling assignments, sometimes he was right on target. For example, when Lepper asked Andy and the rest of the class to become reporters and go out into the Oakland neighborhood and study the houses and the people, then render the details of an interior as it ought to be with chairs, fireplace, windows, curtains, lamps, etc., Andy's imagined interior could not have been more perceptive or brilliant as a drawing in itself. It suggested Van Gogh's bedroom study. But when he was asked to create a vitrine (display case) containing a re-creation in three-dimensional detail of some past epoch for a cultural, anthropological study, Andy did not seek out some recognizable thing like the Cro-Magnon caverns in France; rather he created an arbor of perfectly symmetrical, 'lollypop' trees with flag-like leaves made of red, gold and silver ribbon. It did not belong to any known past epoch or culture, and Andy would not explain what he had done.

Classmate Arthur Elias first met Andy when he returned from his years in the army. Elias said the classes in the art school were small, and he got to know Andy, Eleanor, Philip and the others very well. They were all in Sam Rosenberg's class. Rosenberg taught them the fundamentals of putting oil on canvas and how to use tempera. During an interview in 1978, Andy said that Rosenberg influenced him more than any of his other teachers. It is possible that since Andy was to become a conceptual artist, he wanted his concept area, where Lepper was his college mentor, kept inviolate and unknown, but he was quick to give Rosenberg credit because Rosenberg had encouraged him and admired what he was doing. So there seems to be a consensus of memories that would indicate Andy had the support of both Lepper and Rosenberg. But, according to Elias, there were conservative teachers whose opinion of Andy's work was negative. Some of them felt that it was subversive, outrageous and fanciful. Andy had begun some drawings that were strongly inspired by the work of the decadent *fin-de-siècle* artist Aubrey Beardsley. Professor Howard Wörner, who taught illustration, apparently expressed his misgivings to Lepper, who told Pearlstein, and Andy's classmate persuaded him to find some more appropriate influence, which turned out to be Ben Shahn.

Arthur Elias recalled that Andy may well have come into some difficulty on 'Judgment Day', which fell at the end of each semester:

> 'Instead of being graded by the teacher of a particular course, the whole faculty would arrive at a grade for the specific student. The teacher who headed a class would have one vote. This is not terribly fair, in a way. And it is possible there were some people who didn't quite approve of Andy. He had some people who liked his work very much, and there were others who didn't. There were some very strong supporters – Rosenberg, and Lepper, but Lepper not so much. Professor Wörner would be against Andy.'

Years later, when fame overtook Andy in New York, it was always Lepper who had to deal with reporters and scholars who came to Pittsburgh seeking details about Andy's life as a student. So it devolved on Lepper to sustain some sort of delight on Carnegie Tech's part that Andy Warhol was a product of their school, and in the wake of Andy's death, there was one final, amusing moment in the Warhol/Lepper saga. Lepper recalled:

> 'On the morning of the day before the funeral, the *New York Post* sent in an elite team of reporter and photographer to do the story. They visited the family, the undertaker [Andy was buried in Pittsburgh], Schenley High School,

some bars in McKeesport [Andy's mythologizing would live after him], and me. For me they had, you have guessed it, a Campbell's Soup can. I held the Campbell's Soup can with a vacuous and simpering smile and was committed to posterity. I was appalled next day to see this horrible image staring at me – fortunately from page three. The story ended with a quote from the professor, "I should have flunked the bastard. . . ." I am pleased to think that this episode is vintage Andy tradition and in a small and perverse way worthy of his memory.'

When Andy, Ellie and Philip completed their sophomore year at Carnegie Tech, Ellie and Andy had reached a financial impasse. Typically, Ellie had done well scholastically and she was high in her class; but she had exhausted her family's resources, and it is likely that her older brother Sidney, who was then taking graduate courses, was tapping all available family funds to complete his own art education.

For reasons unknown, Julia had decided not to pay for Andy's third year at Carnegie. Andy must have been in an agony of indecision. Unlike Ellie, he was not a professor's favorite. His grades were marginal. That summer of 1947, his oldest brother, Paul, began hauling fruit through the streets of Oakland and other boros of Pittsburgh. They picked up the fruit in bushel baskets at the central wholesale market very early in the morning and then set out. Later, Andy recalled selling cantaloupes to housewives for a nickel.

Philip and his fiancée, Dorothy Cantor, who was then just through with her freshman year at Carnegie Tech's art school, had gone in with a thirty-year-old painter named John Regan and rented a Victorian barn for the summer for ten dollars. Their classmate, and Andy's second closest male friend, Arthur Elias, had joined them. When Andy was not selling fruit, he set up his easel alongside his friends in the barn, and it was doubtless this contiguity of artistic impulses that decided Andy to continue on at Carnegie Tech for a third year.

Although Pittsburgh was a far cry from Greenwich Village, it did have its 'Villagy' types. Some were the genuine article, like the Balcomb Greenes. He was an important abstract expressionist from New York, who came to Pittsburgh one term each year to show art slides and lecture in a course he called 'Humanities, Arts and Civilization', which Pearlstein recalled as always putting Andy and himself to sleep (although Greene never seemed aware in the darkened slide-show atmosphere). As one of the several jobs Ellie took to support herself and save money towards her eventual graduation from Carnegie Tech, she helped Greene with the slide projector.

The Greenes (he called his wife 'Peter', although she was Gertrude Glass, the sculptress) had helped a local woman, Betty Rockwell Raphael, open a gallery called 'The Outline', where every Sunday night during that fabulous summer of 1947 the avant-gardists, including all the artists' barn's tenants, Ellie, Leonard 'Pappy' Kessler and his sister, Corinne 'Corky' Kessler, would convene for a cultural event. Pearlstein described these gallery affairs as 'marvelous programs . . . and we saw Maya Deren, filmmaker and dancer, a lot of experimental film, John Cage, and all of these were exciting. . . .' They saw their first Afro hairdo on the exotic Deren and their first ever real Picasso painting, possibly borrowed from the Museum of Modern Art.

Others in Andy's circle that summer were Gene Feist, who had been Ellie's boyfriend for a while and who was interested in experimental theater, and Sorietta Silverman, who hoped for a classical singing career. In 1954 Sorietta would introduce Ellie to her future husband, Avrom Blumberg, after her own affair which Avrom had foundered.

Funds were pulled together for Andy's last two years at college. He earned part of the tuition and applied to a special scholarship fund set up for that very purpose – to see talented students of limited financial means through to graduation.

In the summer of 1948, Andy and Philip went to New York on an exploratory trip. They stayed with George Klauber, a former classmate from Carnegie Tech who had returned to his native Brooklyn after little more than a year in Pittsburgh. Klauber believed that they both determined during that visit to make their careers in Manhattan.

Andy's senior year was chaotic. He was rapidly moving towards the blotted ink style that would change the look of advertising art in the decade just ahead. Lepper had him and the class doing some aspect of 'Human behavior as recounted by masters of the short story and the novel'. Indirectly, Lepper was making Andy more literate, since he was not drawn to reading anything longer than a magazine article until he was forced to digest all of Robert Penn Warren's novel *All the King's Men*, based on the life and sudden death of an American political demagogue, Huey Long. As Lepper stated, it was an 'inculturating experience' for Andy and a number of other students. In this instance Andy made an illustration of one of the more violent confrontations in the book. He also depicted a scene from a short story by Katharine Anne Porter, a drawing that has some of the centrifugal force of a Thomas Hart Benton work.

Ellie would not return to the campus as a student until 1951, but Andy would drop by her apartment casually, often for dinner. Not so casually, afterward they would do his tougher assignments. Lepper said he was convinced there was 'a cabal of girls doing his essays for him', but it was really only Ellie. Their close friendship was never a sexual one, although she always had an affair going on with some boy. Andy got to know most of them. Through the years of their intimate association, Ellie had become aware that Andy was homosexual. There was no room left for doubt about it. As Avrom Blumberg, the man Ellie eventually married, recalled:

> 'Ellie was decades ahead of her time in being understanding. . . . She had impressively wide acquaintance within the arts with gays. She was tolerant and never critical and sensed that this was not a matter of choice but of nature. . . . It was her way to accept the entire person with his faults and assets. She was only critical of people who were intolerant or thoughtless toward others. Not so curiously, she never mentioned Andy's sexual habits and obviously accepted him, the entire package, as a friend.'

So there were these intimate friends in whom he could confide – Pearlstein, Elias, Leonard Kessler and his sister, Sorietta Silverman, Gene Feist, Dorothy Cantor, and Ellie, of course. With them, he had opened up rather like one of those small Japanese clamshells, so popular in the 1930s and 40s and bought at Woolworths, which Andy liked to drop into a glass of water, where a paper flower of the brightest hues would 'grow' in a flash from the opened shell towards the surface. Sometimes, attached to its stem would be the American flag. It was the sort of absurd dime store plaything he loved. And he could share with these friends certain formerly secret obsessions, like Garbo. All of them, from Ellie to Philip, knew how he identified with the enigmatic film star. Most of them also knew that he was developing a similar obsession with the young novelist Truman Capote, to whom he wrote fan letters although he had seen only his photograph, the slightly wicked one, recumbent and staring languidly at the viewer from the back cover of his book *Other Voices, Other Rooms*.

But his friends knew that there was far more substance to Andy than these impersonal infatuations might suggest. He had developed instincts about where his art was taking him. The commercial art world he was about to enter was really an interlude, a means to an end. Professionally, he identified with no mysterious and remote film goddess, nor with a gay literary figure like Capote, but with the Dadaist Marcel Duchamp, whose notorious porcelain urinal, bought from a bathroom fixture store, mounted on wood and called *Fountain* (done in a series of five, one of which Andy would one day own), was refused by the Society of Independent Artists in New York in 1910.

With Duchamp in mind, Andy submitted a self-portrait to the senior art show which he entitled *The Broad Gave Me My Face But I Can Pick My Own Nose*, and the title itself doubtless caused the curator of the show to refuse to hang it. The Arts and Crafts Center showed it instead, where according to one observer 'the public flocked to see it'. One other student work was even more popular, and that was Andy's poster for the Progressive Party and its candidate Henry Wallace. While his allegiance to Duchamp can be seen as a radical connection, his political interests ended with the art work he did for Wallace and would do for other democrats, renegade or otherwise.*

Besides Duchamp, there was another Frenchman whom Andy

---

* Andy only voted once in his life – in New York – and regretted it, since he was promptly called for jury duty.

had come to admire. Jean Cocteau was an artist of many parts. He was also gay and unashamed about it. There seems to be little doubt that it was Cocteau's example that successively led Andy Warhol into serious art, film, magazine publishing and consummate self-promotion. As a young man of many parts, he decided that he wanted to learn dancing. Leonard 'Pappy' Kessler's sister 'Corky' was studying modern dance, and she volunteered to teach Andy all the basic movements. He even joined the Modern Dance Club at the college, and later turned up in a picture of the group as its only male member. In the years of Andy's most intense celebrity, he told a reporter: 'I never wanted to be a painter; I wanted to be a tap dancer.' But, as with Cocteau's excursions into many fields, dance was a temporary enthusiasm with Andy. He never went back to it, although a closeness developed between 'Corky' and Andy that differed markedly from his friendship with Ellie. With Ellie, his alliance was more complex, originating as it did in protectiveness and gradually becoming one of motherly affection and concern, while 'Corky' treated him like a brother. She was the one who changed his name to André, considering it more appropriate for an artist.

Julia Warhola must have had mixed feelings about Andy's years at Carnegie Tech. From the time he began his studies there, she was increasingly left out of his life. The old closeness was gone, although at one time or another she met all of his intimate friends. For those four years at least, he no longer needed her. Gene Feist described the Andy of those student days:

> '[Ellie] sort of mothered him a great deal. . . . She was always saying "Did Andy have breakfast? Did he have lunch? Who's taking care of him for supper? . . ." He was always kind of fey. Not in the way they say it today . . . and I remember he did a kitten book and he would walk around and, if he liked you, he'd say, "Do you want to see my kittens?" And he'd reach for the book. The main thing about him was, in relation to being with Ellie, he was naive, he was not sophisticated, he was not corrupt . . . and he was not a manipulator of people. He was, as Shakespeare would say, "an innocent". And he appealed to the maternal and paternal instincts in people in those days. And later, ironically enough, he reversed the roles, and he became the all-listening, all-absorbing,

all-taking-in of other people's problems. How he reacted
to them I don't know. But he had that benign look.'

Of course, Ellie and Andy used each other relentlessly. Ellie had
rebelled against her family and moved out, a step Andy admired
but could not emulate. His fantasy of stepping away from his
Czech roots into a purely American situation – i.e., one's own
studio apartment – had been fulfilled by proxy in Ellie's last
move. And Andy's own recognition of his homosexuality and
developing a circle of male dance friends, most of whom were
gay, was a far more liberating thing in Ellie's eyes. She was
a bohemian like Andy, but she was hobbled by her ties to
conformity. Little touches in her studio apartment suggested that
frustrated rebel streak – small squares of colored cloth tossed over
the furniture and the lamp (suggestive of Blanche duBois and her
paper lampshade).

But Andy and Ellie were alike in seeing business in art, and art
as a business. Ellie collected 'found objects'★ and worked them
into useful articles. She shopped at Army and Navy stores and
bought wholesale lots of binocular cases, Second World War
surplus, and, again in Gene Feist's words:

> 'She would put a long leather thong on them and turn
> them into women's pocketbooks and sell them. . . . She
> took graham cracker boxes with stained bottoms from
> the oil and then drew little calligraphic sketches around
> them . . . and [her art work] was this kind of minutiae,
> almost myopic, and she wore glasses and Andy was
> myopic and wore glasses.'

She also collected all of Andy's early work she could get her hands
on. She seemed to know better than anyone, save Andy himself,
the destiny that lay ahead for him. After she graduated in 1952
and was settled into a teaching job, during vacation periods, she
worked in New York and she would drop by the stores where
Andy had done the windows and take away parts of his displays
after they were dismantled and save them.

★ Found objects are things that already exist, such as plumbing pipes, car
fenders, beer cans, etc., that become part of an art work.

★★★

As Andy's school years moved towards their close, it became apparent that something fundamental had happened to his personality. Rather than avoiding his peers, as, with only a handful of exceptions, he had done in high school, it was now obvious that he wanted people around. Other people – schoolmates in particular – became necessary to him. It was as though he feared being alone. When he walked across campus, it was nearly always with somebody. He rarely had much to say, but he expected a great deal from others. Once, as Leonard 'Pappy' Kessler walked him across the campus grounds, Andy turned to him and said: 'Entertain me.' Gossip and conversation had become as necessary to him as his weekly ration of movies.

A question must therefore be addressed when writing of Andy's life: Could anyone who so depended upon others and their presence to see him through the day and into the night truly be considered an outsider? The answer must be yes, and for a very simple reason – Andy's perception of reality was clouded by his childhood years of withdrawal. He often spoke of not living the moment as it was happening. It was as though it were happening to someone else. As subsequent events would show, this meant that Andy was little interested in close attachments that involved his physical participation. Here again is a clue to his future artistic development. He found that he could come close to reality, to real everyday living, through others, through gossip about the most intimate details of their lives. And he learned that, like his idol Duchamp, he need not create something. He could take a photograph from *Life* magazine, trace it, simplifying it as he did so, and come up with something original.

Andy's most visible contribution as a class member during the senior class's last weeks was a little dance he did in the class show, which was a parody of Rodgers' and Hammerstein's *Oklahoma*, called *Oaklandhoma*, after the section of Pittsburgh where the school was situated. He danced with one of the girl students. At a party afterwards, Professor Lepper reprised one of the 'hit' songs, 'Juniors Bustin' Out All Over', and his students thought it was fine. 'A very daring thing to do,' recalled Lepper, since nothing is worse, in his view, than an egalitarian professor hamming it up before his students.

Andy had made a place for himself at last among his peers. He

no longer could be thought of as freakish. Acceptance had made
him look less weird. He wore chinos and white shirts like many
of the other youths. Of course, he was a long distance from being
one of the campus 'wheels'. His set was not a fashionable one.
His friends were students on the outer fringes of campus social
life who had formed their own tight little circle. They were the
first of a number of sets of friends that Andy would go through
as his life progressed. Although he would not know their like
again – after all, they all had attended their first modern dance
program together, when they saw Martha Graham's company do
Appalachian Spring; they had heard together the strange mixture of
sounds and silence in the music of John Cage – nostalgia was not
part of his make-up. It was as though he regarded life as a train
ride with a number of stops along the way, and these were people
he had met and studied with and played with during an extended
stopover. Yet among them, he was admired, cosseted, and made
to feel like a very special human being.

He was also leaving another group of friends, all male and
some of them dance students. With few exceptions, they were
all homosexual. Somehow Andy had come out to them or they
had seen their own kind in him.

Still, there was no sense on Andy's part that he would be
leaving his friends behind. All of them spoke of New York, and
especially of Greenwich Village, as the place where they would
regroup.

Weeks before graduation, the plans for New York had become
crystalized. As the favored student of the faculty, Philip Pearlstein
had got to know Balcomb Greene nearly as well as Bob Lepper.
Now Greene proposed that Pearlstein sublet the Manhattan apartment of an artist friend of his who was about to go to Europe.
Philip told him that he would be sharing the place with Andy
Warhola, and that seemed quite all right. It was extremely cheap,
under forty dollars a month, and a walk-up, but Andy especially
was ecstatic about the prospect.

TWO

With their BFA (Bachelor of Fine Arts) degrees in hand, Andy and Philip got ready for their departure from Pittsburgh. Neither one would ever live there again, and in his strange effort to erase Pittsburgh from his biography Andy would tell interviewers that he had come from Philadelphia, Cleveland, McKeesport, and even Czechoslovakia.

During those final days before their departure, Philip was spending most of his time with Dorothy Cantor, his fiancée. It was obvious that the young men were altogether dissimilar in their sexual preferences, but they were oddly alike in other ways. Both were physically slight, Pearlstein being actually short, and they rarely had anything to say. Both were good listeners, however, and they watched whoever was speaking with an unblinking stare. They would make ideal roommates, since each would do his own thing quietly without distracting the other. They already had tested their compatibility when Andy moved his drawing things over to Pearlstein's house and they worked together because, in Pearlstein's words, 'Andy's nephews had begun destroying his drawings at home.'

New York was the mecca for the arts in America, and both Philip and Andy knew that they belonged there. Their instincts could not have been more on target. They became New Yorkers for life, and the city was theirs. As the most gifted men in their class, Pearlstein was convinced that his talent would make him a successful painter and Andy, against all odds, hoped that his would make him famous.

Waiting for them in New York was George Klauber, their former classmate, who, in their eyes, had already succeeded in the world of commercial art. He was the man they aspired to be like at that juncture of their lives, and he was the one who would open many doors for them in the big city. An affable man, who smiled as he talked, with the twinkling, wide-awake eyes of a pixie, Klauber exuded charm and confidence. Years later, he would take special pride in the distinction his Pittsburgh classmates accorded him by asking for his help – he became mentor to both Andy Warhol, the best-known American artist of the twentieth century, and Philip Pearlstein, the most influential painter of the human figure in contemporary art.

Klauber knew then that the two young men were gifted. He described them as being

> 'straight arrow. They did what came naturally to them. They never took great chances. But they drew marvelously, and Andy specifically drew as beautifully then as he did all the rest of his life, with a surety and sensitivity that I think was conspicuous to me at the time. I remember a self-portrait he did where I can just see those wonderfully long fingers that he had . . . and Philip the same way. Philip was a little more mannered perhaps, but it was a personality. And I never saw a personality in my own work as I did in Philip's and Andy's. Andy would never overwork anything. It was that statement and it was made, and it didn't need to be changed. It was second nature for him to draw. I've always found most people draw as they talk . . . it's as though they are talking. And yet Andy was so expressive in his drawings.'

But to Andy and Philip, Klauber was the big New York success. Klauber had first studied art at Pratt Institute in Brooklyn for a year and a half before he was drafted for army service in the Second World War. When he came back from the war he was a much more sophisticated artist. He had spent some months in Paris studying and using the models at the Sorbonne, the Lycée Louis le Grand and Le Grand Chaumière. Inexplicably failing to get into an illustration course at Pratt because of an obstinate dean, he transferred to Carnegie Tech's art school, where he found Andy and Philip in the sophomore class.

The three men had become very close during Klauber's year in Pittsburgh. After that year, when Klauber decided to return to

New York and Pratt Institute for reasons that had as much to do with Pittsburgh's provinciality as Klauber's perseverance, he got into the illustration course at Pratt, and, in his words, 'as soon as I got out of school, I found a job as assistant to the art director of *Fortune* magazine, Will Burtin. I worked as a special assistant to him and also on his freelance work.' When Burtin left the magazine to open his own studio, Klauber went with him. That is where he was when Andy and Philip arrived in town to stay.

There were friends other than Klauber waiting for Andy in New York. They would thin out over the next few years, making him feel friendless and alone, a new feeling for the grown-up Andy, whom college had spoiled a bit thanks to Ellie and Philip's crowd. His drift into alienation needs some explanation. According to nearly all of his friends of this period, he believed that he was terribly unattractive. Klauber, for one, believed that Andy was sexually frustrated throughout the fifties. He was seeking a mate, but he had to settle for something else – friendship.

One of his old friends from Carnegie Tech's modern dance group, Victor Reilly, met Andy within hours of his arrival at Penn Station. An actor friend, Charles Rydell, accompanied him, and Andy made no secret of the fact that he thought Rydell was sensational-looking. He was tall, wavy-haired, broad-shouldered, with a strong resemblance to the young Charlton Heston, except that Rydell's features were much more refined. Within a few years Rydell was in the off-Broadway musical *The Threepenny Opera*, and in the 1960s he was cast as Hercules in the Broadway musical *By Jupiter*.

He described Andy then as being

> 'like a machine in that he never said much, although when you got to know him well, he would joke . . . but he was like the Isherwood thing, *I Am a Camera* – he would record everything around him. . . . I do remember we went to a restaurant . . . then we just walked. I remember us walking along Central Park West and talking, in pouring rain. At Andy's memorial service, I told somebody that I met Andy on his first day in New York and that he was so boring I didn't see him again for ten years. I was just joking. . . .'

Over the years, Andy's crush on Rydell became a joke between them. More than a dozen years later, and on the brink of success in musical comedy, Rydell was snatched from the jaws of fame by a millionaire lover and he rarely acted again, except occasionally for Andy and a few road company musicals. But he always kept a small place of his own as an assertion of independence.

Andy's 'boring' side emerged early, presumably on his first day in New York. He later would write that he liked 'boring things', and there is a clue here to his methodical serial work (two hundred and ten nearly identical dollar bills etc.). It also reveals what newspaper people, especially gossip columnists and celebrity reporters, already know – that you don't have to be fascinating to become famous. Fame is often extraneous to the personality of the famous individual. He may have been consciously emulating his pet obsession, Garbo, about whom he knew everything that had been printed. Once Garbo visited Gertrude Stein's companion, Alice B. Toklas, in Paris, and Toklas asked if she would like to see Stein's collection of paintings, including a number by Picasso. Toklas turned on the lights above each painting, and Garbo sat in the middle of the room, shifting her gaze from painting to painting, making no comment until her eyes had finished their 'tour' and then saying with finality, 'Thank you.' That was the sum total of her conversation, and after she had gone, Alice B. Toklas had a comment of her own: 'Mademoiselle Hamlet.' Garbo's friends, few in number by her choice, found their relationship with her often tedious but excused this deficiency in her. She never had anything to say to the press and very little to say to her friends. The Press called her 'The Sphinx', and her friends 'difficult and retiring'. One of them, the insouciant novelist and playwright Anita Loos, said that Garbo's favorite reading matter was movie magazines, and so it was with Andy, but for a different reason. Anita described Garbo's preoccupation with the fan monthlies as rooted in her intense interest in what was being written about herself and her peers. Andy devoured them as reflections of the glamor of Hollywood with which he was besotted.

Rydell called Andy 'this quiet little guy . . . but with enormous presence. . . . He was not the most attractive man in the world,

but something about him compelled you to stick around.' On
the other hand, Pearlstein, who was heterosexual, found Andy
very attractive and thought it had something to do with his
air of helplessness. 'Helpless and vulnerable . . . people became
interested in him.' Pearlstein went on to describe how Andy was
dressed upon their arrival in New York: 'All he had to wear that
first summer was a heavy white corduroy suit, which rapidly
became rather yellow. It was a very hot summer, but we always
wore neckties.'

While Andy admired 'chic and glamorous people', he emphasized in himself a kind of gaucherie, a sort of grown-up 'Raggedy
Andy' thing. Early in their months together in New York, he
even appropriated stories of things that had really happened to
Pearlstein. Pearlstein said: 'One of the art directors I went to
wanted to see my work . . . and I opened my portfolio and a
roach crawled out. We lived in apartments that were crawling
with roaches. We'd put out an empty soda bottle and in a couple
of hours it would be filled with roaches.'

In the more innocent forties and early fifties, roaches were
just about the only residents New Yorkers ever talked about
as totally undesirable, and among much of the population their
extermination came up frequently in conversation. Andy wanted
to be thought of as a New Yorker, and Pearlstein's humbling
experience made a good roach story.

As for Pittsburgh, Andy never looked back. He had made a
clean break with his past there, and no one, in or out of the
media, would ever be told a straight story about what had
transpired in his life before Manhattan. Once, as artist Ed Plunkett
recalled, Andy attended a party given by ex-Pittsburghers, and
he puzzled some of them – especially those who remembered the
shy student at Carnegie Tech – by affecting an effete languor. In
those days, sometimes he tried on a new personality and then
chucked it.

The young men settled into the subject arranged for Pearlstein
by Balcomb Greene. It was an artist's cold-water flat on the
sixth and top floor of a walk-up building on St Mark's Place
near Avenue A. Then it was the lower East Side; today, it
is part of the gentrified East Village. Pearlstein remembered
it as a tenement section mainly populated by Poles and other

Eastern Europeans. 'There were peasant types around,' he said, 'and bread was in big baskets . . . .We'd go out once in a while for a bowl of soup or something. It didn't take much money to survive in New York then.' A nostalgic glimmer could be seen in Pearlstein's eyes as he continued: 'Now my daughter is an actress and she earns a living doing proof-reading at night. And all her money goes into paying rent. Rents are horrendous.'

They lived frugally, but they were far from being impoverished. 'I guess we each had about four hundred dollars. It was a lot then,' said Pearlstein. And so it was, and much more money was to come in at the end of their first week when Andy picked up his first fee as a free-lance commercial artist.

Klauber had lined up some prospects for them. Pearlstein thought that his own portfolio was 'too geared towards ideas' for most prospective employers, and things were leaner for him in their early New York days, but he described Andy's portfolio as 'stunning and geared towards illustration'.

But Andy did not draw on Klauber's contacts that first week. Like nearly every repressed gay American male, Andy, in a boyhood spent almost entirely without companions, depended upon the movies to keep sane and 'normal'. Twice-weekly visits to the local movie-house brightened his life with glamor and elegance. The first thing he did in his search for work was to go through the 'yellow pages' listing of magazines. The name *Glamour* magazine doubtless leapt out at him, and he went to them entirely on his own.

There, in the Graybar Building, he was informed that the art director was a Mrs Fredericks. 'I greeted a boy with a big beige blotch on his cheek, possibly going up to the forehead,' Tina Fredericks recalled of that first meeting with Andy.

'He was all one color, weird. There seemed something other-earthly or offbeat, different for sure, elfish, from another world. Later, when I had a more realistic view, I found him shrewd – Paul Morrissey told me he always went to auctions to bid on his own work to keep his prices up – and I found out at the funeral, I think it was John Richardson who spoke about his going to church every week and working with the poor on holidays, and that was a real surprise, and I was very moved by that.'

The 'wash' over the side of his face reminded her of something by Helen Frankenthaler, and, by contrast, he carried a big black portfolio.

The portfolio did not overwhelm her, but she was caught by a 'charming' abstraction of an orchestra playing done on gray paper in tempera. She thought it would look nice in the nursery she was planning – she was five months pregnant at the time – and she asked if she could buy it. 'He had a breathy way of talking,' she said. 'His voice was slight, unemphatic, whispery, covered over with a smile. When you read his writings, you can almost hear him speaking in that voice.'

'Oh,' he said. 'You can have it.' But she insisted on some token amount and paid him ten dollars for it. The painting was signed 'André Warhola'.

Thus began a professional relationship that would lead by an indirect path to Andy's final, successful assault on the nearly impregnable bastion of modern art. It can be said that it was not an intimate association. Neither one learned very much about the other personally, and what Tina Fredericks did learn about Andy did not especially charm her. 'The men who were always around did not have much use for a woman,' she said. So Andy never knew that this attractive young woman in the navy blue gabardine suit, with a smart white beret (lady editors always wore a hat in those tradition-bound days) was a German-Jewish refugee born in Berlin, whose father, Kurt Safranski, had wound up in America working for Richard Berlin, second-in-command at the Hearst publishing empire; nor had Andy yet met Berlin's daughter, Brigid, who would become one of his closest female confidantes. Safranski, a publishing genius, had designed the dummy of a picture weekly that Hearst turned down as too expensive, and the project, complete with the red block and white letters of the magazine's name (which turned out to be Life) in the upper left corner, went to the Luce company. Andy had been a fanatical fan of Life as well as Look and used them as major sources for much of his commercial work, frequently tracing or copying things from them, but he never knew that his first commercial art employer had anything to do with it.

Tina then asked, 'Can you draw anything else? Something we could use?'

'Oh, sure,' Andy replied confidently. 'I can draw anything.' And so he could, of course.

'How about a shoe?' She needed drawings of about six shoes, so she gave him the trial assignment, a paper bag full of shoes, and told him to bring the drawings in the following day. 'Overnight was what we insisted upon. We were always in a rush.'

Andy stayed up half the night working on that first assignment. He would never correct anything. If he thought a drawing was not just right, he started over again. But he failed to grasp what Tina Fredericks' needs were regarding his shoe drawings. She smiled as she recalled her first glance at the result.

> '. . . he'd drawn the shoes, but he'd given them a lot of character. He made them look as though they had been worn by someone for years, with wrinkles and rumples and all kinds of funny shapes.'

So she told him they would have to have 'sell' and look brand-new. 'Do them again,' she told him.

When he came back the next day, they were beautiful. 'Perfect,' she remembered.

> 'He took instructions perfectly. Then the way they were laid out – they were on one page and the next eight pages were an article on the various aspects of success for a career girl. We put these shoes on ladders, and he really did that charmingly, so we used those on the next eight pages. When we weren't working on something, I didn't see Andy that much, but he occasionally did something for us. Condé-Nast paid very little, but it was a good beginning, and I think the going rate was about a hundred dollars a page. I don't know exactly what we paid for those little sketches. But appearing in Condé-Nast magazines led some place. You would get other advertising jobs. Geri Stutz was the shoe and accessories editor at the time, and when she went to

I. Miller later on, she brought Andy with her. After that,
she went to Bendel's and she is now a publisher.'*

Despite Andy's scruffy appearance, and possibly because of it, he
made a lasting impression on Tina Fredericks and nearly everyone
else who employed him. Beginning that first summer of 1949,
Andy became a kind of character, easily described by the art
directors and ad agencies, sometimes with a little patronizing
laugh, but none of it did him any harm. He courted receptionists
with a single rose gallantly handed to them as he entered; he
courted secretaries. Doors opened all over town through this
essentially cornball technique. Pearlstein was a little astonished
by the volume of work that came Andy's way, but the fact
that it had been so easy for him did not surprise him. There was
work for *Glamour*, *Vogue*, *Harper's Bazaar*, the *New York Times
Sunday Magazine*, *Seventeen* (where Miss C. P. Pineles presided as
art director and began using Andy with some regularity). There
were book jackets for half a dozen publishing houses and album
jackets for Columbia records. Soon, he was on a level with
Mary Suzuki, Dagmar Freuchen, Jack Bodie, Richard Decker,
Ben Shahn (who was still doing commercial work), Maurice
Sendak (before he became a classic children's book author and
illustrator), Lynd Ward, Bill Charmatz, R. B. Hawley, Suzanne
Szasz, and Dink Siegel. Unlike most of them, he worked at
befriending his clients. He devised what became a ritual to achieve
this, drawing on his shy look, his elfin demeanor, his semblance
of naiveté, his child-like pleasure in giving presents (May Baskets
on May Day, Easter eggs, home-baked pastry from his mother's
oven), even his shabbiness as 'the poor, struggling artist'. Like
a professional panhandler about to go out on the streets, he
'dressed down' before making his daily rounds: shabby shoes,
faded, soiled corduroys, later replaced by chinos, an old necktie.
For a time he was forced by an oculist to wear opaque glasses
with just a pin-hole to see through, which made him look blind
as well.
    The Easter eggs were decorated by his mother after her arrival

---

* Geraldine Stutz founded Panache Press, which in the late 1980s published
facsimile editions of several of Andy Warhol's privately printed books.

in New York sometime in the winter of 1951–2. She demonstrated once again that she had a primitive genius for art. He
began designing and having printed his little promotional books
of cats, cherubs and other fey creatures, all published in editions
of one hundred copies by Seymour Berlin and then hand-coloured
by friends, who were as much taken in by his poor-boy routine
as the receptionists, secretaries and art directors had been. These
little books were handed around to prospective clients as advertisements for himself and to old clients as gifts.★

Pearlstein went several weeks before connecting with a decent
job through Klauber. Meanwhile, Andy was going from one
free-lance assignment to another. If he experienced profound disappointment over his failure to succeed in the sexual marketplace,
in the world of commercial art he had already made an impact. It
was something that Pearlstein had expected to happen. He said:

> 'Andy always seemed like nobody else. At least in the
> art way. From the very beginning he seemed much
> better than anybody else in the class. I never felt com-
> petitive in any way. I was always interested in how that
> talent would grow. It was really quite gratifying . . . I
> may have done my bit toward bringing that out. My
> gift to the world. I'm sure if he hadn't gone to New
> York, all sorts of things would still have happened, but
> I was a part of all that. It was nice to see it happen.'

At first, Andy was too busy to do any serious drawing or
painting, but he was full of energy and somehow he managed
to begin doing some large ink and watercolor wash drawings
derived from Capote's writings. It was an extension of what he
had been doing earlier in the year at school with Katherine Anne
Porter and Robert Penn Warren, but with Capote he became truer
to himself and he allowed Aubrey Beardsley's influence, for one,
to creep into his work once again.

All of his serious art in the 1950s consisted of clean line

★ Because there were only 100 copies printed of each title and because they were
hand-colored, each of these books today has value as an art work. Warhol
was unique in promoting his work in this original way and may have been
influenced by the example of Walt Whitman, who was his own publisher of
early editions of *Leaves of Grass*.

drawings, some with color, some without. There was a deceptive simplicity to Andy's early work. It masked his true obsessions – the beauty of the male figure and male feet, usually bare. There were many cherubs, naked but naive; many butterflies; stylishly crude sketches of legends like 'the Divine Sarah' (Bernhardt). While George Klauber believed Andy to have been closeted, at least to the public, in the fifties, he came on very strong to some new male acquaintance who was especially comely.

As someone who was very much a part of New York's gay subculture, he moved freely in the theatrical, art and fashion worlds, which had not yet meshed with the ambisexual, bicoastal disco set.

In the fifties *haute couture* was often in the hands of women. Coco Chanel was as powerful as Dior or Mainbocher, and women headed up the powerful fashion magazines, with Diana Vreeland among the most prominent. Vreeland would come into Andy's orbit permanently in the seventies through her friendship (and one-sided affair) with Fred Hughes, who was Andy's second-in-command at the Factory. But at no time was there a strong woman looking out for Andy in this tough-elegant scene. In Pittsburgh, Andy had been protected by Julia Warhola, Ellie Simon and others. In New York, he was liberated and lonely, moving into unknown waters, swimming alone. He knew he was going to have to make it on his own, although his eye was always cocked for a handsome lifeguard.

Andy and Philip followed what was happening in the art world by going to shows at galleries and museums and reading the reviews and commentary, but both of them were moving in directions that were different from what was then currently fashionable, although they made half-hearted bids to keep *au courant*. Philip finally worked out a style that was later called by his biographers abstract expressionism, but he abandoned it soon after his work began to sell and returned to the terribly honest renderings of the human figure that he preferred.

Ellie Simon had no intention of remaining behind in Pittsburgh, and in the autumn of 1949, she moved to New York, sharing an apartment on West 74th Street near West End Avenue with a former classmate at Carnegie Tech, Leila Davies. Her arrival did not mean that she and Andy would resume their old relationship. Andy no longer needed her help, and they led very separate lives in Manhattan, although Ellie worked at keeping their friendship alive, seeing him as often as she could.

Since Andy was accepting almost more assignments than he could manage, it was becoming obvious that he needed an agent to keep his fees up, especially as the signature 'Andy Warhol' was now turning up all over the place. According to Philip, he had stumbled upon the magical name when he received a bill in the mail addressed to 'Andrew Warhol', with the last 'a' of his name dropped in error. For a time he used exactly that name, abandoning the 'André' of his final months in Pittsburgh, but by 1951 he had become 'Andy' professionally. One afternoon a woman named Fritzie Miller was visiting the studio of Will Burtin, George Klauber's employer. Fritzie Miller had been representing her commercial artist husband and several of his friends. Andy was there that day visiting Klauber and Burtin. Miller was introduced to someone she described later 'as this slender boy in paint-spattered clothes, holding a hand-painted Easter egg.' The egg was a gift for Burtin, and it was doubtless one of the same batch he made up with his mother's help at the time he gave Tina Fredericks one. 'Andy,' Burtin said, 'meet Fritzie. You need her.'

Andy had been using an informal agent, a man who had volunteered simply to take his things around. Now the man phoned Andy in great annoyance and complained that he heard he had got an official agent. Andy was afraid that this man was coming over to beat him up. The fears of his childhood were a long time a-dying. Andy phoned Miller in great distress, and she told him, 'Listen, Andy, forget it. You don't owe me anything.' But about a month later Andy phoned her again and asked her to represent him, which she did for nearly a decade.

Although Andy was too young to have served in the recent war, he was part of the immediate post-war art world. Thirty years earlier, the peace after a similar world conflict had sent his kind to Paris. But Hitler had changed all of that. It is ironic that the cultural legacy of that frustrated artist would be that the heart of modern painting crossed the Atlantic. Hitler's ominous legions made refugees not only of Jewish artists but of scores of gentiles as well – Marcel Duchamp, André Masson, Fernand Léger, Jean Tinguely, Max Ernst, Salvador Dali, Piet Mondrian, and Joan Miro.★ These artists knew that the warped spirit behind Nazism was anti-art. Only a few major painters elected to remain on the continent, among them Braque, Picasso and Matisse. Jewish refugees like Marc Chagall and Jacques Lipchitz seasoned the exodus. Then there were painters from South and Central America, notably Matta (Roberto Sebastian Matta Echaurren), the Chilean-French painter from Santiago, who pioneered Surrealistic drawings and who turned to Expressionism in the 1950s (e.g., *The Birth of America*, 1957). His canvases of mural size may have given a heroic dimension to what was to become the New York School. He lived in New York from 1939 to 1948.

In those post-war years, all of these artists continued to paint and sculpt in New York, finding America, and particularly New York City, congenial to their work. In truth, it was easier for most of them since they had distanced themselves from Hitler's war and its aftermath. And their influence was so profound that it changed the face of American art.

So New York was the beating heart of contemporary art in the late 1940s. Significantly, one of the major commercial galleries in the world, Marlborough of London, opened a branch in New York that was soon on a par with its parent in sales and importance.

The New York School of painting had already begun to form upon Andy's arrival in the city. Helen Frankenthaler, exactly Andy's age, was there if not yet known, as were Jasper Johns and Robert Rauschenberg. Franz Kline and Willem de Kooning were ready to give the movement its shape, and Jackson Pollock, Ellsworthy Kelly, Mark Rothko and Hans Hoffmann ensured its international impact. The outlines of the School were easily spotted on a museum or gallery wall – there were sweeping abstractions, large flat color fields, splashes and drips – and it had a name, Abstract Expressionism.

In his heart of hearts, Andy did not like Abstract Expressionism. Over the next decade, he would make occasional stabs at,

---

★ These artists were following the paintings themselves, their own and those of their predecessors. Wealthy art patrons and museums in America had bought up the greater part of European art produced in the twentieth century, and when a Léger retrospective was mounted in the Louvre, say, the museum would seek loans of American acquisitions, without which they would have no show.

or incorporate into his work, such elements of the movement as he felt it could stand. But it was always a self-conscious effort. He preferred his sensitive blotted ink drawings of cats, cherubs and beautiful boys; his influences (Beardsley, Cocteau, Lautrec, Balthus, Demuth*) were of another time.

The summer flew by. Andy and Philip continued to go to museums and galleries, but they rarely discussed art. Perhaps it is significant that Andy Warhol seemed to have no strong opinions about what was happening in the New York art world. Pearlstein never heard him voice any. If one is to deduce anything from his future serious art, it would seem that he was willing to move with the mainstream, if he could, and if he could not, then he would forge his own way. The men saw a lot of double features on 42nd Street, and they would talk about them on the walk home (they walked everywhere, eschewing subways and buses; in those closing days of the 1940s, the streets of New York and even Central Park's lanes were safe). Sometimes Andy was quite critical of a film, but Pearlstein found something worthwhile in all of the movies. It is likely that Andy was so critical because he had already decided that at some point he was going to make movies himself.

Philip found Andy a congenial roommate. They were often as silent as two cats stretched out near a warm grate. During his evenings away from Sutnar's studio and on weekends, Philip painted. He was doing paintings 'ahead of their time . . . crazy, symbolist stuff.' An art dealer, Harry Saltpeter, looked at his work and encouraged him to keep at it. Andy was trying to finish several drawings from Capote's work, enough to make a series, but he was working ten-hour days at his commercial assignments so his serious art was slowed down. Following a pattern set in Pittsburgh, he attended mass at least twice a week. Sometimes, he spent a social evening over in Brooklyn Heights with George Klauber and his friends. It was understood by both roommates that these were always all-male affairs, so Philip often remained behind.

* Balthus (Count Balthazaer Klossowski de Rola) was noted for his nude adolescent girls, often in erotic poses. Charles Demuth was a watercolor painter from Lancaster, Pennsylvania, who used the line and wash technique employed by Andy for his Capote drawings. Demuth illustrated works by Henry James, Poe and Zola.

They enjoyed their neighborhood just off Tompkins Square Park. It was only later, in the sixties, as the city began to feel the impact of the drug culture and people hurried through crime-ridden streets, that the Polish peasants sunning themselves in the park were displaced by junkies making connections. It became known as 'Needle Park', and it was no longer safe for the locals still living nearby. But by the time it went 'bad', Andy and Pearlstein were both prosperous and living in separate establishments in good neighborhoods. Today, Tompkins Square Park has been reclaimed and is a part of the restored East Village.

Andy's commercial work had to have been different from that of his rivals to attract all the commissions he was getting. Besides the blotted line, which gave his ad drawings a printed look, or the sort of look one finds in a child's primer, there was the simplicity and the elegance. Some say that he was influenced by Ben Shahn, others by Matisse. Andy would never credit anyone, but Pearlstein did claim that Andy created the blotted line style:

> 'He invented it, simply because he wanted to make variations, so he made the drawing on good paper, and then added water [water-resistant] paper hinged to it and then would draw [retrace] a couple of inches over the original drawing and then would re-wet the ink and blot it with another piece of paper. Just blot it. But there was a master drawing and there were several copies done by this blotting technique.'

Thus we see how Andy could deliver two copies of a guitar drawing to the publishing house for the Spanish textbook *Madrigal's Magic Key to Spanish* in 1952. He tops off the chapter headings with little, blotted-line drawings of fruit, the devil, a doctor, a monkey that looks almost human, because there is a line from the eyebrow to the nostrils suggesting a human nose rather than a flattened simian one. The duplicate guitar drawings were required for the spine and for inside the book.

But it does seem unlikely that Andy invented the style. Dudley Huppler, an artist friend of Andy's, did some early drawings, portraits of Andy and exceptional likenesses, which utilize this same blotted-line technique. Some of the Huppler drawings surfaced at the auction of Andy's things at Sotheby's in New York in 1988.★

Andy employed a similar style in illustrating *The Amy Vanderbilt Complete Book of Etiquette: A Guide to Gracious Living*. Vanderbilt had become *the* authority on manners, although Emily Post's book, laying down the rules of another, more rigid time, was still in print. Andy was essentially ignorant of proper social behavior. He knew nothing about how to live graciously and, in fact, for a number of years had shared apartments with his mother that had nothing but bare mattresses on stark bedframes, a work table, a kitchen table with unmatched chairs. He was the poor boy who had made it, and manners and gracious living were customs of a foreign land. Small wonder that Amy Vanderbilt found his simple renderings of social situations fresh and charming. They made a perfect combination, and several years later she would ask him to illustrate her cookbook.

★ The Huppler work was pointed out to me by Andreas Brown of the Gotham Book Mart. Brown is a Warhol scholar and produced a definitive catalogue of his early work. He bought two of the Huppler drawings at the Warhol auction.

THREE

At the end of August, Andy and
Philip found themselves a larger, considerably more comfortable
apartment by answering an ad in the *New York Times*. It was a loft
space over a truck garage between Eighth and Ninth Avenues on
West 21st Street in the Chelsea district. The loft had been leased
to a modern dancer, Francesca Boas, and had been renovated
by her and her roommate, Jan Gay, into a studio-theater with
a proscenium arch at one end. Boas was the daughter of the noted
anthropologist Franz Boas, author of the definitive work *Primitive
Art*, first published in 1927. She was presently using her studio
for dance therapy with disturbed children. Pearlstein recalled that
'These kids ran around screaming their heads off. Primal screams.
She was probably one of the pioneers of that. I think she played
around with Andy's mind. . . . It was during the day, but I think
they had long conferences.'

Boas lived with her companion in a space behind the pro-
scenium arch and was still on the premises much of the time.
So was Andy, who still worked at home on his assignments.
During their coffee breaks they had long talks, and she found
Andy, in Pearlstein's words, 'so intriguing'. Philip observed a
'metamorphosis' begin and said, 'Andy Warhola became Andy
Warhol.' This may be a simplification, but certainly the process
of change began then.

Boas had a hand in releasing that persona in Andy which he
had held in check in Pittsburgh and in his first months in New
York. She encouraged him to go farther out in experiencing
life, particularly the rich variety of New York life. It was the
beginning of a remarkable and perilous journey that would take
Andy Warhol farther out than any of his peers and finally take
him beyond the edge. In the years ahead, only one fellow painter,

Larry Rivers, could approach Andy in complicating his life with relationships that were as challenging and as demanding as his art. Others were boozers or had other crippling dependencies, but only Warhol and Rivers collected people as fascinating subjects to explore personally.

Their characters could not have been more different. Andy was passive, quiet, always watching. Rivers was volatile, noisy – he even played a jazz saxophone – forever actively engaged in one personal relationship or another. Both were born in the 1920s, although Andy had the edge in youth, being five years younger, and both were fascinated by homosexuality. Andy could not help himself; he had been gay since he could remember. Rivers approached male love by choice, or so it would seem. He looked at homosexuality as something 'that seemed too much, too gorgeous, too ripe.' Rivers was 'straight' as the world and most of his peers perceived him. He was at home in the Cedar Street Tavern, a super-macho hang-out for abstract expressionists, some of whom, including Jackson Pollock, were brawling alcoholics. At least one of Rivers's friends insists that none of his homosexual affairs or encounters was serious in intent; they were just something that emerged spontaneously when he was drinking. Here may be the place to put to rest that ancient fallacy – that drinking makes people do things totally out of character. Alcohol is simply a release. Yet Rivers was married; he had a son and stepson. He genuinely liked women, and it seems evident that he saw them as sexual creatures as well, which Andy never did. Furthermore, Andy was already categorized as part of the gay world, even though he was perceived even in that first year in Manhattan as someone completely harmless. Because of his look of innocence and his seeming helplessness, he was acceptable to everyone.

Even in the gay world, Andy was not clearly pinned down. Despite its outlaw status in 1949–50, the homosexual underworld demanded considerable conformity. You either did this or that, and you became known for what you did sexually as well as what you wore – leather for sado-masochism, not yet modish but beginning to be taken up by gays, who would remain in the forefront of male fashion throughout the century; suit and tie for 'dressy' men's bars (not yet called gay bars except by a handful of avant-gardists); casual masculine attire for closeted cases like Andy and those who chose to look 'normal'.

What was a distinct difference between Andy and Rivers, as their parallel journeys progressed, was their relationships with others. Rivers attempted to live his experiences on the deepest possible level, including a long friendship with the poet Frank O'Hara, while Andy, when he was finally liberated and totally himself in the first of his Factories ten years later, rejected personal commitments in favor of watching others play out their brawling, fractious entanglements. It was safer, or so he thought at the time. But there was obvious envy of Rivers in Andy, who described Rivers's personality as 'very Pop – he rode around on a motorcycle and he had a sense of humor about himself as well as everybody else.' While Andy may have felt too little, Rivers felt too much. Around this time (1951), he slashed his wrists, but survived. One of Andy's favorite painters, Fairfield Porter, painted Rivers with taped wrists.

Andy and Pearlstein shared their large end room with Boas's huge dog called 'Name'. When they had to leave, about eight months later, Andy was sorriest to leave Name and her puppies, born in their room. More than a dozen years later, when a street person on amphetamines was brought to the Factory by Andy from the San Remo café, a hang-out for unpublished poets and speed freaks, he changed the man's name from Billy Linich to Billy Name, in silent honor of his long-lost canine mascot (Linich never learned the true origin of his name). Billy Name became a kind of mascot, too, never leaving the premises, and soon made himself indispensable.

Sometime during their ten months together, Pearlstein observed Andy writing little notes to somebody. When he discovered that they were being written to Truman Capote, he was surprised. Although Ellie Simon had known that Andy had begun this one-sided correspondence back in Pittsburgh, Philip had not been aware of it, and he was certain that Andy did not know Capote. Later, Andy would write:

> 'I met Truman Capote through his mother years ago. Truman was just a little bit older than me, but a lot more famous. I wrote him fan letters from Pittsburgh and when I moved to New York, I tried to meet him. I did some drawings for *Other Voices, Other Rooms* and called up Truman and asked if he wanted to see them.

Truman wasn't interested. But his mother was. When
I got to their apartment on Park Avenue I realized she
just wanted somebody to drink with.'

Truman remembered their first meeting a little differently. He
said that he began getting fan letters from Andy, one nearly every
day for months. The most 'creepy' one arrived in their mail box
with no stamp, and then Truman knew that Andy had found the
building where he lived with his mother and stepfather, Nina and
Joe Capote. Truman glanced down at the street and saw Andy
leaning against a lamppost, 'staked out there'. This made him
very angry and he complained loudly to his mother about it.
But she felt sorry for Andy and went down to the street to invite
him up. Not long after he arrived in the apartment, where Andy
met a rather frosty Truman, Nina Capote picked up her purse and
invited Andy to go around the corner to have a drink with her.
   Andy continues his version:

'She took me to the Blarney Stone on Third Avenue
and we drank boilermakers and talked about Truman's
problems. Then, one day out of the blue, she called me
up and told me to stop bothering Truman. She wasn't
that well and eventually committed suicide.

'Truman has had a strange life. His father ran away
right after Truman was born. He married eight more
times but never had any more children. All his wives
were rich when he met them and broke when he left
them. Truman's real name is Streckfus Persons. He's
from New Orleans. Capote was his stepfather's name.
He was Cuban.

'I didn't see much of Truman in the fifties. Sometimes
I ran into him with Cecil Beaton. They were best
friends, and I knew Cecil a little bit.★ Truman was
always nice to me but never that friendly. Recently,

★ The magazine editor George Davis introduced Beaton to Capote. Later
Beaton wrote of him: 'I found him a very remarkable person, a genius and
although only twenty-three years old had the maturity of a man of sixty . . .
I like him a lot, as well as being impressed and think if he lives (his blood
doesn't flood easily in his veins – or some other such awful thing happens to
him) he will make a contribution to the world' (Beaton to Greta Garbo).

Truman told me that he always liked me because I
was nice to his mother – when I drank with her he
didn't have to. But he said he felt sorry for me then.
I didn't know what he meant. I was exactly the same as
I am now, but I wasn't famous.'

Andy leaves out a significant part of the story. When Truman
got fed up with his mother's neuroses and alcoholism, he would
check into the Plaza Hotel. Andy kept close tabs on Truman's
movements, and he would sit in the lobby, dressed as a dandy
with vest and tie, hoping that people would mistake him for
Truman. It was a lunatic idea. While Truman was as slightly
built as Andy, Truman looked like a beautiful boy.

The two accounts spell out the differences between them.
Truman knew at once that Andy, like many others, including
several married men, had an enormous crush on him. He had
had this sort of attention all of his life, and it would continue well
into his thirties when alcohol, baldness, and a weight problem
robbed him of his attractiveness. But in 1949 he was the 'doll'
of the moment and he did not find it at all unusual. Since the
publication of his first book in 1947, with the notorious jacket
photo by Harold Halma, he had received a steady stream of
letters from young gay men, saying how much they admired
him, and often enclosing photographs of themselves. But Andy
was the most persistent and possibly did not even know that he
was one of a multitude. These fans were people whom Truman
studiously avoided. He most enjoyed the company of the rich and
successful. Tycoons, their wives, mistresses or male lovers were
his dish. Super-rich women especially became his 'best friends'
and confidantes until he speared them all to the heart in his *roman
à clef*, *Answered Prayers*, which he never finished, partly because
of his dismay at his ex-friends' outrage when portions were
serialized, and mostly because he could not shake his dependency
on alcohol and prescription drugs.

Once he could afford them, Andy was attracted to losers.
Over the next quarter of a century, much of his income from
his succession of Factories supported speed freaks, transvestites,
young hustlers, female hangers-on, and unpublished poets, all of
whom found a haven at Andy's workplace. Not until he was
shot by one of these misfits did Andy reappraise his predilection

and realize that now, as someone as rich and famous as Truman Capote was, he, too, could cultivate and regard as friends tycoons, their wives and their lovers. But it was almost as though Andy climbed up the social ladder because he had been made afraid of those on the bottom.

In a very important sense, Andy did not 'blend in' very well with the upper classes. He always seemed a little outside things, and he was, of course. But Truman became not only their bedmate but their jester and, finally, their Proust, and Cecil Beaton became their court photographer. Beaton expresses regret over having missed a Warhol party in 1965, probably one Andy threw at the Amusement Pier in Santa Monica, which Beaton described as 'a fantastic orgy with people making love on the revolving horses and being photographed betimes for an advanced movie.' Later, Beaton asserted, Andy visited him at his hotel and stole a glass, which he thought 'nice'. (This is one of several documented accounts of petty thievery in Andy, although at that time he was surrounded by speed freaks, nearly all of whom stole routinely to support their addiction.) From society's viewpoint, Andy was still the kid in the street in front of the candy store with his nose against the glass, except that eventually he had a camera and tape recorder in hand to conceal his discomfiture.

Truman and Andy might not have agreed on the facts of their lives when those lives converged, but they could not deny that they were both very theatrical in their respective fields. As a consequence, Truman was constantly making the rounds of the television talk shows. When Andy entered the period of his most intense celebrity, lasting twenty-five years, he was equally ubiquitous socially, although television hosts quickly learned that it was a mistake to ask him on a show because he had so little to say.

Unlike Truman, Andy courted fame as though it were not already his. He was obsessively concerned with his appearance. Never good-looking, when he was at his best, in the mid- sixties, with all his essential features refined as much as possible, he was passably unprepossessing. When that no longer worked, he cultivated a *counter-image*. This was something Truman could appreciate, since he attempted something akin to it when he was no longer decadently cute. Andy's semi-punk, spikey silver wig was calculated as part of this counter-image. He latched onto

punk years before it became the vogue among the young –
with the Warhol look, and with his own rock band, the Velvet
Underground, eventually being called 'the Godfathers of punk'
(although their music was more raw sound than real punk). But
despite their contemporary eccentric images, there were significant differences in the way the world regarded Truman and
Andy. Truman gleefully thumbed his nose at the straight world.
'I'm gay,' he seemed to be saying, 'and if that bothers you, you
can go fuck yourself.' While Andy, sweet Andy, always smiling
and looking even gayer than Truman, remained 'officially' in the
closet his whole life, trying to persuade the world that 'he could
be anything'. Certainly Pop Art (in which he became the central
figure) was in the main a homosexual movement, but even some
of those artists who were gay were embarrassed by Andy's look a
good deal of the time. Andy knew that he was 'swish' in manner,
and said: 'I certainly wasn't a butch kind of guy by nature, but I
must admit, I went out of my way to play up the other extreme.'

Eventually it became impossible for Truman to ignore Andy.
Andy's fame had eclipsed his own and he was turning up everywhere and they were constantly bumping into each other. Ever
conscious of beautiful males, Andy became concerned in the late
1970s about Truman's preference for men older than himself,
Truman himself being then well past fifty. 'Truman is always
getting himself involved with these old guys!' Andy exclaimed.
'They're not very attractive, and they're *so* dull!' By that time,
Andy obviously had sufficient self-confidence and self-esteem to
deplore both dullness and unattractiveness. Andy asked a public
relations consultant named Joseph Petrocik if something could
not be done to find Truman a young boyfriend. But that was
not Truman's cup of tea, and Petrocik himself, who was about
Truman's age, and his companion, Myron Clement, who was
only a little younger, became his saloon companions and saw
him through the heartbreaking episodes with booze and drugs
that lasted until his death in 1984. During this final disintegrating
spiral, Andy approved of Truman's efforts to reverse it by having
a face lift, hair transplants and major work done on his teeth.
'Why, Truman,' Andy told him, 'it's a new same old you!' The
tone was finally familial.

They met frequently in those years at the most popular disco
in New York, Studio 54, where men could dance with men and

even have sex on an upper balcony and where, in the dim light, both straight and gay couples carried on.

Late in life, Truman also made several pronouncements on the subject of Andy Warhol. In a bestselling biography of one of his 'Superstars', Edie Sedgwick, Truman contributed:

> 'I think Edie was something Andy would like to have been; he was *transposing* himself into her *à la Pygmalion*. Have you ever noticed a certain type of man who always wants to go along with his wife to pick out her clothes? I've always thought that's because he wants to wear them himself. Andy Warhol would like to have been Edie Sedgwick. He would like to have been a charming, well-born debutante from Boston. He would like to have been anybody except Andy Warhol.'

And then in a discussion about people's obsession (including Andy's) with Garbo, who was often referred to as 'the Sphinx', Truman said: 'Andy's a sphinx without a riddle.'

So in the end there was an accommodation made, and they accepted each other. Andy was now filled with amused concern, and Truman was coldly analytical as always, seeing Andy's self-protective masks and costumes as efforts to escape from himself, a self that, in Truman's view, was abhorrent to its inhabitant as well as shallow.

Andy never showed any evidence of having low self-esteem, so Truman's view that Andy thought himself abhorrent is quite incorrect. As for considering himself 'shallow', he did come across in that way to some interviewers and others who never got close to him. Yet he aspired to become another Matisse, which is scarcely an ambition in one with low self-esteem.

Pearlstein saw a very different Andy. 'Andy was a workaholic,' he recalled.

> 'He used a table across the room from me. He did several versions of each of his assignments, showing all of them to the art directors, who appreciated that. He studied the results carefully when they were printed for the effectiveness of his work and then he'd apply the results of these self-critiques to his new work.'

On his side of the room, Pearlstein would be painting at his easel
every evening after the day's work was done at Sutnar's studio.

They played phonograph records while they worked. Back
in Pittsburgh, Andy's taste in music was much the same as
his friends'. He liked the popular records and worked hard at
developing a taste for classical music. Those were the years of Nat
Cole, Frank Sinatra in his 'comeback', Peggy Lee, Lena Horne,
and Dinah Shore. It was the tag end of the swing era, and rock
and roll was beginning to be the 'hip' thing with teenagers. Andy,
at twenty-one, was not so distant from his own teens that he
could not connect with their music. He preferred Bill Haley and
the Comets to Johnny Ray, who was becoming the pop music
idol in the early fifties. In truth, Andy never moved very far
away from this stage of his life. He preferred to be around young
people.

FOUR

'As soon as I became a loner in my own mind, that's when I got what you might call a "following". As soon as you stop wanting something you get it. I've found that to be absolutely axiomatic.'

The Philosophy of Andy Warhol

Suddenly it turned out that Francesca Boas, Philip and Andy's leaseholding co-tenant, was behind in her rent to the landlord of the loft building on West 21st Street. In April 1950 they were all evicted, despite the young men having paid their own rent on time to Francesca. They were all out on the street – Philip, Andy, Francesca and her friend, and Name and her puppies. Andy was most distressed over losing Name.

There was nothing to be gained by Andy finding a new apartment with Pearlstein. Philip was getting married that summer, and, of course, the newly-wed Pearlsteins would be getting their own apartment.

Andy was invited to the wedding. Dorothy Cantor Pearlstein, still feeling some of her friend Ellie's concern over Andy and his helplessness, may have expressed to her new husband some guilt over Andy's abandonment. His aura of helplessness persisted even in New York. After the wedding, Andy phoned her frequently and at all hours, and she became, by phone, what Ellie had been earlier and what several men and women would be in the future for Andy – a confidante.

But all of that happened a couple of months later. At the time of their eviction, Andy was in a state of near panic. He had never lived by himself in his life, and while countless gay men were always advertising for roommates in the *New York Times*, he could not imagine living with a stranger.

Leila Davies had moved with Ellie from West 74th Street into a ground-floor apartment on 103rd Street and Amsterdam Avenue with Andy's former classmate and friend, the dancer Victor Reilly, whom Ellie had introduced to Leila. Ellie had already decided that she really did not like living in New York. The war within her between her wish to be liberated and her desire to live in a conventional environment was being lost to the forces of conformity. She would only stay about a week in the new place before returning to Pittsburgh. There were four male roommates sharing the place when the girls moved in. Andy moved in at almost the same time at Leila's suggestion. So for several days, Andy and Ellie shared the same roof, Andy on a daybed in the dining-room. The apartment comprised the entire ground floor, with the two girls in one bedroom, three men in the second bedroom, and one man in the living-room. The other men sharing the place were Jack ('Mitch') Beaber, also from Pittsburgh and then with the American Ballet Theatre; Joey Ross, who was working in musical comedy; and a serious artist named Tommy Quinlan who was supporting his career through an advertising job. An exotic mulatto beauty named Mata, a dancer from the Caribbean, was visiting Reilly that week. There were people coming and going all the time, some of them visitors, others semi-permanent roommates.

Ellie had realized during Andy's first year in Manhattan (and her own, too) that he had abandoned his former reticence about his gayness, but both Ellie and Leila thought that he was virtually friendless except for themselves and his new roommates. She was pleased to see before her departure that all of the men liked Andy, despite his complaint about them in his future memoirs, and Leila was a good and loyal friend. Leila and Andy did a lot of casual walking around Manhattan together. She said they would make an excuse to go out: 'It might be to pick up the paper, but then we would just walk, for blocks and blocks. We walked all the way to midtown and back. New York was very different then.' The others included Andy in their inexpensive amusements, which sometimes included going to the movies. But they were all poor, young, ambitious, and every one of them looking for a break.

Both Ellie and Andy were bohemian in their need to be around people in the arts, but the streak of orthodoxy within Ellie that was now taking her back home would ignite a very real war within her one day. When she returned to Pittsburgh, she took up a teaching position, while taking evening courses at Carnegie Tech, doing her leather work and spending her summer vacations in Provincetown working on her enameled pieces for Milton Hefling's boutique there. Unlike Andy, she remained relatively poor, and when she became engaged to physicist Avrom Blumberg, he was touched by her efforts to conceal her near poverty. When they attended a play, as the lights went down she put on a pair of glasses with the temple leg broken and hanging down 'like a lorgnette'. But Avrom found her to be 'a delightful mixture of zany humor and sensitive observations', and they seemed compatible in every way.

When they finally married in 1954, her sympathetic husband knew that she not only had to continue with her boutique creations but keep in close touch with that artists' world where she felt most at home. In 1959 Avrom took a sabbatical from teaching physics, and he and Ellie sailed to England (she was afraid of flying) and spent a month in London, with side trips to Cambridge and Oxford. She sketched places they visited, and seemed to be enjoying herself. She was much moved by their visit in Amsterdam to the house where Rembrandt had lived. Avrom remembered:

> 'We did not map out an itinerary but decided to plan our trip along the way . . . we knew we wanted to spend time in France and Italy also and perhaps in Israel and maybe even the Soviet Union . . . . We stayed in Paris for a month. As a hint of things to come, one day Ellie's hands became very, very cold and she wanted to return to our hotel for a while. We rested and went out again, without any problem . . . . After Venice we went to Siena and Florence and then met Philip Pearlstein, who was in Italy with Dorothy and their first-born, William George, on a Fulbright. Philip had gone up north to buy a Volkswagen and asked Ellie and me if we'd like to go with him and Dorothy on a motor trip to and around Sicily to look at early Greek and Roman ruins . . . . On this trip the cold-hand symptom became

more pronounced. Ellie suffered spells of acute panic and yet didn't want to spoil the trip for everyone . . . . When we finally got back to Rome she was exhausted and we decided to go to a sea resort in Fregene, for a two-week rest. It became obvious that leaving our room brought on the attacks.'

Pearlstein and Dorothy realized that Ellie was quite ill when she 'had her first siege of not wanting to leave her hotel room in Syracuse.' Somehow, Ellie and Avrom managed to visit Israel, persuading themselves that they had heard that there were expert doctors living there. In Jerusalem a psychiatrist identified her condition as anxiety and recommended they return at once to America. When they eventually moved to Illinois in the early sixties, they had already fallen into a pattern of rarely going out. In Chicago, they found a new therapist through the Institute for Psychoanalysis. Edoardo Weiss was one of the last close associates of Sigmund Freud, and he correctly diagnosed her illness as agoraphobia, a morbid fear of being in open or public places. Weiss ferreted out what was behind her anxiety. In Avrom's words: '. . . it had to do with her feelings toward her parents. She seemed to resent it that her gentle and capable mother was just a housewife after her first child, and worried that she might fall into that trap also.' Perhaps to exorcize this resentment, they tried to have a child, failed, and then adopted a five-day-old boy, whom they named David. When Ellie developed cancer, Weiss learned of it and refused to take any more money for her therapy.

Thus it was that in the sixties, the decade of Andy's great success, Ellie Blumberg, his first champion and mentor, was in seclusion and decline. While his life became a kind of non-stop party, Ellie remained behind her closed door. Cancer killed her in September 1967, nine months before Andy was gunned down and nearly died.

Andy's contacts with Ellie became fewer after she left the 'art commune', where they were all living on West 103rd Street. Once, she dropped by there to see him, accompanied by her artist brother, Sidney Simon, who was on his way to a Rhodes scholarship abroad. In the early fifties, she visited Andy with Avrom when Andy and his mother were living on lower Lexington

Avenue. Andy's apartment was cluttered, but he wanted them to see the transparent plastic 'lace curtains' he had stuck to all the windows, a curious decorating item from the thirties' depression, and Avrom recalled that Mrs Warhola told them that she was planning to stay with Andy until he got married. Both Ellie and Avrom accepted this improbable turn of events with polite interest. But future contacts were few in number, and the old friends drifted apart. They were so out of contact by the time of Ellie's death that Andy was not invited to the funeral.

Eight years after her death, Andy published a kind of memoir which he called *The Philosophy of Andy Warhol* (1975). In that book, Andy went into his early days in Pittsburgh, but Ellie, their circle of friends, and her crucial role in making him see that he was a sensitive artist and not a freak were totally ignored. His high school was mistakenly or deliberately moved to nearby McKeesport, suggesting that he was reinventing his life. The book was not to be taken as fact, although it often was. The myth about himself that appeared in *The Philosophy* was a distillation of inventions he had passed along to interviewers. His published writing came closer to the facts when he acquired an amanuensis, an attractive blonde woman named Pat Hackett, who, like Andy, loved cats and seemed totally at home in a Warholian world. Hackett first performed this function in a book about the Warhol Sixties (*Popism*) and, after his death, would pull his 'diaries' together from a daily capsule commentary by Andy dictated to her over the phone.

Andy's first Factory assistant, Gerard Malanga, would say: 'Basically he's a liar when he's being interviewed.' 'I'd prefer to remain a mystery,' Andy declared in the 1960s. 'I never like to give my background and, anyway, I make it all different all the time I'm asked. It's not just that it's part of my image not to tell everything, it's just that I forget what I said the day before and I have to make it all up over again. I don't think I have an image, anyway, favorable or unfavorable.' Of course, he was wrong in this last statement. In the remarkable phenomenon that Andy Warhol became, image was all.

Ellie's place in the Victor Reilly apartment was quickly taken by another, and so was Leila Davies's when she moved. Andy was to write that he shared the place with 'seventeen different people . . . and not one person out of the seventeen ever shared a real problem with me.'

> 'They were all creative kids, too – it was more or less an Art Commune – so I know that they must have had lots of problems, but I never heard about any of them. There were fights in the kitchen a lot over who had bought which slices of salami, but that was about it. I worked very long hours in those days, so I guess I wouldn't have had time to listen to any of their problems even if they had told me any, but I still felt left out and hurt.'

A shut-out look sometimes appeared in Andy's eyes when his sexual frustration was most acute, but there are photographs as evidence that on other occasions the fierce lines of tension left his brow and eyes, and his mouth, wide and a bit vulgar, like the mouths of Van Gogh's 'potato eaters', shrank in size; he smiled a lot. Intimate friends could tell – *Andy's in love*. And they usually knew with whom. George Klauber said that he knew

> 'damned well that [a mutual friend] had Andy at his house countless times when they were working [on the little promotional books for Andy, among other things]. I somehow believe they never had sex, but I believe Andy wanted to. He was so circumspect about his sexual preferences and acts. He'd ask for every detail about your own, but never tell you one. So he is [sic] a voyeur in the true sense of the word. I remember he was madly in love with a photographer and he used to go on dates with him, but whether they ever had sex?? This photographer was married. At the time [the 1950s], that would have been a little eccentric. A fashion photographer, the fashion world. . . . Certainly in terms of his interests, I find it hard to believe that he ignored the opportunities that subsequently presented themselves. Now they may not have presented themselves in the period of the early fifties because he always seemed to be quite frustrated. One time I almost found myself trapped.'

It seems clear from the testimony of friends that for a long while

Andy gave up trying to find a lover and did become, in fact, a voyeur available at all times to watch. This was only a step removed from his legitimate role as artist – all artists are voyeurs by the nature of their work. Later, as he got some power and influence as an artist and celebrity, that would change. But then he had to accept the fact that he had problems.

'He had terrible skin,' Klauber explained. 'It was just strange. His [facial] skin had lighter parts and darker parts. . . . I always thought Andy wore make-up because his skin was so white.' He could be fiercely burned in the sun and, at the beach, he used a man's black umbrella to protect himself. His figure was slight, a little over five feet eight inches, and usually slender as a boy's. But he had an older man's face, so those men who liked boyish types might find him attractive only from a distance, which did not help much in making a connection.

He would phone someone* and talk out this problem – his inability to form a close relationship. He felt that some of his defects were correctible. In the middle 1950s, a plastic surgeon removed the large beige discoloration from his face, and a bit later he had his slightly bulbous nose, which was of the W. C. Fields variety but had nothing to do with drinking, refined. The operation, on which he pinned most of his hopes to become desirable, failed to make him handsome – a bitter blow.

Sensitive about his baby-fine, thinning hair, in 1951 he acquired his first hairpiece. It was brown and undistinguished-looking, but a year or so later he purchased a better one that was blond as his own hair had been. He would not be seen in the trade-mark silver wig until the 1960s.

Andy knew that male beauty and wit were passports to popularity in the gay world. He had a droll sense of humor, which he would sharpen over the years, although one of the girls living at the Reilly apartment remembered him as being inarticulate and 'non-verbal'. Once again his refuge was the movie-house, and he joined the others in the Reilly menage in going to several huge and slightly tattered old movie palaces on upper Broadway. They chiefly enjoyed musicals, and they all had a crush on Judy Garland. At their social gatherings, he sat quietly and watched.

* For several years his telephone confidante was Dorothy Pearlstein; then, in succession, it was Charles Lisanby, Ted Carey, Henry Geldzahler, David Bourdon and Brigid Polk.

Once, the actor Hurd Hatfield, who was socially active among
artists and dancers, and who had starred in the film version of
Oscar Wilde's *The Picture of Dorian Gray*, attended one of their
parties at Reilly's invitation.

Andy's favorite bar in those days was the Winslow on the East
Side off Madison Avenue. It was considered 'elegant' as gay bars
go, and everyone there was in a suit and tie. He did not buy his
first leather jacket until around 1954 when the Brando look was
'in'. Some of the Winslow's habitués were actual fops. They were
all carefully barbered, and a look of arrogance was not frowned
upon. Andy was not so shy he could not engage an attractive man
in conversation at a bar, but inevitably when he asked to buy the
man a drink, acceptance of which was the first big step towards
agreeing to a night together, he was rebuffed. As a consequence,
he preferred to accompany a friend to the Winslow, but one who
would not abandon him if some 'trick' presented himself at his
escort's elbow with a proffered drink.

On Christmas Eve 1950, Andy and Klauber, with some of
Klauber's male friends, attended a showing of the French film
Forbidden Games, and then went back to Klauber's Brooklyn apartment to party. Klauber recalled: 'We had picked up a Christmas
tree on the way. We set it up in my apartment and we were
dancing, and that's when Andy met Ralph Thomas Ward. His
nickname was "Corkie".'

Ralph Ward was good-looking, about Andy's age, and Andy
got a serious crush on him. But apparently, it was Andy's
gifts as an artist Ralph Ward was interested in, not his person. The two men collaborated on two of Andy's little privately printed books (*A Is an Alphabet* and *Love Is a Pink Cake*)
and spent many hours together in Ward's apartment, but no
very solid friendship was ever formed and Klauber said that
Ward told him he thought Andy was a 'boorish peasant'. Ralph
was living with a writer who had been Isadora Duncan's secretary at one time, and Ralph's friends knew just about everyone
of importance in the dance and art world. So there was no
chance of Andy ever scoring with Ralph Ward. Indeed, it became
a pattern in his life of falling in love with men who were
already attached, but never having the ability to attract them
away from their partners. Some of the tension created by that
sexual dilemma doubtless spilled over into his art work and

helped him become the most successful commercial artist in New York. Not only did he put in the hours to achieve this by default, but on canvas or drawing paper he had the talent to be the best, the most sought-after, the man everyone wanted.

Five years after his initial meeting with Andy, Ralph's friend died in Paris with Janet Flanner (*Genet*) by his side. Immediately upon hearing the news, Andy phoned Ralph, not to offer condolences but to inquire what he might have been left as an inheritance. This inquiry infuriated Ralph, who found this materialistic streak in Andy hard to forgive.

The 1950 Christmas party took a calamitous turn when Klauber stripped down to his undershorts because, as he put it,

'I never could stand the flannel trousers popular then . . . I always took them off when I danced. It used to be a joke. There Ralph and I were waltzing around when I crashed into a drafting table where I had been doing my Christmas cards and something cut me in the side. It was an incredible cut. I have the scar here. It cut the tendons, I think. When you call for an ambulance in New York City, you get the police first. They came immediately. I was bleeding. Andy was very upset and left immediately, but waited downstairs for Ralph, thinking that he and Ralph could go off together. Unfortunately for Andy, Ralph came with me to the hospital because I needed someone in attendance. . . .'

Early in 1951, Andy abandoned his former distaste for strangers; he left the 'Art Commune' and began sharing places through ads in the paper. He was all over town, but none of them worked out. In 1977, he wrote:

'To this day almost every night I go out in New York I run into somebody I used to room with who invariably explains to my date, "I used to live with Andy." I always turn white – I mean whiter. . . . At the time of my life when I was feeling the most gregarious and looking for bosom friendships, I couldn't find any

takers, so that exactly when I was alone was when I felt
the most like not being alone.'

★★★

In the way of mothers who are close to their sons, Julia Warhola
figured out, from the brief phone conversations she had with
Andy and the absurd number of changes of address, that he was
unhappy. Sometime towards the end of 1951, she showed up on
lower Fifth Avenue, where he was living alone, with a suitcase
and several shopping bags of belongings. 'I've come to live with
my Andy,' she announced. Andy – facetiously, one supposes –
said she could stay until he got a burglar alarm.

Julia Warhola often referred to herself as 'an old peasant woman'.
The late Patrick O'Higgins described her as looking a little like a
Buddha, 'a solid, square figure of a woman with her hair pulled
back in a gray, almost white bun. She wore house dresses and,
when she went out, a babushka over her hair.' As Andy got
older and fiercer in feature, there was an uncanny resemblance
to her, except that Julia had a resolved look on her face that
served to soften her features, while with Andy there always
seemed to be a question in his eyes – *Are you friendly? What are
your intentions?*

O'Higgins asserted that Andy shared the only bedroom in the
two-room apartment with his mother. That is credible in light
of their closeness throughout his childhood, but it should not be
forgotten that they kept very different hours. She retired early and
got up at dawn. She was, in fact, not a very visible presence in
Andy's life. His new friends, unless they were constant visitors,
would meet her briefly and then she would retreat to the television
in the front room. Emile de Antonio, who met Andy in 1958,
described her as 'ectoplasmic. When she did float through, Andy
would sort of guide her away.'

She got up every morning before dawn, usually at five o'clock,
and fixed coffee, which was kept a-boil all day. Then she began
her compulsive cleaning. What was odd about the cleaning was
that neither she nor Andy had the faintest notion of how to pull a
presentable household together. But she kept Andy's clothes clean
and off the floor. He managed to keep his accumulating piles of
canvases and art work in corners or closets.

Sometimes her other boys, John and Paul, would come up for
a weekend. John would do odd jobs for Andy – some shelves

that needed installing, new paint on the walls, a window that kept sticking. John was bemused and impressed by the way his mother scooted up the stairs to her quarters. The climb did not seem to bother her at all.

Someone brought her a pair of Siamese cats, male and female, and she seemed content – she had her beloved Andy to look after; she had her cats, which proliferated and began to dominate their successive residences, and she had her church. She went to St Mary's, where the priest was from her province in Czechoslovakia. She would go at least twice a week, and a portrait of Christ and a crucifix were above her bed.

Julia was extremely intelligent, according to her surviving cousins and family and others who got to know her. While she never intruded in any way in Andy's career, she kept a close and observant eye on what he was doing professionally. Around 1953, she was asked to sign some of his work because she had bold, distinctive handwriting. Soon, she was signing nearly all of Andy's work, and doing the calligraphy in his promotional books, so all of Andy's assistants got to know her fairly well.

Andy's attitude towards her was indulgent up to a point, but he was more considerate of her after he was shot than before.

Andy attempted to find some way whereby they could coexist. Her presence meant that his sexual partners, when he found them, would either have to take him home, which they almost never did, or he would have to utilize his work space. Until he had his first outside studio, this was impossible, of course, and it must have led to the sexual frustration about which George Klauber has remarked.

Julia's kittens and cats were all named 'Sam', according to Andy, but her favorite was named 'Hester'. At some point in the fifties when Andy found a home for one of the kittens with a friend, the kitten began to cry 'for its mother', so he gave Hester away, too, to be with her kitten. Julia may have agreed to this at the time, but she never quite recovered from the loss of Hester, and then the man took her to be spayed and she 'died under the knife'. Andy told his Diary that he gave up caring at that point.

Not spaying the cats and allowing them to multiply must have helped relieve the loneliness that was Julia's lot much of the time. Siamese cats often have identical coloring, although the spots of brownish-beige may vary; they all have blue eyes. Surrounding herself with them has a kind of Warholian logic to it, and there are other clues that point to Andy's most significant *idea* as coming in part from his genes. Neither Andy nor his mother saw anything wrong with stacking cans of grocery products in the kitchen on open shelves for easy access. The Zenith box the television came in made an excellent place to store rolled-up art work. There were identical cans stacked up in the kitchen and identical cats bouncing around the rooms.

In the late 1950s, when Andy finally bought a townhouse 'because of my mother', there was some spill-over of attractive hangers-on at his studio (then a firehouse in the East 80s). Julia saw numerous 'beautiful boys' around her son, as they were coming or going, and the truth seems to be that she missed very little that went on.

Andy's unpredictable and sometimes surprising unorthodoxy probably came from his mother. If there was a difference in their impassive natures, it was that Andy's impassivity was natural, developed in part because he did not want to feel too much, because he had been hurt by others. In Julia, there was the pacifying factor of her faith; she prayed a lot and counted on the Lord to see her through. She was then in her sixties and had seen great turmoil in her life – death and wars and the Depression – and yet she seemed untouched by it.

PART TWO

TAKING

MANHATTAN

FIVE

By the end of 1951, with his mother permanently established as part of his household, Andy became an authentic New Yorker in every way that counted. He knew the gallery dealers on West 57th Street better than he knew his neighbors in his building. He spent far more time out of his apartment than ever before. Perhaps he wanted to reassert a kind of independence from his mother that had been compromised upon her arrival. If he even vaguely sniffed out a party, he always finagled an invitation.

He adored Horn and Hardardt's automats, and usually tried to be out on the streets drumming up assignments so that he could go into one. His favorite was on Sixth Avenue at 46th Street. He loved the way everything was dispensed impersonally, although once in a while he would see a hand placing a slice of pie in its cubicle. But he loved that, too – that little instance of man working with the machinery.

He recognized the fact that the Avenues, which were north and south, were tunnels of wind from New York harbor, and he tried to avoid them on windy days because of his wig.

That year the Korean War was being fought by many American boys his age, but he was never asked to serve. He was simply never called up, although he was registered with the draft board back in Pittsburgh. It seems a certainty that he would have been classified 4-F and turned down because of his boyhood ailments that had left him looking far more delicate than he in fact was. So he had skirted the issue of his homosexuality. In fact, he never would have to confront it in any public way.

He was not in close touch with any of the Victor Reilly art commune, but he did remain in contact with Victor's friend Charles Rydell. If there was any common denominator in Andy's interests

it was his strong identification with any alienated human being.
The recent Billy Wilder film *Sunset Boulevard* had impressed him
enormously. Its central character, Norma Desmond, was rejected
by her peers because she was past fifty and no longer a sex
siren. Even Marilyn Monroe had risked Hollywood's rejection
when it was revealed that she had posed nude for a calendar
shot. She also claimed to be an orphan. Charles was the son
of a prostitute and an alcoholic father, and had been raised
in a home for abandoned boys in upstate New York. Andy
saw no reason why Charles, with his handsome face and great
smile and his resonant, masculine voice, couldn't make it to the
big time. Andy was constantly talking up Charles's assets as a
performer to people, but it did not do anything for the young
actor's career, presumably because Andy knew practically no one
in show business.

    Greta Garbo was living in New York in the East 50s, and once
Andy saw her shopping along antique row on Madison Avenue,
but he was terrified of her finding out that she had been spotted
by him. A few years later, they met at a beach picnic on Long
Island and he drew a butterfly for her and handed it to her. She
looked pensive as she held it, but after she had gone he found the
little drawing crumpled on the ground. He took it home to show
his mother just the way he had found it and called the art work
'Butterfly Crumpled by Greta Garbo'. Sometime in 1951, on a
visit to Brooklyn, he asked George Klauber to take a snapshot of
him in a Garboesque pose, and he sat on the ground with elbows
on knees, holding his face with his hands in the manner of Garbo's
classic photo by Steichen.

    In those obscure years, Andy never relaxed in his pursuit of the
famous. Once again, George Klauber:

> 'He used to call up all the time asking to be introduced to
> famous people or to meet people, and for some reason I
> did have a large coterie of friends, but my friends weren't
> famous. But he gleaned certain connections that were
> famous, and he would always jokingly tell me to intro-
> duce him to someone, but I doubt that I ever introduced
> him to anybody famous, certainly not to anybody as
> famous as he has become . . . as far as his contact with
> such people, not with me. They weren't forthcoming.'

Andy never made a connection with a great celebrity until he was famous himself, except for Capote, Cecil Beaton and a handful of other men of his own kind.

Klauber gathered all of his 'not-famous' friends together at a big bash in the early 1960s after Andy had become a great success as the central figure in the Pop Art movement. There were, as Klauber recalls, 'wall to wall people because I wanted everybody to meet him.' Andy brought two friends, including gallery dealer Sam Green. Klauber adds:

> 'That was my last social encounter with Andy except for a time when I went with a friend who had been invited to the Factory on East 47th Street to surprise Andy. The party was crowded and Andy stood in the silver-foiled room, the center of the action, and he looked right through me.'

When Klauber found the party boring and went to leave, he said his goodbyes to Andy, but Andy's handshake and acknowledgment were those he would have given any stranger who dropped in and there was no indication, not so much as a little nod of the head, that they ever had met before. It seemed so weird to Klauber that he thought 'Andy might have been on something.' Around that same time, Philip Pearlstein, who had been out of touch with Andy by then for several years, went to the Factory in the company of painter Ad Reinhardt. Pearlstein said:

> 'He came over to ask about my wife. And he asked how many children we had now. I have two daughters and a son. None of them ever met Andy. His orbit was very different from mine.'

From these drastically differing accounts of Andy's behavior once he had arrived, one can only speculate about motives, but it seems probable that Klauber represented rejection to Andy (Klauber had been a witness to his failures at obtaining a meaningful relationship with another man before he withdrew from the fray), while Pearlstein represented all that was best in his

early days in New York, and, of course, he was the husband
of Dorothy, who had been Andy's telephone confidante.

By 1952, Andy felt confident enough about his serious art,
which then consisted chiefly of individual drawings of young men
and fifteen large ink drawings with a wash based on the work of
Truman Capote (whose published work by then consisted of his
novel *Other Voices, Other Rooms*, and his book of short stories
A Tree of Night). The Hugo Gallery on East 56th Street and
Madison Avenue was then concentrating on the work of young
artists just starting out. The dealer owner was Alexandre Iolas and
his partner was David Mann. Mann met Andy in the spring of
1952 when, as he recalled, 'this young man, quite pimply-faced
and poor-looking, wandered into the gallery and said, "Would
you like to look at my things?" ' The gallery owner, Iolas, was
about to leave for Europe and he suggested that if Mann liked the
drawings, they could do the show in June. Mann continued:

> 'I looked at them and I really liked them very much.
> They were more interpretive than book illustrations.
> They were large drawings. We stuck them on a wall
> a couple of months later. It was a June show.'

Andy designed the posters for it. All of his friends, who by then
could be counted on his two hands, came, and he was thrilled to
have his work shown in Manhattan even though the event was
lightly attended and it was not 'a one-man show'. Painter Irving
Sherman made his debut at the same time on an upper floor of
the gallery. The show ran from 16 June to 3 July.

Mann was impressed with the show and with Andy. Later, he
would open his own gallery, the Bodley, where Andy would have
three successive shows. The critics were invited to look at the
Capote show and James Fitzsimmons, writing in *Art Digest*, said:

> 'Andy Warhol's fragile impressions [reminded him of]
> Beardsley, Lautrec, Demuth, Balthus and Cocteau. The
> work has an air of preciosity, of carefully studied per-
> versity . . . . At its best it is an art that depends upon the
> delicate *tour de force*, the communication of intangibles
> and ambivalent feelings.'

Mann recalled that:

'Very few people came because it was pretty much the
end of the season . . . . I remember that Truman [Capote]
came and looked at them. He loved them . . . . He came
with his mother. They both liked them very much . . . .
The next thing I knew, Andy told me he'd won some
kind of poster contest. I think it was for NBC, a series
of programs they were doing against drugs. He did one
of his black-and-white drawings. They used that and
that kind of shoved him to the forefront. He started
his series of shows with me [at the Bodley], which
I loved doing, but they were always kind of crazy.
Lots of people came and the sales were minimal, but
Andy very quickly started a good commercial career.
I got him a couple of commissions. I remember one
was for Bristol-Myers. They were doing their lipstick
and someone else was doing an eyelash mascara, and
the art director came to me and said, "Listen, your
show is very interesting. Do you think you could get
him to do something in his style for us?" The people
at the ad agency said, "This is crazy!" but they liked it.
For the mascara, he had a whole blank page, one eye
and two fingers holding a brush, reminiscent of those
shoe things he did later for Geri Stutz at I. Miller Shoes.
We became very good friends. He took a series of flats. I
remember a place he had on Fifth Avenue. It was in one
of those old buildings that used to be for men's tailoring
and manufacturing . . . . His broken-line drawings were
starting to become very well known.'

SIX

In the summer of 1953, Andy moved to another floor-through apartment on East 75th Street under the Third Avenue E1. Julia was given the front room adjoining the living-room, where the television became an addiction for them both. Later, Mrs Warhola would say, 'I'm so scared of this television, it makes me very nervous . . . . I'm scared to death about it.' But that was after the violence of the sixties when she had watched coverage of the Vietnam war with its needless carnage and body bags and coffins, and then the succession of assassinations, including the two Kennedys and Martin Luther King. For Andy, it was different:

> 'When I got my first TV set, I stopped caring so much about having close relationships with other people. I'd been hurt a lot to the degree you can only be hurt if you care a lot.'

Andy ran into Philip Pearlstein on the street one day and asked him if he would like to assist in a rush job, illustrating a cookbook. They had not been in frequent touch, but relations had remained cordial, and Philip agreed to help. Andy's commercial art assignments sometimes threatened to engulf him, and he had not yet hired a regular assistant. He was always dashing to meet a deadline. But he was now in the habit of laying out the design and then finding another artist to execute it under his direction. By the end of the 1950s he was spending more time in taxicabs rushing from one art director to another, picking up assignments, than he was at his drafting table or easel. In his studio, another artist, usually one of a succession of assistants, did the actual drawing, while Andy checked it out to make sure it conformed to his idea and design. He had in fact become a cottage industry and was by then the highest-paid commercial artist in New York, as much for the number of jobs he accepted as for the extremely high quality of the work itself.

When they went back to Andy's apartment, Pearlstein observed how much Andy resembled his mother, who was wearing a babushka that day, and he recalled that there were many Siamese cats running all over the place. 'They were on tops of tables and in pulled-out dresser drawers.'

Andy and Philip worked in a room behind the living-room and at one point Pearlstein overheard Julia in the next room remark, 'Look what they're doing to that good man,' referring to the red-baiting Senator Joe McCarthy.

The rush job on the cookbook was not the first collaboration for the former roommates. When they were classmates back at Carnegie Tech, they decided to do a children's book, which was to be called *Leroy*. It was about a worm inside a Mexican jumping bean. Pearlstein wrote the story and Andy illustrated it. But in designing the cover, Andy misspelled *Leroy* as *Leory*, which Philip thought was 'nicer', so *Leory* it remained. Philip said: 'I don't know what happened to it. He once told me that he gave the story to somebody who was dancing, as a dance. I don't know if the dance ever came off.'

As he was leaving, Philip was offered a pair of Siamese cats by Andy, which he took home to Dorothy. They kept them for several years. The Pearlsteins would soon be living in a townhouse on the West Side, which they bought for only $25,000, the former owner being so eager to sell that she advanced them the down payment. Since his marriage, Philip had spent eighteen months at New York University getting a graduate degree in art history. Unlike Andy, he had steeped himself in art tradition, so eventually there would be connections between his work and the art of the past, especially the disciplined work of the great masters who ran strict ateliers, working with models every day and choosing them for their reliability as much as for how they looked. He was slowly working his way towards the human figure. Interestingly enough, in 1952 he had done an expressionistic oil of the comic strip hero *Superman*. The painting anticipated the subject matter of Pop Art but was in no way Pop in style. Pearlstein's *Superman* appears to boil up in dark blue storm clouds over a darkened city. He was about to do a series of Anselm Kiefer-like landscapes. Holding a rock he had collected from one of his and Dorothy's trips (she was very much a partner in his undertakings), he would explore the facets of that rock on canvas, extrapolating from the fragment and building up an imagined landscape of cliffs and crevices. Tree roots were done in much the same way, and the resultant forms were within the Abstract Expressionist aesthetic. Pearlstein later explained something of what he was doing:

> 'The rules of the game are determined when the artist decides what kind of faithful record of which aspect of the experience shall be made. For, regrettably, the artist cannot transmit the total experience. The displayed forms themselves become only a point of departure . . . .'

By the beginning of the 1960s, Pearlstein had struck upon the subject matter that would make him one of the leading figures in contemporary art – the human form.

Around the time he was helping Andy with his cookbook, Philip was doing layouts for *Life* magazine. The full-bleed photographic layouts (i.e., with no white margins) of that periodical, with its 'close shots' of people with elbows and feet missing (off the page), tops of heads gone (out of camera range), may have inspired him to paint his nudes with the same ruthless disregard of the whole figure. In a sense, it was like Andy's later use of polaroids except that Philip worked from live models and painted them directly, with some arbitrary frame in his head.

Andy had begun his drawings of young men that would later be the components of his *Boy Book* series. Like all of his work, they were simply drawn, but they were unmistakably sensual. Most of them were drawn from life, and he often asked his unpaid models to lie down or drape themselves casually about a chair or the end of a sofa. They were as desirable-looking as Pearlstein's nudes were homely. It would be fair to say that Andy's work was from the heart, an area where the vision is often obscured.

Many of Andy's boy drawings were clothed, but it scarcely mattered. He was interested in the delicate line of the throat,

the thrust of a bare foot and slender ankle, the parallel curves
of a compact rear end – certainly as provocative as the pendulous
breasts of a Renoir or Rubens female. The drawings are rather
in the manner of Jean Cocteau's sketches of Raymond Radiguet,
but they are not libidinous and, in their sensitivity, suggest the
half-nude young girls of Balthus.

New York was full of attractive young men. Most of them
knew it. They were aware of eyes pausing for a few moments
on their pretty faces, their lower frontal torsos, yes, even their
tight rear ends. The trained eye skilfully slid over all three items
within the compass of about three seconds.

Andy would ask a number of these young men to pose for him.
They were encountered casually, often in public places. Alfred
Carleton Walters was a librarian working in the picture collection
department of the New York Public Library. In addition to
tapping *Life* and *Look* magazines as sources for his art, Andy
spent many hours in the Public Library on Fifth Avenue and
42nd Street searching for material. Sometimes he would trace
what he found, using ordinary tracing paper; at other times he
would tear out the page and conceal it with his note paper or
even inside his clothes. Librarian Walters was attractive, and the
men quickly struck up a friendship which led to Walters' coming
to Andy's place to pose. Scores of these drawings of Walters were
done over a period of several months.

Walters recalled Andy playing records while at the easel. 'I
can remember hearing *The Golden Apple* [a musical comedy] a
thousand times. He just played it over and over . . . .' The hi-fi was
always on high volume, and when he wasn't playing Broadway
show tunes, it was his favorite Bobby Rydell singles. It became
clear in time that he played this loud music as a distraction,
something to turn off his brain while his gifted hand – which
painter Robert Rauschenberg would call 'a curse', presumably
because drawing so effortlessly kept Andy from growth as a
painter once he was established – recorded the lines of Walters'
body and face.

And Andy needed distracting. As a young male in his mid-
twenties with a healthy interest in his own sex, he needed the
music to deflect his thoughts from bed to sketch-pad.

SEVEN

Sometime late in the year 1953, George Klauber invited Andy to accompany him to the apartment of Bert Greene, a former classmate of Klauber's at Pratt Institute. Greene lived on West 12th Street in the Village, and he was about to launch an off-Broadway theater operation to be called Theatre 12, after his own street, of course. By 1954, Andy was spending much of his spare time with the group.

Off-Broadway was a phenomenon of post-war American theater that had begun in earnest at the end of the 1940s. As theatrical production costs mounted, fewer and fewer risky ventures were being undertaken. New playwrights, people like Jack Gelber and, later, Edward Albee, were not being launched on Broadway because their language could offend the out-of-towners, on whom Broadway producers depended for the profit beyond production costs. Samuel Beckett, considered by many at the time as the greatest living playwright, was not then produced on Broadway because his themes were too dark, too dismal, and his language too bold. The big Broadway names like Tennessee Williams and Arthur Miller were acceptable because they had shaped their work to be generally inoffensive. If Williams, who was gay, felt it necessary to inject a homosexual note in *A Streetcar Named Desire*, it was so disguised as possibly to seem like a case of poetic vapors or even epileptic attacks. The possibility that Brick, in *Cat on a Hot Tin Roof*, might have had a homosexual love for his best buddy is sanitized by Brick's coming close to an alcoholic breakdown over the mere possibility. Whenever Williams' commercial successes deluded his producers into thinking the public would accept unadulterated Williams, with touches of cannibalism and other exotic aberrations, the public was profoundly offended and the plays quickly closed. And, of course, Arthur Miller, being not only straight but writing in blue-collar prose, could be counted upon to draw in the customers because he was writing about the dark underside of the American dream.

So Beckett, Gelber, Albee, and a host of other playwrights, both young and middle-aged, were seeking a stage in New York other than the commercial Broadway theater. Some regional theaters were already committed to producing new plays and revivals of Strindberg, O'Neill (and even unproduced work by that master), Ibsen, Shaw . . . the list was endless. Yale had such a theater; there was the Alley Theater of Margo Jones in Texas; there was a new one starting up in Minneapolis.

The off-Broadway theater movement in New York was initially launched by a handful of very brave producers. There was the Living Theater of the Becks (Julian Beck and his wife, Judith Malina); the Jan Hus Theater, begun in a former church building on the upper East Side by impresario William Gyimes; the Artists' Theater under the direction of Herbert Machiz; and The Circle in the Square on Sheridan Square under the direction of Ted Mann and much later absorbed into the larger off-Broadway operation called The Public Theater managed by Joe Papp.

The Becks introduced Jack Gelber's *The Connection*, a harrowing study of a junkie with such blunt language that some critics called it obscene. The critics did not know what was down the road. The Gelber play was so realistic that it is said that some members of the audience fainted during the performance and the Becks had to employ a nurse to handle such emergencies.

Each of the off-Broadway houses specialized in something a little off-beat to attract playgoers. The Becks did new plays as well as 'unexpected' works by Pablo Picasso and the poet William Carlos Williams. The Jan Hus became a home for Gilbert and Sullivan repertory as well as original musicals such as *The Man with a Load of Mischief*. The Circle in the Square revived O'Neill and plays by Tennessee Williams that did not hold up on Broadway, such as *Summer and Smoke*, and it introduced exciting new players like Jason Robards and Geraldine Page. Theater 12 had an interest in German Expressionism, and they had been studying the work of Bertolt Brecht with a view to staging something of his.

On Andy's first visit to Theater 12, which was then located in the large living-room of the apartment shared by Denis Vaughan, the group's director, and Bert Greene, they were reading Congreve's

The Way of the World aloud with parts assigned. When Vaughan asked Andy to read, he readily accepted. Ever resourceful, Andy did not hesitate to pick up the text and begin. Vaughan described the impression he made: 'Andy was pretty stupid – which nobody ever says about him. He was about as dreary and colorless as anybody could possibly be. I mean, he faded into the woodwork, and the only thing that showed was his red nose.' Vaughan and Greene shared the view that Andy was not very bright. What they failed to see, since Andy was so pitiful as an actor, was his genius for using the ideas of others, for appropriating exactly what was needed from someone or something that was at hand. They only saw Andy, the bumpkin. They failed to notice his campy outlook, and were unaware that he was ready to take from them if they were only willing to give.

Vaughan was not only unimpressed by Andy's delivery, but he thought he was very bad-looking. 'He looked as though he'd been on the sauce forever.' Apparently, Klauber had erred in bringing Andy. George had proved useful as an actor. Undaunted, Andy told Vaughan that if they could not use him as an actor, he would design some sets.

Andy's first stage design was supposed to represent Sardi's Restaurant and Bar for *The Days of the Bronx*, a new play by William Larner about an over-the-hill singer trying for a comeback in New York. Fitting this 'spare time' work in with his numerous, rush commercial jobs was not easy. For a while, it seemed evident that he could not meet the deadline for the set's completion (scrambling to meet deadlines was a problem throughout his life). On the day announced for the first performance, Andy rapidly sketched some black-and-white drawings for the restaurant set and created a cardboard bar. The set was a success, and Vaughan described it: 'The sketches that he did and the other things were very, very reminiscent of the shoes he was sketching for I. Miller.'

He did a series of drawn designs for James M. Barrie's *The Twelve Pound Look*. A brilliant poster artist of the day, Aaron Fine, was also a playwright, and it was for his play, *My Blackmailer*, that Andy did his most sensational stage design. Vaughan said the sketches were done on a set of screens that worked very well. They utilized his by-now famous blotted-line technique.

Vaughan's theater group went on to stage Kafka's *The Trial* in 1955 at the Provincetown Playhouse in the Village, where it had the longest off-Broadway run of any play up to that time.

Although Andy's participation was limited, he brought the group one of its most vital forces when he introduced Vaughan to Lois Elias, wife of Arthur, his classmate. The Eliases were just back from three years in Paris where Lois had studied mime with the teacher of Marcel Marceau. She became Theater 12's most resourceful actress, always got rave notices, and finally became one of the group's producers. She credits Andy with bringing her into the New York theater.

Despite the presence of such luminaries as Mildred Dunnock, and Viveca Lindfors in one of their productions, Vaughan and Greene left the theater in 1965 to manage a catering business in Amagansett called The Store. In fact, they published *The Store Cook Book*, which had quite a success. By then, Andy was long out of their lives, and they never went to the Factory.

Many years later, Andy's German biographer, Rainer Crone, wrote that German Expressionism had affected Andy profoundly, especially through his contact with the work of Brecht at Theater 12. This would appear to be in conflict with Vaughan's feeling that Andy did not seem bright enough for something like that to make an impression; but Vaughan *had* been drawn into the experimental group because of his interest in German theater and Brecht's *The Good Woman of Setzuan* and *The Caucasian Chalk Circle* had been read aloud by the Theater 12 players. Furthermore, Kurt Weill and Brecht's *The Threepenny Opera* was one of off-Broadway's biggest hits at the Theater de Lys on Christopher Street, a short distance from Theater 12. The Brecht–Weill collaboration opened in 1954 while Andy was still involved with the group, and ran for six years. One of his close friends, Charles Rydell, was appearing in it, and it was a 'must see' for everyone in town. Still, Crone's interpretation of events may be dubious. Andy assimilated Brecht's theme of alienation (of people, one from another) from his own experiences during his first years in New York, years marked by social rejection. He did not have to learn it from Brecht.

On a lighter note, Vaughan's partner, Greene, learned that Andy collected male pornography, and once showed him some reproductions of drawings of husky, nude males. Andy said they were by Cocteau, but Greene insisted they could not have been done by Cocteau, whose male nudes were always slender and languorous. Andy was not convinced.

Andy's enthusiasm for Theater 12 lasted well into 1954. In the months of his association with them, they relented on the acting and gave him small parts, but he was 'a downer'. Except for a production in London in the early 1970s, Andy never ventured into the theater again. But more important than the theater work itself was one friendship that grew out of that connection. A scenic designer, Bill Cecil, invited Andy to a party where he met Charles Lisanby, a scenic designer for television productions.

Lisanby and Andy immediately became best friends, and Andy spent many hours in Lisanby's company over the next five or six years. They began drawing together in Lisanby's 15th Street apartment, usually on weekends. They would buy fresh flowers at a stand and then bring them back to draw. Lisanby himself became a frequent subject for Andy's *Boy* series. One especially fine profile shows a sensual face with rather full lips and slightly sloe eyes, perfect features in all, with a rather thin neck, suggesting a slender man. Born on a farm in Kentucky, Lisanby fascinated Andy with his mixture of eager forthrightness and sophistication, and he was impressed with Andy's candid and raw ambition to be famous.

By 1954, Andy was no longer leaning on his Pittsburgh classmates for friendship. He not only had Lisanby, but he had acquired a small entourage of good-looking young men. He would contrive to meet them after his work was done and he rarely went anywhere without them, except for his junkets about town with Lisanby. Around this time, a small coffee house named *Serendipity* opened on East 58th Street. It was started by three young men, Stephen Bruce, a farmer's son from upstate New York, and two boys from Arkansas, Calvin Holt and Patch Caradine. The place opened in September, and Andy discovered it right away. He had begun what was to be a lifelong practice of dropping by any new interesting place that opened in Manhattan. Then, the establishment was only open from five p.m. until midnight, because the three men had other jobs (Stephen was a buyer at Macy's; Calvin was working at the Latin Quarter; and Patch was writing material for performers at Le Reuben Bleu). When Andy first came by, Stephen Bruce recalled that he was surrounded by beautiful people,

Julia Warhola with sons John and Andy (on the right), c. 1930 (Amy Passarelli)

Andy's uncle and aunt, John and Anna Zavacky, having fun by exchanging hats c. 1916 (Amy Passarelli)

Zavacky Family c. 1915. The children in the centre of the front row are Andy's grandparents (Amy Passarelli)

Andy aged 17 (Amy Passarelli)

Andy as a student in Pittsburgh, c. 1946 (Amy Passarelli)

Family portrait: back row – John Warhola, second row – Julia Warhola and Andy, front row – Julia's sister Mary and son Paul with Paul Jr and Eva Warhola (Amy Passarelli)

Andy framed in the window of the student union, a carriage house on the Carnegie Tech campus, c. 1948 (Philip Pearlstein)

Professor Robert Lepper, who taught conceptual art at Carnegie Tech Art School (Robert Lepper, photo by James Klingensmith, *Pittsburgh Post-Gazette*)

Andy's college friends relax between classes. From right, Philip Pearlstein, Arthur Elias, Ellie Simon, George Klauber and Liz (Gruse) Dixon c. 1947 (George Klauber)

Andy with George Klauber at Andy and Philip Pearlstein's apartment on West 21st Street, 1950 (Philip Pearlstein)

Ellie Simon on the steps of the Metropolitan Museum of Art, New York,

Andy on the beach with Corky Kessler, who taught him to dance and gave him the name 'André', which he used during his first year in New York, c. 1950 (Philip Pearlstein)

Leonard Kessler, Dorothy Cantor (later Pearlstein) and Andy on the Carnegie Tech Campus c. 1949 (Philip Pearlstein)

Ted Carey, Andy's best friend in the late 1950s, c. 1958 (Richard Banks)

Andy in Manhattan, 1950 (Philip Pearlstein)

The 'Art Commune' on West 103rd Street, Manhattan, 1950. From left: top row – Mata (a girlfriend of Victor Reilly's) and Jack Hudson; second row – Joey Ross, Victor, (Buddy) Reilly, Tommy Quinlan, Dale Blosser and Ellie Simon, kneeling, front – Jack (Mitch) Beaber, and Andy (Avron Blumberg, photo by Leila Davies Singeles)

Actor Charles Rydell, friend to Andy from the day he arrived in New York until his death, c. 1960 (Charles Rydell)

Nathan Gluck, who helped Andy with most of his commercial art (Nathan Gluck)

Emile de Antonio, who encouraged Andy to become a serious painter, and persuaded Eleanor Ward to give him a show (Emile de Antonio, photo by Cinda Firestone)

Tina Fredericks, Art Director of *Glamour* magazine. She gave Andy his first commercial job. (Tina Fredericks, photo by Richard Rutledge)

Richard Rutledge, fashion photographer and prime mover between the worlds of fashion, photography and commercial art, *c.* 1950 (Tina Fredericks)

Eleanor Ward of the Stable Gallery and her assistant Alan Groh at Eleanor's home in Old Lyme, Connecticut, *c.* 1958 (Buzz Miller)

Eleanor Ward with Andy's friend Buzz Miller (Buzz Miller)

Gerard Malanga with Andy – the first day on the job at the Firehouse,
June 1963 (© Archives Malanga)

Painter Richard Banks, friend in the 1950's and colleague at *I. Miller Shoe Co.*
1989 (Richard Banks)

Ed Plunkett, artist and friend to Andy in the 1950's (Ed Plunkett)

'mostly handsome young men. He had an entourage of boys constantly. He wore a tweed jacket usually, with a white shirt, a knit tie, dungarees and loafers. Then he came in many times with Charles [Lisanby]. He would come in with all the sketches he did for I. Miller Shoes. I would look over his rejects. He would always come in during the afternoon before we opened. We would look at his work and he'd say: "Oh, they liked this" or "They didn't like this" or "They picked the wrong one." And so I got the idea . . . I said, "Let's frame them and we can sell them." So that's how it started. We sold them for $15 and $25. I framed them in very simple gold frames . . . and I kept asking Andy for more. So he started doing them with color. We were Andy's first "Factory". He'd bring in these four or five guys and he had pens and inks on the table, and then he would do the butterflies on the shoes and water colors. Those were all done at Serendipity.'

Andy was still wearing his strange glasses with cardboard behind them and a little hole to see through. Bruce described him as having a 'slightly red, bulbous nose. His complexion was raw and red. As he got richer, he had a lot of work done on his face.'

About a year after Andy's meeting Lisanby, in 1955, Geraldine Stutz, who had worked for *Glamour* magazine with Tina Fredericks, went to I. Miller Shoes to become head of their retail division. Geri Stutz, like Fredericks and David Mann and half a dozen others, was always on the lookout for work to throw Andy's way. Now she decided to employ him as the shoe company's only illustrator for their advertising, which regularly appeared in the *Sunday New York Times* and other newspapers around the country. It was a sinecure that would make Andy moderately famous and rich. Stutz described his work as blotted-line drawings that had

'style and grace . . . . They were full of fantasy, but they weren't fey. There was nothing coy or cutesy about them. Each one had a full life of its own. Andy would take an idea and do something. Shoe advertising, most advertising, was very literal up to that particular time.'

It was Andy's later friend and champion Emile de Antonio who said that Andy was famous before the world knew he was famous. The I. Miller Shoe Company gave him his first solid acknowledgment that he was something more than just one of the busiest commercial artists in the city. It was chiefly through his work for them that he turned on the advertising world to the fine drawing that began dominating the ads in magazines and newspapers from then on. Andy and a handful of other first-rank commercial artists set a new standard, and the rest had to measure up to it. Copy was spare in major ads after Andy came on the scene. It was also tied closely to the design. Advertising had acquired a seriousness that commanded respect. An artist did his very best when doing a commercial design; the hacks no longer found a place for themselves.

In 1955, Pushpin Studio was founded. It was a design firm that used distinctive illustrative styles and references to popular culture as well as to earlier art works, and its market was predominantly middle-class. The consumer and the artist were walking together.

Once again, Andy's work was being compared to that of Ben Shahn. CBS art director Lou Dorfsman said that Andy's work had 'Shahn's kind of linear treatment'. Shahn's advertising art stressed the interrelations between serious art and ad art, and he approached all his commercial work seriously. With Shahn as the pioneer, Andy completed the task of erasing the line separating art and commerce.

It became an artist's medium, and Andy's contribution did not go unrecognized. One of his I. Miller series of ads would win him a medal from the Art Directors Club in 1957.

Richard Banks, who was raised in a pristine Palm Beach, Florida, in the 1930s and 40s, had been brought to the I. Miller Shoe Company as a designer. He had the same skills as Andy, but he was soon assigned to

'designing all the windows for I. Miller, which, regrettably, paid me much less than Andy was getting paid. But quite often Andy would have to utilize one of my drawings in his ads, or I would have to utilize an ad from the *New York Times* in my window design . . . . Geri Stutz had a lot of my drawings as well as Andy's on her walls that were framed. But the one who really

created that look was the art director at that time for I.
Miller, Bob Israel, who later became an art director for
Esquire, who really is a genius. Andy would make a little
drawing like this, but then, by God, he would put in a
leg and Bob would blow this up and the leg would be
coming down two columns of the side of the *New York
Times* and the foot would go across the whole bottom
so you suddenly had this new art direction which really
Andy had nothing to do with. The drawings of Andy's
were there and they were wonderful. They looked new,
and nobody had been doing that kind of bumpy line that
we both had got from Aubrey Beardsley and a couple of
other artists we admired.'

Perhaps there is some envy in this comment, but what Banks
is saying most strongly is that Andy's great success was not
something he did all by himself, that there were others, now
unsung, who contributed to the Warhol look in advertising.

Despite Andy's 'lost soul' complaints in his writings about this
period in his life, he was moving constantly in gay circles. They
were also the fashion and design world, the photography world
and that world of the demi-monde who were neither here nor
there. He had his covey of beautiful boys, and if there were few
bedroom connections, he had subsided into a certain resignation
about his chances.

Nearly everyone who ever met Andy remarked on his voice, on
that soft, tentative delivery. Richard Banks, who had met Andy
before their mutual employment by I. Miller Shoes, said:

'I had come up from Florida. It was snowing and I wanted
to meet Andy because I knew of his work already. Here
was this kind of goony guy, talking this baby talk, and
he said, "Oh, you've got a suntan. Were you in Florida?"
His voice was a bit like Marilyn Monroe's. He did that
kind of thing, and he said: "What color is your bathing
suit?" and I said, "Turquoise." Then he said, "Gee whiz!
Why didn't you wear it to the party?" Finally you got
used to it, but it didn't amuse me, and I think Andy
knew that it didn't because I knew there was a little
computer brain in there going ninety miles an hour. I

never liked the gag, but other people liked it, so. . . .'

People often wished he would hold it – all those gees, gollies, and goshes – but he was not expected to be a raconteur or even a moderately interesting conversationalist. He had something even rarer to contribute; he had a child-like absorption in what anyone was saying to him. Somehow he made anyone who happened to be standing or sitting next to him feel that he really cared that the boiler in their building had conked out more than two weeks ago during an early freeze. He might say with genuine interest: 'What did you do? Did you stay in bed a lot?' At the moment you were speaking, nothing else seemed to matter to Andy. Small wonder he became such a popular party guest.

Like many artists, he was not a profound thinker. He seldom ranged very far for ideas. What he could not glean from friends ('Have you got any ideas?'), he took from right under his nose. It was the latter source that prompted him to do the series of fantasy shoes or 'Golden Shoes' series. These were shoe drawings, as he imagined they might be on the feet of famous personalities.* There was a *Truman Capote* shoe – unmistakably a woman's shoe – with allusions to his then running musical comedy *House of Flowers*; a *Judy Garland* boot, a gold affair with several fleurs-de-lys affixed to the calf, toe and heel, a white feather stuck in the buckle, suggesting peace after her many private and public wars, and a golden spur to show any mount that she meant business. The *James Dean* boot is plainly derived from an old eighteenth-century design, indicating that Andy looked upon Dean as a romantic in the tradition of Sir Walter Scott rather than as a contemporary rebel in the Brando mold. (Dean was not yet a dead legend when the drawing was done, but was an overnight screen sensation to millions of teenagers and a good part of the gay population. His hold on the latter group was derived from the inside knowledge that Dean was himself gay and his stage appearances prior to Hollywood in N. Richard Nash's *See the Jaguar* and André Gide's *The Immoralist*, as adapted by Ruth and Augustus Goetz, in which Dean played the amoral Arab boy.) There was a boot drawing in honor of singer *Kate Smith*, who was then riding a wave of popularity on television

---

* It is generally believed that Andy derived the shoe and boot designs from *The Romance of the Shoe, Being the History of Shoemaking in All Ages, and Especially in England and Scotland* by Thomas Wright (London, 1922).

and was becoming a patriotic legend with her version of *God Bless America*, which Irving Berlin asked her to introduce. An elongated pair of golden slippers (one with a fleur-de-lys on a bow, and the other with a golden compact mirror) was called *Christine Jorgensen*. This drawing was unusual because most of Andy's other designs were for one foot only. It shows us the extraordinary length of Christine's feet and composes an affectionate tribute to the first American male (formerly George Jorgensen) to have a sex-change operation in Denmark, becoming thereby a celebrity of the day, with a published memoir, a movie and personal appearances. But film stars dominate Andy's selection of celebrities. His galaxy went back as far as *Anna May Wong*, an oriental *femme fatale* of early talking pictures. One splashy drawing was his *Elvis Presley* boot, as spangled as the singer himself.

EIGHT

Nathan Gluck was one of the artists Andy often employed as his assistant and became nearly full-time for a period of ten years. Gluck assisted Andy in doing the shoe designs, and said that Andy used large German-made gold foil sheets with pre-cut designs such as fleur-de-lys, stars etc., which he punched out as needed. Andy's impersonal approach to art was already in its ascendancy.

There seems little doubt that Andy had a foot fetish. He often drew the bare feet of his volunteer male models, and, a bit later on, he started to draw the feet of famous persons, but did not get very far, which is surprising, since he later met with little resistance when asking men to allow him to sketch their penises. Perhaps he stumbled upon something a little bizarre about the human psyche – most men are not averse to having their cocks drawn, but men and women are shy about exposing their bare feet for posterity – all of those hammer-toes and fallen arches, perhaps. Diana Vreeland, one-time editor of both *Vogue* and *Harper's Bazaar*, was among those who declined, saying, 'My feet are too small.' But Andy did manage to sketch the feet of Cecil Beaton, opera star Leontyne Price, and ready-for-anything Tallulah Bankhead.

When Andy felt he had enough shoe drawings for a show, in December 1956, David Mann mounted it at the Bodley. Mann recalled: 'We got enormous publicity when we did his "Gold Shoe" show. *Life* magazine took it up and did those in gold. It was really a big push for Andy.' *Life* published all of the gold shoes, calling them 'Crazy Golden Slippers', in a two-page spread that appeared in January 1957 in their up-front and highly visible *Speaking of Pictures* section.

The magazine exposure gave Andy his first real 'publicity high'.

He did not even mind their calling his art 'a hobby'. This was heady stuff, for his work had now appeared in a nationally – and even internationally – circulated magazine. He was now even with Philip Pearlstein, who had appeared in *Life*'s pages just after the war. *Life* called him a 'commercial artist', and said that 'while drawing shoes for advertisements, Andy Warhol . . . became fascinated with their designs and began to sketch imaginary footwear as a hobby . . . . Recently Warhol exhibited them at New York's Bodley Gallery, priced at $50 to $225 each. To his astonishment, they were eagerly bought up for decorations, and Warhol is now busy creating a whole new set of crazy golden slippers.' As with most publicity, the figures were exaggerated and there was no panic to buy the goldfoil drawings. But some did sell, and he gave Lisanby the *Julie Andrews* lady-like design because Lisanby knew her as a show-business colleague.

When the lease expired on East 75th Street, Andy and his mother moved to 242 Lexington Avenue, between 33rd and 34th Streets. The apartment was situated over Shirley's Pin-Up Room, which Andy described as:

> 'where Mabel Mercer would come to slum and sing "You're Adorable" . . . the building was a five floor walk-up and originally I'd had the apartment on the fifth floor. Then, when the second floor became available, I took that, too, so now I had two floors, but not two consecutive ones.'

Mabel Mercer, it should be mentioned, sang more than old pop standards at the Pin-Up Room. She also did original musical settings of A. E. Housman's poems. So while the neighborhood may have seemed something of a 'slum' to Andy, the crowd at Shirley's Pin-Up Room was mostly erudite and not the usual saloon clientele.

The apartment had two large rooms, one in the front, where Andy had his drafting table; there was a kitchen in the middle, and a large room and bath in the rear, which he shared with his mother at first. Leonard 'Pappy' Kessler, Andy's classmate from Pittsburgh, who was now a children's book illustrator in New York, dropped by one afternoon and got corraled into helping

Andy 'straighten the place'. They shifted piles of drawing paper, much of it already used, from one corner to another, and a $700 check surfaced for a job Andy had done about six months earlier. Money was casually handled by Andy. When he dined out, often he pulled dollar bills out of his various pockets and even his shoes to pay the bill. He always left the waiter a good tip and a little stack of Hershey chocolate kisses from his hoard.

Bruce, Andy's friend from Serendipity, volunteered to decorate the place. His partner, Calvin Holt, had an apartment on the 3rd floor at 232. Bruce bought for Andy a big club sofa and chairs.

> 'I put white café curtains, and of course I hung a big
> Tiffany lamp in the middle of the dining area . . . . It
> was on loan [Andy did not buy it, telling them it cost
> too much] . . . . I never met his mother and I don't think
> my partner Calvin did either. I think she was real but
> he was always saying, "I'll have my mother sign this"
> or "Why is this misspelled? It's the way my mother did
> it." She must have been a wonderful character.'

Tiffany lamps were the principal decor at Serendipity. They were able to buy them at antique shops for five dollars a piece. The men did so well with the small place that within months they took a larger space at 225 East 60th Street, where they would remain. They painted the walls and ceilings white, with white tables and the colorful Tiffany lamps as accents. Overnight, they became 'an underground success' with, in Bruce's words, 'The elite of New York. We had all the principal fashion designers, people in the theater, society, all the editors from *Vogue* and *Harper's Bazaar*, photographers, and the advertising world.'

The partners gave up their outside jobs and opened the place for lunch. Andy kept dropping in several times a week. On one occasion, he asked Bruce to pose for him, and Bruce remembered 'there were twenty-three line drawings. They have a title, "Playbook of You, S. Bruce from 2:30 to 4:00 p.m. 1954".' They showed Bruce in profile, head poses, and in a crotch view. 'Then he saw my ice-man coming with a block of ice, so he asked him to sit down. In the midst of all these drawings there's a picture of my ice man.'

Sometimes Andy seemed a little desperate to establish his

credentials as a suitable partner for the good-looking Lisanby. He gave him a photograph of himself taken at fourteen in one of Woolworths' photomat machines. It shows an angelic boy with blond hair, looking younger than his years. 'Cherubic,' Lisanby described it. This was at a time when Andy was very conscious of his slightly bulbous nose. He had had the large stain on his face removed, but had not yet had his nose job. It was while he was close to Lisanby that he had his nose trimmed and his hopes of becoming an Adonis shattered when it failed to make him handsome.

But Lisanby cherished the photo. He recognized the motive and he acknowledged to Andy that he had indeed been a beautiful boy. He tried to reassure Andy in other ways, by befriending Andy's cats, and by collaborating with him on a little book, *25 Cats Name* [sic] *Sam and One Blue Pussy*, printed in 1954. Lisanby chiefly supplied the title, although it would lead to yet another myth about Andy – that he owned twenty-five cats. Even in the book, there were only seventeen, plus one kitten.

Lisanby and Andy's other friends could not fail to notice that Andy was beginning to collect a small entourage of beautiful young men. Andy's efforts to be handsome enough to compete had failed but by surrounding himself with 'beauties', he managed to convey an enormous attraction. One of his most perceptive friends, Stephen Bruce, co-owner of Serendipity, observed that:

'As he got more popular and richer and more accepted, he had a lot of work done on his face . . . . I guess he felt slightly inferior, and the wonderful thing that he did was to use his art as a way of meeting people . . . . He would say "You're such a beautiful person, I want to draw you." And that put him on the same footing, with his talent and their beauty, because I know that he was constantly surrounded by beautiful people and he had to keep them interested because he was truly a talent. You know you don't want to be bothered with someone who's not talented because there's not an exchange and it's not fun.'

★★★

In the summer of 1956, Andy ran into Pearlstein on the street and Philip found Andy's mood 'very up'. Andy told him that he was leaving the very next day on a six-week trip around the world. Philip was pleased to see him so prosperous, but not especially surprised.

The lengthy world tour was Lisanby's idea, since he was a frequent world traveler and now included Andy in his plans. It was a major event for Andy, since he had never been out of the country.

They flew from Idlewild Airport in New York to San Francisco, where they caught a flight to Hawaii. They went on for three weeks in the Orient, arriving in Tokyo in late June. From there, they took side trips, including one to Kyoto, where Andy drew three Japanese ladies in traditional dress and hairstyles and an ink portrait of the cosmetic tycoon Helena Rubenstein with two Japanese maidens in kimonos in attendance. From Japan, they flew on to Manila, Hong Kong, Java, Bali, Cambodia (where they visited Angkor Wat in the company of commercial artist Floyd Davis and his artist wife, Gladys Rockmore Davis), then Singapore and Calcutta, where Lisanby came down with a fever and an Indian doctor gave him antibiotics. The fever did not subside, so they aborted a trip to Nepal, where Andy had wanted to visit Buddha's birthplace as well as the city of Katmandu, and they wound up in Cairo at the height of the Suez crisis.

The Egyptians had repudiated their treaty with Great Britain in June that year, forcing the British to withdraw. President Nasser had nationalized the canal by the time Andy and Lisanby arrived in mid-July. Nasser was trigger-happy and extremely nervous about foreigners landing on Egyptian soil at that time. Lisanby recalled that they were removed from their plane and were taken into a small room, where they were shown a Nasser-inspired documentary film, a piece of propaganda. Armed soldiers were everywhere – it was like a South American country on the eve of a coup – and Andy was visibly terrified. But when their plane was refueled, they were allowed to take off. Lisanby was still ill and the presence of the soldiers in Cairo had made Andy uneasy, so they decided to cancel their plans to visit the Valley of the Kings.

They arrived at the Grand Hotel in Rome, where Lisanby recovered. Andy demonstrated his loyalty and affection for his friend by staying indoors with him until he was well enough to go out. Then they made a ten-day excursion to Florence. In both cities, they toured the museums and monuments exhaustively, and

Andy was much impressed with both the antiquities and the Italians themselves.

Later, in Amsterdam, they browsed through the bookstalls along the canal. There, they found some children's books with illustrations of fairies dressed in flower petals. One was called *Flower Fairies of the Autumn* by Cecily Mary Barker. When they got home, Andy did one of his little promotional books, which he called *In the Bottom of My Garden* (after a Bea Lillie song, 'There are Fairies at the Bottom of My Garden'), with amusing, pseudo-naive versions of cherubs, a violin-playing cricket and other fey caricatures based on seventeenth-century drawings by Jacques Stella of small, naked boys playing in close bodily contact, and more elaborate and stilted illustrations found in Jean-Ignace Grandville's *Les Fleurs animées*, published in 1846.

Andy's amusing caricatures are deservedly considered a major part of his early work. While they have the simple outlines of comic strip art, they are at the same time both crudely primitive and extremely sophisticated. Probably he was influenced by the Swiss artist Paul Klee, who not only used a transfer method similar to Andy's blotted line, but also did whimsical paintings not unlike what Andy was doing in these drawings. For example, Grandville's violin-playing cricket is accurately based on a real cricket. Andy's identical pose, borrowed from Grandville, could have come off the screen of a Disney cartoon except that it is too crudely drawn to pass muster as good animation art. Andy deliberately drew this series like a gifted, decadent child. His mother signed them, and they are of a piece with his caricature of Sarah Bernhardt done in 1953, and *Love Is a Pink Cake* of the same year, done with Ralph Ward. But they are quite unlike his finely drawn books, also done with Ralph between 1953 and 1955: *A Is an Alphabet, A House That Went to Town*, and *There Was Rain in the Street, Snow of the Day*.

Andy's naive art and his own collection of American folk art, which he began pulling together then, are related.* He acquired portraits done by American primitivists, carrousel horses, cigar store Indians, and quilts, among many other things. His own quarters on the second floor at 242 Lex became cluttered beyond description. He kept only a small space to work in.

* For further background on Warhol's folk art, see *Folk and Funk: Andy Warhol's Folk Art World* by Sandra Brant and Elissa Cullman, New York: Museum of American Folk Art, 1977.

Andy's drawings for *In the Bottom of My Garden* have an erotic
verve and disarming simplicity, for example, a girl cherub in an
aproned dress has a pink cat's head visible above the apron at her
mid-section, and the caption reads: 'Do you see my little Pussy.'
The captions were Lisanby's.

There seems little question that a very real and enduring affection
developed between Lisanby and Andy, although it can in no way
be translated into sex. The signs of that affection were subtle ones,
going beyond the time they spent together. Lisanby's initials would
appear around the corners of Andy's work, C.L. for I. Miller Shoe
ads, as well as in fairly obscure corners of his window designs
for Bonwit Teller. It was the closest Andy would come to a
lasting male bond with someone with whom he had everything
in common except looks.

Perhaps Lisanby sensed that if he were to accommodate Andy
sexually, despite the lack of physical attraction, everything would
change between them. That is certainly a common fear among
intimate friends, gay or straight. Andy seems to have made his
own feelings clear enough. But if a love affair had materialized
with someone like Lisanby, who could not materially gain from
such a connection and thus was not opportunistic, as some of
Andy's future friends would be, Andy might well have changed
course in the direction of his art. Andy Warhol was a paradox, but
not an indecipherable one. While he would insist time and again
that he put nothing of himself into his work, and even on occasion
tried to convince people that there was nothing inside himself to
put there, his own passivity, which was a hunkered-down reaction
to rejection, might have been blown out of him by a major love
affair. It never happened, and Andy would write later, after the
trauma of the shooting, that life always had been 'half television',
as though it was happening on a screen. He was describing a
condition that author Colin Wilson made the subject of an entire
book, *The Outsider*, published the year of Andy's and Lisanby's
trip. As someone who felt that his life was not quite real, Andy
was the classic 'outsider'. Colin Wilson explains:

> '. . . . The Outsider wants to be free; he doesn't want
> to become a healthy-minded, once-born person because
> he declares such a person is not free. He is an Outsider
> because he wants to be free. And what characterizes the

"bondage" of the once-born? Unreality, the Outsider replies. So we can at least say that, whatever the Outsider wants to become, that new condition of being will be characterized by a perception of reality.'

Wilson's book was much discussed among gay men in 1956. It struck a responsive chord within the alienated – blacks, gays, women, and especially artists, who had been Outsiders for generations in America. Andy Warhol would be one of the prime movers in bringing this neglected group inside the American Establishment. Certainly he was the one who made art news exciting to the media.

It doesn't matter much whether Andy read the Wilson book or not. It was discussed by his friends, by other artists, by other gays. Had he known it, and perhaps he did, Andy would have appreciated the rather remarkable way in which the book was written – on the run on scraps of paper during Wilson's time as a street person who slept in London's parks by night.

Lisanby was good for Andy's ego. He genuinely admired both Andy himself and his drawings. Any sexual frustration Andy may have felt was siphoned off with his sketch pad. It was Lisanby's recollection that the sketching never stopped. He recalled an eight-millimeter movie he took of him while on their world trip 'sketching and being surrounded by monks', and then in Bali

'the little children came to watch what he was doing. I must say, we created a sensation in a few of those places because they weren't quite ready for two strange Americans, wandering around and making drawings.'

They went to gallery shows together and, in 1956, they saw Philip Pearlstein's one-man show at the Tanager Co-op Gallery on Tenth Street. The show included several landscapes Pearlstein was doing in an abstract expressionist mode. Andy liked the show, and he was very curious about the gallery. The Tanager had launched a movement wherein artists banded together, rented a space, and had one-man shows in succession. Initially, these cooperatives met with some success, but the idea fell apart when the gifted among them, Pearlstein included, were invited to join major established galleries, and all that was left was the second string of not-so-talented artists.

Pearlstein's success at the Tanager – it had got extensive coverage by the art critics – reminded Andy that he was still in the business of promoting himself. The Bodley Gallery and the Serendipity Shop and Icecream Parlor gave him space as a kindness. Only rarely did anything sell, and then it was for prices that embarrassed him. His latest 'vanity' publication had been a beautiful book of drawings from his *Boy Book* series as well as of children, which he called *A Gold Book*. It was oversized on gold paper with black ink. Lisanby posed for several of the drawings, including one in which just his head is seen, with a rose between his teeth. The book was splendidly printed, with colored tissue paper between the pages. But as beautiful as the book was – and Andy saw that it got around town – in the context of Andy's situation at the time it was only self-promotion. Some would treat it as the work of a dilettante. Something more drastic had to be done.

So in 1957, around the time of Pearlstein's second one-man show at the Tanager Gallery, Andy suddenly became obsessed with the notion that he, too, should have a show. His *Boy Book* drawings were accumulating, and he had no interest in dilettantism. He wanted to share these drawings with the world.

To Andy, that was what art was all about – hanging on a wall in a gallery or museum or in somebody's living-room. Andy approached Pearlstein about his joining the Tanager. The gallery had what Pearlstein called 'a certain cachet'. Besides him, Alex Katz was at the Tanager. Katz was to take his subject matter from a source Andy would draw on later – celebrated personalities in the art world.

Andy selected the best of the *Boy* drawings and took them over to Pearlstein. Some of them showed boys kissing each other. Pearlstein was in a terrible spot. He felt that it was a dead certainty that the drawings would be turned down because of the provocative subject matter. But out of loyalty to his old school chum and roommate, he felt that he had no choice but to take them in for his colleagues' inspection.

'They hated them,' he said. Pearlstein described the drawings as 'aggressively treated', a strange phrase to apply to work that had only affectionate intent. Quite obviously, what Pearlstein meant was that homosexual love as depicted by Andy was too open to be tolerable. Some critics would call the drawings blatant, and conservatives would call them outrageous since, in the light of prevailing attitudes in the mid-1950s, they were a political statement. They were saying 'Gay is beautiful' a good dozen years or more before such a statement was acceptable.

It must be asked if Andy expected a rejection. How could he reasonably anticipate approval from these men, most of whom only recently had wrenched themselves from the macho grip of Abstract Expressionism or were still practising it? Andy's drawings grew out of a gay sensibility that in another dozen years would be unexceptionable, and would help solidify the reputations of an artist like David Hockney, and a bit later, photographer Robert Mapplethorpe.

But this was 1957, the Eisenhower years, the quiet time when activists for whatever cause were few in number, and the only gay activists (a label that would never be applied to Andy) were middle-aged men and women, usually in the upper middle class, banded together to win some measure of acceptance and tolerance for the homosexual with their group called the Mattachine Society.

The word 'gay' had not even come into common usage. It was still being applied to divorcees. Only homosexuals, always in the advance guard, were using it. Joe McCarthy would die that year, but the 'ism' he created was still around, and the country was still in a muddle about it – 'fags were commies' and vice versa. On one or more levels, all homosexuals were in the closet ('I have this fag friend. He's not obvious. I think you'll like him'). Men of this kind who were pushing thirty often married in order to 'pass', to get that promotion as 'one of the boys' and get invited to dinner by the boss, or join the country club. They fathered children. Their 'adulterous' flings were often in 'tea rooms' (public lavatories*), where they were sometimes arrested and ruined for life. That was 'gay' life in the closeted fifties.

Yet Andy was hurt by the rejection at the Tanager. His friendship with Pearlstein was abandoned. Pearlstein was to say: 'I think he felt I had let him down, and we were seldom in touch after that.' Andy gave up telephoning Dorothy Pearlstein for any reason.

* In England, just as euphemistically, they are called 'cottages'.

The *Boy Book* drawings were put away, and within a year or two few of Andy's publicly shown drawings and paintings would touch upon the subject. It was a pity, because nearly all of these studies were done from life with a ball-point pen. They have a tremendous vitality. They are of living persons drawn spontaneously and they are not based on photographs, which would become the norm for Andy's portrait sources in the future. The public view of Andy Warhol as seen in his art would be that he was totally involved with painting commonplace things, from comic strips to soup cans, or with celebrities in stylized silkscreens drawn from old publicity photos (*Marilyn*) or polaroids taken by Andy (*Liza Minelli*). Yet the general perception of his person, as he projected it in the sixties, would be quite different, and with his films he would once again attempt to impose his liberated sensibility on the material, this time with more success.

Andy pushed aside or pushed back into the closet anything that would reveal his private self. He studiously avoided saying anything that could be construed as accurate biographical fact. He gave trivial answers to significant questions. In sum, he began a studied process of pretending that this complex creature whom we have been reading about up to now was, in fact, a vacuum. By never answering a biographical question with any grain of truth and by giving nonsensical answers to questions about his work, he may have felt that he was creating the right climate for his soup cans, his electric chairs, and his skulls to be received. In this regard, he is a bit like the court jester who, during a plot against the king, plays the imbecile and then seizes the crown. But one wishes that he had not been so obsessed with his looks; he might have kept public attention where it belonged – on his work. Plainness (and enormous ears) never hobbled Noel Coward, and Andy with his dry wit, so unexpected, kept that part of himself mostly private. Andy's sense of humor was never a part of his public image.

In the mid-to-late 1950s there were signs of change, of rebellion, of a move towards galvanic shifts in American manners and morals. In Venice, California, and in the North Beach section of San Francisco, the Beat Generation was in flower. They had an eastern annex in the Village. Their chief spokesmen were Jack Kerouac, a New Englander of French-Canadian extraction, bearded and myopic Allen Ginsberg from New Jersey, Peter Orlofsky, Gregory

Corso, Kenneth Rexroth, Chandler Broussard, William Burroughs
and Lawrence Ferlinghetti, the last a bookseller in North Beach
who provided a hang-out for many of them, and it was almost
defiantly a male revolution. Burroughs' work was profane, often
homoerotic, and always sexually violent. He was the American
counterpart to France's Jean Genet, 'the sexual outlaw'. Andy's
later glimpses of gay love in his films were child's play (almost
literally) compared with Genet or Burroughs.

The Beats wanted to experience life intensely and they routinely
experimented with alterations of consciousness through drugs
(psychedelics and marijuana); they were against the collective
anxiety (the Bomb, the Big Brother syndrome, etc.), denounced
what they called an elite intelligentsia, and they attempted a kind of
anti-literature. Kerouac, the most popular among them as a writer,
may have been the least gifted, since his ideas, which spilled from
his typewriter in a diarrhetic fashion, were neither profound nor
very interesting; but he was terribly photogenic. He was also an
alcoholic, which is always a colorful touch, and booze would
contribute to his early demise. His rambling, autobiographical
paean to the wandering life, *On the Road*, in which he and his best
buddy, Neal Cassidy, are the thinly disguised leading characters,
became the Beats' bible. It was also a powerful influence on late
teenagers, who heard its siren call and took to the road.

The Beatniks (the name derived from the Beatitudes in St
Matthew's Gospel) believed that America was too wrapped up in
consumerism, in upward mobility, and in the shallow pursuit of
success and pleasure. The Beats espoused a kind of Zen buddhism,
and Ginsberg in particular fell into Zen trances with an 'ommm'
mantra that was especially impressive. They wanted to experience
life without baggage, so they espoused poverty, which was easily
come by for most of them, communal living (*crash pads* were
another option wherein the Beatniks simply showed up at one's
house or apartment, often sleeping on the floor), and sexual sharing
of partners, a point stressed in the literary work of Jack Kerouac.
Like nearly all the Beats, Kerouac had a decided preference for
male company when he was not trying to be domestic in a
relationship with a young woman. Not so incidentally, they
were all pacifists, which would be an important connecting link
with the slightly later Hippie movement. Their literary idols
were homosexual or otherwise outsiders – Walt Whitman, Hart

Crane, Rimbaud and Celine. They used women badly, as badly as rock stars with their groupies. Some were homosexual: others were simple misogynists. Another faction, more bizarre and coming so late in the movement that it blended into the hippies, was mostly heterosexual, and was led by Ken Kesey, a novelist (*One Flew Over the Cuckoo's Nest*) with a penchant for being the Big Chief. His tribe of Beatniks, called 'Merry Pranksters', survived into the sixties and were progenitors of the Hippie movement. The Pranksters' wanderings in a day-glo painted bus were chronicled by writer Tom Wolfe in his book *The Electric Kool-Aid Acid Test*.

Andy was not literary, although the auction of his personal possessions after his death revealed that he had an extensive library, including many biographies that were not about film stars, popularly believed to be his obsessive concern. He also read popular fiction and books that were of topical interest, so he may have read *On the Road*; but whether he did or not, he knew that Kerouac was handsome even before he met him, since he was photographed by the media nearly as much as a film star. Andy knew that Ginsberg and Orlofsky, who often traveled together, were gay. So was William Burroughs, whose *Naked Lunch* kept him in drugs and paid his hotel bills, when he was a wandering junkie for several years, made him a fortune and brought him the kind of notoriety Andy could appreciate.* All of them wound up at Andy's Factory as guests during the sixties. Jack Kerouac, Peter Orlofsky, Allen Ginsberg, and Gregory Corso all appeared in *Couch*, a mostly nude and pornographic film Andy made in 1964, showing several dozen varieties of sex on the battered red couch that was a fixture in the 47th Street Factory.

The Beatniks were older than the Hippies, but they stood for many of the same things. While the Beats were more interested in jazz and poetry and the Hippies in rock music and peace, violence swirled around them. Hooligan bikers, including the Hell's Angels, sometimes got mixed with Beat communes, confusing everyone involved, and a kind of improvized drug mafia imposed itself on the drugged-out Hippies, leaving some of them dead. First, pot (marijuana) and acid were in and love beads, and grown-ups in the

* For the record, Burroughs had a son by a common-law wife, but he became a spokesman for the homosexual community in the 1960s. He shot and killed his wife during an episode with drugs in 1951. It was ruled as an accident.

more 'swinging' circles (how dated all these words sound now) assimilated all. Then it was cocaine.

By 1962, when Andy broke through with his 'statement' in a major one-man show, the Hippie movement had taken over Haight-Ashbury in San Francisco and the East Village in New York. For the young, it set the tone for the decade. So strong was its influence that the term 'hippie' would survive in the dictionary to describe any young person, or in fact any person with some 'hippie' traits (such as living arrangements, including free love and partner sharing; long hair on young men; beards and/or pony tails on men; granny dresses on girls; Indian sweat bands; nudity in public places; nursing babies in public places; marathon rock concerts or 'gatherings of the tribes'). This mostly youthful, communal way of life, free of any moral restraint, was perhaps the most fascinating part of the social upheaval that paralleled the escalation by Kennedy and then by Johnson of the Vietnam war.

The hippies did produce the Flower Children and certainly influenced the anti-war movement that helped bring the Vietnam war to a halt by the early seventies. Coming one after the other and nearly flowing together, the Beats and the Hippies buried Eisenhower complacency forever and shook up America. But they did considerably more. They awakened sleeping dragons that have yet to be destroyed. Drug use that once seemed a 'hippie' thing moved into the general population.

Despite his difficulties with the law, that great propagandist for hallucinatory highs, Professor Timothy Leary, was not yet out of favor and, in 1964, would drop by Andy's Factory for an approving tour of the premises.

All of this paralleled Andy's rise to commercial success and international fame. And perhaps alone among the great success stories of the second half of the twentieth century, Andy Warhol refracted rather than reflected all of this, one influence and then another being bent to suit his own needs as they passed through him. He thought that sexual liberation and mysticism were fine, but was bored by people who were into mantra-chanting. He thought the drugs were okay, as long as the druggies did not expect *him* to get stoned. And he was non-violent from birth.

Charles Lisanby was around throughout all of this and it was to lead to his disaffection. His friendship with Andy gradually dissolved when the first of the Factories was opened and the street people began to drift into the studio and into Andy's life. Lisanby could not accept any of that. He thought these people were basically leeches and emotional cripples. He could not accept their casual and frequent use of drugs. Andy had crossed over into a world he wanted no part of.★

★ Andy kept in casual touch with Lisanby for a while after their closeness evaporated. In 1962, when Andy was doing his series of Marilyn Monroe silkscreens, he phoned Lisanby just after the November opening of his one-man show at the Stable Gallery. He told him: 'The Museum [of Modern Art] just bought *Marilyn Monroe* and they're going to be famous. And I want to give you one of them.' But Lisanby did not like the *Marilyns* and foolishly told Andy that he did not have the wall space, and he just did not want one. It was a treasure lost for Lisanby.

NINE

In 1957, Dick Banks, Andy's old colleague from I. Miller Shoes, introduced Andy to the most important friend he would have in the fifties, after Lisanby. Ted Carey was a strikingly handsome, blond scion of a limousine-for-hire empire. Although he had family money behind him (to buy art works, for example), Carey worked to support himself as a commercial artist in textile design. Banks explained how it happened:

> 'Ted was my lover, and he liked Andy's work. We all admired it . . . . And Andy came over Sundays to draw me when I lived around the corner from him on Lex. I knew a lot of celebrities, and Andy got very excited about this. Through Carl Van Vechten, I had just met half of the world. I knew Tallulah, and Mabel Mercer was my great friend [she often had a singing engagement at the Pin-Up Room under Andy's apartment], Gloria Swanson, Aileen Pringle, all the ballet dancers . . . .'

It used to annoy Banks that Andy worshiped celebrities merely because they were celebrities.

> 'You know people because you enjoy them. The only friend of Andy's I knew to be constant was Carrie Donovan, the fashion editor at the *Times*. Carrie is only interested in fashion, in where the hem-line is, and is not an intellectual. But she was a great help to him in the fashion world. She opened up the doors of *Vogue* to him.'

And apparently it was through those open doors that Andy met such famous people of that world as Diana Vreeland and finally Halston, the designer.

Banks had left the fashion world, because he did not care enough about where the hem-line was, and became a successful portrait painter to the Palm Beach-New York-Newport crowd. His portrait of Rose Kennedy was much reproduced, and his full-length study of Gloria Swanson had the place of honor on her living room wall until her death. But Andy held on, working for *Vogue, Harper's Bazaar*, and the *New York Times Sunday Magazine*. He was also still getting a $50,000-a-year retainer from the I. Miller Company, and he was not yet into big spending.

Once, Andy and Banks were attending a party where they both noticed a beautiful boy, 'an expensive boy', as Banks described him,

'the kind of boy you'd see in New York or Paris or some place, probably a European boy, and Andy whispered: "Oh, look at that beautiful boy!" and I said, "Andy, you have to be one of three things to have that boy, if you want him. You have to be able to afford him, which means that you have to be rich, or very famous, or you have to be beautiful, which is like doing it in the mirror, and you're none of those things." But he took me at my word, and in a couple of years, he was at least two of them.'

Banks heard that Andy had hired a publicity man, who had handled Richard Avedon, the photographer. He was a press agent who only had one client at a time, and his fee was $20,000 a year. Within weeks, Andy's name was appearing in the papers every day, and that continued on and on. Such publicity certainly became a significant component of his international reputation.

Even Leo Castelli, Andy's art dealer for many years and a shrewd analyst of the art scene, believed Andy was a genius at self-promotion. But it seems highly unlikely that he did it entirely on his own. So Banks's theory about how Andy's snowballing publicity began has some merit, because Andy's name began appearing in gossip columns as well as in art news and periodicals with more regularity than other artists'. The only thing distinguishing him from his peers at the time was this unrelenting stream of publicity.

But Andy did not rely entirely on the media. His techniques in cultivating helpful people did not change much from his early days in New York. He still gave such people things. When Banks introduced him to Stuart Preston, art critic of The *New York Times*, Andy began giving Preston drawings, and soon the man's kitchen and bathroom walls were covered with them. In fact, Andy became known for being generous with his drawings and his and Julia's kittens.

Like many city-dwellers, Andy and Julia had given their cats significant status in the household. For many years they had the run of their apartments, but as Andy's reputation grew and people began to come around to see his work, he began giving kittens and even mature cats away to friends. They were down to only two just before they left East 75th Street, and this pair included 'Cross-Eyed Sam', which they had the longest. Andy liked to tell a story about 'Cross-Eyed Sam' going crazy every time a fire engine left the firehouse next door.

Julia must have missed her large family of cats very much, since around this time she did a series of drawings of cats, which Andy had printed up by Seymour Berlin. The book was called *Holy Cats by Andy Warhol's Mother*. On the dedication page, in her remarkable, bold handwriting, she wrote: 'This little book is for my little Hester who left for pussy heaven', and a sweetly smiling Hester in ghostly, broken-line outline form is seen with a fanciful feathered head-dress, crowned for her goodness, no doubt. On subsequent pages, she drew a series of amusing cats in 'pussy heaven'. 'Some pussies wear hats,' she writes, with a spring-like bonnet on a very fat cat shown between two daisies, and 'Some wear chapeaux', showing a couchant cat, surrounded by about forty 'purrs' written out and a fat little angel pointing to it. She did not forget the 'bad cat', for she drew one mischievous cat head, captioning it: 'And once in a while one of them goes to the devil.' Serendipity, the now fashionable bohemian restaurant Andy favored, especially for lunch, showed the *Holy Cats* drawings, as they had the I. Miller rejects and the fantasy shoe series earlier.

Sometime after Philip Pearlstein helped Andy with the cookbook drawings in 1953, Andy decided that he needed a regular assistant. His first was Vito Giallo, and they quickly fell into a routine: Andy would show Giallo what he had drawn the night before; Giallo would take these originals and then make the stylized blotted-line copies. 'Whatever came out was okay,' Giallo said. 'I'd finish a drawing, and he'd initial it – it was almost too easy.'

In 1955, Giallo left to open an antiques store, specializing in old jewelry, and Andy became not only a sponsor but one of his best customers. Another artist, Nathan Gluck, replaced him, and the work routine remained the same, although there was less social contact with Gluck. 'He usually would call in the morning and say he'd got some work,' Gluck recalled.

> 'I'd spend anywhere from three to four or five hours drawing material he had brought back from clients – jewelry from the *New York Times* and various other things. This lasted from '55 to '64 or '65. It tapered off about '65. Ten years. I would draw the things, make lay-outs, draw the material, then he would work over it, leave it as it is or make corrections or deletions, and then he'd blot it. If he was too weary, he'd ask me to blot it. His mother used to sign his work. If she was too tired or if she was asleep, I would sign it, imitating her penmanship.'

Gluck, a genial man, and quite unlike most of Andy's associates through his career, nearly all of whom had a hyper thrust about them, described his own situation with Andy as a simple arrangement, and he felt he was adequately paid for his work. He never got any credit for what he did, nor did he expect any. 'Some people around me thought I was being used, but I never thought so. I was like one of the people down in the bull pen of an agency and Andy was the art director.'

He found Andy an even-tempered boss, who rarely lost his temper. What surprised him were the gaps in Andy's educational background that were often apparent (he did not know how much Andy had been helped by Eleanor Simon and others in getting through school).

'He was never well-read. I always wondered if he

acquired a veneer of sophistication when he became
so very famous. He began to go to the opera, but I
thought it was because he knew Charles Lisanby, and
I would have to sit down and tell him the stories of
the operas. He wouldn't bother to read them, and he
would mispronounce them. He would say, "I'm going
to see *La Boheem* tonight," and I would have to tell him
the story. So I've always wondered, say, when he was
with the Rothschilds, what would they talk about? He
was never much of a conversationalist except for gossip
and chit-chat. But basically he was a good soul. I was
very pleased when I went to St Patrick's to the mass
[Andy's memorial mass], that every Thanksgiving and
on Christmas he would go to some church and feed the
hungry and the needy.'

Gluck seemed concerned that some people said that they had been
dropped by Andy or that he had been dropped by them:

'As you go through life and you develop, you move
into different spheres and you go through people, not
intentionally. You see some people who may interest
you more and you see others a little less, or not at all,
but to say that you were dropped or cast aside is a sort
of personal viewpoint and a lot of people have an ax to
grind regarding Andy.'

Gluck compared Andy's reliance upon assistants to do the actual
work to the atelier of Rubens or other Renaissance painters. 'Who
knows how much they really did themselves?' he asked. A few
years later, Andy confided to Gluck that 'it's too hard to paint',
which seemed to be why he liked to silkscreen and 'grind things
out', including all the serial silkscreen work. Gluck saw these
slight variations of the same thing as related to the blotted-line
technique, where Andy accomplished the same thing manually
because each copy was a little different. Gluck suggested that
Andy had always been moving in that direction. 'There were
also the little promotional books he had printed up. Those
were multiples.' Gluck stopped working for Andy when Andy
turned his back completely on commercial work because he felt

it would stigmatize him once he was established as a serious artist.

By 1965, Gluck was gone from Andy's life as totally as all the others – Eleanor Simon, George Klauber, Ralph Ward, Charles Lisanby – that long procession going back from just yesterday to his school days. Andy felt no need to hang onto old friendships. He seemed to have no stake in continuity and none at all in useless loyalties. Still, if some old friend was met on the street, he was always cordial. But his train was moving on, and, curiously, all he kept was his baggagē – he never threw anything away.

★★★

Andy was now thoroughly cosmopolized. He knew New York far better than he ever had got to know Pittsburgh, and the city, at least that part of it that was dedicated to fashion and graphic art design, knew him. He was in his late twenties, but he felt boyhood urges – on a walk down a crowded street he would pull out a cap pistol and begin shooting it off, scattering a few people and getting baleful stares; he would take a bag of birdseed from his pocket and hand some to a person, telling him or her to plant it 'and birds will grow'. It might have been 'yokel boy makes good', except that it had a serious undertone to it; he wanted to experience some of the fun he had missed when he was growing up.

Ted Carey was a witness to some of this, but his amusements were more decadently adult. He had become a fairly constant companion to Andy by this time, and, on the side, was chalking up a remarkably long list of conquests in the gay world. He had a beautiful face and a slight and unimpressive body, and he was daringly promiscuous. He would spend whole weekends cruising the 'tea rooms' at Grand Central Station. He had an open relationship with his current lover, an Englishman. During sex, which Andy was often invited to watch, Carey would go into a kind of moaning swoon and his eyeballs would roll up like one possessed. Andy found all of that fascinating.

It was Ted's suggestion that Andy should move on from his boy drawings to 'famous cocks'. Perhaps lending celebrity to cocks is a practice unknown to the general population, but it is certainly a part of the gay subculture. Dick Banks had a 'famous cock', and Andy agreed with Ted that he would begin this series with Dick as his model.

'It started out as a little dinner party [Banks remem-
bered]. So I carefully chose some bright red, see-through
underwear which I put on under my pants. I thought
that would get Andy going. And Ted had his current
lover, an Englishman, named, I believe, John Mann,
and Miles White, the costume designer and [unnamed]
who came from the old [radio manufacturing company]
family, who was the black sheep of the family because
he was an absolutely screaming blond faggot, who lived
above the Blue Parrot, the gay bar, and he'd solicit out
the window above the bar entrance. A terribly funny guy
. . . . And there was Andy and myself. So we had a little
sit-down dinner, and, the night before, Andy had been
to the opening of the opera . . . . and Andy couldn't talk
about anything but the celebrities who were there. . . . I
asked him what was the opera? He had no idea. Who was
the composer? No idea. Who conducted? But I knew it
had been Thomas Schippers, Menotti's lover, and I was
beginning to see more red than my underwear.'

After dinner, Miles White and the radio manufacturing scion left,
and Miles later told Banks: 'Oh, migod, if I'd only known what
was going to go on, you'd have never got me out of that apartment.'

After they had left, Ted said, 'It's time now to draw Dick's cock.'
But Andy demurred, which was a little surprising, and said 'Oh, I
forgot to bring any of my drawing things. Oh, I couldn't do it.'
He had forgotten that Banks, as a commercial artist and painter,
had everything he would need. Banks told him, 'Andy, you just
sit right down here. Here's a pad. Here's the pens and the ink.
Here's everything you need.'

Then Banks sat down with his legs spread apart and told
Andy:

' "Okay, Andy, here it is. Take it out, if you want to."
So he unzipped my pants. It was the only time I ever
actually saw him . . . and he saw the red underwear,
and he said, "Oh, gosh! Gee!" and I said, "Well, take
it out," and he did and he touched it. By God, touched
by Andy Warhol! . . .

'Ted had one of those French glove-hands with jointed
fingers. You put gloves on it. They're pretty wooden
things. So Andy made an arrangement with a rose and
this glove hand, this wooden hand around my cock. By
this time, it had got hard. In those days, it got hard if
you just looked at me . . . . So Andy began drawing, and
Ted stood behind him, and it was like art school. It was
a surrealistic movie. Ted would say, "Oh, Andy, the
volume, and the way you've placed . . . and the density
of the black hair next to the thigh, and the cock . . . ."
It was like a critique as he drew, and Andy would do
that . . . . So I said to John [Mann], "If there's going to
be a hand, you hold my cock." Then there was another
drawing done.'

The scene rapidly escalated into serious sex. Banks was blown,
with Andy drawing furiously and Ted supervising the art work.
Banks likened his running commentary to 'going to a porno film
and discussing the value of the acting.'

The first two or three drawings were quite controlled, but then,
Banks recalled,

'They got looser, little action shots, and by the time we
were sitting on each other's faces, Andy screamed: "I
can't take any more!" and picked up the pad. And I said,
"Oh, no, you don't. For once I'm going to get one of
those drawings," and I got the drawing I wanted.'

That turned out to be the very first cock drawing by Andy, the
first in an important series that has been much discussed but rarely
seen by anyone. The drawing as a piece of art is as fine as any of
those clean-lined sketches in ink done by Andy during the late
1950s. Banks believed that Ted Carey got one of the drawings,
too, and that John Mann probably now owns it.

Once begun, the cock series became important to Andy. At
social gatherings, he would flatter some man by asking forthrightly
if he could draw his cock sometime. It was an entirely serious
undertaking on his part and he was unthreatening enough to get
away with it. His subjects would drop by his studio, the sketch
was done, and nothing further was intended. It has been reported

that later, as he increasingly relied on polaroid photographs as the basis for his work, pictures were taken and the sketches done from those. But there is considerable undocumented rumor about this series, although it seems to be a fact that quite a few penises of the famous were added to the collection over the years. Several of his 'crotch' drawings have surfaced – one drawing of a young man reclining with his shorts open revealing an erection was shown at the Grey Art Gallery on the New York University campus in April 1989.★ But there has been no public showing of Andy Warhol's 'cock drawings', and their whereabouts is unknown to the author.

As for their propriety, everything under the sun is a proper subject for an artist, if he chooses to do it. Michelangelo, whom nearly all gays have claimed as one of their own, was equally interested in meticulously drawing male genitalia in numerous paintings. In modern times, only in cartoons would a figleaf be used to cover a subject's manhood. Painter Larry Rivers, whom Andy much admired, a bisexual who never has been called 'gay' by either art historians or his peers, painted and sketched his friend, the poet Frank O'Hara, in frontal nudity poses. He also did a 'family portrait' of his son and stepson in a similar fashion alongside his clothed mother-in-law. In 1969, Rivers executed a light-box construction showing one black and one white penis with the stenciled legend 'America's No. 1 Problem'. A ruler at the bottom of the box shows us that each penis is nine inches long, nine being the 'magic' length for an 'impressive cock'.

The 1960s, Andy's decade, was, as nearly everyone knows, a time of change, of upheaval, but sexually it was an upheaval that did more to free people from old hypocrisies than to hurt anyone. Gays saw no danger in what they were doing; in fact, they saw less danger. They were enjoying themselves and not hurting anyone. No babies were being made, despite occasional fraudulent headlines in supermarket tabloids. No homes were being wrecked except those few where the husband was gay, and declared himself and suddenly found a hostile wife. But even that was rare, since most wives stood by their men, gay or otherwise, when it was a question of fundamental personality and not a rival.

★ *'Success is a job in New York . . .': The Early Art and Business of Andy Warhol*, Donna De Salvo, Curator.

By the time of Andy's death, the politics of AIDS had changed attitudes about 'cocks' within the gay community as well as within the general population. Cocks had become dangerous; they were killing people. The American government invested millions of dollars urging its people to use condoms during sex. Celibacy became a way of life for numerous gays. Gays and straights adhered to monogamous relationships. Still, death came to many of Andy's friends while they were under forty, including Ted Carey, who died of AIDS in the mid-1980s.

But back in 1957, Andy was no different from other gay men. He was obsessed with cocks. Fellatio, which was his own particular pleasure, would become a pattern in his films, from *Blow Job* (1964) to *The Blood of Dracula* (1972). In 1968, for a literary quarterly, *Intransit*, he contributed the following★.

> I don't think he's badly sized at all.
> He can only tell us.
> He could show us. When that little man goes you can
>   (show us, for . . . sake and then we'll
> all judge
> He's getting nervous, he's getting all
> Well of course . . . .
>
> How big is it? Did you ever measure it?
> (S) No.
> I mean as a child you must have. You mean you you
>   (kids didn't play the games
> . . . . how big is it? . . . .
> Well this is only a clinical study for heaven's sake.
>   (What do you think this is? What do
> you, what do you think I'm going to do s– swoop down
>   (on it.
>   (Don't be silly. I mean you've
> gotta learn if if it doesn't reach a certain size
>   (you we we just have the proper excercises [sic]
> that's all.

Conversation around Andy was ribald, yet he seemed innocent to

★ From *Intransit: The Andy Warhol-Gerard Malanga Monster Issue*, 1968.

everyone. He lived nearly sixty years, long enough to see his own kind liberated in the late sixties, a movement that was politicized in the seventies through the Stonewall Inn riot, when gays harassed by the police fought back and won instant respectability; but he saw that movement losing ground in the eighties. Andy must be given credit through his films for helping with that revolution, and he has in large measure. To most gays, he is Saint Andy. To many in the straight world, he poses a question, but is without exception acceptable.

During the winter of 1958–9, Andy's first New York employer, Tina Fredericks, was dividing her time between a house in the Hamptons and her apartment in New York, where she was winding up her years in publishing. On the rebound from her breakup with a man on Long Island, she began seeing a great deal of Emile de Antonio, a soft-spoken former professor of English literature (at the College of William and Mary) with an independent income and on familiar terms with nearly everyone of importance in the New York art world. During her affair with de Antonio, she had looked on as he, whom she and everyone who knew him called 'de', brought a very young Frank Stella from obscurity at Princeton University to the beginnings of a major career as a painter and found him a gallery. When Tina had moved from *Glamour* magazine to the *Ladies Home Journal*, she had discovered the genius of photographer Diane Arbus, and she introduced Arbus to de. de promptly took Arbus to the New Yorker Theater to see a revival of Tod Browning's *Freaks*, and Arbus' eccentric genius was unleashed. Tina also had looked on for years as Andy struggled for recognition and some firm foothold in the world of serious art.

Tina's close relationship with de soon ended, and he was not surprised. de was essentially a romantic (he eventually married six times), and admittedly an alcoholic. During one of their last meetings, she brought up the problem of Andy Warhol, whose work de did not know, and that same week she brought the two men together. It seemed a very casual meeting, but it was a bridge Andy had been seeking, and now he could cross over to the world of serious painting with de leading him by the hand.

PART THREE

THE
INNOVATOR
AND THE
FACTORY

TEN

'**I** was an [artist's] agent in a sense,'
Emile de Antonio said. de and Andy shared a trait of considering
their personal histories as irrelevant. Where they differed was in
their public images – Andy liked people to know he was around,
and de would like to ease in and out without anyone noticing.

> 'I had my own money. I didn't really have to do that, but
> [Robert] Rauschenberg and [Jasper] Johns were starving.
> I suppose Jasper today brings the highest prices of any-
> one, as he did in a recent auction, more than Pollock. I
> got them work with Reynolds Metals, where a friend of
> mine was an official, and they used to do windows for
> Reynolds Metals and they did windows for Gene Moore
> [of Tiffany's and, earlier, Bonwit Teller]. And I knew
> Philip Johnson, so I got Gene Moore the job of doing
> the Christmas decor for the Seagram's Building. Philip
> was instrumental in getting that building built. That was
> what I would call "the gay underground", in a sense.'

Andy was part of this 'gay underground' – the business of gays
helping gays to get work, an interesting allusion coming from
de Antonio, who could not have been more heterosexual, and
was known in art and literary circles in New York as much
for his women as for his prodigious appetite for alcohol. So it
was especially hurtful to Andy to be largely rejected by both
Rauschenberg and Johns in most of his friendly overtures. 'It's
in that book about the sixties [*Popism*] that Andy wrote,' de
explained.

'He claims that we were having dinner at 21. I've eaten at 21 dozens of times but never with Andy, but he likes to change things. And he asked, "Why don't Bob and Jap [Rauschenberg and Johns] like me?" And I said, "Because you're too swish. Too campy." Now Bob and Jap were gay; they were even living together, but they wore three-button suits and they would even have women for dates and masked who they were, which I found interesting and amusing and ridiculous,★ whereas Andy was always terribly swish, but also much more chaste. Andy played that swish thing for everything it was worth. I came from the kind of background – I'm not gay – even before the word 'gay' was used and when gay people called themselves 'fags', I never liked the word. I'm not judgmental about people except in the harshest way for political reasons, but I'm never judgmental because of who people sleep with or who they read. I'm judgmental about [a family in national politics] who hide their gay son and talk about another kind of virtue. That I find repugnant. If you're gay, it's fine. And if you're not gay, that's fine, too. You can be a swine as a gay or as a non-gay.

'Andy was a great salesman. My studio was across the street from his. He was at 860 Broadway, and I had a huge floor-through loft at 857. We used to look out the window and wave and then go out on the street and have lunch. And he'd come out, and he'd have about fifty copies of *Interview*★★ under his arm . . . . He said, "I'd like to give these away to people on the street," and he gave every one of them away. About half of the people he gave them to said, "Oh, can I have your autograph, please?" and he said, "Sure." He was always selling himself, and at the same time seemed to be never selling himself, which is absolute genius. He was wonderful at promoting his shyness . . . that extremely diffident, shy look, generally looking away and then looking up at you. It was a very effective selling tool. People really liked it. People who

★   For the record, Rauschenberg was married at one time and has a son.
★★ The magazine founded by Andy in 1969.

hated gay people loved Andy. He managed to transcend everybody's . . . . I mean, he was remarkable. What he said in the book was really true. He valued my opinion because I did know those other guys so well – Jap and Stella and Rauschenberg, who were already established. And John Cage, who I think is *the* seminal character in American arts in post-World-War-II America, was a close friend of mine. I lived in the country then with another wife . . . I had a house and a lot of land, and John lived there then and he had no money at all. His ASCAP* check back there in '52 or '53 was, I think, eleven dollars. He came to our house every night for dinner. And I was the head of a Foundation. I was very young, but I had a lot of time. I wasn't doing anything – drinking. I decided that this idiotic Foundation should spend some money and put on a concert by John with a little dance by Merce [Cunningham].'

As casually as this, a concert of music by John Cage with choreography by Merce Cunningham was sponsored by de Antonio in the distant suburb of Rockland County during a terrible thunderstorm, with traffic advisories warning people to stay home. But de was such a persuasive impresario that a loyal group of artists drove out from the city despite the weather, and Rauschenberg and Johns were so impressed with de's resourcefulness that they made him their agent. He represented them in their dealings with Gene Moore in display, and he promoted them with galleries, where he knew just about everyone.

It was that kind of support which de Antonio had offered Andy in his last days as a commercial artist. de saw beyond the obvious incredulity of the public to the significance of the work itself – music, painting, whatever it might be. Andy later wrote that 'The person I got my art training from was Emile de Antonio . . . de was the first person I know of to see commercial art as real art and real art as commercial art, and he made the whole New York art world see it that way, too.'

De Antonio realized that Andy was not in close touch with any

* The American Society of Composers, Authors and Publishers, the oldest and most powerful of the performance-tabulating organizations, collecting royalties for its composer members.

legitimate group of painters or successful creative types besides
some theatrical and commercial designers, although he insisted
that he wanted to be. de recoiled from many of Andy's friends.
Some of them were involved with the Judson Church group,
which a little later fell into the talented hands of the Reverend Al
Carmines. The Judson was doing some interesting experimental
theater and dance in those years, and Andy's association with it
gave some of Andy's friends an air of seriousness, but since they
never were paid anything to speak of, he was becoming a meal
ticket for several of them. de liked Andy's art and he liked Andy,
but he never did like his friends.

ELEVEN

Perhaps merchandizing was in Andy's blood. There had been merchants in the family for generations. There was Uncle John who ran a general store back in Butler when Andy was visiting there on a regular basis. But Andy always hustled after dollars. Long after success and fame came to him, he would prod prospective clients for a portrait as though he were staving off the wolf from the door. One day, he startled de Antonio a bit by asking, 'Wouldn't it be wonderful to have an underwear store?'

Such a commercial enterprise as that was just about the last thing de would ever undertake, but politeness being second nature to him, he inquired, 'What kind of underwear store are you talking about?' Then Andy, in his breathless, eager young fourteen-year-old voice, said, 'Well, an underwear store of famous people. You'd have Tab Hunter, fifteen dollars, but twenty-five dollars if it was dirty. Fifteen washed, but twenty-five unwashed.' de became convinced that Andy was testing him at such moments. 'He would judge you by making that kind of statement,' de said. What hidden aspect of de was Andy probing? Possibly his gift for being ever unabashed.

By 1959, Andy badly needed a house. No ordinary apartment could contain all of his own work, which was accumulating but not selling, and the things he was collecting. The excuse he gave his friends was that he wanted a place for his mother, and it was true that when they moved, she took over the English basement (ground floor) and never had to climb stairs again.

Most of his canvases were rolled up, unstretched, and stacked in corners and in closets. But he was becoming a serious collector of the art of his contemporaries. He had the work of Magritte, Picabia, Jasper Johns, and a double portrait by Fairfield Porter he had posed for with Ted Carey (he had bought out Ted's interest in it); and soon after he moved into the house, he acquired a crushed car by John Chamberlain.

His huge retainer from I. Miller Shoes was continuing, and he made perhaps twice that from his freelance work annually. He could easily afford the handsome brownstone near the corner of Lexington Avenue and 89th Street, next door to the National Fertility Institute.

de recalled that Andy's new house was full of shoes, which he was collecting along with all the other things. One pair was strange, very small with high heels. 'What are these?' de asked. 'A prop of some kind?' Andy explained that they were Carmen Miranda's, bought at auction. They were four inches long, with five-inch heels.

It was around this time that it became clear that Julia had a drinking problem. She now seemed to be sipping whisky in her quarters most of the day. de Antonio, who knew all the signs from personal experience, said that Andy bought Cutty Sark whisky by the case, and since he knew that Andy was not a heavy drinker he assumed it was for his mother.

Andy overlooked it and apparently abetted it by being her supplier. What bothered him far more was the prospect of becoming suddenly poor. He simply did not trust his financial success. He was apprehensive about the burden of maintaining a townhouse. de knew that he was buying all sorts of things, including some good art works – a Rauschenberg combine, more Jasper Johns drawings, and another Magritte. de also knew that he was fearful of the specter of poverty, so he asked Andy if he would like to take on some more window display work that paid extremely well. Andy seemed grateful for the suggestion and soon afterwards he was doing windows for Tiffany's and Bonwit Teller. As he had done with Johns and Rauschenberg, de sent Andy to Gene Moore, who was then in charge of retail display at both stores.

Moore liked using Andy. He said:

'He worked hard and made it seem easy. On the surface he always seemed so nice and uncomplicated. He had a sweet, fey, little-boy quality, which he used, but it was pleasant even so – and that was the quality of his work, too. It was light, it had great charm, yet there was always a real beauty of line and composition. There was nobody else around then who worked quite that way.'

Unlike Jasper Johns and Bob Rauschenberg, Andy felt no shame about doing windows even though he was now one of the best-known commercial artists in town. Johns and Rauschenberg were then much poorer than Andy, used a pseudonym, 'Matson Jones', and worked as a team. But Rauschenberg was especially inventive with this line of work, and de recalled sitting in on a photography session for which the two men designed the setting. It was a winter scene and 'Matson Jones' had to create a 'snowfall' for Dick Rutledge, the most admired fashion photographer of the day. de recalled the episode in Rutledge's studio:

'Two stories high. A Japanese youth as an assistant. Very elegant, sitting in the late afternoon with two or three of the most beautiful models in the world all sipping Dom Perignon with Dick.'

This bra ad would win the *Art Director*'s award for Rutledge and it appeared in the *New Yorker* and other magazines.

'Bob and Jap designed a snow scene for Dick. Ruth Ebling, who had the greatest boobs in the world, posed in fragile lingerie.'

The designer team tossed down handfuls of 'snow' and Rutledge utilized strobe lights to get off shot after shot. The effect was sensational.

Andy was more consistently reliable than 'Matson Jones'. His employer at Bonwit Teller, who worked under Moore's supervision, was Daniel Arje. Arje recalled:

'Andy, of course, just adored the idea that he had the *whole notion* of what windows were about – here today, gone tomorrow, and the immediacy and the *reportage* and the journalism of it was, of course, right where his head was at.'

The Lexington Avenue house worked well for Andy. Despite its size (it was four stories), clutter seemed unavoidable around him. While his apartments had always looked bare of any real furniture, now he began acquiring antiques. He continued to amass what became a major collection of contemporary art: the work of Larry Rivers, Jackson Pollock, Grace Hartigan, and Robert Goodnough.

His young librarian friend, Alfred Carleton Walters, was still in touch with him, and was apparently an overnight guest occasionally for he gives us this view of a typical day:

> 'He would get up in the late morning, and his mother would make him some kind of breakfast. He would finish up some little thing that he was doing. He would put on his "Raggedy Andy" clothes . . . with his shoelaces untied and things like that. His tie was all askew, and off he would go with his portfolio . . . .'

Andy never could manage a tie properly, and back in Pittsburgh he had frequently cut off the end that did not come out right. He had a boxful of tie ends.

> 'He would then, after that was finished, and let's say, this was in the afternoon, he'd go to some very expensive pastry shop in New York, and he'd buy the most extravagant pastries or cakes possible, let's say.
> 'And then, he might buy a record . . . . Sometimes he would eat all the stuff right away the minute he got home; éclairs and what have you. And, then, he would work in the evening. Again, his mother would make dinner . . . .'

Walters adds that he went to parties often, sometimes two in one evening.

Another friend, artist Ed Plunkett, described an Andy who, when they first met, would attend a mixed party with an *outré* remark upon his entrance, something like: 'I forgot to bring my butterfly on a leash.' But by the end of the fifties, he had refined his image. He put aside 'Raggedy Andy' on party occasions. Art critic and writer David Bourdon met him in the late fifties. He remembered that

> 'Andy was very social. He circulated among tons of people. I first met him in '58, and we became close friends in 1962, but in those intervening years I would run into him at parties . . . . I found him a very, very attractive character. He just looked so unusual, with a sly sense of humor . . . . I had no interest in Andy as a commercial artist because I studied art history and I thought I knew the difference between serious art and trivial and I thought that his art was just totally trivial and beneath notice . . . . It was only much later that I began to see how really charming and delightful Andy's work in the fifties really was . . . it has so much style and flair and wit . . . . But at the time, it seemed pretty cornball because this was the heyday of Abstract Expressionism . . . a time when serious artists were slopping paint all over the big canvases and when you went to somebody's apartment and saw a tiny watercolor drawing of a cat, it just looked hopelessly innocuous. And it wasn't until I heard that he was doing soup cans that I called him up and for the first time expressed an interest in his own work . . . . He was always so grateful when anyone expressed an interest in his work and so from the moment that I really expressed a lot of support for his art, we became good friends. That was '62.'

Bourdon found Andy a slightly different social animal from the one Plunkett had known. For one thing, Andy was now moving in circles where he often ran into the very famous. But he was still in awe of them. Bourdon explained:

> '. . . I had heard that when Andy went to parties and saw a celebrity, he would just freeze. And he was certainly that way during all of the sixties when I was running around with him.'

Despite his quiet mien, Andy stopped a party cold upon his entrance. 'It's Andy!' everyone would say, much as the patrons at the Cedar Street bar would exclaim 'It's Jackson!' whenever Pollock arrived.

All of this contrasts oddly with an entry by Ned Rorem* in his published *The Final Diary*:

> '. . . Fled to Stella's [Adler]. Now I had mentioned to no one I'd be there. So later when the doorbell rang (interrupting converse with the twelve selected nonbohemian guests, she in lamé pyjamas, they in graying temples like all authors of best sellers), I was nonplussed to hear that my "guests have arrived". In the foyer stood Andy Warhol with four disheveled sidekicks, all silent, glassy-eyed, placing me in a false position. Without waiting to ask how they knew I was there, I slammed the door. Whereupon Andy phoned intermittently to the party for the rest of the evening. Picasso would not permit such dreary liberties. Party-crashing stops at seventeen. Had I let them in they would not – with the spirit of a Gregory Corso – have romped about goosing actresses, but stood like statues. It's the new style . . . .'

This entry was written by Rorem in 1965, and there is no doubt that the incident happened. But Andy was then, and for a period of more than six years, traveling with a group of underground film players and 'speed freaks' (amphetamine addicts). One of his intimates at the time was underground film star Taylor Mead, who could be socially quixotic in the name of camp. On one occasion, when he, Andy and others descended upon a friend who was renting a cottage from Eleanor Ward, the gallery owner, Mead donned a kimono and greeted Ward's arrival at a party with 'I'm Eleanor Ward and who are you?' Ward was so shocked she never went back to her Connecticut cottage again and eventually sold it.

Still, Andy now had some solid friendships with a handful of upper-strata art world people. There was Ivan Karp, who was a

---

* Ned Rorem is an American composer, but he is probably better known as a diarist, and has published three volumes: *The Paris Diary*, *The New York Diary*, and *The Final Diary*. They are noted for their candor, style and natural egoism.

kind of scout for gallery owner Leo Castelli; short, dandyish, and, by his own admission, imperious Henry Geldzahler, who had come to New York in 1960 and as curator of contemporary American art for the Metropolitan Museum was touring the artists' lofts with Karp to get a firm notion of what was happening on the New York art scene; and, not least, de Antonio, who lived just five blocks away from Andy's house.

During the Christmas holidays in 1960, de invited Andy to drop by his place for a drink. de recalled that 'I had this lovely apartment with a fireplace that looked out on a tree-filled street.' Andy arrived with Ted Carey. de liked Carey and it was his custom to invite only congenial people to small affairs such as this one. On this occasion, he had invited

'a mixed couple – the husband was gay and the wife was mostly a lesbian. She was a well-known psychiatrist and psychoanalyst. She had well-known and famous people as patients. The woman was wearing a brand-new, fashionable Dior black dress and a fur hat. She looked remarkably nice in it, and Ted Carey was really nice-looking, and Andy always saw everything. In a sense, all the modern painters in New York were conceptual artists, instead of that other thing which had to do with the hand and the color of Cézanne's day, playing with the canvas and spending a lot of time. Andy had ideas. He could visualize that dress on Ted, so they went into the bathroom and changed clothes . . . . Ted was fantastic-looking, and Andy was pleased, but he never showed his pleasure except for that shy smile. But if you knew Andy, you knew how much it meant to him. It had come out the way he thought it would.'

On a nice day, Andy and Ted would sit at a table in the Central Park Zoo cafeteria, a fairly respectable spot, to watch people go by. Cruising gays often spilled over into the cafeteria area from their usual turf on the west side of the Park. While Andy may well have given up competing in the 'marketplace', he liked to be out where 'the beauties', as he called them, were promenading. It seems probable that he, like the hero in Jean Cocteau's novel, *Le Grand Écart*, 'Ever since childhood . . . had felt the wish to *be* the beautiful people whom he saw – not to make himself loved by them.' If Andy asked one of these 'beauties' to pose for him, and the three of them went off together, predictably, the drawing session would turn sexual between Carey and the stranger, but that was fine, too, with Andy. He participated with his sketch-pad and no longer skittered away when such a scene developed. A friend of Andy's in the early sixties, Buzz Miller, said that such trios became commonplace in Andy's life – Ted and the pick-up in bed and Andy nearby sketching the scene.

TWELVE

Historians look for signs and markers, events of sufficient weight and impact to divide one epoch from another. On the evening of St Patrick's Day, 1960, a significant 'happening'* occurred in the garden at the Museum of Modern Art in New York. It gave everyone a strong hint of the tone the decade just begun would take.

It consisted of one contemporary artist, the Swiss Jean Tinguely, setting up in the sculpture garden an elaborate piece of junkyard sculpture, which Tinguely called, satirically perhaps, *Hommage to New York*. The work utilized rusty pipes, numerous old electric fans, a very ancient baby buggy, and nearly eighty other bicycle and wagon wheels, a battered player piano, glass bottles and a large inflated metereological balloon. When Tinguely turned on a switch, the thing began chugging, hissing, smoking and clattering its way to self-annihilation. As Governor Nelson Rockefeller and dozens of other distinguished guests watched, and three television network crews filmed the event, Tinguely had to intervene, since a good part of the contraption clung to life. His assistance did the

* *Happenings* were performances or artist-involved shows that were peculiar to the 1950s and early 1960s. Artist Allen Kaprow, who staged a number of them, is credited with giving them a name. Kaprow had moved from the flat canvas on which he had painted abstract expressionist work to 'environments' consisting of crumpled cellophane, strips of colored ribbons, Scotch tape tangled with tinfoil, plastic and Christmas tree lights, while several tape recorders played electronic sounds. Kaprow was inspired by Jackson Pollock's huge drip paintings to evolve a theory that such large works 'ceased to become paintings and became *environments*'. He urged artists to go beyond canvas and immerse themselves in 'a thousand other things . . . all will become materials for this new concrete art.' His inventory of suggested subject matter included old socks, a dog, smoke, water, movies, paint, food, electric and neon lights, chairs, and he readily admitted it was derived from a visit to Bob Rauschenberg's studio. Later, he said that 'Happenings are events, which, put simply, happen . . . they appear to go nowhere and do not make any particular literary point.'

trick, and the thing continued on its charted course to the scrap iron graveyard from which most of its parts had come. As the assembled guests stared at the smoking, twisted ruin, Tinguely's *Hommage* had succeeded in making a very strong statement. Marcel Duchamp, Andy's patron saint, did not attend, but he told the press that it was a healthy idea to 'destroy art before it's too late'.

Picasso and others had distorted the human face and body, which the Cubists flattened and boxed, and the abstract expressionists had internalized the human experience and then projected it from their feelings in bursts of action upon the canvas with swirls or drips of color or black and white. Modern art had reached a point where it was no longer necessary to understand it; it only needed to be seen. The Tinguely event was a harsh commentary, and the point taken was that the 1960s would be radically different from the decades before. Tinguely himself would be starting with a clean slate.

Andy knew in his heart that the sixties belonged to him, though it might take some maneuvering to get the public and the critics to fully grasp this. The idea, the Warhol idea of giving the public the thing that was so recognizable that reflection or any form of interpretation would be superfluous, was there in his head. He simply had to put it on canvas.

Just as Andy and Pearlstein had studied, painted and lived together long enough to use the same approach, albeit towards different goals, both of them almost religiously disavowing any interpretation of the subject matter, so did Jasper Johns and Robert Rauschenberg study, paint and live together in a consanguinity that resulted in a new direction for modern American art. While Johns asserted that there was no emotion behind his work, which consisted in the main of versions of the American flag, targets (concentric circles and a bullseye), and maps of the United States, there was an acute intelligence, possibly even a *cold-blooded* intelligence, evident in their execution. Johns was a seemingly humorless, very serious man who kept his feelings to himself at all times, although he had the look of a man who might be suffering from occasional bouts of depression. Rauschenberg had an altogether different personality. He was a moderately handsome show-off with some American Indian blood who liked center-stage. If Johns's brilliance crept up on the public and surprised them, Rauschenberg set out to show everyone that he was gifted. Rauschenberg's major work at the time was a series of drawings based on Dante's *Inferno*. He took his symbols from *Time* and *Life* magazines, and from *Sports Illustrated*. He drew his central characters – mother, father and children – from one ad for golf clubs. For Virgil, he snipped out a photo of Adlai Stevenson, and Richard Nixon turned up being boiled in a river of blood. The technique was *collage* (the use of images found in magazines and elsewhere and affixed to the work of art unaltered) and some free-hand drawing. It is fairly easy to see that John's *Targets* and *Flags* are as cool as their creator and Rauschenberg's *Inferno* as volatile as the artist himself. But between them, the work of these men was the transitional force that gave us Rosenquist, Warhol, Lichtenstein, Dine, Wesselmann, and Oldenburg.

Andy needed some prodding to get into the fray on his own. de Antonio was the one who insisted. 'You've got more ideas than anybody around,' he told him. When Andy had finished his first two canvases, he called de in to see them. Andy writes:

'At five o'clock one particular afternoon the doorbell rang and de came in and sat down. I poured Scotch for us, and then I went over to where two paintings I'd done, each about six feet high and three feet wide, were propped, facing the wall. I turned them around and placed them side by side against the wall and then I backed away to take a look at them myself. One of them was a coke bottle with Abstract Expressionist hash marks halfway up the side. The second one was just a stark, outlined coke bottle in black and white. I didn't say a thing to de. I didn't have to – he knew what I wanted to know . . . .

' "Well, look, Andy," he said, after staring at them for a couple of minutes. "One of them is a piece of shit, simply a little bit of everything. The other is remarkable – it's our society, it's who we are, it's absolutely beautiful and naked, and you ought to destroy the first one and show the other.'

★★★

That conversation liberated Andy, and the painting never stopped for a period of about three and a half years. His statement had been made, and it was fairly simple. You take an everyday object, render it on canvas exactly as it is, put a frame around it, and call it *Coke Bottle, Superman* or *Nose Job*. It was Duchampian, but it was also in a direct line from Johns's flags and targets.

Nose Job was a duo profile of a woman's face 'before and after' a plastic surgeon had taken the semitic, aquiline hump from the nose's mid-point. It might be said to have been inspired by Andy's own facial refinements, but it had no more to do with him personally than the Campbell Soup cans he began painting almost immediately thereafter. He later said that he liked Campbell Soup and consumed some of it daily.

Another champion now joined de Antonio in encouraging Andy's new art. Henry Geldzahler was first introduced to Andy and his work by Ivan Karp, who thought Henry was 'a very bright kid who was an odd combination of sophistication and adolescence'. Henry had gone from Harvard right into the Metropolitan Museum as a curatorial assistant in twentieth-century art. Since there was very little of such art hanging in the Metropolitan, his job was to scour the lofts of Manhattan and see what the contemporary artists were doing. Almost at once, he and Karp saw the emergence of what British art historian and critic Lawrence Alloway called *Pop Art*. It could be seen in the billboard-sized paintings of car fenders and girls' smiles of James Rosenquist down at Coenties Slip; in the constructions of Claes Oldenburg; and now, when Ivan took Henry there, in the coke bottles and comic strip blow-ups of Andy Warhol.

When Henry and Andy met, it was the beginning of an intimate friendship almost immediately. For some years, Andy relied upon the telephone to keep him in close contact with the handful of friends he depended upon, and, as Henry recalled, 'It was the very next day. We were together several hours each day, including a lot of telephoning . . . .' Henry saw Andy's work as thoroughly American and attributed much of this bias to Andy's wish to get as far away from his foreign (Czech) origins as he could.

Ivan Karp had met Andy at Leo Castelli's Gallery when Ivan had shown him and Ted Carey a Jasper Johns drawing of a light bulb, which they bought for $350. Ivan remembered the meeting because he had heard what Andy was up to. Castelli had Roy Lichtenstein's paintings of comic strip subjects in a back room, and 'they were both working with cartoon subjects and commercial imagery. It was at this point there was this tremulous tension for launching this new vision, and Castelli resisted the idea, thinking there might be a bad client reaction.'

Leo Castelli, born in Trieste, had read no comic strips; the images were foreign to him; the colors were bright; the Ben Day dots, used by Lichtenstein to approximate the newsprint's way of handling shading, seemed extraordinary. Castelli was excited by them, and he trusted his eyes, but not always his own judgment. That was why the Lichtensteins were in the back room. When Andy saw them, according to Ivan, 'he turned paler than he usually was, which was blanch white. Then he asked me to come by his house and look at his own work.'

Lichtenstein had used a little pressure to get Castelli to take him on.

'They were in the back room about a month and a half . . . . Ileana [Sonnabend, formerly Mrs Castelli], who had split with Leo, and Irving Blum, who was on the west coast, both asked me to go with them before Leo did, so I went to Leo and I said, "Well, I'm getting all these offers. Do you want me to go with them?" So I sort of forced his hand a little bit.'

When Henry Geldzahler liked what he saw at Andy's studio, Ivan must have felt his own judgment confirmed. The works of Lichtenstein and Andy had struck him as 'really strange, unreasonable, outrageous. I got chills from them.' Later, Henry would say that Andy Warhol 'was really the unconscious conscience of the sixties.'

Henry and Andy were an odd pair – the slight Andy with the pale, homely peasant face, and the short, pear-shaped Geldzahler who looked like an antique photograph from the Edwardian era. If Henry was a dandy, Andy wore shoes that looked ready for the dustbin. Andy was terribly insecure about himself physically and no longer made much of an effort to find a partner. Henry had a companion installed in his apartment from the moment he had settled in Manhattan. He was as forthright about pursuing someone he liked as any lord of the manor. He was on the party list for functions all over the place, from patronesses about to endow a museum to painters in their lofts celebrating everything from the sale of a painting to the advent of a new girlfriend or lover. Andy needed Henry Geldzahler at that point in his life.

The 'happenings' contributed to the advent of Pop, but not in any direct sense. As Claes Oldenburg stated through the 'voice' of Ray Gun: 'We are just a little tired of four sides and a flat surface.' If Andy took the things on billboards, news-stands and movie marquees for his art, Oldenburg's eyes were on the trash cans and gutters. Like Andy, he did not interpret what he saw. The things that stimulated him were

> 'the beauty and meaning of discarded objects, chance effects . . . . The city is a landscape well worth enjoying – damn necessary if you live in the city. Dirt has depth and beauty. I love soot and scorching. From all this can come a positive as well as a negative meaning . . . . Look for beauty where it is not supposed to be found.'

'The Ray Gun Manufacturing Company' was his metaphor for the city of New York itself. While sometimes he sculpted an actual weapon (*Western Ray Gun in Holster* and *Study for Ray Gun Rifle*), New York was an infernal place where the Statue of Liberty was the outsider's symbol of it. To anyone like Oldenburg, who really knew what the city was about, a weapon was its symbol, a weapon of self-defense as well as one of aggression; a phallic assertion. The Ray Gun Mfg. Company 'sponsored' *The Store*, which in its fully realized state turned his studio into a general store where in stiffened paper, kapok, and canvas, he recreated the cheap staples of life just outside his door – bargain underwears, chintzy dresses, hamburgers, vulgar striped ties and gym shoes.

Andy acquired several works by Oldenburg, all among his 'lighter' things – *Shrimps on Fork* (sculpture), *Design for a Bowling Alley in the Form of a Cigarette and Smoke* (drawing), and *Three Hats* (charcoal and pastel). As he put together his art collection he was far more interested in his earlier rival, Roy Lichtenstein, and bought numerous paintings, drawings, and pieces of sculpture (the latter mostly of an 'Art Deco' design in brass). There was the same kind of breezy wit in these pieces that audiences would be drawn to in revivals of the twenties-period comedies of Noel Coward. Lichtenstein's delightful round painting, *Laughing Cat*, became the logo promoting the huge Sotheby's auction of Andy's entire collection following his death.

Andy and Lichtenstein were moving in on the same territory at virtually the same time. Lichtenstein recalled the influences that might have played a part in this:

> 'It was a kind of object, merchandize something. There were a lot of influences to deal with here. De-mystifying and the vulgarization of art, I suppose. In retrospect, I can see how these were all influences.'

Like Andy, Lichtenstein had done window design briefly for a department store in Cleveland, although he had no hand in the creative end. He did drafting for architects. He also said something that inadvertently might clue us in on some of his later subject matter:

> 'I worked at Republic Steel doing product development . . . . It was more engineering. I mean, I had taken a certain amount of that. I never worked as a commercial artist. The closest I got to it would be the window display. I did very little of a creative nature. I was just dragging things through the store. [My background] has been slightly distorted. People would like to think you were one [a commercial artist].'

The years at drafting and engineering emerge in Lichtenstein's precision and in the architectural shapes on many of his paintings. While Lichtenstein sees the convergences in his and Andy's work,

> 'They have completely different roots . . . coming from completely different points of view . . . . We had a lot in common. Both [of us] were using what would have been considered debased subject matter to make art and the *same* subject matter. It just happened that we didn't hit the same cartoons.
>
> 'I did Mickey Mouse and things like that early, but I

went on to things that were sort of generic like a pretty
girl, a handsome guy. They're very close to the originals,
with significant changes, or made up . . . . *Vernacular* is a
good word [to describe the subject matter] . . . . [The Ben
Day dots] were done with a dog-brush that had regular
plastic tines that pushed [paint] on the painting [surface].
Then I made my own stencil out of aluminum. And then
I used perforated metal . . . . They got sort of neater . . .
Cartoons have their own tradition. It has nothing to do
with what anyone was doing in art school . . . .'

The two artists would acquire their international reputations
through the Castelli connection – Andy, at first, through his
show at the Ileana Sonnabend Gallery in Paris. Lichtenstein thought
that it was 'only because of Leo's international-mindedness. He
felt it was important to be everywhere . . . . Before us [Andy and
Lichtenstein], nobody was moving in that direction. Nobody was
promoting it.' Lichtenstein commented on Andy's 'cinematic way
of working and many attitudes that were really of his time, and
that would not have happened before his time, and all those things
are really there.' Certainly it was this manner of Andy's – the
serial images, framing up the commonplace – that ensured him
an audience in Europe and, not much later, the Orient. Germany
had several collectors who got interested in both Lichtenstein
and Warhol. As a consequence, there are many Warhols and
Lichtensteins hanging in Frankfurt.

Lichtenstein also thought that 'replication is a part of what it
[Andy's art] is about in a way.' It did not bother him that he
turned out one work at a time, and it was unique, while Andy
turned out dozens of *Marilyns*, soup cans and dollar bills. 'Andy
liked that idea. He called it The Factory. As though he wanted to
be a robot or something,' Lichtenstein said.

Beyond the comic-strip imagery, they were thinking along
the same lines. Lichtenstein painted what he was to call 'false
masterpieces'. He took paintings of Picasso and Mondrian and
did his versions of their paintings. Andy first did his *Double Mona
Lisa* in 1963, and he did absolutely nothing to make it his own
work except that he did not add anything to da Vinci's image.
This was to become one of the primary forces at work in Andy's
silkscreen paintings. Like Duchamp, he took what he found and

put his signature on it. This was typical of Andy's work in the sixties. It was related to Rauschenberg's taking a drawing by de Kooning and erasing it and the erased work thus becoming a 'Rauschenberg', which he signed and which was last sold for approximately $50,000. But it was also something else. It was picked up as part of a serial image. From *Double Mona Lisa*, Andy moved on to *Four Mona Lisas*, all framed up together. Duplication led to an extension of power of the original work that was copied. *Marilyn Twenty-Six Times* is the most valuable *Marilyn* from an auction point of view. Exceptions were when Andy drew on his Byzantine Catholic background and made the *Gold Marilyn*, a single colored silkscreen of Marilyn's face surrounded by a field of flat gold paint, bringing home more obviously than the other works the point that Warhol was dealing in iconography.

THIRTEEN

There was yet another circle of friends around Andy now. They could not very well be overlooked by Karp, Geldzahler and de Antonio. de shied away from them, but Henry attempted to fit in with them, and Karp, in his jovial way, studied them with some interest. They were bizarre enough to mark Andy as more than just bohemian. Because of them, it is certainly possible that Leo Castelli hesitated for a time in fulfilling his commitment to himself (if not to Andy) to take Andy on after the successful Stable shows. We are speaking, of course, of those first Warholian groupies, the speed freaks from the San Remo and the Judson Church, dancers too spaced out to dance, poets too befogged to write anything important, handsome kids too involved with pills to realize that there was a whole world out there from which they were disconnected.

Andy did not embrace them because of their addiction. They just happened to be hanging out in the places where he chose to be – especially the Judson Church theater activities, which were exceptionally innovative. It was interesting to see how the Judson crowd divided up – the really gifted ones were not hooked on anything but eventual success, so someone like Tom O'Horgan would meet Andy, but would be too concerned with his theatrical projects to bother hanging out at Andy's place.

Stanley Amos, who seemed almost as proper if not as Edwardian as Geldzahler, was one of the first to lead Andy in their direction. Born Stanley Corin in London, England, he was a big man (well over six feet tall) with a permanent slouch, and he had a modesty that obscured the range of his acquaintances and artistic interests. There is no doubt about his concern over the drug use that occurred around him, but he seemed to have adopted a stoical attitude towards it. Drugs were a reality that had some very sweet and dear people enthralled. Stanley could not stop the drugs, nor their use, but he could feed the often gifted users and give them a roof over their heads. Stanley was a kind of saint, and Andy saw him as such. Artist Ed Plunkett had introduced them in 1958.

Like Andy, Stanley was 'more at home in Bohemia than anywhere else. I've been around a long time. I've always been interested in the decorative arts.' He was drawn to people as passionate about life, and especially New York life, as he was. He shared a loft with playwright Tom O'Horgan (*Hair*, the musical). The people around him, those he really loved, almost always had sweet personalities. He found Andy to be

> 'a very reverberating personality. A sweeter than sweet person. I was involved in the Village theater – the Café Cino and the Judson Church both before Reverend Carmines took over and after. Being involved with art and artists began when I was a student and it's gone on ever since.'

Stanley leaves unspoken his many attempts to sustain starving poets, painters, playwrights and dancers. In significant ways, he influenced Andy to do the same. These creative people, most of them male, were taken in by him and given shelter and food. The addicts among them, some of whom were notorious thieves, only rarely stole from him. Stanley regrets none of it, and, like Andy, remained in love with the city after more than thirty years of seeing it change.

> 'New York is considered dark and dangerous. I find it relaxed and cheerful. People in the art world and even the advertising world treat me with great generosity. I think even New York society is wonderful.'

Many of Stanley's young friends survived on literally nothing. A few of them got money from home, but that soon went, as it always does with addicts. One of the dancers Stanley helped was a man he described as 'beautiful'. Andy used nearly identical words in writing about him, saying he was 'a very intense, handsome guy in his twenties.' His name was Freddy Herko, and he danced or choreographed at the Judson whenever he could, meaning that his life see-sawed between functioning and long bouts with amphetamines when he would sometimes disappear for brief periods. Stanley said of him:

> 'He was sweet and nice. Crazy? Yes, we were all crazy. We were all unpredictable, but his craziness was poetic. We were all involved with living as an art form . . . . Freddy was quite wonderful even when difficult. There was a magical intensity about him.'

Andy further described Freddy as someone

> 'I was absolutely fascinated with . . . . He was one of those sweet guys that everybody loved to do things for simply because he never remembered to do anything for himself . . . . He was brilliant but not disciplined – the exact type of person I would become involved with over and over again in the sixties. You had to love these people more because they loved themselves less.'

Stanley recalled one instance of Freddy turning 'life into an art form', when

> 'we were with a group of people walking along the street and we came across a half-wrecked church. It was on the lower East Side and Freddy went into a store and bought a penny candle. It hadn't got a roof anymore and where the altar had been he took the candle and lit it, and took his clothes off though it was quite chilly, and danced as long as the candle burned. That was a wonderful dance.'

When Freddy could pull himself together, he might spend as long as a month sharing a flat with Billy Linich, who was about to come into Andy's life and who was almost as deeply into speed as Freddy was. But somehow Billy seemed immune to the befuddlement that enveloped most of them, including Freddy, and the drugs simply kept him going nearly all of the time so that he rarely slept. Freddy kept his franchise as a member of the Judson troupe by occasionally choreographing something. Stanley recalled one memorable performance:

'It was at the Judson Church, which was all dark, and slowly a glow appeared on the balcony and over a disc of light was a figure [of a woman] inside a chiffon veil, and the figure picked up handfuls of glitter and let them drop between her fingers and just went on doing this as the light grew stronger and stronger and more and more glitter was just raised and dropped and raised and dropped from inside the chiffon veil, and gradually after a minute or two the lights slowly faded out again on the figure with slower and slighter gestures in raising and letting the glitter drift through the fingers.'

Andy observed one particular thing about Freddy and the other A-heads★ he came to know. They shared a 'classic symptom: intense concentration *but* only on minutiae . . . your brother might be dropping dead right next to you, *but* you would have to, say, get your address book recopied and you couldn't let any of that other stuff "distract" you . . . he [Freddy] was never able to see his choreography jobs through to the finish. . . .'

Billy Linich or Billy Name, as Andy had rechristened him, was Freddy's particular friend. But Freddy was one of the street people, who 'crashed' other people's 'pads', a surviving vestige of the Beat Generation. Stanley had some of Freddy's things stored in drawers, including many bags of glitter and feathers and things he used in dance. In fact, Freddy's belongings were scattered all over lower Manhattan.

After Andy's year at the Firehouse in the east 80's, which he had subleased as his studio, he had taken a large factory loft in a building on East 47th Street. Andy and everyone else began calling the new studio 'The Factory'. Billy Name was now established there as the only permanent resident, and he, too, kept a trunk with Freddy's things in it – flowers made out of broken mirrors, feathered hats, costumes and a few clothes. Mirrors especially fascinated Freddy. He had an aunt in Manhattan and when he would drop in on her, he would be energized by the tall mirrors in her parlor and start leaping about in an impromptu dance in front of them. His aunt, who understood him and loved him,

★ Amphetamine users or speed freaks.

would hug him whenever he landed. Andy and Gerard Malanga accompanied him on one of these visits. The aunt gave Freddy some cash as they were leaving, and then pressed dollar bills into Andy's hand and Gerard's, thinking they were in the same boat as her nephew.

This was the Factory crowd surrounding Andy when 1962 arrived, the year he stepped out of the wings onto center stage. Besides Billy, Freddy and Stanley, there were Rotten Rita, the Duchess, Eric Emerson, Ondine (Robert Olivio), Ronnie Cutrone, and Jimmy Smith. The Duchess was then fat, and played the role of lady bountiful, managing to supply most of them with pills and injections, for a 'quick fix', which was her own special need. She also had another name and life. She was Brigid Berlin (later Polk), the heiress daughter to Richard Berlin, Chairman of the Board of the Hearst Corporation. She and her sister, Richie, had been not quite disinherited. Their parents were aggrieved by their behavior but in those years still gave them funds to live on, which, of course, went at once. She would walk around the Factory nude to the waist on many occasions, contributing as much as anyone to that peculiar decadence that marked Andy's Factories in the sixties, causing the premises to be raided frequently by the police, who always went away puzzled. Naturally, they never found anything in the way of hard evidence. Decadence can't be carried back to the precinct house.

Except for Andy and Stanley, they were one and all speed freaks. Andy would find some of them salvageable, others not. Ondine became a Warhol Superstar when the filmmaking began. Cutrone was only a kid sixteen years old, but he grew up literally on the premises to become a full-time art assistant to Andy. Eric Emerson was not quite a superstar but he appeared in many Warhol films, including *Lonesome Cowboys*. Eric had the innocent features of a boy off the farm, but he lived for sex and pills or injections. He slept with nearly everyone, being bisexual, and he even made one of Warhol's superstars, Jane Forth, pregnant. She kept the child, possibly because Eric was so physically beautiful.

It may be assumed that when the Duchess was out of her family funds, Andy paid for the several hundred pills that she got almost daily, as well as the needles and their contents. Brigid Polk was married briefly to a man who preferred booze and other gentlemen to herself. He often wound up the night curled up asleep in front of Charles Rydell's door, but Charles rarely took him in unless it was freezing. But she, too, pulled out of this tailspin and, by the time Andy was shot and that whole little world collapsed, was off drugs.

But some were beyond help. Eric wound up dead on the street next to his bicycle. He had not been struck by a car, since the bike was untouched, and Andy believed that he had overdosed somewhere else and whoever he was with panicked and carried his body outside and into the Avenue. Jimmy Smith soon revealed himself to Andy as beyond help. Jimmy regularly stole from his friends, and Andy in his indulgent way called this 'moving things', but when it became apparent that nothing was safe around him at the Factory, he was banned. Besides stealing everything not nailed down, while on a high he would paint everything he could touch. Cutrone, who was especially close to him, called Jimmy

> 'a great action painter. He would take your whole house
> – and you know, coffee, mustard, ketsup, all your paint,
> everything, and splatter it all over the entire floor. . . .
> You'd be furious at him. Then you'd be just about to
> hit him with a pipe when he'd say "Wait! Stop! Isn't it
> beautiful?" And you'd look at it and you'd go: "It's really
> great!" Now Andy wouldn't allow that kind of insanity
> to go on at the Factory.'

So Andy visited Jimmy in Cutrone's apartment – neutral territory – and never disavowed him.

FOURTEEN

Art dealers are almost always maligned by artists, who consider them a necessary but burdensome evil. Marisol, the Venezuelan-born artist and sculptor, called them 'leeches', and Marcel Duchamp gave them a similar label, 'lice on the backs of the artists'. A few are considered gentlemen by nearly everyone, including the artists they represent. Leo Castelli belongs in that elite group. He was certainly the most significant dealer in contemporary art in the world – for money generated for his artists and for the influence he wielded.

Andy probably looked at Castelli as the art world's equivalent of Hollywood's Metro-Goldwyn-Mayer. It was the place for the *crème de la crème*, and he would not be satisfied until Castelli represented him.

By 1961, Castelli already had Rauschenberg and Johns in his stable, which meant that he took on artists who were not yet fully comprehended by the art establishment but who were transitional forces and, with Castelli's influence and power in the marketplace, they would become the bridge that would support the sweep forward of the pop art movement, which had not even been named. Castelli relied on inspired hunches to a degree, but he also leaned upon several advisors: David Whitney, a young curator and art consultant who had already met Andy, Richard Bellamy, now a friendly rival with his new Green Gallery, and, not least, his own assistant and chief talent scout, Ivan Karp.

It was Karp who brought Castelli to Andy's studio to look at his pop things. Castelli remembered that day in the summer of 1961:

> 'We went to the house that he had in the nineties . . . eighty-ninth and Lexington. He lived there with his

mother and I went to see what was going on with
Ivan. And we went there after I had seen the work
of Roy Lichtenstein. He [Lichtenstein] had come to the
gallery from New Jersey with a stack of paintings, one
very large one, too, on the top of a station wagon. He
brought them into the gallery and Ivan and I had been
very surprised, but had liked them, and then we tried to
figure out what they were.'

Castelli laughed, and in that laughter there was intelligent wonder,
too, at how he trod that fine line between perpetrating a great joke
on the public in selling them fool's goods and persuading them to
buy something new and marvelous.

'But they would be rapidly understood and then we took
him on. So when we went to Warhol, we already had had
the experience of Lichtenstein, of the first pop artist, but
we didn't know at the time that he was a pop artist. The
term had not been invented . . . . This visit [to the Warhol
studio] must have been immediately afterward. What
we saw there were coke bottles and some comic strip
paintings. I think Dick Tracy was there already, which
is now in the collection of Si Newhouse. And certainly
I remember the coke bottle image. There were other
odds and ends there, which now explain themselves.
Among other things, there was a big rocking horse,
no, rather than a rocking horse, it was a carrousel. It
was there dominating the room. And then the paintings
– the coke bottle, but not serial coke bottles, just one,
and the comic strips. It may have been Dick Tracy or
Annie. Well, it seemed to me that he was doing about
the same thing that Lichtenstein was doing, using comic
strips and also commercial images, and I said on the spot
. . . or perhaps we talked it over with Ivan and then gave
him an answer . . . . I said that what he was doing was
very similar to what another artist was doing whom we
already had taken into the gallery. So I said, do you
know about him [Lichtenstein] and he said he had never
heard the name, but he was curious. So I described to
him what Lichtenstein was doing, and he said, "No, I'm

not doing the same thing," in spite of the evidence . . . .
And I said, "Still, it seems very close to me, and I don't
know whether I can take on now two artists who do
something which is so similar." Little did I know that this
was becoming a great new movement. Then I asked him,
"Is there anybody else who saw your work?" and he said,
"Eleanor Ward at the Stable has seen it and she likes it
very much and she would like to give me an exhibition."
So I said, "Well, why don't we do that. You have your
exhibition and then we'll see." And he said, "Well, fine,
but you're very much mistaken. You'll see." And we
had a Lichtenstein exhibition about the same time as she
[Ward] had her Andy Warhol exhibition . . . .'

But Andy was bluffing about Eleanor Ward, and very hurt and
angry. It comes through in his tone with Castelli. Alan Groh, who
had become Ward's assistant at the Stable Gallery, had known of
Andy's work all along. They went out socially, and Andy was
especially fond of Alan's roommate, the Broadway dancer Buzz
Miller. They were a frequent foursome – Andy and Ted Carey,
and Alan Groh and Buzz.

One night over dinner, Andy told them he wanted them to see
his new work, so they all piled in a taxi and went to the Warhol
townhouse. Andy showed them all the new things – the coke
bottles, the comic strips. Alan was impressed, and persuaded his
employer, Eleanor Ward, to go with him to look at Andy's work
later that week.

Eleanor Ward studied the work carefully, but was non-com-
mittal. When she and Alan got outside, she told him that her
background in the world of fashion (she once had worked for
Christian Dior in Paris) made it impossible for her to consider
taking on any painter who was so well-known as a commercial
artist.

It was in the air – these pop art images – and Castelli would be
the man most deeply involved in promoting the movement. But
in truth Castelli almost always engineered his own revolutionary
connections. He had a reputation for being ahead of everyone else,
so Lichtenstein and the others sensed that he would be the single
dealer who could help their cause.

The presence of Lichtenstein at the Castelli Gallery thus worked against Andy for at least two years, years when the Factory became notorious as a place where street druggies, drag queens and other artists rubbed elbows.

David Herbert, another gallery person, was a former art history professor. Like Alan Groh, he had met Andy at a party. He had left teaching because he wanted 'to get closer to the creative act'. At this time (1961), he had his own gallery after years with both the Betty Parsons Gallery and Sidney Janis. Herbert made a profound impression on Andy by seizing his thumb and closely scrutinizing his nail. 'Oh!' he exclaimed. 'You have the most marvelous fingernails! What a marvelous thumb!' Now no one ever had complimented Andy before on any portion of his anatomy, and he was dumbfounded. 'From that moment on,' Herbert recalled, 'we became friends.' Not so incidentally, Herbert had clean-cut, scholarly good looks, and he was very popular in both straight and gay society and, of course, the two groups blended in the art world, except for the hang-out of the Abstract Expressionists, the Cedar Street Bar, which was the artists' equivalent of your local redneck beer hall. Andy asked if Herbert would come by his house for a visit.

Herbert was much impressed with the house itself.

> 'It was not in a slum; it was a good neighborhood. And I knew enough about Andy to know that it had been acquired by dint of hard work in the fashion world. His house was filled with Art Deco, Japanese screens. I could tell he was interested in many, many things.'

But it was his paintings that Herbert had come to see.

> 'He brought out maybe ten rolls of canvas, and he rolled them out on the floor. I was stunned. I was absolutely stunned. . . . This was something totally different. It was really original. I didn't know whether I liked it or not, but that wasn't the point. The point was that I was confronted by something totally original . . . I felt it was very, very important. Being in the art world, I knew that it was exceedingly difficult to get new work seen and promoted, so I said: "For God's sake, Andy. Don't show these to anybody, not until you get them properly

presented . . . paintings should be stretched." '

Herbert gave him the name of a man, 'Bernie', at one of the best
frame shops in the city, and Andy got everything stretched.

The revolution was happening without the man whom everyone came to regard as its leader. Andy and Lichtenstein were far
from being the only American artists involved with commonplace subject matter. Tom Wesselmann was doing montages of
kitchens and bathrooms, and combines* using real lawn-mowers
and painted canvas showing the cuttings (grass and leaves). Claes
Oldenburg and George Segal were representing the artifacts of
Everyman, and, in Segal's case, the man himself, in clay; plaster
and stuffing (for the Oldenburg soft sculptures). Castelli had been
turned in their direction by Jasper Johns with his flags, maps and
targets, and by Rauschenberg with his combines. But Castelli
resisted James Rosenquist's billboard-sized fragments of the same
genre (automobile fenders, toothpaste smiles) because Rosenquist
was framing up several disparate items on one canvas so that some
'mystery' evolved for the viewer to ponder. Castelli thought that
this 'mystery' was too close to surrealism, which had had its
day. So Rosenquist went to Dick Bellamy at the Green Gallery
(financed by major collector and taxi tycoon Robert Scull). And
Andy was all over the place.

Allen Stone hung a few of Andy's things in his gallery. In the
spring of 1962, Sidney Janis included Andy in his show called 'The
New Realists' that included nearly all of the artists mentioned. This
was a fairly bold move on Janis' part, and it resulted in all of his
Abstract Expressionists leaving his gallery in a collective huff.

Andy was frustrated, but he was far from despairing. There
was now a 'Warhol network' within the art establishment and
the antennae were out there probing and checking. There was
de Antonio talking up Andy's work to anyone who would listen;
there was Henry Geldzahler, whose opinions on contemporary art
were making him a legend in his own time; there was Ivan Karp,
forever smiling with a cherubic impudence; and there was David
Herbert, who didn't smile quite so much but who was in deadly
earnest about those things he believed in.

---

* Art works combining paintings and sculpture, with occasionally real objects
(wooden boxes, etc.) as part of the sculptural component.

Herbert brought two Los Angeles art dealers, Irving Blum and Walter Hopps, to Andy's house to see the work. Blum was a man with an impressive physical presence. He was about six feet two with the shoulders of a fullback, but he revealed himself as being out of character when he spoke. His voice was as soft as Andy's own. Straining to listen, I heard him say: 'My first reaction was I was mystified by them. They were the cartoon paintings, done simply. My partner, Walter Hopps, and I left without committing ourselves.'

Months later, Blum was back in New York on another matter and he went to visit his friend Ivan Karp at the Castelli Gallery. Karp showed him some transparencies by a new artist he wanted him to know about, and Blum quickly told him, 'I've seen these – Warhol.' 'No,' Karp said, 'Lichtenstein.' Blum made the connection and was so impressed with Lichtenstein that he arranged to show his work later that year at his Ferus Gallery on the coast. But before leaving New York, in order to confirm that Andy and Lichtenstein were doing the same thing, he phoned Andy's house and asked if he might drop by.

Just a few weeks prior to Blum's visit, a friend of Andy's, Muriel Latow, had suggested he paint something familiar (he had told her something of his problem with the Lichtenstein comic strip images), and she added: 'Something like a can of Campbell's soup.' The very next day, Andy began painting a remarkable series of Campbell's Soup pictures. There were thirty-two varieties at the time, so he painted thirty-two cans of soup, one for each flavor. It was this series that Andy now showed Blum, who recalled:

> 'These were canvases and I was moved by them. I liked them, and I spent a long time looking at them. I made arrangements to show them at my gallery later that year. The show was controversial, but there wasn't much critical comment. I do remember someone down the block stacked up some real cans of Campbell's Soup in his window and advertised them at .29¢ each. Several of the paintings sold . . . and, yes, I later did buy them back. I got this idea, it just came to me, of their value, and I phoned Andy and said that I wanted to keep them as a set and he thought that was a fine idea, and then I proposed

paying him in instalments. I wasn't that well-off then.
And we agreed that I would pay him $100 a month for
ten months and pay him $1,000 for the set. I still own
them today, and they are at this moment at the National
Gallery in Washington on loan.'

So Andy finally had his one-man show. He did not go out for the
opening, but some of the notoriety of that first exhibition filtered
back east and was something of a hot item along the gallery gossip
circuit. de Antonio was privy to all the art world gossip and he felt
convinced that this *succès de scandale* at the Ferus Gallery might be all
it would take to convince Eleanor Ward that she should think again
about Andy. But when de Antonio told Andy what he was about
to do, Andy was not so sanguine. He knew that Henry Geldzahler
had approached her after Alan Groh had brought her to Andy's,
and she had turned him down without explanation.

But something in Andy's psyche must have told him that this
was going to work. Eleanor Ward was Andy's kind of woman:
'an absolutely beautiful, aristocratic woman. She could easily have
been a model or a movie star – she resembled Joan Crawford –
but she loved art so much, she just lived for it.' The word that
Alan Groh, her long-time associate at the Stable Gallery, used
to describe her was 'reminiscent'. Like Andy, Alan's heroines in
his youth were movie goddesses. He was drawn to Eleanor like
a moth to the flame. She was Bette Davis in the way she faced
the world; Kate Hepburn in her classy style; Joan Crawford as
she emerged from the hairdresser; Greer Garson when she never
deigned to talk prices with a client. She was also Margo Channing
when she turned into a hostile drunk and Norma Desmond when
she made an entrance at one of her openings or anyone else's.

Ward was an upper East Side New Yorker bred to be the rich
wife of a stockbroker, which she actually became for a brief time.
After two failed marriages and a stint in advertising, she wangled
an interview with Christian Dior, who gave her a job in his Paris
salon.

Dior was closer to the gallery world than any of the other
Parisian designers. He had once run his own gallery before
turning to fashion and had shown paintings by Dali and posters
and portraits by Jean Cocteau. Dior was sympathetic to Ward's
gallery ambitions and urged her to open her own in New York.

'You have the instinct, the taste and the eye,' he said.

Like de Antonio, Ward was equally at home in Greenwich Village and Southhampton, and she moved easily through the world of the cultural elite – media moguls, show-business tycoons, fashion leaders. She had a friend who was close to the Shubert family and learned that a large stable next door to the Century Theatre between 58th Street and Central Park South was vacant. There were three complete floors connected by ramps (for the horses) and, as the Stable Gallery, it would become the largest such space in New York. With the help of a backer named Gilbert (married to a Rockefeller), she renovated the stable and turned it into the handsomest gallery in town.

The first Stable shows were not very successful. Very little sold, but the rent was only $300 a month and she hung on. In 1953, Groh joined her. He was a southerner from Virginia and his easy-going temperament survived Ward's volatility with equanimity. The important thing about their association was that they shared a sense of knowing instinctively what was exciting in the New York art scene.

Despite the smell of horse piss (which made even a child of the Depression like James Rosenquist call it 'quaint' rather than important), there was considerable excitement in the art world whenever a Stable opening was coming up. One of the first transitional artists to show there, Robert Rauschenberg, begged her for a job and she put a broom in his hand, and shortly afterward told him that he was 'lousy' at his job. But she gave him a show long before he went to Castelli – his black-on-black and white-on-white paintings. With such a range of sensibilities as that, it is not surprising that she aroused some negative opinion. Ward was in de Antonio's mind when he later wrote: 'Most of the dealers I knew were sluggish in ideas, greedy, blind, and looking for complex and dramatic versions of the master-slave relationship with painters.' But, it must be added, this was written after de Antonio and Ward had had a serious love affair that had foundered, and from that prolonged encounter there remained a residue of bitterness and even a sense, on his part, that 'she was probably just a bit of a dyke.'

In those early years, Ward was committed, as many dealers were, to Abstract Expressionism. In the Stable Annuals, where the works were chosen by the artists themselves, were major paintings by Jackson Pollock, Willem de Kooning, Franz Kline, Robert Motherwell, Philip Guston, Ad Reinhardt, Jack Tworkov and Richard Stankiewicz in shows from 1953 through 1957. Critic Clement Greenberg wrote that the Annuals exhibited 'the liveliest tendencies within the mainstream of advanced painting and sculpture.'

Andy knew the Stable well from its earliest days. Since Alan Groh had become a friend along with his companion, Buzz, he was kept apprised of everything that went on there. Buzz partied with Andy even more than Alan, and said that Andy was a much sought-after guest since he was like 'a little animal. Everyone wanted him to be there. Sometimes he would bring treats from home like cookie boots and hand them around.'

When Andy was turned down at first because of his reputation as a commercial artist, he became extremely sensitive about the issue and hid all of his commercial work, which did wonders in straightening his studio but demonstrated his wounded feelings. He later wrote: 'But if you wanted to be considered a "serious" artist, you weren't supposed to have anything to do with commercial art'; and then he added about de Antonio: 'de was the only person I knew then who could see past those old distinctions to the art itself.' And it was de who finally settled the Stable Show, in August 1962.

de had arranged to meet Eleanor Ward at Andy's house, and the three of them sat around Andy's studio drinking for an hour or so. Finally, de was the one who cut through all the niceties of the rendezvous and said: 'Well, come on, Eleanor. The point of all this, after all, is are you going to give Andy a show or not, because he's very good and he should have one.' Then Eleanor took out her wallet and held up a two-dollar bill, and she said: 'Andy, if you paint me this, I'll give you a show.'

Alan Groh and Buzz Miller were staying on Fire Island that week and Alan got a call from his employer. Eleanor told him that de Antonio had taken her to Andy's studio to see his work and she planned to have a Warhol show that autumn.

As relations between Eleanor Ward and Andy heated up, she became as possessive of him as she was of her other painters. She began calling him her 'Andy Candy'. She buttered him up on every occasion. No matter. Andy knew that this was the big time.

By this time, the Stable was no longer in a stable. The handsome old building next to the Century Theater was being torn down, and the gallery was now located on East 74th Street, where Eleanor kept the parlor floor as her living quarters and had the gallery upstairs. After her usual panic calls to Alan Groh upstairs greeting the important guests at Andy's opening, Eleanor made her dramatic entrance up the staircase, looking her movie star best, and Andy's New York career was launched.

The critics came since they could not ignore a major Stable show. Their reactions were mixed, but mostly on the positive side. They saw the Red Elvis, the Campbell Soup cans, which had become one of Andy's favorite subjects, and the Marilyns in 'various flavors', as Alan described them. Andy had painted his first Marilyn silkscreen in August, soon after her death. One of them shown at the Stable was the *Gold Marilyn*, which sold to Philip Johnson, who then gave it to the Museum of Modern Art. Noted collectors Burton and Emily Tremaine bought a double image of Marilyn, which is now in the Tate Gallery in London. Nelson Atkins bought Andy's first silkscreen portrait of an athlete, Roger Maris. The first 'disaster' painting Andy did, *129 Die*, was bought by Henry Geldzahler before the opening, but was allowed to be hung since it was the first of an important series.

Leo Castelli was there, of course, and he became convinced at once that Andy was right, and that his work differed substantially from that of Roy Lichtenstein.

> 'It just astounded me, and I felt like an idiot not having taken him on. He had Elvis and Marilyn and Brillo boxes. Just an astounding show. So I said I had made a grievous mistake not taking him on. . . . And then the question was how to get him back without doing harm to my friends and all that. So Andy said, "Don't worry. I'll take care of it." '

But Andy did not take care of it. His feelings had been hurt, and where his pride was concerned, wounds took a long time to heal in Andy.

All of the other important dealers came, and, interestingly, a number of art scholars and historians were there, perhaps to see history in the making. One of them, Gene Swenson, perceptively wrote later that 'Warhol simply likes the people he paints.' The show was such a sensation, Andy's fame began that night, and perhaps it was that – the fame – coupled with his wounded pride that kept him from Castelli for nearly two years. If the Castelli Gallery was, to Andy, the art world's equivalent to Metro-Goldwyn-Mayer, he was like the star brought to Hollywood by RKO (Fred Astaire), who, after he achieved huge success there, moved over to Metro when they needed him more then he needed them. Previously, Andy was a New York celebrity known for his commercial art. Now he was suddenly famous for his serious art.

The most persistent images everyone took away were the Campbell Soup cans, done in a variety of 'poses', and the Marilyns, which were all the same image, but varying in colour from silkscreen to silkscreen. Andy's instincts about subject matter were sound. He might have chosen a grocery item like the Green Giant, but well-known art work was on that can and he chose instead the Campbell Soup can with no art work at all except for a 'gold seal of excellence' and the name. Of course, there were the Coke bottles, and he had obliged Eleanor by doing a multiple series of two-dollar bills, but the Campbell Soup and Marilyn silkscreens would dominate the show and become the persistent Warhol images in the years ahead.

The first Marilyn silkscreen painting was done about a week after her death. Certainly it was inspired by her suicide. Andy had a morbid fear of death, and there were dual forces working in him at the time he set about to do the Marilyn. As the son of middle-European Catholic peasants, death had a powerful impact on him. As a young gay male obsessed with glamor and movie star iconography, film star deaths were particularly eventful to him. Consider the way film companies themselves managed such events. When Jean Harlow died, the studio handled the circus-like interment at Forest Lawn Memorial Park; they publicly announced that a double would be used with her back to the camera to complete the last Harlow film, *Saratoga*. On the opening day of the film's run across the nation, Metro-Goldwyn-Mayer saw that each patron received a silver medallion with the cameo likeness of the late star stamped on them.

It was in this spirit of memorializing a woman who had stood for many of the things that Andy stood for – an appreciation of sex as a healthy thing and an admiration of the naked human body with the same child-like innocence that Andy felt – that he completed his first silkscreen paintings of Monroe. He was turning her into an icon, the way Metro did with those Harlow medallions, and he was taming the painful reality of her death by replicating her image; and he was to do that image so many times over in the future – there is no truly accurate count of Andy's *Marilyn*s.

The specter of death also prompted his silkscreens of Elizabeth Taylor. During the year-long production of *Cleopatra* in Rome's Cinecittá Studios, she had collapsed and lay near death. She stood for the same sexually liberating beliefs as Marilyn had, and through Andy's popular silkscreens, Taylor became an icon of the twentieth century. It may have been difficult for the living Elizabeth Taylor to cope with being consigned to the iconography of history through Andy's art.

Andy had begun doing silkscreens earlier that summer.* His first attempts were portraits of film actors Troy Donahue and Warren Beatty. In this process, Andy would clip out a photograph from a magazine or newspaper of his subject, have it enlarged and the image transferred as an emulsion onto silk. It was a process altogether reliant upon photography for its basic image, and what Andy did then was apply color with a squee-gee so that each finished silkscreen on canvas was slightly different from the others. Some of the colors were very bright, and gold and silver were used frequently. Silver was Andy's favorite 'color', and silver panels were often used to make a 'pair' of canvases with a silkscreen image next to the blank silver panel.

Andy may have been influenced by Matisse's legitimizing a 'hands off' approach to his art. In old age, Matisse had turned to doing prints, using the stencil process. Andy worshipped Matisse's memory. Matisse's designs were so brilliant that he said he had to put his sunglasses on to look at them.

The photo Andy chose for his Marilyn silkscreen is one from the early 1950s, taken when her studio was promoting her as a temptress. It was probably used as publicity for her first starring

* Andy says in *Popism* that he did his first silkscreens in August, but he first had experimented with Troy Donahue, which had taken several days, and then went on to try the process again with a portrait of Warren Beatty. Since Marilyn died on 5 August, his first designs had to have been done before this date in late July.

vehicle, *Niagara* (1953). In that film, Marilyn played a shallow, sex-obsessed adulteress who wore too much makeup and vulgar, flaming red dresses. Andy's permutated colors used in his various silkscreen pulls of Marilyn suggest a cheap, peroxided blonde with too much lipstick, smudged.

Andy was not the first artist to hit upon the idea of Marilyn as the mid-century metaphor for woman. De Kooning had painted a series of abstract expressionist portraits beginning with *Woman I*, which evolved through the years 1950–2. *Woman I* is a formidable, fierce-visaged creature, in some ways resembling an armored tank. It has volume and its bulk seems to be covered with a grey metallic sheath. Others in the series followed. Meanwhile, Marilyn had become the greatest sex symbol in the movies (around 1954), and de Kooning painted the only woman in the series to be given a name, calling her *Marilyn Monroe*. De Kooning has softened his palette, the colors are brighter, the metallic sheath is gone. His *Marilyn*, while far from beautiful, is a breakaway from the stern-visaged creatures which preceded her.

Throughout the 1960s, Andy's many silkscreens of Marilyn (all from the same *Niagara* portrait) had found their way into the homes of the rich and museums everywhere (the going rate for one large Marilyn silkscreen on canvas soon rose to $10,000). But at the end of the sixties, something had happened to the Marilyn myth. With the publication of *Norma Jean* and other books that took a sympathetic view of her, her posthumous reputation changed from victim to folk heroine. What Andy thought of this change in his most famous subject has not been recorded, but those of us with a stake in keeping Marilyn's image undistorted have to confront a *fait accompli* with Andy's *Marilyn*. It is everywhere, and no matter how beautiful the 'flavors', it serves to refute all the documentary evidence that Marilyn was far from being the bitch-goddess whom Andy portrayed – a version of her, incidentally, that her studio was trying to promote throughout her stardom and that she herself was rebelling against.★ The truth about Andy's *Marilyn* is that it is probably not a matter of attitude or approach to the subject at all, but rather a matter of process and technique. Andy declared many

★ *Norma Jean*'s celebrated jacket photo of a pensive Marilyn holding a red rose to her bosom showed an opposite view of her. There is a child-like vulnerability, the look of a frightened doe, in this tender pose. Cecil Beaton took the portrait.

times that he emptied his mind of any thoughts or emotions about what he was painting.

   More than anyone of his time, Andy Warhol made photographic art respectable. With Troy Donahue, Warren Beatty, Natalie Wood, Elvis and Marilyn, he had plunged into silkscreen photo portraits and he never would paint a canvas conventionally again. His technique would vary from the portraits that resembled rough, unretouched photographs, the most famous being a series of 'photomats' (*Ethel Scull*), to silkscreens on canvas that had a painted look because so much color was used (*Liz* and *Liza Minelli*).

   The late taxi tycoon Robert Scull was then (1963) the most assiduous collector of pop art in America. His wife Ethel, who would take over the collection and augment it upon his death, was the subject of Andy's first deliberate attempt to move art into total mechanical reproduction.

   Her husband had asked Andy to do her portrait, which, as she told de Antonio,

> 'sort of frightened me, naturally, because one never knew what Andy would do. So he said, "Don't worry, everything will be splendid." So I had great visions of going to Richard Avedon [the fashion and celebrity photographer].
>
> 'He came up for me that day, and he said, "All right, we're off."
>
> 'And I said, "Well, where are we going?"
>
> ' "Just down to Forty-second Street and Broadway . . . I'm going to take pictures of you."
>
> 'I said, "For what?"
>
> 'He said, "For the portrait."
>
> 'I said, "In those things? My God, I'll look terrible!"
>
> 'He said, "Don't worry" and he took out coins. He had about a hundred dollars' worth of silver coins, and he said "We'll take the high key and the low key, and I'll put you inside, and you watch the little red light." The thing you do the passport with, three for a quarter or something like that . . . and I froze. I watched the red light and never did anything. So Andy would come in and poke me and make me do all kinds of things, and I relaxed finally. I think the whole place,

wherever we were, thought they had two nuts there. We were running from one booth to another, and he took all these pictures, and they were drying all over the place.

'At the end of the thing, he said, "Now, you want to see them?" And they were so sensational that he didn't need Richard Avedon.

'I was so pleased, I think I'll go there for all my pictures from now on.

'When he delivered the portrait, it came in pieces [one colored panel for each photo], and Bob [her husband] said to him, "How would you like . . . don't you want to sit down at this, too?" because there were all these beautiful colors.

'He said, "Oh, no. The man who's up here to put it together, let him do it any way he wants."

' "But, Andy, this is your portrait."

' "It doesn't matter."

' So he sat in the library, and we did it [assembled the thirty-six variously-colored photomat pictures of Ethel]. Then, of course, he did come in and did give it a critical eye. "Well, I do think this should be here and that should be there." When it was all finished, he said, "It really doesn't matter. It's just so marvelous. But you could change it any way you want."

'What I liked about it mostly was that it was a portrait of being alive and not like these candy box things . . . .'

Gerard Malanga recalled that twenty photomat strips were 'edited down' and that Andy 'made a selection and we fabricated this huge painting of smaller paintings on canvas that were stretched and then put together . . .' – by someone else, if we are to believe Ethel Scull. Gerard adds: 'Later, we did Bobby Short [with the photomat]. I don't think it has ever been exhibited. We did it for him, and I remember Marie Menken filming us doing this at the Firehouse.'

What Andy had done was to bridge the gap between commercial art and serious art. He had made art into a business, and business into art. Or, as his friend Stanley Amos said, 'The studio was his workplace and he was the manufacturer.'

PART FOUR

ART

AND

LIFE

FIFTEEN

Andy's townhouse was, in his words, 'a total mess', at this important juncture in his life. 'The canvases were spread out all over the living-room and the ink from the silkscreens was getting on everything. I knew I had to rent a studio to paint in.'

The solution was an abandoned firehouse on East 87th Street within walking distance of Andy's home on upper Lexington. A man had leased the building from the city and he offered to sublet part of it to Andy. He had found his studio, and now he needed an assistant who knew something about silkscreens.

Willard and Marie Maas were underground filmmakers with a large apartment in Brooklyn Heights. They were frequent partygivers, and Andy went as often as he could. There was something a little savage in this couple that he found amusing. They were both heavy drinkers, roaring drunk at times, and they engaged in violent disputes at these affairs, shouting unspeakable obscenities at each other. Edward Albee is said to have modeled his George and Martha on them for *Who's Afraid of Virginia Woolf*. They were very free sexually and Stephen Koch recalled a time soon after he was introduced to Marie when she grabbed his crotch, which was unnerving, to say the least. Another of their friends was a curly-haired Italo-American just out of college, Gerard Malanga. There is some evidence from Ivan Karp and others that Andy already knew Gerard, having bumped into him at poetry readings or somewhere around the Judson-San Remo axis. Gerard was a poet himself and sometimes gave readings around town.

According to Gerard, it was in June 1963, at the Maas's Brooklyn Heights apartment, that these two men, who together were destined to make art history, first met. Charles Henri Ford introduced them, Ford being a poet himself as well as a painter and filmmaker. He was also actress Ruth Ford's brother, and, for a time, film star Zachary Scott's brother-in-law. Like Henry Geldzahler and de Antonio, Ford was one of Andy's serious friends and supporters, not just someone who hung around the Factory crowd, an important distinction because the serious friends tended to remain loyal to Andy and he to them for a very long time, while the superstars and hangers-on tended to change every two years or so, when they would be gone, either eased out, departed for fresher fields, or dead. In the event, Ford learned that Andy was looking for an assistant to help him at the Firehouse and, at a poetry reading the following week, he brought the two men together to discuss the possibility.

At first, Gerard tried to continue with his studies out at Wagner College, but that meant he was almost always late for his afternoon of work for Andy. In Gerard's words:

> 'The intention was that it was going to be a summer job, but the job was so interesting and Andy invited me to come out to California that September because he was going to have a show of the Elvis Presley paintings which I had worked on that summer. It was too good a thing to turn down. So the job lasted seven years.'

Gerard tried returning to college in January 1964, but too much was happening around Andy, and Andy was seeing to it that Gerard was involved in all of it. So in the summer of 1964, Gerard gave up college and never returned.

The handsome, curly-haired Italo-American had a real flair for the job and worked long hours alongside Andy, who was still a 'workaholic', putting in about ten hours a day. Malanga was paid the minimum wage, then $1.25 per hour. He said later that he probably could have got $3.00 an hour if he had asked for it, so there was a decent work ethic in him, and Andy must have realized it. On the other hand, he seemed a little desperate to project and protect his own sexual identity. Once, Andy overheard him on the phone telling Charles Henri Ford, 'Frankly, I think he's going to put the make on me.'

A very real affection developed between Andy and Gerard. There seems small doubt that Andy explored the possibilities of having some sexual attachment as well, but he must have bumped into Gerard's admiration for beautiful women. What they did develop between them was a symbiotic relationship, with Andy drawing on Gerard's Italian romanticism and adventurous spirit, and Gerard slipping effortlessly into nearly every corner of Andy's life.

When international fame was about to overtake him, the surface of Andy Warhol seemed the most important thing at the time. Probably with the encouragement of Malanga, he adopted what was known as an 'S and M' look. So did Gerard. They wore black leather jackets and black boots. Most of the time, they wore a kind of French sailor's teeshirt with horizontal stripes. Andy's blond wig had lightened perceptibly and was denser than before. Within a short time, Gerard bleached his hair to a shade of golden blond.

A 'Factory crowd' began to form around Andy. The hangers-on from the San Remo café and the Judson Church were always about, and there were new faces brought there by Malanga. Malanga's circle was bohemian but more serious than Andy's. Andy's crowd was wilder and, for the most part, younger. If one seeks for a comparison in the arts, this was not the world of Larry Rivers but closer to that of the poet Max Bodenheim, who was murdered along with his wife in 1954 and who gravitated, like Andy, to losers and misfits, one of whom would do him in, because he could not help himself. In Andy's case, with hindsight it must be said that he could have helped himself.

The complexion of the Warhol crowd was etiolated and its spirit decadent. They all seemed adrift, cut loose from the moorings most of us are attached to, disconnected. Andy plugged them in, if only for a time. He connected them with the insular life at the Factory if not with the world. Looking at this bizarre crew individually, nearly all of them were hanging on by their fingernails to whatever would get them through the day. Andy certainly took on some of their survival methods. It was at this time that he began to take Obetrols, which he claimed were for weight-loss, but his intake rose from the half pill he said he was taking to several a day. He said later that he got only two hours' sleep for a two-year period beginning in 1964. The pills kept him hopping and he moved non-stop from a day's work into an evening of partying.

If he believed that his reality was 'half television' and not quite real, the Obetrols did not help except to screen out the humdrum element of his working life. He was also on the phone several hours every day talking to Henry Geldzahler or the Duchess (Brigid Berlin) or Charles Rydell. Henry believed that he needed that 'funnel' between himself and his confidantes. The telephone became another screening device between Andy and reality.

There were many self-destructive people around Andy and that fact kept many of his old friends away from continued close contact. de Antonio, Lisanby, Alan Groh and Buzz Miller, and even Ted Carey, began seeing less of Andy except at gallery openings or an occasional party. Some of the most careless ones lasted a remarkably long time. Eric Emerson, he of the altar boy's face, was constantly on cocaine or heroin or qualudes and kept insisting that 'I want to be with the angels', as though he carried a vision that the pills would help fulfill. He was often pulled back from the brink by someone in the Factory crowd and he managed to survive nearly a dozen years before he finally got his wish.

If one seeks for reasons, Andy had been an outsider for so many years that perhaps now he wanted to gather up all the outsiders he could find and bring them inside the sanctuary of the Factory. But it was not an especially congenial crowd. They nearly all remained loners who happened to be under the same roof. There were fights; there was bickering. Petty rivalries broke out. Andy seemed to enjoy his role as peacemaker. He was creating his own world, his own Order, and the acolytes, though often stoned, were never less than reverent.

SIXTEEN

When Gerard Malanga joined forces with Andy, the major silkscreen works, the paintings that compose the platform on which Andy Warhol's reputation rests, began to roll off their improvized assembly line at the Firehouse studio. The process is best described by Malanga:

'The very first painting I screened was a 40″ x 40″ silver Elizabeth Taylor portrait at a shutdown firehouse that Andy rented from the city for $100 a year. In making the Elizabeth Taylor painting, masking tape was shaped to the contours of the face directly on the canvas to create a stencil that followed the lines of a transfer-rubbing. Then we would fill in the flesh tones, eyebrows, and lips by hand with Liquitex. When the paint dried, the masking tape was peeled off, resulting in shaped colors. Andy remarked to me once that his paintings looked more like Alex Katz paintings before the silkscreen was applied. The last step in the process was to screen in the black paint. The paintings were a step-by-step transformation of photography into painting.'

Gerard had learned the craft of silkscreens when he worked for a textile chemist in the manufacture of men's neckties. He had a quick mind, was personable if you did not mind a dreamy remoteness, and he certainly was prescient. He could have earned more money elsewhere, but he somehow divined that this was more than an ordinary job. He was an indispensable part of a creative process.

After a long session with the silkscreens, Andy and Gerard would walk the three blocks over to the townhouse, where Julia would make lunch for them, usually a 'Czechoslovakian-style hamburger stuffed with diced onions, sprinkled with parsley, and always on white bread, and with a 7-Up on ice.' They could work at the Firehouse only in daylight because it had no electricity.

Poetry was Gerard's great passion. He wrote it; he listened to other poets; he wanted to share this music inside him with the world. It doesn't matter that it was overly romantic. What mattered was that the poetry was forthright; it defined who he was. Andy saw this, and encouraged him. He accompanied Gerard to poetry readings, and there were countless evenings spent together. A bit later, when Andy was forced to travel to a museum show in a distant place, Gerard went with him. They shared the same motel room, though Andy knew that Gerard was interested in girls, rich ones if possible. His dream seemed to be to find some beautiful patroness, an heiress perhaps, and live happily ever after with the poetry subsidized and flowing out to the world. And just as Andy understood what he was about, Gerard knew better than anyone what Andy was about. Some months after Andy's death, Gerard summed the man up as well as anyone before or since: 'The secret to Andy's success was his own self-effacement.'

Andy was forced to vacate the Firehouse only a few months after Gerard began working there. The City had sold the building and Andy got an eviction notice (second-hand, since another man owned the building). It was time for a move anyway since the Firehouse was so primitive, he rarely showed any art work there, and one stormy night the roof leaked so badly a number of Elvises were ruined by water and had to be done over.

That was how the Factories began. Someone told Andy there was a vacant loft floor in a hat factory building on East 47th Street near Second Avenue. It sounded right to him, and when he saw it, he took it on the spot. Someone had made hats in that space before him; now he would make art in the same impersonal way.

The Scene began. In a way, it was Andy's nest. It was the alternative to settling down with some loving partner who never showed, although Andy's eye was always cocked for the Right One's appearance. But even if the improbable had happened, it was too late to change things by much. Andy lived by a philosophy worked out through much pain; his sensors had been attuned to keeping some distance between himself and others. Henry Geldzahler said that Andy could become truly engaged with living when he met someone new, had some new crush.

But they ultimately failed the test, each and every one of them. He might even seem like everyone else. 'Gosh! He's bee-you-tiful! Isn't he beautiful!' Such an encounter could escalate into what seemed like an affair. But these crushes always bumped into defenses that were by now impregnable.

Billy Name lined the walls of the Factory, including the john, with Reynolds Wrap silver foil, bought in wholesale quantities. Silver became Andy's favorite color. It had not been the case before; he had seemed obsessed with gold foil in the fifties – the golden slippers, the Gold Book of drawings. But when you are creating a Scene, gold is déclassé. Silver can be today's or something as nostalgic as a hip-flask or the screen at the local bijou.

One of the best descriptions of what the Factory was like came from Ingrid Superstar, who at the time all of this was pulled together was selling refrigerators in north Jersey:

'. . . there's a big wide arch of aluminum foil on the ceiling with white on each side with pipes, and then there's a ladder behind the couch that Gerard is laying on smoking a cigarette. He misses things. And one side of the wall is painted silver and part of the wall by the window is in aluminum foil and there's a big old dilapidated hog jaw with a red couch over there, and there's silkscreens all over the place and wrapped up whatever they are . . . there's a big clock that, of course, doesn't work, and there's a mirror over on that side. . . . It really looks like a loft and an all-purpose workshop, and then in the back there's a sink, of course, with no pipe and the water has to run out in a bucket. And there's all sorts of paints . . . there's a bathroom and . . . the toilet never flushes, and if it does flush, you have to be afraid that it runs over. Plus there are some pretty disgusting, obscene drawings on the wall, which I'd rather not go into. And there's a dressing-room in the back with all kinds of crappy clothes – the crappiest is Gerard's coat . . . . The floor is silver – just about everything in this inevitable plastic palace is silver, except for the lights . . . and there's a red light over the exit sign at the door. I wonder what the red light denotes.'

Life at the Factory had a pattern. Anyone over thirty was probably a person of substance – another artist who had made it and heard that something unusual was afoot over at Andy's loft; Charles Henri Ford was a surrealist poet, an artist, and a collector; Gregory Battcock was an art and film critic and commentator on contemporary culture; David Bourdon was an art critic with the *Village Voice* and, soon, *Life* magazine. The kids were nearly all on speed. Really heavy drugs were discouraged, although some of the regular hangers-on like Eric Emerson would reputedly take anything that was available.

Ronnie Cutrone was about sixteen years old and might qualify as the youngest person to hang out at the Factory on a regular basis. Ronnie's drift towards the Scene is best told by him:

> 'I was friends with a group of people. I guess it was sort of an art crowd. There were dancers; there were the Theater of the Ridiculous [Charles Ludlam] people to be specific. Do you know who Harry Katukis is? There was the Café Cino in those days, which was the underground theater at the time, and I used to hang out with a lot of them. And there was this one person, George Milloway, and he had met Andy a few times. In those days, the Factory was on 47th Street and Second Avenue, and it was open. It was completely open. I mean, almost anybody could go in and visit if they were brought by somebody else. So I was just brought up there to hang out, to watch him paint, to listen to music, and I was in art school. No, I was still in high school actually. So after class, I would go hang out at the Factory. I was sixteen, I think. I'm thirty-nine now.'

Ronnie admitted that he was on speed and said that the drug scene clearly attracted Andy.

> '. . . Andy caught wind of this, and wanted to come over and do a movie, but I never permitted it. And I was making friends with real maniacs, real crazies, like second-storey men [burglars], who were great artists actually, but you know my house was inhabited by thieves.'

Since most of the men around the Factory were gay, Ronnie experimented with that, but it did not work. He was far too interested in girls. And there *were* girls at the Factory of a special kind that seemed to exist only in the sixties – frizzy-haired, lots of make-up on a blanched face, skinny (making Brigid fairly extraordinary), and often flat-chested. Almost none of the boys was bad-looking and some of them were 'beauties' hand-picked by Andy at the Judson or San Remo or the Café Cino. One particularly moving photo surviving from that era shows a young man in jeans, obviously stoned out of his mind, fishing through his pockets for subway change but clearly finding this chore almost beyond his present capabilities.

Andy never sensed that any of the young crowd drifting in and out of the silver-foiled Factory could be a threat to him. There seemed to be safety in numbers, but in his remoteness, in his passivity, he seemed to be alone even among the dozen or so people who always surrounded him.

There were tens of thousands of photographs taken in Andy's series of Factories, but one is singular. It shows a Factory girl aiming a pistol at Andy's head. It might have been Andy's cap pistol, and it was certainly a prank, but this was after an incident at the Firehouse studio when a small but determined woman whom Andy and the others knew as Dorothy Podber came in off the street leading a large dog. She took a revolver out of her purse and shot a clean bullet hole through half a dozen *Marilyn* silkscreen canvases stacked together. Then she walked out without saying a word. Andy simply asked, 'Who was that?' and later, he sold the bullet-soiled silkscreens without repair. They became known as the *'Shot Marilyns'* and two years after his death the *'Red Shot Marilyn'* sold for nearly four million dollars, the highest price ever paid for a Warhol painting. Ondine (Robert Olivio), a gay speed freak from Queens whom Andy met at the San Remo bar and who later became an important Warhol 'Superstar', thought at the time that the silkscreens had been damaged and said, 'There's nothing that Andy doesn't sell,' but Andy knew better than anyone that the bullet holes had made these *Marilyns* unique.

Brigid Berlin, alias the Duchess, chose to walk around bare-breasted, possibly as part of her rebellion against the outside world in general (and not just against her parents and the Establishment). Outside, nudity in a woman was permissible in the right places when she was sylph-like. Brigid was fat, so her bobbing boobs were a statement in themselves. When Cecil Beaton came one day to photograph the Factory regulars, Brigid is topless in the second row. Brigid was someone Andy believed in, overlooking her quirks – she had a series of 'trip' books, huge scrap-books holding her 'rubbings' of people's scars (which were done as one would do a rubbing of a tombstone).

Andreas Brown came to New York in 1967, when he bought the Gotham Book Mart. Brown had nearly as much interest in art as in books, and he organized and hung a show of Brigid Berlin's polaroids, one of the first such shows in New York, during the 1969–70 season. But his first awareness of her scar obsession upset him a little, although he is not easily disconcerted. Brown recalled taking his secretary, who was a beautiful blonde, to dinner in the Village one night:

> '. . . and we'd been there about twenty minutes and Andy marched in with a group of, I would guess, eight or ten people, including Brigid [Berlin] Polk, and of course Andy knew who we were and Brigid knew. My secretary was extremely attractive, a model at one time and that kind of person always attracted Andy. You know he liked glamorous people. Brigid at that time was compiling what she called her "scar book". It consisted of blank pages and she would carry around an ink pad and if you had a scar on your body, the idea was to take an impression of the scar, using the ink pad . . . and then you would sign and date the page and explain how you acquired the scar.'

She did rubbings of men's cocks the same way, and had a belly-button book. At almost the same time, she was making taped recordings of her sexual encounters as well as her visits to the toilet. During one luncheon with Andy and Charles Rydell at the Algonquin dining-room, she turned on her recorder and treated the other diners to assorted sounds from the commode – obvious peeing into the toilet bowl, and then the flushing sound, which turned all heads in their direction. But Andy knew that she was a gifted artist, and he indulged her in all these eccentric pursuits. She was to have the distinction of surviving longer than anyone ever to become part of Andy's inner circle, and as of 1989 was still working at the Warhol headquarters in Manhattan. She took the last name 'Polk' as her 'Factory name' because she was forever poking herself or someone else in the fanny for a quick fix of amphetamine – 'taking a poke', she called it. The name stuck; no pun especially intended.

Richie Berlin, her sister, was typical of the other Factory girls, skinnier than most, in fact, but she did not fall in love with Andy the way Brigid did. She affected a boyish look, but she did not ingratiate herself in any way with Andy. Later, she said: 'I feel best when alone with pocket money, quite thin, agile, and slightly vicious . . . . I've always believed in live high, die, and have a wonderful corpse.'

Ondine, or Robert Olivio, came into the Café Cino from Queens. He was gay, but he ran with dangerous people. He was frankly attracted to lowlife. Ondine and his hoodlum friends seemed very colorful to Andy. In that sense, he and Andy were alike. They never sensed that any of the psychopaths or neurotics with whom they surrounded themselves ever would hurt *them*. But by the end of the sixties, Ondine was living in Pittsburgh, in a reversal of situations with Andy. He had fled from both drugs and his thieving companions.

Gay amphetamine addicts, called 'speed queens', were tolerated but not necessarily admired by Andy. But Ondine was different. He was able to stand a little away from the Scene and analyze it; his comment was often bitchy, and it was invariably funny. Andy loved his company. Later, Andy would write that Ondine was 'the most fascinating character' he met in the sixties.

Of Eric Emerson, the bisexual 'altar boy' pining for eternity, Ondine would say:

> 'Eric presented many faces to many people. If he could use you, he was so sweet . . . . I thought that Eric was wonderful at first. I thought he was the nicest person I had ever met . . . . But this will tell you something – Eric and Warhol had had a fight, and Warhol had planned a tour. *The Chelsea Girls* was going to the Cannes Film Festival or something. And Andy asked me to go with them, and I was really tied down to New York. I didn't want to leave my drugs and my friends and all that stuff.

So I went to Eric and said: "Listen, Eric, Andy wants me to go to Europe. Why don't you go in my place?" And he said, "Andy and I are no longer friends," so I said, "Well, look, I'll bring you in and re-introduce you, and you two can make it up." And he said, "Well, as long as you're going to do that, why don't you take my apartment?" It was a nice apartment on the West Side. "I'll set it up with the landlord and with the Super that you're going to take over for this month. Then after this month, you'll have to pay [the rent]." And I said, "Wonderful!" because the apartment was like two streets away from Rotten Rita's, and Rotten was my best friend. So I moved in with all my clothes and my accoutrements, whatever I had, my hats, my furs or whatever. I had told Andy that Eric would be a good person to take on the tour and so forth and they became friends again. After the plane left, the landlord come up to me and told me that I'd have to leave the apartment. I said, "This is my apartment." And he said, "Oh, no, it's not. Mr. Emerson hasn't paid the rent in like six months . . . . You have to go, unless you want to pay the back rent." . . . Eric was a horrible, horrible, manipulative little bastard.'

Jimmy Smith, who liked to clean out friends' apartments as already described, and who loved to redo the decor with mustard or spray paint or whatever was handy, was an ex-lover of Ondine's. Ondine described Jimmy as: 'Not a very good burglar because his feet were so big. But he was a wonderful lover and a great friend, and he was a lot of fun. He liked to intimidate people with guns . . . . Just a great guy.'

So the Factory was an exotic place to see. Several artists began dropping in frequently, among them Marisol, the Venezuelan artist and sculptor who did witty parodies of middle-class families in blocks of wood with plaster faces. She was often called 'pop' in her subject matter. Later, she said that she and Andy never had a conversation together. Often, with the record-player playing rock music at speaker-busting levels, the din made conversation pointless. Sometimes, it would be Callas singing *Norma*, *Carmen* or her famous *Lucia*. Andy had them all. Marisol got the idea that

one of Andy's 'interesting' ideas was to be disliked. She said: '. . .
people came up to me all the time and they tell me how much they
hate him. They don't even know him . . . . They just don't like his
art and his personality.'

In art circles, Marisol was known as someone who liked to
be by herself, which excluded the casual drop-ins whom Andy
tolerated so voluminously. But among her peers, she moved
in the same circles as Andy. They were often photographed
together. She was thought of as part of the Factory regulars.
Unlike Andy, she had tempestuous affairs – with artist John Grillo
and others – that would become gossip-fodder when they became
public shouting matches, usually when a party was at its peak.

There were other significant persons in 'Andy's crowd': James
Rosenquist, Claes Oldenburg, and, of course, Henry Geldzahler
and Ivan Karp. Karp was a rock music fan and introduced Andy
to rock impresario Murray the K's Brooklyn Fox shows.

Oldenburg and his wife, Pat, had their own crowd, so there was
a time in the early sixties when Andy did not yet sense that he was
the epicenter of sixties culture. Oldenburg and Andy were nearly
identical in extracting their art from their immediate environment.
Rosenquist altered it a bit by fragmenting it, so that you were never
given a whole of anything, only parts, and then in conjunction with
disparate entities.

Lichtenstein occasionally joined the partying at Andy's or
Oldenburg's, but he kept some distance (about forty-five miles,
to be precise) between his work and Manhattan. He was teaching
painting and design at Douglass College, which was the girls'
school at Rutgers University in New Brunswick, New Jersey.
He had a wife and child. He was in that sense out of it.
But his academic colleague, Allen Kaprow (who created the
first 'Happening'), introduced him to the others in what was
becoming a movement. And Ivan Karp had helped him rethink
what art really was, helping to liberate him from the past.
Lichtenstein took a studio on Bond Street in the financial district
sometime in this period, which was more of a statement than
a convenience to him. He wanted to be thought of as a New
York painter, but he was too bound up with his family to
stay away very long. As it developed, Lichtenstein fought to
hang onto traditional values in his private life while his increasingly public art was at the forefront of the Pop revolution.

Jim Rosenquist tried to have it both ways. He liked to party; he was as bohemian as Andy. As for culture, he said:

> 'I guess my living-room furniture was my culture, and after winning a scholarship at the Art Students League, I was sort of dropped into a place with no money, totally broke. I had a hard time in New York. I was dislocated from my previous lifestyle, which like any other person in the midwest was pretty ordinary. Then for instance, in New York, I ate in the Automat all the time, which was automated. I never rode in cars; I always rode in public conveyances. So I was sort of dislocated from my recent past and at that time the Beat Generation people were around and they used to move around a lot. They seemed to live rather well on nothing. They took pride in wearing second-hand clothes, second-hand everything – second-hand coffee cups. Their values were displaced into something different. They were very poetic, some of them . . . . There were Miles Horst, Larry Rivers, Alan Ginsberg. I met Jack Kerouac once. William Burroughs I met a few times. So my values changed a great deal when I'd lived in New York about a year.'

Both Andy and Rosenquist used their working-class origins to project Manhattan personalities of a naiveté that could be disarming. Perhaps it was Andy's awareness of this similarity or the large scale of Rosenquist's work, but Andy frequently told his Diary and other people that Rosenquist was his favorite Pop artist; and at the time of his death, Andy owned several major Rosenquist paintings. Rosenquist even anticipated Andy with his soup cans – in 1960 or thereabouts, he had done a big painting called *In the Red* showing two pairs of feet standing in a puddle of tomato soup.

After Rosenquist went with the Green Gallery (before finally settling down with Leo Castelli), he began to see a lot of Andy. He recalled being photographed with him at a party given by Ethel Scull:

> '. . . in a tuxedo with a short haircut. I wish I had a picture of Jasper Johns doing the Twist. He'll never twist again . . . . I hung out with Andy for a while

and I remember we went to see *Goldfinger* and *Winnie the Pooh* the same night, and a strange coincidence – Andy, Bob Rauschenberg, Marisol, Henry Geldzahler and myself would always show up at the same parties for a long time. A lot of them would be black tie, and why I'll never know. There were so many parties, we'd go to one party for the hors d'oeuvres and then Henry would say, "Are we seeing you at the next dinner?" "I think so," I'd say, and then the main course somewhere else. And somewhere else for dessert. Constantly like that for a period of time . . . . Andy always used to stand near any movie people. He'd stand in back of them. He was very shy and he'd stand near them. I was in an ad as a cowboy for a Volkswagen truck advertisement and this guy wanted me to be some other person in another photograph, and Andy said: "Oh, you should do it." I think he'd secretly like to have been an actor or was an actor and wanted to be outside of himself and something else.'

It was this fine imbroglio of Andy's friends – artists and millionaire hostesses and dealers on the one hand, and the unpublished poets, second-storey men and speed queens on the other – that must have started him thinking about the possibilities of film. The thing about the Factory hangers-out was that they were rootless, adrift, disconnected with the real world. Somehow they had come to him and he had got them involved in a kind of daisy chain of relationships within the Factory. These spaced-out people looked to Andy for guidance and approval, so he became a sort of surrogate parent of an ideal kind. He never told them not to do anything; he encouraged them to do what they wanted to do. When Billy Name had converted one of the two toilets into a darkroom, the regulars could duck inside and have privacy for a 'quickie' sexual connection. Andy was used to drawing from life, certainly the things immediately at hand, and here was a Hogarthian world of outsiders filling up his Factory space and spilling down to the street. It was impossible to capture it all with drawing pad or canvas.

Andy told Charles Henri Ford about his interest in acquiring the equipment needed to make movies. Ford recalled:

'. . . I took him to Peerless with Gerard, and there he tried out a Bolex. And I remember his using it, the first time, he brought it home and just opened the lens and just waved it around the room without even looking at it. But he had decided from the beginning he was going to make "bad" movies, like he was always talking about bad art which was another word for pop. He could make as bad movies as anybody.'

Ford was making 'bad' movies at the same time. A bit earlier, he had filmed Andy with the actress Jean Seberg at the Firehouse studio before the first Factory opened. Ford also had filmed

'a thing of Claes Oldenburg putting up pop-sicles and taking them down. And Robert Whitman and Jim Rosenquist. I had the idea at that time to be a still photographer – to me movies move too much, they make me nervous, they move so much. So, when Andy did his first movie, of *Sleep*, it never moved at all; he might have taken that hint.'

SEVENTEEN

'The reason I'm painting this way is because I want to be a machine. Whatever I do, and do machine-like, is because, it is what I want to do. I think it would be terrific if everybody was alike.'

Andy's commentary, coming as it did in the revolutionary sixties, sounds anti-humanist in a way that would deeply offend every artist, going back to the cave painters, who strove to express a vision, a personal view, of the life around them.

But it does not seem so dire when placed in the context of a decade when old ideas and even laws were failing, as Americans tried to cope with racial strife amid new and stringent civil rights acts, passed quickly once President Johnson took over from a slain idealist who could speak of great dreams but not get Congress to budge on any meaningful legislation. All of this was played out in a mood of wry irony against a backdrop of escalating warfare against a people almost none of the Americans understood. The Vietnamese were trying to throw off their colonialist shackles while the American military presence was attempting to impose a corrupt regime of its own in the name of democracy. It was certainly that schizophrenic demon that President Johnson was trying to exorcize when he announced after winning the 1964 election and settled into a four-year term that he would not seek reelection.

It was in that climate that Andy first took up Henry Geldzahler's idea to do *129 Die in Jet*. If Henry had not handed him that front page to paint, there seems little doubt that Andy would have found something equally horrific. His friends gave him ideas that he already had in his head. They simply articulated them and got the machinery going.

Andy had been moving in this direction ever since his *Marilyns*. He was moved by her death to do them, so he told us. And it might not have been any different if he had done the first of them a year earlier and had said that he had been moved by her life. The *Elvises* belong in this canon only in hindsight. They were done when Elvis was alive, and while surely Andy had heard of the 'Memphis mafia' surrounding the singer and had read, as we all had, the lurid accounts of his affairs, all of that goes with super-celebrity and not with tragedy.

Why, among our contemporary masters, did not Lichtenstein, Rauschenberg, Johns, or Oldenburg do such a series and not Warhol? Johns, of course, had touched upon things wrong with our world more than once, and Rauschenberg tried to pin down on his canvas some of it (*Dante's Inferno*). Oldenburg's *Street* and even his *Store* gave us the seamier side of Metropolis. But only Warhol saw the most evil, the most tragic, the most heart-rending events impersonally, and, like a sculptor chipping out of a block of stone a wondrous thing, freed the front pages from the dustbin of history and put them, undiluted by the slightest hint of interpretation, on our museum walls. There is nothing to be gained by looking to Freud for guidance. Better to look to Camus and Brecht, to the existentialists. Warhol was a society reject. He had come to a liberal city full of hope as a gay young male. But what he sought there – acceptance and love and, yes, even admiration would not be found except through his art.

The flattening of his emotional response to tragedy came little by little. It first surfaced when he phoned Ralph Ward to ask if his dead roommate had left him anything rather than to attempt to console him. It was full-blown by the time John Kennedy died. Emotionally he had become what he said, often enough, he wanted to be – a machine. He was the impersonal recorder of the terrible things happening to us. When he did the *Tuna Fish Disaster*, the *Electric-Chairs*, the *Race Riots*, the car crashes, *Suicide*, he was the unfeeling recorder. His being gay and unwanted because he was not beautiful has given us a series of art works recording peak moments of our so-called civilized society when ethics failed us.

'I am for an art that is political–erotical–mystical, that does something other than sit on its ass in a museum,' said Claes

Oldenburg. Oldenburg had opened his 'store' in December 1961, stocked with real-looking items, so real that small boys would come in to shop-lift rather than look, as the regular gallery goers were doing. How chagrined must a young thief have been when he discovered outside that he had helped himself to a sausage filled with kapok and covered with stiffened fabric. Oldenburg also created a city *Street*, frighteningly close to Manhattan's seedier sections.

In England, there was a parallel Pop movement, but it differed from its American counterpart in one major respect. Like Rosenquist's fragments, it was subjective and not impersonal. The Warhol image was bare of any association. It was for the eye to see and not the mind to ponder over.

Dubuffet remarked as early as 1947 that 'What interests me is not cake, but bread.' He was referring to art stripped to its essentials. This is what Andy was doing, and Tom Wesselman, Jim Dine, and Oldenburg. Lichtenstein seemed to be more cautious, as though weighing just what direction he should go with his bold cartoon lines and ben day dots.

English Pop was altogether gentler than the American variety, but the English pop painters were obsessed with America, its manners and its fads, in the late fifties and early sixties. It is probably important that the major American pop artists were born at the beginning of the Great Depression and grew up in a society in which all the little elegances and fancy touches had been swept away. The English chose to look at that stripped-bare world when they drew on American life for their pop subjects. For the Americans, it was not an intellectual exercise but a recording of what they had seen around them.

Andy's pop subjects annoyed people more than anyone else's. His were more Duchampian than anybody's. If a machine could have created silkscreen paintings of coke bottles, soup cans and dollar bills, Andy would have paid its inventor to set the thing up in his studio.

But he was also becoming known to the man in the street. Henry Geldzahler tells of an air conditioner installer putting a unit into his apartment, seeing one of Andy's *Marilyn Monroe* panels and asking 'Is that an Andy Warhol?'

Since this recognition came so early in Andy's career it could have nothing to do with the notoriety that by the end of the sixties had made him into an internationally known celebrity. By then, anyone who read a newspaper tabloid or gossip magazine knew who Andy Warhol was.

But surely it was the *inside* gossip of the art world that kept Andy from Castelli's favor for such a long time. It was hard for a civilized and urbane man like Leo to take seriously anyone who kept such raffish company, certainly not in the way he took Roy Lichtenstein seriously. Oldenburg could claim to be one of the street people, record it, and be accepted as a true artist. Andy simply immersed himself in that subterranean world, and even if the street people conceded that he was their king, how could the straight world care very much?

The body of Andy's work that emerged between 1961 and 1963, a period of less than two years, said a great deal about him that he was unwilling to reveal then or ever about himself. The early crudely done ads for false teeth, nose jobs, back of the *Police Gazette* and *True Confessions* ten and twenty liners, the Marilyn of the sex queen Fox ads, the soup cans, coke bottles, and the other signposts of a society sold out to the merchants and cut off from the philosophers except for Sartre and other I-told-you-sos, all of this declared that Andy was a man very much alone. There are no connections here except to a disposable world. There is not one single suggestion that here is a man who feels anything at all. He is not numb; he has turned off. The eager young artist of the early fifties who drew those marvelous young men from life, those fanciful shoes and boots, the pears and calla lillies, which fairly shouted their sensuous origins, had stifled all of those emotions.

Andy was deliberately moving towards a mechanized art, a hands-off technique, because he no longer wanted to feel anything at all. If his responses seemed vague, he was simply riffling though the pages in his mind for some *appropriate* comment, and not always finding it. Essentially, his life in the sixties was a buttoned-down reaction to the dashed hopes of the fifties – all that intense, but frustrated sexuality; that concentrated drive for fame that eluded him except in the narrow world of fashion and commercial graphics.

His art after those twenty months or so of pop masterworks would be echoes of those fecund days until the late seventies, when, with the help of a brilliant silkscreen technician, Rupert Smith, he would suddenly emerge as one of the great colorists of his time, creating a dazzling body of late work (*Endangered Species*, *Cars*, etc.) totally different from the commonplaceness of the earlier great paintings.

Pop Art was becoming important enough in the sixties to be covered by major art critics; it had also crossed over and become topical news, although reporters were inclined to ridicule it or be very patronizing. In London, a dealer on Duke Street named Robert Fraser was showing a great deal of it, but it would be towards the end of the decade before the Tate Gallery would hang a major American show (*Manifestations of Pop Art*).

Roy Lichtenstein was the first American to be seen abroad to any degree. The Castelli connection had led to major museum interest in him. In Lichtenstein's work, one could see all of the major elements of Pop: the stress on recognizable elements of the environment; the pieces of technology or industrial life as works of art; the familiar seen in a new way.

Andy pretended not to care about his own situation. His friends knew that he desperately wanted to be with Castelli, too. He had to remember that Leo Castelli had told him that after his first Stable show, 'then we'll see.' But more than a year had gone by and he was still waiting to hear from Leo. After his Stable show and the one on the coast at the Ferus Gallery, Irving Blum of that establishment planned a second show. This one would feature the double-paneled silkscreens of *Liz* and *Elvis*. It would coincide with a major retrospective of Marcel Duchamp's work at the Pasadena Art Museum.

If it had been Andy Warhol and not Roy Lichtenstein who was getting all of this international attention, it is possible that Andy might not have turned to filmmaking as early as 1963. But it must be said that Lichtenstein took his art far more seriously than Andy did.

Here again, Andy was unconsciously following in the footsteps of Cocteau. What both men took very seriously indeed was fame. Lichtenstein was expanding the range of the pop image as far as it would go, crossing over into abstraction in several significant instances. He soon would turn to pop sculpture, working in an Art Deco fashion in brass. He was far more interested in acceptance for his art than in the pursuit of fame.

Henry Geldzahler sensed what was happening, and when he

bumped into the underground film actor Taylor Mead outside the Metropolitan Museum, where he worked, it must have occurred to him that if Andy was planning to change his direction – and Andy told Henry everything – he should have the best available talent around. Mead had appeared in a number of critically acclaimed underground films, notably for Ron Rice. Henry knew as well that Mead was the same gentle but sly rebel that Andy was. He was convinced that they should meet and he took him at once to Andy's house nearby.

Like a number of the people Andy was to bring into his group of underground film players (or Superstars, as Chuck Wein, a Warhol film associate in the mid-sixties, began calling them), Mead was from the upper middle class. His father had been a Detroit Democratic bigwig for a couple of decades. He was untypical of those men surrounding Andy in being more colorful and unique in appearance than handsome. He was as slight as Andy, but he had one drooping eye that threw his face off-balance while giving him great character. He probably loved his cats more than people. Taylor had become popular with underground film audiences, especially for a Ron Rice movie called *The Flower Thief* that had become a cult classic.

When Taylor was taken by Henry to Andy's house, he was given the 'royal treatment', and even got to meet Julia, which was fairly extraordinary. The truth was that Andy had begun to see the value of a little troupe of Warhol players that could make his films in rapid succession. There was a touch of fey comedy in Taylor which Andy knew he could exploit. Despite his eccentic appearance, Taylor was as self-involved as all the other people now surrounding him. Taylor would write in his diary: 'The radio doesn't like anyone but me listening to it. . . . After I become a great film star I intend to remain as spoiled as I am . . . . I feel that I'm on the verge of something big – something so big that it might not happen.' But he was known to hundreds of New Yorkers as he made his daily amble through the city streets, and he knew nearly all of them by name.

Andy had begun attending nightly screenings at the FilmMakers Cinemathèque, located in the Gramercy Arts Theater on 27th Street, and the Film-Makers Co-operative with screening facilities at 414 Park Avenue South.

The leading figure in underground film at the time was Jonas

Mekas. Someone approached him sometime in very early 1963 and said: 'Pretty soon Andy is going to start making films. He's sitting here every night, he's seeing all these films, I think he's going to make his own.'

When Andy first set up his Bolex to make a film, he was still thinking more as an artist than as a filmmaker. He conceived a plan for a film, and what was seen on the screen a few months later, when all the technical work was done on *Sleep* (1963), was a virtually motionless six-hour view of a well-built man sleeping. His motorized Bolex was set up in front of a relaxed John Giorno, who was a poet and teacher. Andy had the notion that continued exposure to a given familiar subject created a state of desirable boredom. He often said that he liked to be bored, and he must have felt that others shared this feeling. In order to create such a long film, he had the technicians cheat a little. He told writer Stephen Koch: 'it started with somebody sleeping and it just got longer and longer. Actually, I did shoot all the hours of the movie, but I faked the final film to get a better design.' While shooting, he set up the camera in various positions, opening with a view of the sleeping torso shot from the feet towards the chest and abdomen; then we get a close-up of the breathing abdomen; close-up of the face, etc. The finished film was looped (the sequence exactly repeated several times to artificially stretch out the length – 'for the design').

Almost no normal person could sit through all six hours of *Sleep*, not even Andy when Jonas Mekas tied him to a chair (he managed to wiggle free). With this first film, he was creating not simply a multiple image like the *Marilyns* and the *Dollar Bills*, but a sustained view of human flesh in the most inactive state available to a filmmaker – sleeping. Lest any reader feel that he was putting his viewers on, it should be emphasized that as his body of film work began piling up, there was some question whether the films should be reviewed by art critics or film critics. As a result, *both* kinds of critics wrote on his films, and even Leo Castelli, once Andy went with his gallery (finally!) in 1964, investigated ways in which the films might be exhibited in a museum setting.

Very soon after *Sleep* was made, Jim Rosenquist was out for the evening with Andy and Henry Geldzahler, and suddenly Andy said: 'Let's go and see my movie.'

'So we all get into a cab and we go downtown and we go in the theater and he asked, "Is there anybody in there?" And the ticket-girl says, "Well, two people came but I think they left. There may be somebody in there and then there may not be." So we go in there – it's a big theater [the Gramercy Arts] and we sit in the back and there's John Giorno sleeping, and he had been sleeping for two hours at that point . . . . I think there was one other person in the theater. No, I think the theater was empty. So Henry he got up on the stage and [Rosenquist demonstrates] he started dancing like Porky Pig in front of the movie, and there was nobody there. We stayed about two hours. We were just bull-shitting about what each other was doing. And then I went home. While I was looking at John Giorno . . . I thought the poor bastard was dead. He's dead. Then I saw a tear start to grow out of something, and I thought, Thank goodness he's not dead. Then I went home and I went to sleep and I thought, "Gee, now I've got to go under for eight hours." It made me think about what I was doing, somnambulating or sleeping. It was so peculiar. I never thought about sleeping before.'

PART FIVE

FILMMAKER, PATHFINDER

EIGHTEEN

In October 1963 Andy set off for California in a station wagon with Wynn Chamberlain, Taylor Mead, and Gerard. Chamberlain was the 'magic realist' painter who rented Eleanor Ward's Connecticut cottage and invited all of Andy's delinquent entourage out on weekends. Neither Andy nor Gerard knew how to drive, so Taylor and Chamberlain shared the wheel. Andy was a little amazed to find that Taylor could really drive a car. He seemed so puckish, helpless and out of sync with the normal world.

They had the car radio going full blast all the way across the country. Andy would make them play even the most overplayed records on the 'top forty' list at this same level out of a fear that the driver might doze off.

Andy had brought his Bolex along and he had every intention of making his first film while they were on the coast. On the day of their arrival, film actors Dennis Hopper and Peter Fonda threw a party in their honor at the Hopper home. Hopper had an interest in contemporary art, including Pop. He did some painting himself and he was becoming a major collector. Andy liked the slightly crazed look in Hopper's eyes, a look that would be exploited in such films to come as *Apocalypse Now*.

At the party, Andy met 'everybody in Hollywood I'd wanted to meet'. He loved the films of Troy Donahue, and the film star was aware that Andy had done a silkscreen portrait of him the year before.

On the following day, a young woman named Naomi Levine arrived. Andy had told her of his plans, and as an underground filmmaker herself with a strange sort of crush on Andy (apparently she believed that he would respond to her), she had been alerted to the possibility of taking part in Andy's first filmmaking experience.

She was attractive in a hyper sort of way and some of her own films were considered brilliant, if a little uneven. Taylor said of her: 'She's very pushy. She's also so good.'

The show at the Ferus was well-attended, and the *Elvises* in the front gallery and the *Lizes* in the back created a considerable stir.

Andy's first sculptures were seen at the Ferus show. Andy had sent Irving Blum a box of various stretched candy bars, Baby Ruths predominating, which Blum had got instructions to cut and hang profusely around the walls of the gallery.

There seemed to be no significant critical reaction, but quite a bit of media attention, as though it were a freak show. Andy had not yet moved from the scandal pages to the art news.

Blum's former associate Walter Hopps was now curator of the Pasadena Art Museum and had organized the Duchamp retrospective. It opened soon after Andy's arrival, and they all went to the opening together – Blum, Andy, Taylor, Gerard, and Wynn Chamberlain.

Someone took a candid photo of Andy and Marcel Duchamp, the two champions of the commonplace. Duchamp was a hero to Andy from his earliest days in art school. And once Andy had discovered Duchamp, there is little doubt that he was overwhelmed by one Duchampian idea – that anything can become a work of art because the artist says that it is. What he understood at once and did not act upon was Duchamp's titling such a work with some more poetic name. A urinal became *Fountain*, and it became bona fide art when the artist signed it; Duchamp signed the *Fountain* as 'R. Mutt'. Andy eschewed the poetry and simply called his painting *Ethel Scull* – or a dozen years later, *Skulls*, when that was exactly what was depicted.

Jasper Johns, Robert Rauschenberg, and Joseph Cornell tapped into other Duchampian notions. Of the three, the most intellectual response to Duchamp is Johns's. His career seems to be his own idiosyncratic reaction to the entire oeuvre of Duchamp. His recent work suggests that he finally has matured to the point where he can represent Duchamp's androgynous references without dropping any of his own defenses. Cornell picked up on the voyeurism; the secrets in the box or romantic mysteries beyond the peep-hole. In slightly different ways, Rauschenberg and Andy delivered the same Duchampian message. Rauschenberg adds some original art work and makes it more complicated, and since art is *supposed* to be difficult to the degree that you have to think about the image and what it means, his reputation as the most influential artist of the latter decades of the twentieth century seemed, before Andy's death, to be secure. His former close friend Jasper Johns now brings higher prices, and seems to have surged ahead of most of his contemporaries. Andy lived long enough to see this beginning to happen as he followed the art market closely. Andy never struggled with 'significance' and that simplicity seems to have made it clear suddenly to many critics not only that he was *the* artist of our epoch but that history might well one day refer to the last third of the twentieth century as 'the age of Warhol'. If that happens, then the entire twentieth century will have been dominated by art that is mainly machine-made – first by Duchamp with his readymades and then by Warhol with his photo silkscreens.

At the Duchamp show, Taylor was barred at the door because he was wearing a sweater that was several sizes too large for him and hung down about his knees, with the sleeves pushed up so that his small hands were visible. He also created a little incident when the news magazine photographer snapped the shot of Duchamp and Andy. 'How dare you push me aside!' Taylor screamed. 'I'm a prince. My father used to boss two million people.' He was very good at such sudden confrontations, so good, in fact, it was scary. Everyone stared. They had all been noticed. Taylor subsided, pleased.

Taylor danced with Pat Oldenburg, who was there with Claes. They had moved from New York to California earlier in the year, a stay that was only temporary. It seems probable that Naomi Levine was there, also, since she not only had touched base with Andy but she was staying in Santa Monica with the pop sculptor John Chamberlain and his wife, and all of them would have been interested in Duchamp. Levine later said that Andy

> 'invited me to all kinds of parties and he just kept taking me around to all kinds of people, and every time I looked at him he had his hand on me. At that time I was very free and I never wore clothes, it was very hot, I just wore this big purple scarf, so I would jump into the water and that's the sort of thing he liked.'

This account is totally at odds with Viva's recollection three years later when she said that Andy cringed at being even touched and would moan and shrink away ('the proverbial shrinking violet') if he even thought that someone planned to touch him. Levine is fantasizing, perhaps to satisfy her very real crush on Andy.

Taylor saw the great curiosity in Andy early in their association. 'It was as though he said, "What's happening? . . ." and "there's something out there." ' He also loved little ironies he could put into his films. They emerged as wry little asides. Incongruity was another of the devices Andy began to use in his filmmaking with this first 'location' endeavor. Taylor, the slight, pixie-like Taylor Mead, was cast as Tarzan. Dennis Hopper, who had an average build, was Taylor's stand-in. Naomi Levine played Jane, of course.

Andy shot the film at John Housman's house, with one scene done at Claes Oldenburg's house, where Claes squirted Taylor with a garden hose to drive him out of his yard. Pat Oldenburg and Wally Berman play small roles in this two-hour film. Taylor added sound to the film with his tape recorder.

Taylor remembered a

> 'knock-down drag out fight with Naomi because she wanted to cut out parts of the film where she was exposed in the tub for a quarter of a second. She said, "Oh, my father would be offended" because her vagina was exposed. It was a shot of a woman getting out of a bath, and I felt, aesthetically speaking, it would have harmed the film to cut it. I'm like Andy. I don't believe in cutting anything. I think it's all valid, especially when you're working with crazy people like we were . . . are. So I was fighting to protect myself.'

A few weeks later, back in New York, Jonas Mekas was planning to show the movie at his Film-Makers Cooperative, and he seemed about to let Naomi cut the film, probably because she was a respected filmmaker herself, despite her run-ins with the law over nudity in her own movies. Taylor was furious:

> 'I'm not into zen, I'm not that religious to think the world can walk all over you. But I wouldn't let her cut

that film, and I resented Jonas sitting by . . . He didn't care that Naomi was about to wreck a film.'

Although he never dreamed of living there, Andy loved Los Angeles, and agreed with Taylor when he said that the city 'was ahead of the East. Pop Art was in the air.' Certainly, the outsized consumer icons, such as diners in the shape of enormous hot dogs, a huge bulldog housing a fast-food operation, larger-than-life pink elephants in front of night clubs, made Andy feel right at home. He said that he thought Los Angeles was a plastic society and one that he wholeheartedly approved of.

Taylor said that he and Andy's small troupe attracted a great deal of attention whenever they stopped to eat. To the truck-drivers and ordinary users of the western highways, they seemed to be a traveling freak show.

'Andy took speed. He took Obetrols, and once threw one pink Obetrol in a ditch when we were stopped by police. I took speed legally, black beauties with tuonal to come down. I was using qualudes . . . thirty a month. One black beauty would keep me up two or three days. Everyone was on uppers and downers but they were terribly active . . . . Andy was stunned by Las Vegas.'

Soon after they got back, *Tarzan and Jane Regained Sort Of* was given one or two showings at the St Mark's Theater (next to the St Mark's Baths, which Taylor thought very appropriate). It was not exactly a hit, but Andy loved bad reviews. According to Taylor, he would give a cheshire cat grin and say, 'Oh, they hate it!'

Of course, there was no money to be made from those early films. Andy subsidized his filmmaking with some commercial work, which continued well into 1964, and the sale of his art work. He and Gerard were turning out *Marilyns* and *Elvises* by the dozen, and they were sold immediately. But he was becoming obsessed with filmmaking, and it was becoming clear that his interest in silkscreen painting was more perfunctory than inspired. But it no longer mattered. Hands-off art was meant to be that way.

Andy was almost never alone now that he had Billy and Gerard at the Factory, and he was pulling together a film company. Naomi Levine thought that his work was an excuse

to be with people, but she felt that Andy's people were a bit
different:

> 'I think it's something like being very close to people he
> feels are good. Even though most of his characters are
> really crazy – I mean they're people I can't be with for the
> most part – some of them have a kind of sweetness.'

Levine felt that Andy exploited their freakiness and was personally
very conservative.

> 'I found it when I was with him, I started seeing how he
> provoked people with his passiveness into their becoming
> sort of freaky. But if you talked to him and related
> to him, you had to relate to him on a very simple,
> conservative line, i.e., our conversations were never like
> any deep considerations, like very straight . . . . And he
> used to say, "Oh, I really like Tuesday Weld." He liked
> very conservative women. I think he used all this freaky
> stuff to make his business off of . . . . He's very passive.
> I think he's very feminine . . . . He's very involved in
> that kind of having a good life. You know like going
> to good restaurants and buying the most expensive ice
> cream all of which is kind of nice, but that's him. He's
> not bohemian at all.'

Levine revealed that Andy had a short fuse about many things.

> '. . . if I say anything nasty to his face he gets terribly
> angry. Most people have a certain tolerance, like if he
> says to me, "You're neurotic," or something, I'll start
> to discuss it, but if I say that to him, he'll say, "I'll talk
> to you sometime, someday," and he'll hang up.'

On the other hand, Charles Rydell found that 'things rolled off
Andy like water off a duck's back.'

> 'He would sort of sit there zen-like and buddha-like and
> nothing would faze him, so he tried to instill a little
> of that in me. He'd say, "Well, Charles, why do you

care?" and I'd say, "Andy, I'm not like you. I've got
to get things out. I've got this sense of injustice, when
somebody steals from me after I've helped them." And
sometimes it occurred to me that maybe I've been doing
that as a trick, giving Brigid enough rope so that I could
get mad at her and relive that old thing [in his boyhood]
and accuse her of stealing . . . .'

When he was a small boy, Charles had been put in a boys' home
because his father was alcoholic and his mother and aunt were
'thrown out of Pennsylvania because they were prostitutes'. Some
money was stolen and the head of the home wrongly accused
Charles and then he had to run a gauntlet of paddles. He never
got over his sense of injustice.

Charles smiled as he recalled how a kind of 'Reaganomics'
existed around the Factory. Andy never paid his film Superstars and players anything, so they were always in need of
funds. Charles helped Brigid Polk with money and put her
up at his small apartment at 20th and Park frequently. She and
her sister Richie had their photos posted at the cash registers in
Bloomingdale's, so when they were out of funds, they had to
cadge meals and pocket change from Charles. He put up Taylor
Mead on occasions and helped him out. So the system worked this
way: Charles was being kept by the filmmaker and railway scion
Jerome Hill, and Charles in turn often kept Brigid and Taylor.

Andy was sometimes vilified in magazine pieces and the tabloids
as a skinflint, a commercially-minded man who would do anything for a dollar and regularly exploited everyone around him,
who he expected would work for nothing or next to nothing
because he had deigned to call them his friends. There was just
enough truth in this comment to alter the public view of Andy
Warhol. No underground filmmaker paid his players anything,
but when Andrea 'Wips' Feldman committed suicide by leaping
from a fourteenth-floor apartment a few days after a showdown
with Andy over money, Dodson Rader, a celebrity journalist,
built a strong anti-Andy piece for *Esquire* magazine around the
incident. Feldman had a certain undirected talent, which was
evident in the extensive role she had in Andy's most financially
successful movie, *Heat* (1972), but she was totally adrift, far more

so than the other Warhol players, into drugs, and she had the same exhibitionist tendencies as Eric Emerson – she showed off her ample breasts at any and every opportunity, and Eric exposed himself just as often.

The sixties New York subterranean world of pre-punk boys in leather and chains, frizzy-haired girls, open-shirted hustlers, transvestites and the long-haired aesthetes who traveled with them, occasionally could be seen ducking into a coffeehouse or a disco or one of their cafés or bars. Andy Warhol was the only artist with a growing international reputation who moved everywhere with an entourage of these people as his companions. This marked him as different. One would hesitate to say 'tolerant'. He seemed one of them, went out of his way to be one of them. Just by being seen in his company, they moved into the elite group of 'Andy's entourage'.

It might have been his polarity to the Cedar Bar crowd that had given him this notion, but Andy was genuinely fascinated by this particular kind of outcast. Let us agree with those who called him a voyeur to this degree: he enjoyed watching their lives unfold and get ensnarled in his immediate vicinity. And in their spaced-out way, they felt safe in his company. When they occasionally overdosed fatally, it was usually off the premises. No one can recall anyone dying within the Factory.

Yet Andy was not perceived by those who knew him well as callous or uncaring. David Bourdon, who was as close to Andy as anyone who held a salaried job, said that he was

> 'not at all insensitive. But he could be very cold and callous toward people who he felt had wronged him or who had been disloyal, and it was just like he was a refrigerator slamming the door on them. They were out, and he was very unforgiving. His public stance, to my mind, was always that he was a forgiving person, that he never held grudges, but in private on the telephone you should have heard the way he would lambast people and talk about how awful they were, and how they were cheap and crooked and no good.'

Obviously, Andy had feelings, and they could be hurt. But they were easily assuaged by this wonder that he had created around himself, the Factory.

The Factory rapidly became a stylish gathering place for the downtown 'druggy', 'faggy' set, as David Bourdon described them.

> 'Within just a few months, it was a big scene there, almost like a railroad station in a medium-size city. . . there was a lot of running around exchanging drugs, stealing boyfriends from each other. The Factory became a popular rendezvous.'

It became one of the major attractions for visiting film stars and members of what was called in the sixties 'the jet set'. Judy Garland and Montgomery Clift were there the same night, but not together, and there was far more interest among the visitors that night in the Warhol 'Superstars' like Edie than in these very real luminaries.

Andy was still a workaholic. He drove himself and Gerard fairly hard. But he also played hard, and his days away from the townhouse were long. He was really living two separate lives – away from his home he was in close contact with misfits and extremely successful dealers, artists and a smaller, faithful band of hard-working technicians like Gerard, and underground film people like Paul Morrissey and Taylor Mead. That was his Factory life, and then from midnight until mid-morning there was his life as a homebody with a mother who made him turkey sandwiches when he arrived home, no matter what the hour.

Julia was alone much of the time. It was not until the seventies that Andy hired two Filipino sisters to do the household work, cleaning and cooking. Julia attended her church as often as she could, and she got very close to her priest. He must have known better than anyone just how isolated she was.

Andy's late arrivals did not seem to bother Julia, and she was always up and ready with a sandwich or whatever he wished. Except for his mid-morning breakfast, that was the sum of her intimacy with her Andy. Afterwards, he would disappear upstairs to his room, his telephone and his television. They had two sets now. They no longer watched television together.

As Julia entered her seventies, she developed heart problems and blood pressure that had to be medically controlled. She was rarely seen now by Andy's friends, and she napped a lot. She learned not to go upstairs from her basement quarters when Andy had guests in. He told her that it was 'business', and she accepted that.

The upstairs regions must have seemed foreign to her anyway. They were beyond simply 'straightening up'. The women at the Factory have supplied us with the best descriptions of both Julia and the house at this time. Viva, an actress who came on the scene in the middle sixties, described Andy's building as having

> 'a lot of junk piled up on the stairs inside the front door. There was an old John Chamberlain crushed car sculpture on the landing, blocking it completely, so if you wanted to go upstairs you had to go around through the living-room. The living-room had an old American cigar store wooden Indian in it, along with a bubble gum machine and some other early American antiques. The room beyond the living-room was completely blocked and filled to the ceiling with paintings. There was an old desk in the room, the kind with a lot of secret drawers and cubbyholes, and the entire room and everything in it was covered with a layer of dust.★ Old lace doilies were on the arms of the couch. That was the only room I was allowed to see.'

Around this same time, Ultra Violet, another actress and 'Super-star' created by Andy for his films, was very curious about his mother and told him that she wanted to meet her. 'She doesn't have the right clothes,' he said, intending her no doubt to believe that meeting someone as fabulous as Ultra Violet would require a very special wardrobe.

But Ultra was quick to say: 'That's easy – let's buy her some . . . . Your mother needs some good clothes and a woman's touch in choosing them.' Andy responded that they would not be able to understand each other, his mother being Czech and Ultra being born Isabelle Dufresne, a Frenchwoman.

Ultra would not be denied and the next day, she had a cab waiting at the curb of the Warhol townhouse. She wrote that:

★ This is in sharp contrast to the compulsive cleaning by Julia described by de Antonio as he remembered the apartment in the 1950s.

'Andy comes out first, then a strong-looking older
woman dressed in black. She has pale skin, ghostly gray
hair, a large nose. She wears beige low-heeled shoes with
comfortably rounded toes. She carries a shopping bag for
a purse.'

In the cab, Ultra gave Julia a small bottle of perfume, telling her 'A
lady without a scent has no future.' Julia smiled and said, 'Thank
you, thank you.'

At Macy's, they finally settled on a black pleated dress, even
though Julia protested that it was too expensive. They wound up
buying her three dresses. Andy wanted to buy her a mink coat,
but she thought such an outlay of cash scandalous and refused
even to try one on. Much later, he got her one through bartering
a silkscreened painting with a furrier.

Julia's lot was not entirely miserable, and she never thought of
herself as anything but blessed. When her other sons came to New
York and stayed at the townhouse, particularly John (Paul rarely
came), she was ecstatic and hummed and sang and joked.

NINETEEN

When she came back from California, almost immediately Ileana Sonnabend planned a major show of Andy's work at her gallery in Paris. It would open in January and she assured Andy that this would mean a great deal in opening up a European market for his art. For a brief time, Andy was diverted from filmmaking to concentrate on preparing silkscreens for the Sonnabend show.

It was while Andy was readying those art works that he heard the news of President Kennedy's assassination over the radio. His reaction to this event is extraordinary in its lack of any normal human reaction to a calamitous event, but it does throw a light on his essential character: 'I don't think I missed a stroke. I wanted to know what was going on out there, but that was the extent of my reaction.'

Henry Geldzahler was nearly as shocked by Andy's failure to react to this tragedy as he was by the news itself. He wanted to know why Andy was not more upset.

> '. . . I told him about the time I was walking in India [with Charles Lisanby] and saw a bunch of people in a clearing having a ball because somebody they really liked had just died and how I realized then that everything was just how you decided to think about it . . . I'd been thrilled having Kennedy as president; he was handsome, young, smart – but it didn't bother me that much that he was dead. What bothered me was the way the television and radio were programming everybody to feel so sad.'

All of this reads back as a callous lack of human regard, but it simply cannot be lifted out of context as a true measure of Andy's character. To understand how Andy rigorously put down sentiment and ordinary human feeling, one must go back in time as far as kindergarten when the other children were staring at him as something different. There was never a friend or acquaintance who did not fail to notice that he was indeed unusual, 'other-earthly', as Tina Fredericks put it. The good friends elaborately overlooked this difference, and it was possible for someone in daily contact with him, like Gerard, Billy or Brigid, to get so used to this unusual man they no longer saw that he was fairly extraordinary-looking. But Andy never got used to the fact, and he lived with it and coped with it; and flattening human feeling was one of the ways he coped.

Prior to his first Stable Show in November 1962, he had done his first 'Disaster' painting, which was a silkscreen on canvas of the front page of the *New York Mirror* showing the shattered wing of a jet-liner with the headline: *129 Die in Jet*. Right afterwards, he had done *Suicide*, from a news photo showing the figure of a person in the air after leaping from a building. Throughout 1963, he was following up on this concept with a whole series of car crashes, often utilizing two panels so that the impact of the dead bodies hanging from car windows or sprawled under the wreck would be distanced a bit through repetition. Various tints were given the silkscreens – green, orange, violet, silver. The race riots in the south, where police dogs were turned on blacks by the Alabama police, were caught in a multiple-paneled series called simply *Race Riot* (1963). At this time, Andy was also doing his first *Electric Chairs*. Within a week or so after the prolonged business of Kennedy's murder, Oswald's capture and murder, the gathering of the world leaders to mourn and bury the American president, Andy began doing his series of *Jackie* paintings, all of them derived from news photos taken either in Dallas or at the funeral. They were first shown at the Galeria Ileana Sonnabend in Paris in January 1964, and as much as anything Andy ever did, they began his international reputation. They, too, fit into his Disaster series.

In April 1964, many of the things that had been shown in Paris were seen in New York at Eleanor Ward's Stable Gallery, in Andy's second big show there. For most critics and gallery-goers, this was their first glimpse of the box sculptures – the Brillo and Heinz Ketsup, Mott's Apple Juice and Campbell Tomato Juice. These piled-up boxes took up at least half of the Stable space. Alan Groh, Ward's associate, ran out for a few minutes just prior to the hour for the opening, and when he returned:

> '. . . who was standing in the doorway greeting the guests but Ivan [Karp, Castelli's assistant], so it was quite apparent at that time that Castelli was going to take over. Andy wanted to be where the art stars were. He wanted to be in the gallery where Rauschenberg and Jasper Johns were.'

There was no way Leo Castelli could resist Andy Warhol any longer. His ex-wife, Ileana, had made Andy's name known throughout Europe. The Ferus Gallery had caused excitement on the coast, and the two Stable shows had made Warhol collectors of eminent art patrons such as the Tremaines and Philip Johnson. Leo put Andy under contract that summer, and began doling out $1,000 a month to him against future sales of his work. That royalty advance would go on a long time, augmented of course until 1965 by commercial art assignments.

Castelli had such an openness to new creative ideas he probably did not think twice about taking on a painter who seemed to be preoccupied with making movies. He said that he could 'stock-pile' the silkscreen work of Andy's whenever he was immersed in film.

Even when *The Chelsea Girls* made some money for Andy, he plowed it all back into new films, so he simply could not understand the complaints of some of his players or Superstars from time to time. Couldn't they understand that they were contributing to something worthwhile? The truth was that most of them could not appreciate this fine point, and some of them were not aware that he was involved in serious art at all. One of them expressed surprise with a mob scene at an opening of a Warhol show in a museum: 'These people really believe Andy's an artist!'

Leo Castelli was, by any measure, a most civilized man. A slight, wiry native of Trieste, he favored double-breasted suits and had a professorial air. He spoke five languages, and as frequently as not, when he picked up his phone to talk business, it was with a European in New York on an art buying trip.

Once, charged with helping to kill off Abstract Expressionism, he told a *New York Times* writer, 'But they were dead already. I just helped remove the bodies.' So much for the old school. As for the new artists like Andy, Castelli was the most generous dealer around. The advances he gave his artists each month kept a whole pack of wolves from Manhattan doors, and Andy was no exception. He did not need the money for housing or food or paints; he needed it to underwrite his filmmaking, which for years would be a drain on his finances.

Castelli came into gallery work very late in life, at around fifty. But he managed to make a long run of it and in early 1989, he was still as busy as ever with two galleries in New York and kept in close contact with galleries affiliated with his own in places like Chicago, Los Angeles, San Francisco and Dallas. Such an affiliation for a gallery outside the hub of the contemporary art market, which Manhattan certainly was, was considered very prestigious for good reasons – Leo Castelli created much of that market.

When Eleanor Ward heard that Andy was leaving her for Castelli, she was very hurt and displeased. She rightly felt that she had gone out of her way to put Andy across with the two Stable shows, and now that the art critics had taken notice, he was going to Castelli's. She may have been a little surprised. While Eleanor steered very clear of any social contact with Andy, leaving all of that in the hands of her associate, Alan Groh, she knew that Andy was getting a reputation quite unlike any of her other artists. He was becoming known for stripping the glamour from the business of art, while at the same time creating a world of his own in his Factory loft, where, it was reported, almost anything went.

Castelli finally saw nothing wrong with any of this, and credited Andy as having a genius for publicity. What Andy had done was to create an art of the commonplace and, possibly but not necessarily, for the common man. On the other hand, the denizens of the Factory were often street people, gay more often than not, and not exactly Main Street, USA. This dichotomy was not lost on Castelli.

Castelli was not even concerned about the hostile critics. As one of the key promoters of the avant-garde, he often was shaping public taste and acceptance, not listening to critics like Hilton

Kramer, who took over as art critic of *The Times* around this time, and who found Pop Art far more significant as a social phenomenon than as an aesthetic one. He considered Andy's art as of no great consequence in the sixties, and even as late as 1987, the year of Andy's death, he considered Andy a commercial artist who

> 'had tapped into something with a canny sense of what the opportunities were . . . . He had a gift for graphic design. He understood how quickly images could be used and used up. He understood the momentum of it [better than Johns and Rauschenberg]. He never put himself forward as an artistic personality. He knew that there was something more to be achieved by being a "dumb artist" than being a smart artist.'

But Amei Wallach, younger than Kramer by about a generation, commenting on Andy's art in 1988, saw the abstract expressionists performing as artists in a heroic way,

> 'and Andy thought that was corny. He was anti all of that at exactly the moment when you no longer had the artists talking to each other and to no one else with no support from society, no galleries, no magazines, no critics, no nothin'. You had a market in the good old American tradition, and the art market immediately took off and became like any other American market. A lot of artists to this day wring their hands about that and say, "That was the end of art." Andy said . . . more than anyone else: "This is an opportunity. This is what America is about," and he put his finger on an America that never had been acknowledged before, certainly not in fine art.
> 'I like to think of it as Levittown and the Jericho Turnpike. The Levittowns were the tract developments made from the eighteenth-century agrarian dream – you know, a little land of your own, the houses are kind of colonial – but real life is lived on Jericho Turnpike, where you have McDonald's and the diners and the big signs and Andy Warhol is Jericho Turnpike and he makes

art about it gleefully, and that was an important thing to do.'

There was a duality in Andy that was perfectly obvious to his friends. He was shy and uncommunicative at public functions, even a small dinner party with 'outsiders' (non-Factory people), but he was at total ease with his street friends like Billy and Ondine, the Duchess (Brigid) and Rotten Rita. Ondine, who gave faggoty names to everyone he liked, called Andy 'Drella', which he said was a combination of Dracula and Cinderella, and soon everyone, or nearly everyone, at the Factory was calling Andy 'Drella'. It was quite apt, since Andy's passive control over all the activity surrounding him seemed very Count Draculish, and as the hot new artist from the commercial art world (the back alley of the art world), he might only have until midnight when the jig would be up and Cinderella would turn into poor Andy Warhol again.

A series of film portraits was undertaken by Andy. The Bolex was attached to a tripod and Billy Linich (usually) would operate the camera at Andy's suggestion. The pop artist Robert Indiana appeared in a forty-five minute portrait called *Eat*, in which a hatted Indiana slowly consumed a mushroom. Jim Rosenquist was sat in a chair and 'the camera slowly moved around me or maybe I was in a swivel chair and I was moved slowly.' Henry Geldzahler was asked to smoke a cigar for more than an hour and a half.

> 'Andy sat me down and turned on the automatic camera and then left. He came back to change the reel. I was left to myself, and of course betrayed all the things . . . . But that was Andy's idea.'

The first Castelli show of Andy's work opened on 21 November 1964. Castelli called it 'the Flower Show':

> 'The show occurred at the Gallery at 4 East 77th Street, and there was a whole wall facing you as you come in filled with small flowers, various colors. There were twenty-eight of them on that wall. On the right-hand wall, there was one of those large paintings that occupied the whole wall [also of the *Flowers*]. Then there were four foot by four foot ones. It was a beautiful show. It

was quite successful. People liked the flower. It was an acceptable, nice image. I think I sold practically all of them. The prices were extremely low. I would say the little ones were five or six hundred dollars. And then some people like Jennie Holton bought four of them because that was a nice thing to do, to buy a group of four. They may have been two thousand dollars. Then we had a lawsuit in connection with the *Flowers* because he had taken it from a magazine. Just taken it, and that woman [the photographer of the magazine photograph] claimed that he had stolen her property. Andy didn't want any fuss. I had an attorney take care of it . . . Jerry Ordover. She got two paintings for the use of her image. Then she just returned the paintings for me to sell and I gave her the money, so the case was settled.'

TWENTY

It is impossible to cleanly separate Andy's filmmaking from his art as 1963 waned. They are meshed inextricably, and certainly Andy himself saw some link between the two.

The first films he did upon returning from California were for his 'soap opera', as he called the *Kiss* series. Like *Tarzan*, they were filmed by the Bolex in 16mm, and they consisted of three-minute segments of couples kissing. Andy called them 'soap operas' because Jonas Mekas loved them and began showing them serial-fashion, one each week, at his Cinemathèque screenings.

The very first *Kiss* film showed Naomi Levine and Gerard Malanga in a long, passionate kiss. Then Naomi was paired with poet Ed Sanders. She was still in Andy's good graces, although a few weeks later, she would say something about Andy's 'faggy' obsessions and be thrown out of the Factory. ('Gerry, get her out of here.')

Another girl used by Andy for this series was his second Superstar, Baby Jane Holzer, who came from Long Island society and looked upon her Warhol film career as a lark. She recalled that it began after running into Andy at a dinner party:

'. . . he said to me, "Do you want to be in the movies?" I was quite bored at the time so I thought I would like to . . . we started doing a film called "Soap Opera" which in a funny way was ridiculous . . . I mean I had to kiss boys . . . . And, you know, we were sort of in these horrible old apartments and it was a bit depressing. Not so much that film but there were other films and a lot of other depressing people who were hanging around the Factory at that time.'

Besides those mentioned, others who did *Kiss* segments were Marisol and a critic named Pierre Restany. One of the things distinguishing Warhol films was the consistent use of unprofessional actors, drawing on fellow artists, critics, debutantes, fellow Factory workers, hangers-out at the Factory, with small regard for acting potential. The Italian neo-realists like Rossellini and Fellini had been doing this for years, ever since the Second World War, and Andy may have drawn on Fellini's love of the freakish for some of his films.

Gerry Malanga proved to be especially skillful before the camera, having a self-absorption that caused some sort of sexual current to pass between him and the equipment.

There was one movie, *Dance*, with Freddy Herko on roller skates, which may have been inspired by Andy seeing Bob Rauschenberg do a roller skating number with wings in a Merce Cunningham performance. This belonged chronologically before the California trip, but later was 'lost', or at least unavailable when Jonas Mekas compiled Andy's filmography. The film that does exist, at least in the original print form, is *Haircut* (November 1963), in which Billy Linich (Billy Name) gets a haircut that lasts thirty-three minutes.

Haircut was shot in a badly furnished loft, and opens with three men standing in the further recesses of that space. In the foreground is a burned-out hustler type, bare to the waist, with a hairy chest, the kind of hustler almost anyone with sense would pass by. He wears soiled white jeans that emphasize his genitals. He looks thoroughly bad and is a foretaste of similar 'bad' actors in future Warhol films. Andy had not yet purchased his sound-on-film Auricon camera, so the film was silent. The action begins when the nasty-piece-of-goods begins sauntering towards the dark recesses of the rear of the loft. He looks back at us once or twice, as though we might be in a mood to follow him, but he has no more luck with us than with all the rest met on the street.

The first film cartridge expires in a blur of whiteness and the second small reel begins (Andy picked up on Lisanby's home movie camera work and left all the ragged ends in his early films). Now Billy is seated in a chair and a very ordinary-looking barber begins cutting his full head of dark brown, wavy hair. The hustler type is now seated to the right of the barber chair, wearing a soiled shirt and a cowboy hat, and reading a magazine. In the third reel,

the seated hustler has stripped down again and is seated at a desk
sorting out some marijuana to smoke in a pipe, while the barber
continues working on Billy's hair

The point of it all comes in reel four, with the hustler stripped
bare, but our attention is diverted to Billy, who now stares into
the camera or at us, as though we are impertinent for seeing this
intimate trio. The hustler-cowboy at the desk uncrosses his legs
and we catch a glimpse of his cock. The film ends with all three
men staring at the camera for an intense moment and then bursting
into silent heaves of laughter, and rubbing their weeping eyes (from
mirth, of course) as it subsides and goes to white.

What impresses a viewer of *Haircut* is the manner in which
Andy directs our gaze from one point of interest to another. It
is as though we are instruments and he is Stokowski pulling out
this reaction and then another.

Before there was serious interest in underground films, there
were gay cult classics that were shown in major cities, especially
New York, San Francisco, Chicago and Los Angeles. There
was *Scorpio Rising*, made by Hollywood's journalistic 'bad boy'
Kenneth Anger, which possibly inspired Jack Smith's *Flaming
Creatures*. Andy and Charles Lisanby used to race to a theater
where one of them was to be shown, along with a crowd of
other men. Since they were contraband, too outrageous to be
publicly screened, someone would start a telephone grapevine and
perhaps as many as one or two hundred interested males would
flock to a particular movie-house, usually around midnight after
the last regular show. Andy was fascinated by the films of Jack
Smith, who had become a regular contributor to the screens of
the underground film world in New York in the early sixties.
He even did a film of Jack Smith in the process of making one
of these outlawed movies (*Andy Warhol Films Jack Smith Filming
'Normal Love'*), a three-minute color documentary view of Smith's
production in the making. Andy's own film was considered so
pornographic that it was seized by New York police when it was
out of his hands for screening along with Jean Genet's *Un Chant
d'Amour*.

Thus, it was not much of a step for Andy to make his own male
pornographic film. In late 1963, during a phone conversation with
Charles Rydell, he asked Charles if he would star in a film to be
called *Blow Job*. Charles readily agreed, so within a day or two

Andy called in a friend to be Charles's partner in this exquisitely simple film showing the act of fellatio. Reliable report says that it was Willard Maas, Andy's old friend from Brooklyn Heights and a filmmaker himself, who agreed to do the fellating. Andy set up his camera at the hour he had told Charles he would be filming, but Charles failed to appear. When Andy phoned him to find out what had happened, Charles told him: 'I thought you were kidding. I never dreamed that you really meant me to appear in such a movie.' Nothing Andy said could persuade him to come over and be blown on camera.

It was an emergency of sorts, but one easily cured. Andy simply asked one of the hustlers, who happened to be hanging around the Factory at the time, to oblige him on camera. The finished film ran for half an hour and shows us in close-up the head, neck and collar area of a ruggedly handsome blond young man, roughly twenty years old, or a bit younger, reacting to the actual performance of fellatio upon himself. We only see black leather covering the shoulder of the active partner for a brief moment. What is marvelous about *Blow Job* is that clearly an actual sexual act is being performed on screen but we only see the passive partner's facial reactions. The film is entirely concerned with perceptions. You have to know what being blown is all about to understand the grimacing and fleeting pain crossing the man's face. The handsome young man who took Charles Rydell's place may have been paid his usual fee or perhaps not. It is entirely possible that Andy told him, 'You're going to be famous, kid,' and let it go at that. Years later, he was seen briefly in a crowd scene in a Hollywood production.

Andy's first real sound film was a travesty of Jean Harlow's presence filmed in December 1965, with one of his discoveries, Mario Montez,* a professional transvestite, as *Harlot*, in the classic Harlow 'Grand Hotel' pose reclining on a couch (it was a bed in Harlow's movie). Next to her, a woman holds a small dog in her lap and looks bored, while Gerard and Philip Fagan simply stand by – mute. It is typical of the approach Warhol would take during his first months of talking films – the voices are those of unseen people off camera with the commentary vaguely steered in

---

* Mario Montez, whose name was borrowed, of course, from the film star Maria M., a camp favorite, never wore drag on the street as did later transvestites, Holly Woodlawn, Candy Darling and Jackie Curtis – all Warhol film performers.

the direction of the title character, which in this case is legendary movie stars.

Stephen Koch said that Andy turned out movies at a feverish pace, one or two features a month. Ronnie Tavel, a poet and novelist with a mystic bent (like Billy Name), was Andy's first screenwriter. Tavel told Koch that:

> 'when we organized, there were two a month. He would tell me one day what he wanted; two or three days later, the script was ready and at the end of a week, it was shot. Two, three days later it was processed, so that two weeks was about the time between his telling me what he wanted and when it would be shown in a theater.'

Much of this film work has vanished, although Paul Morrissey, who came in later and in time took over Tavel's function, insists that it all exists and will be seen someday.

Besides Tavel, Andy brought in Buddy Wirtschafter, a professional filmmaker who had been covering gallery openings. Wirtschafter assisted on Andy's first color film, showing Ondine and another Factory person 'mushing their hands in fruit'. Wirtschafter believed that the Warhol films were extensions of his art, that they were ideas or concepts that were more important conceptually than as films to be seen on a screen. He thought that Andy surrounded himself with people who understood what he was doing without being told anything, that if you ever asked Andy what he wanted, he would respond with 'What do you think?'

Wirtschafter came close to explaining Warhol's methodology by saying that:

> 'I think after years on Madison Avenue and so on [in commercial art], you learn how to get away with what you're about and doing without revelation. And this was his means and method. Then he carried it into a world that is really quite opposite, over-revealing . . . .
>
> 'The interesting thing about Andy is that he didn't approach films like a filmmaker, he approached films as an artist, and consequently he used film to extend his art, and art is the idea.'

TWENTY-ONE

The ambience of the Factory may have been decadent – that seemed to be Andy's intention – but it would be wrong to assume that it was primarily a playground and not a work-space. It would be more accurate to say that it was an unusual work-space, often close to surreal. A case in point was the arrival of the good-looking young British artist, Mark Lancaster. In a way, he was a present from the British pop artist Richard Hamilton, who had met Andy at the Duchamp retrospective in Pasadena in 1963. Lancaster came over from Yorkshire on a student flight with instructions to go straight to the Factory. He stayed close to Andy for several years.

Mark was met at the silver-foiled elevator by Baby Jane Holzer, part of the cast of *Batman Dracula*, a two-hour silent film Andy was shooting with the notorious master of the homoerotic film, Jack Smith (*Flaming Creatures, Fireworks*), as Dracula. The young men in the cast of 'walk-ons' were required to strip to their jockey shorts, which were covered with silver foil. Within half an hour of his arrival at the Factory, Mark Lancaster was wearing silver-foiled jockeys and becoming one of Dracula's victims. After their stint before the cameras, the cast sat around in their semi-nudity for a while, 'relaxing'.

Andy escorted Mark about town. He sent him over to Henry Geldzahler, who introduced the young artist to Jim Rosenquist, Robert Indiana, Roy Lichtenstein, Frank Stella and Marisol. Mark helped Andy stretch the flower silkscreens and the blue and black *Jackies*, as well as some *Marilyns*. It is doubtful that he was paid anything. Compensation for work done, except for Gerard's salary and Nathan Gluck's when he was called in to help complete something, was most irregular. Billy Name was given walking-around money and, of course, a place to live – his cot at the Factory. The

Flower, 1964, offset litho, 23″ × 23″

Liz, 1964, offset litho, 23″ × 23″

Jackie III, 1966, screenprint, 40″ × 30″

Self Portrait, 1967, screenprint, 23" × 23"

Vote McGovern, 1972, silkscreen, 42″ × 42″

Mao Tse-Tung, 1972, from a portfolio of ten screenprints, 36″ × 36″

Ladies & Gentlemen, 1975, one from a portfolio of ten screenprints,
43½″ × 28½″

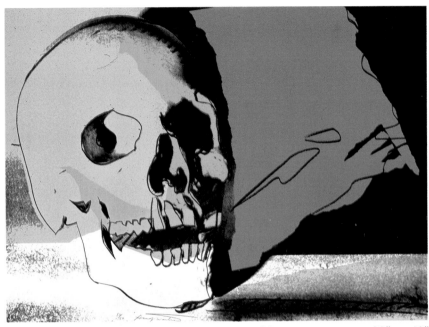

Skulls, 1976, one from a portfolio of four screenprints, 30″ × 40″

Endangered Species: Siberian Tiger, 1983, silkscreen, 38″ × 38″

$9, 1982, one from a portfolio of two silkscreens, 40″ × 32″

Kiku, 1983, one from a portfolio of three silkscreens, 19⅝″ × 26″

Moonwalk, 1987, one from a portfolio of two silkscreens, 38″ × 38″

performers in the early films got nothing, since there was a general understanding among underground filmmakers that there would be no salaries for actors. Andy and Morrissey would come under heavy attack later when they went mainstream with their films and attempted to release them in regular movie-houses. Only Andy and Morrissey seemed to be making any money from the films, with the actors paid either nothing or token salaries. An exception later would be Joe Dallessandro, who was given a modest salary and great expectations, and Sylvia Miles, who managed to be paid a decent fee for her starring role in *Heat* (1972).

Lancaster was compensated in part by being introduced to nearly all the elite art and fashion set, and they immediately took him up and he partied a great deal and did a lot of weekending in Connecticut, Long Island and Provincetown. Once, during a few days' stay in Provincetown, he was punched in the gut by Norman Mailer at a party. It was entirely unprovoked; he had not been introduced to Mailer. But the episode delighted Andy, who grinned and asked Mark: 'Norman Mailer actually punched you? How great! Why?' Mark explained that it was for wearing a pink jacket. Mailer's self-appointed role of being the chief of a dwindling tribe of super-macho males seemed to be the only motivation for this random bellicosity. Within a year or so, Mailer became an admirer of Andy's films, especially *Kitchen* (1965). He was then making underground films himself, although he was hoping, as Andy did a few years later, that they would go 'mainstream'.

Lancaster was such a comely, thoroughly delightful companion, Andy was generous in sharing his company with others. When pop artist Ray Johnson was ill with hepatitis in Bellevue Hospital, Andy sent Lancaster there as a 'get-well present'. But he was also keenly observant, and once he suggested to Andy that he did not think Gerard wanted anyone else to be close to him, and said Gerard had told him: 'When it's one-to-one with Andy, it's very easy, but when you're in a group, Andy creates competition between people so he can watch problems being played out. He loves to see people fighting and getting jealous of each other . . . .' Lancaster indicated that he was well aware of Andy's quietly deployed manipulation of those around him:

'. . . I suppose he also meant that, for example, when we leave here tonight, you'll be going on somewhere, but

> you'll never say who else is invited – you'll just contrive
> in an elegant fashion to make sure the people you don't
> want to be there aren't . . . . And you'll do it all without
> saying a word, or by saying something very oblique –
> some people will realize they have to fall away, and some
> people will just know they can come along.'

Lancaster could say these things to Andy because he was almost
never left out by Andy. In fact, David Bourdon believed that he
was one of Andy's boyfriends. This did not afford him any very
great distinction, however, since Andy had several at the time.

Lancaster made a second film, *Couch*, that was designed to outdo
anything of Jack Smith's. It was filmed entirely on the battered
Factory couch, and it was saturated with male pornography, and
never shown publicly, although in *Popism* Andy said that it was
one of a dozen films he ran at the Dom disco 'turning movies
. . . into all different colors' by slipping gelatin slides over the
projector lens. The idea of the film seemed to be for the men
involved to combine in such a variety of sexual positions as to
boggle the mind. Cheerfully volunteering to perform in *Couch*
in addition to Lancaster were Taylor Mead, Jack Kerouac, Allen
Ginsberg, Gregory Corso, Gerard Malanga and Rufus Collins.
One married couple contributed their bodies to this strange,
voyeuristic excursion – Piero and Kate Heliczer – but did not
appear together. Taylor was so annoyed over this film that he left
the Factory film scene to go to Europe. He felt that the shooting
was too oblique and that no one viewing the film could tell who
was doing what to whom.

Andy thought that Lancaster was putting together material for
lectures on the art scene in America to deliver in England upon his
return home to Yorkshire. Perhaps he did some of those lectures,
but very soon after going back, he became successful as a painter
in his own right, with shows in major galleries. Andy became a
part of his rather colorful past, although they kept in touch over
the years.

Stephen Koch was a writer whose novel *Nightwatch*, while not
a great popular success, had won critical approval. To Koch's
surprise, Andy had read it and had even discussed taking a movie

option on it. Andy's interest in it gave Koch an inside track on
what was happening at the Factory, and in 1973 he would publish
Stargazer: Andy Warhol's World and His Films, a book of astonishing
immediacy and perception that seeks to penetrate Andy Warhol's
psyche. It is not flattering, but it outraged Andy far less than Paul
Morrissey.

Of this particular time in Andy's life and career, Koch said:
'Something very dramatic happened to Andy. His growth and
development took a long time, but in a certain way, he discovered
his way of going in, probably quite quickly. He suddenly *got* how
to be Andy Warhol.'

Andy knew what his mission was. It was a strange message he
would be sending out to the world: 'There is nothing here to
report,' he might have written. But he presented that nothingness
in such a bold way, everyone had to notice.

He was saying it in his art; he was saying it in his films. His films
in particular were not outrageous because they were mostly about
matters seldom discussed in polite company; they were outrageous
because they were so pitifully empty. He was telling us that life is
empty. Life in the twentieth century in America (and in most of
the western world, at least) is filled with signals to others never
picked up, connections never made. We are surrounded by things
we consume so rapidly and with such taken-for-granted disinterest,
they are blips that barely register either in our digestive process
or our awareness. He was recording everything that might even
remotely touch upon this situation. A perfect example was his
eight-hour silent view of the Empire State Building, which he shot
from the 44th floor of the Time-Life Building on 25 June 1964.
Andy now had acquired a sound-on-film Auricon camera, and it
was fairly typical that his first sound film should be of this quiet
monument to Grover Whalen.★ *Empire* was suggested to Andy as a
film subject by a friend, John Palmer. The vantagepoint was a suite
in the Time-Life Building occupied by Henry Romney. At the time
this film was shot, Romney was trying to secure for Andy the film
rights to *A Clockwork Orange*, an Anthony Burgess novel about
random and pointless violence or delinquency. He proposed it as

★ Grover Whalen was the chief promoter of the construction of the Empire State
Building during the deepest heart of the Great Depression (1930–1). He was
the Official Greeter for New York City for many years and maintained his
headquarters in the Empire State Building.

a possible vehicle for Rudolf Nureyev, Mick Jagger and Baby Jane Holzer. It was conceivable that Jagger, then already a 'megastar' in the rock music firmament, might have been interested. He and Andy met frequently, and Jean Shrimpton, a London model who knew Jagger well, was living with David Bailey, a London photographer who had befriended Andy. But Baby Jane's days as Andy's second Superstar were dwindling. She was about to leave 'the scary scene' of the Factory for good, although she would stay friends with Andy.

Empire, it must be said, created the first critical uproar over Andy's films. Some critics insisted that it was a huge put-on, a hoax perpetrated against those culture mavens who considered anything as true art if it bored them silly or was too much beyond their comprehension to even talk about. It is a film that has survived and is considered a must for any Warhol film retrospective. We see the huge building over an eight-hour period – in late afternoon, twilight, night-time. An occasional shadow of a cloud abstractly stains it; lights come on. The background changes from visible sky to pitch darkness.

No one was expected to sit through all eight hours of the film. Ideally, it is a film to be seen in a museum setting, where the viewer stops for a few minutes and stares at this subtly changing image, marveling if he or she happens to be present when the lights go on or a cloud passes.

Empire became the most discussed unseen film of the day. But its success caused Andy to sever his ties with John Palmer, the young man who gave him the idea in the first place. Palmer could not resist telling everyone that he was the major contributor to *Empire*, and so he had to be eased out.

Andy only rarely left the island of Manhattan, and even an excursion to Brooklyn was a big deal for him. Those who were closest to him in the Factory crowd had this sense that Manhattan was the only place where they could possibly survive – Gerard, Ondine, Rotten Rita, Brigid, Richie, the whole crowd. Although Taylor often weekended with friends like Charles Rydell in the Hamptons, where his friend Jerome had a house, he felt ill at ease when he crossed one of the bridges away from his turf.

On 27 October 1964, Ondine was spending an evening in the apartment of his friend Johnny Dodd, who designed the lighting for the Judson Church performances. Dodd's living room had a remarkable panel covering one wall with 40,000 George Washington postage stamps. It was something that Andy coveted, but Dodd never would part with. Freddy Herko had come in, as he frequently did, to take a shower. He had a list of friends' apartments where he could clean himself up twice a week.

His friendship with Ondine went back a long way, and he confided in him. Once, when they were together in a loft apartment above a chicken factory ('Bones and feathers were all over the place', as Ondine recalled it) belonging to one of Freddy's girlfriends – platonic, of course – he began getting into one of her dresses, and he turned to Ondine and said: 'You know, Ondine, I'm a lesbian.' And Ondine responded: 'Well, I've never told you, Freddy, but you know you are.'

That October evening at Johnny Dodd's, Ondine was sitting with Johnny, who had the flu, listening to some opera on the phonograph while Freddy was showering. When he came out of the shower, he asked if he could put on *Swan Lake*. He put on the record, returned to the bathroom, and then they saw him streak through the room wearing only a gossamer scarf about his genitals towards the front of the apartment, which was a floor-through. Freddy's selection continued playing and Ondine and Johnny heard no other sound. Then someone came up to the apartment on the sixth floor and said, 'Do you know who dove out of your window?'

Johnny said 'No.'

'Freddy,' the man said. 'Freddy Herko.'

And Johnny said, 'That can't be. Freddy's in the front room listening to some music.'

'No, he's not. He's splattered all over the sidewalk.' Freddy had simply danced through the open window, landing on Cornelia Street five flights below.

Andy had done three films with Freddy, including *The Thirteen Most Beautiful Boys*, and they were shown at a memorial service held at the Judson Church. One of the Factory crowd said later that Andy had regretted that no one had been down on Cornelia Street to film Freddy's last leap.

In the summer of 1965, I was working on a decade-long project, a study of the life and career of Marilyn Monroe which was to be called *Norma Jean*. I was then in touch with two sisters from South America, Marina and Mercedes Ospina, stunning girls who wanted to break into the theater. One evening I took the screenplay of *Norma Jean* over to their apartment. Over cocktails the girls began telling me about the movie they had made with Andy Warhol earlier that season and which they had recently seen screened. It was *The Life of Juanita Castro*, and it sounded so bizarre, I kept asking questions about it all through dinner and we never did get around to poor Marilyn (I left a copy of the screenplay with them to read). Andy had cast Marina as Fidel Castro, with another actress (Elektra) as his brother Raoul, who was, according to Andy, a secret transvestite.

The Ospina sisters told me that an older woman named Marie Menken had played the title role, and that much of the film was a long monologue delivered by her in which she tells her brother, the Cuban leader, all the things he has done wrong. Andy later said that Menken looked like the actor Broderick Crawford.

The Ospinas laughed when I asked if they planned to do other things for Warhol. Marina was engaged at that point (I believe her fiancé came by before the evening was over), and Mercedes seemed to think that one film for Warhol was enough. It is a pity, because in Mercedes, giving her a decent break in showing off her smoldering beauty, he would have found his Garbo two years before he stumbled onto Viva. But it was not to be in any case because Mercedes was dead of cancer by the age of twenty-six.

PART SIX

THE
GIRL
OF THE
YEAR

TWENTY-TWO

Early in 1965, Lester Persky, whom Gore Vidal called the Wax Queen (out of deference to his biggest account at his ad agency – Six Months Floor Wax), gave one of his numerous and glitzy parties. Persky was one of Andy's 'pals', meaning that he and Andy met frequently at social gatherings of the 'Trash and Vaudeville' set (in Stephen Koch's usual apt phraseology) – art, fashion and the drugged-out scene. There were also the 'beauties', Andy's pretty boys, androgynous creatures for the most part, who went everywhere with him as a kind of decorative bodyguard. Gerard was handsome enough to fit well into this entourage, and was often along, fitting especially into the Persky ambience, where Tennessee Williams and Truman Capote were among the guests.

Andy had even made a film with Persky called *Lester Persky: A Soap Opera*. Persky said that when he invited Andy to one of his parties, he could expect twenty uninvited to accompany him. This is a slight exaggeration; the number rarely exceeded ten or twelve. But even such a number as that indicates Andy's growing dependency on people. And Andy's entourage did not mean that he was surrounded by persons he loved so much he could not move about without them. It was as though through these mostly attractive men (there was rarely more than one woman with them), he created a persona – the ubiquitous social creature known as Andy Warhol. They were appurtenances, just as the silver wig and the dark glasses were.

But at this party, there was a small group of young New Englanders down from Cambridge who had accompanied a young woman who, like Andy, moved about with her cronies. Her name was Edie Sedgwick and she was one of eight children of Francis and Alice Sedgwick, wealthy members of the New York social register.

Edie Sedgwick was boyishly slim, small-breasted, but anyone, especially a perennially star-struck Andy, could see that she was radiant. As slight as she was, she gave off enough energy and intrinsic glamor to light up any room. Andy was bowled over as he watched her do a blend of ballet and rock dancing, all by herself. She was delightfully self-involved.

Edie became at once Andy's Sally Bowles. If a gay Christopher Isherwood could come intimately close to a young woman when he met Sally's real-life counterpart, so could Andy feel something stir in his breast when he saw Edie.

Edie was on the cusp of breaking free of her past and becoming the darling of New York's fast lane, that ever-changing set once called 'café society', then a bit later 'the jet set'. Her past was every bit as cluttered with dead bodies and burnt-out hopes as Andy's was. Her father, Francis (also known as 'Fuzzy' and 'Duke'), was a super-macho, almost gifted sculptor of the Daniel Chester French school (heroic equestrian statuary done in a realistic mode). He overdrank and ran with women. He tyrannized his family, especially his wife, but he was overfond of daughter Edie. His importance in her story cannot be stressed enough. He destroyed his sons through indifference and impossible demands. He alternately terrified and pampered Edie. The smiling waif Andy saw at Lester Persky's was a girl who had just emerged as her own person with no close ties to her family except for a grandmother in Manhattan, with whom she was living at the time as a matter of convenience. She was recovering from the suicide of her brother Minturn ('Minty') and the probably suicidal death of her brother Bobby in a motorcycle crash. All three of them, Minty, Bobby and Edie, had undergone several years of treatment in mental hospitals in an effort to rehabilitate them after the horrors of their adolescent years around their father.

Andy found out most of this in bits and pieces over the next year. What he learned that night was that she was ambitious to find her place in films, that she was 'old family', according to Lester, and Lester told him: 'Here is your next Superstar.' Edie gave off a glow Andy never had seen before in real life.

Among the several young men escorting Edie that evening was one who quietly was orchestrating her life. His name was Chuck

Wein. Wein was an extremely clever manipulator of people, intelligent, and even charming when necessary. While having no plans to become a filmmaker, he did fancy himself a screenwriter. Of course, any ambitions he had for himself were subordinate to what he planned for Edie. He was the Stiller-von-Sternberg in her life, as Andy soon discovered.

Chuck Wein, while not a beautiful young man, was passably attractive, so when Edie came into the Factory to make her first movie with Andy, Wein was not only there, he was very soon ousting Gerard Malanga as Andy's adjutant or 'prime minister'. Andy saw Edie's dependencies very early – she looked to Wein for guidance in planning her day, to get her to places, if not on time, at least before her tardiness became something more than mere discourtesy. She was also into drugs, speed for sure, and possibly other things. But then Andy was taking his pink pills to keep moving. His telephone friends occasionally got calls from him before daybreak – he had gone to bed at one or two a.m. and was up again at four-thirty.

Wein's promotion of Edie had begun back in Cambridge. One of Edie's friends, Sandy Kirkland, recalled that Wein

> 'would be plotting out the next move of their great strategy – whom he was going to introduce to Edie that night, what they could do for her. She would try on twenty-five different outfits, but every gesture was very slow. Do you remember how she moved? Like a Japanese Noh dancer – very dreamlike and slow. Lighting twenty cigarettes and putting them down.'

Kirkland added that Wein had taken over Edie's life.

Wein had the perception to see that Edie related to everyone she met, from the socialite at a jet-set party to the man with the nice smile at the next table in the corner deli. She was everybody's 'princess'. Wein also saw how Andy reacted to her and the intense media hype around Andy convinced him that they were about to make their first significant connection.

Andy was no less perceptive and saw that Wein was vital to Edie. He was part of her clockwork; he helped her run. So Wein not only became 'prime minister', jostling Gerard aside, but he wrote most of the film, *My Hustler*, deferring so entirely to Andy that there was no role for Edie in it. Wein's own sexuality was seldom discussed, but he blended so well with the other gays on the premises, nearly everyone accepted him.

If Andy had his only 'straight' love affair with Edie Sedgwick, no one could have blamed him. She had broken hearts in Cambridge for years and had several swains following her to New York. And Edie seemed to relate well to Andy. She did everything to please him those first months. She stopped wearing the beehive hairdo so popular in the early sixties. She had her hair cut short and then dyed silver to match Andy's. She affected the same look, wearing the striped French sailor teeshirt that Andy and Gerard had been wearing for some time. She usually wore black leotards, matching Andy's black chinos, and she even started wearing boots. When they put on their oversized dark glasses and entered Max's Kansas City, which was becoming a hang-out for underground filmmakers and had for some years been a gathering spot for poets, painters and others, it was said that they looked identical.

Almost at once, they were inseparable. Sometimes Chuck Wein came along, as did Gerard. Ondine, who saw everything, was inclined to like her and had no real complaint about Wein. There was a little hustle in everyone at the Factory, including Andy, so no one could be faulted on that score.

In some ways, Edie Sedgwick lived a lifetime during the year or less that she was close to Andy. This was her 'fifteen minutes of fame', which Andy proposed that everyone would have in the future. She and Andy became such a well-known couple socially that Roy Lichtenstein and his wife Dorothy dressed as Andy and Edie for a costume party, and Roy's standard response all evening to everyone was 'Gee!' and 'Gosh!'

Edie's influence at the Factory went far beyond her own advancement. She had brought a crowd with her, and they all settled into the Factory in one capacity or another. There was Donald Lyons, a good-looking graduate student from Harvard, who was her favorite dancing partner. Lyons became a Factory regular. He appeared with Edie in the films *Kitchen* and *Afternoon*. Danny Sullivan, also from Harvard, became the Factory electrician. Chuck Wein, as we know, became second-in-command.

The most incredible thing about Edie's ten months or so as Andy's most publicized Superstar was that it lasted such a short time and left such an impression. She came in April and was planning her exit the following February.

An entire book, *Edie: An American Biography** was written about her with that brief period as its centerpiece. Andy made this lovely post-deb out of Cambridge and California into a minor legend. Part of the reason for this intense scrutiny is that Andy had become, in a relatively short time, an enormous name in the international art world. Part of his celebrity was founded on his eccentric image, the pale 'shy' silver-wigged man who was constantly being photographed and written about. There was great public curiosity about the true person behind this strange etiolated visage, and in *Edie* the public was at least partially satisfied that what they suspected all along was true. Andy Warhol was a menace to the young who were drawn to him. The book was an excellent documentary of the life of an American that, not by chance, ended in tragedy. It was Dreiserian and it hurt Andy. It hurt him because it exposed a side of him that few would understand – his will not to feel as other people feel. There are babies born with an inability to feel pain. Andy managed to acquire this facility on an emotional level in adolescence and refined it in his early twenties. Who could understand such a thing?

They met in March and within days after their meeting, Andy began shooting her first film, *Poor Little Rich Girl* (what else?). It was shot in her own studio apartment, with Chuck Wein, her eager mentor-promoter, feeding her ideas, and with Gerard's help, Andy shot two reels. When they got the film back from the lab, they learned that it was terribly out-of-focus. They found they had the wrong lens, replaced it, and a week later, Edie repeated everything and it was sharp and clear. But Andy enjoyed profiting by his mistakes in a very literal way – he took the blurry reel and opened the movie with that, as though to show that Edie's life was out-of-focus; then after more than an hour of eye-strain the audience suddenly saw her clear – a revelation!

Andy and Edie were so close that in less than a month after their first meeting, he took her, and Chuck Wein and Gerard, with him to Paris for the opening of his *Flowers* show at the Sonnabend Gallery, where it was to duplicate its success at Leo Castelli's in

* Written by Jean Stein and edited by George Plimpton (1982).

New York. One of the greatest advantages to Andy's 'Factory' methodology was that he could recreate an entire successful gallery show after everything hanging had been purchased and taken away. For Ileana Sonnabend, he did small and large panels of the *Flowers* image in various shades.

They stayed at the Hotel Montana, where Andy picked up the tab. There is a photograph of the four of them on a bed there with Edie in a night-shift, her eyes ringed with fatigue, propped against her pillow. Andy sits on one side of her in a long-sleeved woolen shirt over a black turtleneck. He wears a natural hairpiece, not the spiky silver one that would come much later. Edie is smoking – in bed – the thing that would burn her out of one apartment and a hotel room. Chuck Wein is on the other side of Edie, but he is stroking the open palm of Gerard, who lies in Edie's lap. Gerard's sexuality could not be more opaque than in this shot. While one of Andy's arms brushes against Edie's shoulder, he seems as solitary as ever. In essence, the other three people in the picture are irrelevant to Andy's pose. He could be leaning against a sofa arm. Gerard is looking into the camera, but not as intently as Andy is. Still, there is a warm bond uniting these people and Andy is giving as much of himself as he can.

From Paris, the foursome flew to Morocco, where they stayed for a week at the Hotel Minza in Tangier. On the way, they changed planes with a stopover of six hours in Madrid, where they visited Waldo diaz Balart. He was the son-in-law of Fidel Castro, and he had fled to New York from Castro's revolution with a million dollars in currency in his suitcase. Gerard explained that

> 'the Castro government knew that he was leaving the country with that money and it was their way of getting rid of him – good riddance. We became friends with Waldo back in New York in '64. He appeared in an early film of Andy's, *The Life of Juanita Castro* [1965] . . . . Waldo flew down to Tangier to spend the rest of the week with us down there.'

From Tangier, they decided to go to London. As casually as that they flew there, and the very next day, through Dennis Deegan, who had appeared in Andy's *13 Most Beautiful Boys* (1965), they met Nico, a blonde singer who was hanging out with rock-and-roll people. Gerard recalled that the following fall

> 'Nico called me when she came to New York . . . . I arranged for the three of us to get together for dinner, Andy, Nico and myself. It was at a Spanish restaurant, and it was at this time that Andy and I proposed that maybe Nico should sing with the group [*The Velvet Underground*] because she had a 45 rpm that was released in London by Larry Ogun, who was the Rolling Stones' producer. Her voice was more melodic in those days, not such a drone.'

What Edie could not possibly have known was that in that first month of her life with Andy, in London he had met one of the women who would replace her on his screen – Nico.

Between social engagements with Andy, Edie never stopped making movies from March until late July, when she got a brief break while Andy was on Fire Island making his movie about a hustler. There was the narcissistic *Face*, *Vinyl*, *Bitch*, *Restaurant*, *Kitchen*, *Prison*, *Afternoon*, *Beauty #2*, *Space*, *Outer and Inner Space*, and finally *Lupe*, which was made in December.

It occurred to everyone at the Factory, especially Chuck Wein and Edie, that perhaps she could create enough excitement to open Hollywood's door to Andy. But the movie season of 1965–6 did not produce any breakthroughs as far out as the films of Andy Warhol. Carson McCullers' *Reflections in a Golden Eye*, with its theme of homosexuality, was causing great problems, and although the Code had been abandoned through the courageous stands taken by Otto Preminger and others, Hollywood was not yet ready for Warhol's typical on-screen eccentrics.

When Edie Sedgwick sat in front of Andy's camera for her film portrait, *Beauty #2*, a couple of things are obvious. One is that she may look shy and vulnerable but she adores the camera in the way natural screen personalities like Marilyn and Swanson and the long line of screen goddesses adored the camera; and the other is that Andy's camera adores her. There is an obvious affection as the camera stares at her, a little open-mouthed. We are seeing her through Andy's eyes, of course.

This is more of a 'star vehicle' than her earlier film, *Kitchen*, filmed in a cramped New York cold-water flat. Norman Mailer would see *Kitchen* and say that 'it captured the essence of every boring day one's ever had in the city, a time when everything is imbued with the odor of damp washcloths and old drains.'

For any veteran movie-goer, in Edie there seems to be a screen natural. Surely she could step off this 'underground' movie screen and onto the big Hollywood one. She sits on the edge of her own bed, showing us her long and sensational-looking legs while petting her dog. Next to her is a handsome young Italian (Gino Peschio) who strips down to his jockey shorts. (Males taking off their clothes becomes a fairly constant action in Warhol's films.) She wears dark lingerie – skimpy panties and a bra over her fairly flat chest.

Throughout the seventy-minute film, the off-camera voices of Chuck Wein and Gerard can be heard. Their commentary is intended to provoke her to react, and it does. Her range of emotions is fairly extensive – she is marvelous when she laughs. When she and Peschio finally get into a clinch on the bed, the comments from Wein are mean-spirited, so much so that she abruptly abandons the attempt and sits up in great annoyance.

Much of the film work Edie Sedgwick did for Andy is unavailable as of the spring 1989. Nearly all of it is in storage cans and, according to Morrissey, it would cost a fortune to get prints because of the 'reverse negative' film itself and the primitive sound system that was used. 'But someday, it will be seen. I don't know when, but it will be,' Morrissey said confidently. What is interesting about all of it is that as the years pass and Edie Sedgwick becomes more of a sixties figure, and Andy's art and film become records for the ages, nearly all of the glamor surrounding her image falls away. We are left with a fascinating glimpse of someone who just might have become celebrated for her own sake.

The core of Edie's celebrity problem was that she was as drawn to the druggy scene at the Factory as she was to the filmmaking. There was also the burden of Andy's chronic inability to see Edie Sedgwick in any terms but as an extension of his own fame. She did not care enough about it, and Andy lusted after fame as though it were not already his.

And there was his art. Occasionally, it still commanded center stage. In early autumn 1965, there was a Warhol exhibition scheduled at the Institute of Contemporary Art in Philadelphia. A trainload of Andy's entourage went down for it – Edie and Andy, Sam Green, Walter Hopps (who was in from Los Angeles), Jane Holzer, Kenneth Jay Lane, Isabel Eberstadt, Gerard and Taylor. That evening at the opening, the Press and public stormed the museum, converging on Andy and Edie. The museum people quickly cordoned off the exhibition rooms and removed all the paintings so they would not be destroyed. Of course, few there were really interested in the work. The fans began chanting: 'Edie! Andy! Edie! Andy!' It was terrifying, especially since the Philadelphians are known for their poise. This was Grace Kelly territory, but the crowds were misbehaving in the way of rock fans at a Stones or Beatles concert. Andy and the others finally escaped by retreating up a false staircase that went to the ceiling, where a hole was made for their retreat up to the roof and down into the back alley.

When earlier that summer Andy and Edie were making a thing of trying to look alike, Gerard, who was a gifted photographer, took a picture of them seated in directors' chairs at Steve Paul's nightclub, The Scene, holding a press conference. Edie had her hair styled like Andy's silver wig. She wore no make-up and had powdered her face to approximate Andy's pallor. They were both in black. This parody of twinship could go no further than this. But then it was all forgotten when they wound up the evening at Max's Kansas City, where half the crowd in the back room was connected with the Factory in some way. Max's was the real world, at least as real as Andy ever would find it. It was a place where homosexuals kissed their lovers openly and did not exchange glances in that furtive way dictated by most of society outside. It was a place where pretense was left at the front tables.

When Edie was left out of the cast of *My Hustler*, she did not object very much. And when Paul America, the film's star, realized that Andy was not planning anything else for him and 'took him for a fool', as Paul A. saw it, Edie invited him into her apartment, where he stayed for a month. The torrid stream of films starring herself ceased while she and Mr America spent their time getting high and fucking. He had a history of violence but he was pacified by non-stop sex during their in-house trips that often lasted for days. He felt that Andy had betrayed him, but Edie, who everyone still believed was Andy's favorite, had not.★

The year rolled on that way, and Andy began wondering just how he might be freed of his own misguided infatuation. He did not have long to wait. In October, Edie overdosed with a lighted cigarette in her hand and set her studio apartment on East 63rd Street on fire. She was burned on the back, the arms and legs, and was rushed to Lenox Hill Hospital.

She recovered quickly, and Andy visited her several times. He discussed a new movie idea with her. He was planning to film the suicide of the Mexican actress Lupe Velez, who drowned herself by either holding her head in the toilet and flushing herself out of this world or by vomiting into the toilet and passing out into the bowl and drowning by accident. It was a nice thought, just the sort of get-well present Andy would bring.

In November 1965, *Life* magazine had a spread on Edie in which they described her as Andy's underground movie superstar. This exposure redeemed her in Andy's eyes, giving her a lease on at least one other movie, which indeed turned out to be *Lupe*.

In her growing self-destructiveness, Edie was a natural for the role. And like Lupe, despite being the most sought-after party girl in town, she had no faith in any of it. Despite her fawn-like beauty and her magnetism (surely she was aware that all eyes were upon her every entrance, wherever she went), she had a profound insecurity. It was very much like Andy's when he was lurking about in the fifties, trying to be seen by the 'right' person and yet not seen. Her father, Francis, had made her this way, and yet she had a deep-seated admiration for him and a desire to prove to him that she had become a success at something. So in 1966 she was determined to bring her father and Andy together.

Of course, Andy was terrified. He expected Francis Sedgwick, or 'Fuzzy', as Edie called him, to swallow him whole. They set up a meeting place in the bar at the River Club. The elder Sedgwick spent his time waiting for Andy watching a world heavyweight fight between Patterson and Clay, and Andy was *very* late, trying to postpone this horror indefinitely.

★ A bit later, Paul America threatened to sue Andy and Morrissey for proper compensation for *My Hustler*, and it is said that he was given a check for $1,500.

Ernest Kolowrat, a friend to all the Sedgwicks, was present at that meeting:

> 'Edie brought him in and introduced them. Andy shook hands very limply, very weakly. Fuzzy was very generous, awfully nice. Tried to get him drinks . . . Andy this and Andy that. Andy didn't say anything. He whispered a few things to Edie. The River Club, with that wonderful view of the East River, was very much Fuzzy's turf, and that made Andy very uncomfortable. I don't know whether he shakes all the time. Does he? Well, he was very nervous. Quivering. After the first five minutes Fuzzy didn't say much to Andy, he kind of gave up. We sat around chatting for about twenty minutes. Then Edie spirited Andy out of there – she said it was too much for him. Afterwards Fuzzy and I were standing at the bar and he said to me with a great sense of relief: "Why, the guy's a screaming fag. . . ." '

What Andy was not was either 'a screaming fag' or a corrupter of the innocent. Edie's father betrayed his own insecurities by seeing Andy as a flagrant example of a homosexual. And his daughter was to do something worse. Edie had been on acid (LSD) in Cambridge, and she switched to speed and downers in New York because they were easily available around the Factory. She began daily visits to a 'feel-good' specialist, Dr Charles Roberts, who gave her shots of methadrine and vitamins. So she later announced to the world by way of a movie she made, *Ciao! Manhattan*, which was supposed to be about her life, that Andy had introduced her to drugs.

To the best of anybody's knowledge, no one who came to the Factory was ever introduced to drugs on the premises; they were, one and all, well acquainted with them before coming there. And there was no one, either mentally disturbed, as some undoubtedly were, or addicted, who ever died because of Andy. Half a dozen of his screen discoveries would be dead within the ten years between 1965 and 1975, but it is important to remember that Andy chose for his camera mainly those who were disinclined to cool out and recover from their excesses. Two centuries earlier, simply by using them as models for his work, William

Hogarth was unable to prolong the lives of the wretched poor he sometimes painted or depicted in his engravings.

For Ondine, the Factory was Andy's 'Sandbox'. 'Anytime I went up to the Factory and Warhol wanted to get involved with me, we'd go off and do whatever we did. He was fun, too, in his own way. But he wasn't dynamic.' Sometime in the summer of 1966, Ondine was complaining of his poverty when Edie said that she needed a maid. So Ondine became her 'French maid', as he called his job. He was paid thirty dollars a week to run over from Central Park, where he usually slept by the lake, getting the city dust off himself by a morning swim. He would use the key she gave him to come into her small apartment on East 63rd Street and wake her up. She was sodden with barbiturates and the first thing she would ask for would be some speed, an upper to get her up and going. Ondine always had some and he would comply.

Edie then would start her daily regimen, exercises to keep that slender figure while Ondine played Callas on the phonograph. Callas was more than his idol; she was everywhere he went. He introduced Andy to Callas and from then on the Factory was usually ringing with her soaring mezzo. Edie usually had roast beef and potato salad for breakfast. The speed she either sniffed or put into her coffee. Then her phone calls began. She was often being called for modeling assignments.

Ondine did not have to do any real work. Edie had a black woman for that. His job mainly seemed to be getting her going with his supply of amphetamine and jollying her through her exercises and into a good mood for the day. For this she paid him thirty dollars a week, which was just about enough to keep him in speed. Since he cadged a lot of meals and slept in the park, that sufficed during the good weather.

While Ondine was doing these chores for Edie, he began to sense that things were not too good between Edie and Andy. He heard both sides of the story, of course, since Andy often complained to Ondine about what was wrong in his life, and Edie talked about things she was doing that were counter-productive to her situation at the Factory, to say the very least.

She was seeing something of singer Bob Dylan that summer,

and his manager, Albert Grossman, had given her some encouragement about a career in mainstream movies. A fairly wanton person sexually who enjoyed sex as much as drugs and often used one to abet the other, Andy later thought that she was 'after' Dylan. When she told Andy about Dylan and Grossman, naturally he was angry. He felt he had been betrayed even though the summer passed and nothing came of the Dylan possibility. When she began to complain to him about her 'poverty' when she was supposed to be the toast of New York, Andy advised her to wait it out. He had not really made any money from her films, so he could justifiably call them experimental. But she and Chuck Wein were no dummies and they had figured out that Andy was getting a great deal of additional publicity by exploiting his connection with her, and publicity to Andy was money in the bank.

But his counsel was always the same. 'I'm not making any money from the movies. Be patient,' he told her. And Edie replied: 'I can't be patient. I just have nothing to live on.' The singular courtship, which save for sex was not unlike those pursued by other males in its inner dynamics – long dormant ambitions, the pride of ownership, jealousy – was long over. He spoke to her now as he would to an exasperating child, though it was rare for him to speak to her directly these days. He was frequently in huddles, laying out *The Chelsea Girls*. She was smart enough to know that she was no longer the pivot around which he was building his films. She caused people to worry, and that was the last thing Andy wanted to do. She had another fire at her studio at the Chelsea, but this time she was not badly hurt. Still, signals were going out; her family was getting concerned to the point of threatening to have her committed. All of this gave Andy an excuse to ease away from her. He simply had to. In the way of nearly all of his relationships, Edie was a chapter very nearly finished. He had done Edie Sedgwick every way but fricasseed. It was reminiscent of the way Hollywood exploited a personality that has nothing behind it – no training, no versatility, no depth – career burn-out. The affair with Paul America and the fires gave him an excuse to retreat.

By early 1966, Edie was an unwanted ghost drifting about the Factory. In January, Andy filmed the Velvets with Nico in performance, which according to Gerard Malanga 'was broken up by the New York police'. Reasons for the police intervention were vague. Perhaps the whip dance got out of hand.

Andy seemed to feel no guilt over Edie's predicament. Although she had not physically gone from the Factory, she was no longer getting Andy's attention when she was around. Most other rejects got the point right away and disappeared, but Edie was too lost in her drug reveries to realize what had happened. Edie's friend Sandy Kirkland said:

> 'Part of her understood, but she was still very hurt by it. I can see her in my mind's eye at the back of the Factory, where there was a bathroom, back there alone, abandoned, and she'd be dancing around, spaced-out, weird.'

Nico was not plastic enough to suit Andy's needs as a Superstar. He was still looking for his Garbo. But he did use her with the Velvets most of that year, and on one occasion when he was introducing a paper dress (possibly inspired by Jim Rosenquist's paper suit), he used Nico as his model in a store-window 'happening' at Abraham and Strauss's Department Store in Brooklyn, where Gerard assisted as Andy poured purple paint through a silkscreen to put original designs on the paper dress, worn by Nico. Her son Ari was in the 'happening' as well, and he sprayed paint on his mother's stockings. Andy and Gerard printed 'Fragile' on Nico's dress from the hip down, while she sang or droned one of her ballads. There was some vague bafflement and disappointment in the audience on the street.

Before she had gone beyond the edge, Edie might have broken with Andy on her own and better terms. There were agents interested in trying to sell her to a major Hollywood studio. It could have happened. She was the girl of the year in 1965 in New York – no question. But when she met these agents, or one of them took her to a studio representative, she would come back to the Factory full of complaints. She called the men she had to deal with 'assholes and morons'. 'I can't work with them,' she said. 'I have to be with my friends. I want to be with people I love.' There was not enough ambition in her to cope professionally with becoming a movie star.

Andy discovered Ingrid von Schefflin on 42nd Street, where she was killing time waiting for her bus to New Jersey. Rene Ricard, one of Andy's players, said that he brought this plain-looking girl back to the Factory to teach Edie a lesson. They cut her hair like Edie's and changed her name to Ingrid Superstar. She was not a beautiful woman, and Edie was aware of it.

If Andy was into playing games with her future, Edie was at least aware that that was happening. Bob Dylan had expressed an interest in doing a film with Edie. One night at the Ginger Man in early 1966, Edie told Paul Morrissey that she did not want Andy to show any of her films any more. She had made nearly a dozen of them in the brief months of her reign as queen of the Factory. Andy and Morrissey had finished *The Chelsea Girls*, their most ambitious film, in which Edie had a small role (it marked the diminishing point of her trajectory across Warhol's heaven). Shortly after the conversation in the Ginger Man, she was asking that her small section of the big film be taken out, saying that she had signed a contract with Albert Grossman, Bob Dylan's manager.

Andy obliged Edie and excised her from the film, one of the very few editing jobs he ever did on a film except in camera. In her place he substituted a long close shot of Nico with some music by the Velvets behind it and colored lights crossing her face. It served as an ending for *The Chelsea Girls*, and it was very effective.

Months passed. Andy heard very little directly from Edie, but gossip was brought back to him. She never did a film with Bob Dylan. Apparently she believed from a flirtatious couple of meetings with him that he had taken a personal interest in her, but when she learned that he had gotten married, she could not believe it and went into a fit of trembling. Her old boyfriend Bobby Neuwirth kept an eye on her and even shot a short movie with her pulling her rhino footstool fitted out with roller skates up Fifth Avenue on Easter Sunday. She leashed the rhino to a fire hydrant for a few moments and a policeman jokingly gave her a ticket for illegal parking. It was a delightful last view of the enchantress Andy had met at Lester Persky's a year earlier, but, alas, not her last appearance on film.

TWENTY-THREE

Throughout all this, the rivalry between Gerard and Wein heated up. Gerard had no ambitions to be an *auteur* of film; he just wanted to perform. But Wein boldly stepped into the space next to Andy and his camera. Eventually, it all got too much for Gerard and he went out and persuaded Paul Morrissey to come into Andy's movie-making business. He probably came to regret that move, since Paul got rid of so many people Gerard liked. But, as David Bourdon remarked:

> 'When I learned that so many people held grievances against Paul, it now makes me wonder whether it really was Paul or whether it was Andy and Paul playing "The Good Cop and the Bad Cop", whether Paul was being used by Andy to do all the unpopular things.

Paul Morrissey was a native New Yorker, born in the Bronx. He was also Catholic, taught by nuns and Jesuit fathers from childhood through his graduation from Fordham University. He believed that 'Catholic schools are the only good ones'. Nearly everyone at the Factory was Catholic, whether practising, lapsed or fallen. Ondine, Gerard, Brigid – all from Catholic homes. It was a bit like Andy's having been surrounded at Carnegie Tech by Jewish friends.

But Morrissey had qualities that set him apart from other Factory people. He did not get involved with Andy and his Factory because he heard that there was a colorful and unusual group there; quite the contrary. Gerard had become a friend, and he had urged him to see a Warhol movie he was in called *Vinyl*, which had Edie Sedgwick in a small role. It was playing at the Cinemathèque on a double bill with Andy's *Poor Little Rich Girl*, which starred Edie. Morrissey had only seen *Sleep*, and he had sat through two hours of it. Morrissey was not only dedicated to film, but he wanted to make films that earned money. Like Andy with his art, Morrissey saw serious, art films in terms of how wide an audience they might win; how much money they would earn. When he came onto the Warhol scene, Andy and Chuck Wein were in the middle of making *My Hustler* on Fire Island. Morrissey stood on the sidelines of that one, not really changing the script or the shape of the film. According to Gerard, he took over the sound chores from Buddy Wirtschafter.

Andy enjoyed watching his lieutenants jockeying around for his favor. Gentle Gerard seemed already demoted as Wein followed Andy around and always seemed to be at his elbow. That did not mean that Andy ignored Gerard. Gerard was included in things; he had proved to be a remarkable screen presence. Unlike others who worked for Andy, Gerard somehow had become 'family'. When Andy would get angry over something that Gerard would do, it sounded very much like a complaining brother. But now that it was always Andy and Edie who partied together, somehow Gerard knew that this 'affair' was not going to last, although he liked Edie and he did not especially resent Wein even though he had set in motion the chain of events that would lead to Wein's being eased out. In spite of everything, Gerard knew that Andy's affection for him was deep and that he would never turn against him.

On a personal level, Andy and Morrissey were a study in contrasts. Andy could not contain himself when there was someone attractive around, but Morrissey never betrayed the slightest interest except a little tilt of his head and maybe a side glance at the person. While his nose was far from prominent, he sensed things with it, his nostrils aquiver, and he had a prim, nasal way of speaking.

At the beginning of their association, Morrissey accepted Andy's present obsession with Edie Sedgwick. When he first arrived at the Factory, Andy was busy filming thirty people, and he needed help with that because he complained that he could not fit them all on the screen. Morrissey proposed the extraordinary idea that Andy should move the camera to various positions to get everybody included. He was very low-key at first. It was only later that a little arrogance surfaced that could turn some Warhol people off and cause them later to make accusations of high-handedness against him. In time, he got the reputation as Andy's 'hatchet-man'.

Even more than Andy, Morrissey was obsessed with film-making. While he was still at Fordham, on his own he made 16 mm black comedies. His very first film showed a priest saying mass on the edge of a cliff and then throwing an altar boy over the precipice. It gave his viewers something to ponder. His ground-floor apartment was a store front, and in 1963 and 1964, he showed these short films in his living-room.

Morrissey knew the underground movie *grand seigneur* Jonas Mekas, of course, but he was not convinced by Mekas' insistence that films were poetry. A friend of his named Joseph Marzano, who was with a classical music radio station in Manhattan, lived on Long Island, and he made films with his sister and his friends. Marzano's films had a certain expressionistic flair to them. For a brief period, on Sunday afternoons, Marzano showed his films in a coop art gallery on East 10th Street. Morrissey dropped in and saw them, and Jonas Mekas was always there, and then would write about them in his column in *The Village Voice*.

After four or five showings, the City stopped them because the gallery had failed to get a Certificate of Occupancy necessary for a theater. But the experience had convinced Morrissey that he, too, could find his own audience, so he rented a projector, obtained a few free films from Columbia University and other sources to fill out his program of his own short films, including one he had done with Taylor called *Taylor Mead Sings and Dances Sort Of*. As he had hoped, Jonas Mekas dropped by and later wrote something about them. The City authorities did not seem to notice what he was doing and these store-front screenings went on for a couple of months. Then they stopped him from showing any more because he lacked the necessary certificate. Obviously determined, he lived solely for his movies. If Morrissey was one of the very few Factory people never to be labeled a druggie or involved in their sexual intrigues, the explanation was simple: he got off on making movies.

Since earliest childhood Morrissey was even more dedicated to movie-going than Andy was, and he knew far more about what he was seeing. About a year after his store-front screenings were stopped, a theater on the East Side, which he said was 'called The Charles, Tenth Street and Avenue B, a nice old movie theater seating 700 people with the balcony, took one night a month and said "You bring your film on Monday night and we'll show it." Well, my films were made with a Bolex with no sound and I had just shown them at my place, a Nickleodeon really, but the Charles made it a bigger thing, and more people wrote about it. I finally made a longer film about miracles, miracles that change people, and it ran about thirty or forty minutes . . . . Andy made a few more experiments with his Bolex, having people stare at the camera and things like that. He had some very interesting ideas. By that time, Jonas had started renting off-Broadway theaters on their closed night. There was a place around Twenty-Fourth and that was the first Cinemathèque.'

But what finally impressed Morrissey the most about Andy's movie-making was his purchase of the Auricon sound camera.

'I thought this was really remarkable . . . . He was really the first one to put a thousand dollars or two thousand dollars into a sound camera . . . . And Andy said, "Oh, I saw your films and the lighting was nice . . . . I'm making a film a week and I think I need some help. Why don't you come and help me?" '

When Morrissey showed up the following week, he recalled that

'it was very curious. Andy was always, let's say, insecure about what he was doing. He led a very consistent life, but he had this manifest insecurity. He said, "I never move the camera. I just like to turn the camera on . . . but look, thirty people showed up. To get them all in, you have to shoot from the other side of the studio and everybody will look so tiny. I've got a problem. What'll I do?" So I said, "Just put the camera here, and just go from here to there and then back again. Why don't you try it?" '

It was apparent that moving the camera was anathema to him, but Morrissey was persuasive, and Andy's filmmaking immediately began to change. No longer was it close to the immobility of his canvases, with only subtle movements, but images began to move about the screen the way most movies do.

Unlike the other Factory people, Morrissey moved through his working day as a self-contained, purposeful individual, whose inner life was unknown. If ribaldry and nudity and 'let-it-all-hang-out' seemed to be *de rigueur* among the others, Morrissey was silent about his human needs. In those first years, he never received any money from Andy except what he received back from the films, and since this was very little, he did draw expense money for his travels with the Velvet Underground and the Exploding Plastic Inevitable. There was much speculation about his sex life, but no one ever learned anything specific. It was rumored that he was a conservative; it was even said that he had a Nazi flag hanging over his bed, but since no one from the Factory was a social crony of Morrissey's, nothing could ever be pinned down.

The only reliable character portrait of Morrissey must be obtained from his films and his cinematic obsessions. He had no interest in filming drugged-out faces or drunks; he liked to contrast beautiful young men with older, slightly ravaged men; he liked to depict women as preoccupied with sex, often with bored male partners. If Andy's films were Felliniesque, Morrissey's were X-rated parodies of Billy Wilder.

Upon his arrival at the beginning of the shooting of *My Hustler*, Morrissey did nothing to dislodge Chuck Wein as Andy's film idea man. He was a general who arrived at the battle scene where a colonel was giving last-minute instructions to the troops. Morrissey walked quietly around, saying very little, watching everything. It must have been very unsettling to Wein, but he pretended at least not to notice.

My Hustler was shot over Labor Day weekend, 1965, on Fire Island. It was to star yet another Warhol discovery, Paul America, who had a football player's physique, and he had some problems over his name, which Andy had given him:

'When he gave me the name, I figured it was all right. Except I went through a period of paranoia about it. I

mean, every time I saw that word – and it's everywhere
– I related it to *myself*. The country's problems were *my*
problems. I think that if I weren't called Paul America
it would have been easier for me to register in hotels.
Most of the time the desk clerks said, "Okay, Mr
America." '

Ondine said that Paul A. was 'everybody's lover . . . marvelously
satisfying to everyone. Imagine having that type of curse. People
would go to sleep in his arms . . . Richie Berlin, me, just everyone! He was the personification of total sexual satisfaction.'

The young 'Superstar' had difficulty communicating with
Andy, since Andy never would answer any of his questions
but always asked Gerard to give him his reply. He believed
that Andy took him for a fool. He never appeared in any
other film despite his obvious sex appeal, and a few months
later he was gone from the Factory. He kept in touch with
Henry Geldzahler and soon wrote back that he was living in
a commune in Indiana. Henry's relationship with all the young
people who paraded through the Factory was warmer as a rule
than Andy's. He seemed genuinely interested in them and in what
they planned to do with their lives.

My Hustler was shot from a rough script by Chuck Wein. He
cast the film, and he found the location on Fire Island. The
title character played by Paul America has been brought to the
Island via 'Dial-a-Hustler' by a middle-aged man (Ed Hood), but
the youth is coveted by his neighbors, a mysogynist woman
(Genevieve Charbon, who was a friend and former roommate
of Edie Sedgwick) and another middle-aged gay, who is her
companion (John MacDermott). A bet is made. Both the man
and the woman will make separate attempts to seduce the young
blond away from his 'owner'.

Wein had a sound ear for dialogue. Everything Andy had done
up to this time was very loosely written by Ronnie Tavel, who
was fond of off-camera conversations and narrative. Wein had
moved in the trashy-elegant worlds of both Cambridge and
Manhattan, and a sampling suggested he was not deaf:

' "Where in hell is that woman? God knows what she'll
do with him. Oh, there she is." MacDermott's woman

companion appears in the frame. "Look at her. Will you
look? Disgusting. It's really just disgusting. She really
stops at nothing." '

In the second reel, MacDermott is in the bathroom of the beachhouse. The hustler is about to take a shower, urinate, and then
wait patiently for his turn at the mirror, where MacDermott
is seeking reassurance after an unsettling afternoon. The hustler
waits very close to the middle-aged man who has wagered a bet
that he can be seduced away. The sexual tension between them
rises. There is, of course, nothing more magnetic to watch than
two nearly naked bodies which you know are bound to touch.
At least, that was the audience situation in the mid-sixties before
nudity on the screen was unexceptional and a few years before
homosexuality was laid out on a platter like this for the mass
movie audience to see (*My Hustler* was supposed to be Andy's first
big bid to go 'mainstream' above ground, which it did, earning
$18,000 during its first week in a Manhattan movie-house).

The film was another step forward for Andy towards showing
the world just how marvelous the male body really was. He
had tried in the fifties and had been slapped down. Now in the
middle sixties, he was using film instead of a drawing board
and the momentum of his career was such that anyone who
tried to slap him down now would surely be badly bruised in
the process. Fortunately, Morrissey shared his enthusiasm. It is
just possible that Morrissey saw exposed male flesh as a way
of making commercially successful films, but that is not meant
as a putdown and there even may have been something more
profound moving Morrissey than that, as we shall see when Joe
Dallesandro comes on the scene.

TWENTY-FOUR

Barbara Rubin was an underground filmmaker who was often around Jonas Mekas. However, like Andy, she moved in broader circles than that. She knew nearly everyone in the rock music scene, and she once brought Donovan and the Byrds to the Factory.

It was in Andy's mind to do something in multi-media. He had been much impressed with attempts like those of the Expanded Cinema to mix movie images with live music and action. He wanted to see Warhol movies projected behind a live rock band or on a screen above their heads on tandem projectors showing two images at once while strobe lights pierced the arena like flashes of lightning with gels to color the light. Noise, color and his own movies in exciting combinations – what a marvel that would be. It was with such dreams as this that Andy became as engaged with the moment and as animated as on those occasions when some beauty walked into the room.

On New Year's Eve 1965, Andy and Edie, Morrissey, Gerard and a small rock group called the Velvets, whom Barbara Rubin was promoting as Andy's musical half of his brainstorm, went to Harlem's Apollo Theater to see in 1966. A singer named Lou Reed was the lead in the Velvets. Andy first heard the group when Rubin asked Gerard's help in making a movie of them playing at a small place called the Café Bizarre. Their music was pre-punk, loud and hostile to the establishment, 'beyond the pale', Andy called it, which must have meant that they were some distance from the Beatles in their sound.

Gerard had enlisted Morrissey's help that night of filming. Morrissey was interested to check out just how the Velvets would sound in a real disco. He and Andy had been approached by Michael Myerberg, who had produced '*Waiting for Godot*', about a huge disco he was planning to open in Queens in an old airplane hangar. Myerberg said that he wanted Andy there every night. He even proposed calling it 'Andy Warhol's whatever'. Conferring at a table at Sardi's, Myerberg proposed that the Factory furnish colorful people like Edie Sedgwick to bring the place press coverage. He realized that press hype had made Sylvia Burton's 'Arthur' the *in* place in town. Then Morrissey suggested that rather than having Andy and his people there every night, Andy would sponsor a rock group, like Brian Epstein did with the Beatles. But there at the Café Bizarre, Morrissey and Andy had sat down together and brainstormed all evening about pulling all of these multimedia elements together in a disco they would control. Myerberg was forgotten.

They were also looking for some spot where they could launch Nico, the German singer whom Gerard had met in London in the spring of 1965. When he was not looking for a rich patroness, Gerard was often in pursuit of some damsel in distress. His was a very romantic soul. When Nico arrived in New York with her small boy in tow, said to be the son of film star Alain Delon, Gerard took Andy with him, probably hoping he would be bowled over by her high cheekbones and angular body and possibly see in her a Teutonic Superstar. Gerard must have seen that the moment was ripe to discover an alternative to Edie Sedgwick, or it may have been just a hope that time was running out for Edie, and Nico could be brought in. Andy was complaining to anyone and everyone that Edie was beyond help. He even had told his brothers on a visit to New York that there was nothing he could do for her any more. One day at the Factory on one of de Antonio's infrequent visits, Edie had told him that her mother had come to New York to have her put away in a hospital; de had gone with her to see her mother, hoping to be of some help, but the mother had banged on the floor with her cane and spoken harshly to her daughter.

The Velvets numbered only four members. They included, besides Reed, a freckle-faced girl drummer, Maureen Tucker, a Welshman named John Cale, who played the electric viola and like

Reed was a composer, and Sterling Morrison. Andy told them he was being given a week at the Cinemathèque to try out his live music and light-show idea, and why didn't the Velvets contribute the musical part of it?

Reed's first impression of Andy was that they were

> 'doing what he was doing, except we were using music and he was doing it with lights . . . . Not kidding around. In other words, to my mind, nobody in music is doing anything that even approximates the real thing, with the exception of us. Of doing a specific thing that's very, very real . . . isn't slick or a lie in any conceivable way, which is the only way we could work with him. Because the first thing I liked about him was that he was very real.'

The word *real* is significant here. This is the way Andy wanted to be perceived but so rarely succeeded in being. Andy and Lou Reed had connected upon first meeting, and their friendship would last until Andy's death and even beyond. In 1989, Lou Reed and John Cale would record a memorial tribute to 'Drella', Andy's peculiarly apt nickname. It was a bit strange; Andy said that by the 1980s Lou would not even speak to him in public.

What was a bit ironic about having Nico replace Edie Sedgwick because Edie was lost in a narcotic haze was the fact that Nico was taking LSD.

The first rock music, light and movie extravaganza pulled together by Andy and Morrissey was called *Andy Warhol, Up-Tight* and it opened on 8 February 1966, at the Film-Makers' Cinemathèque on West 41st Street. Danny Williams was running the lights as plotted by Andy; Gerard and Edie were doing the dancing; and Morrissey was projecting the movies and slides.

The performance began with the unreeling of Edie as *Lupe* in its first public screening. In it, as Lupe Velez, 'the Mexican spit-fire' of films, Edie is seen dressing up in her finery, slowly lighting candles around her bed, taking a massive dose of sleeping pills, and then drowning as she retches over her toilet bowl to which she has crawled.

The film ran seventy minutes and the Velvet Underground and Nico quietly moved on stage in front of the screen and the sounds of their tuning up could be heard in the dark. At this moment, Andy, manning another projector, began to show *Vinyl* with Gerard and Edie but with the sound turned off. Then the face of Nico was seen superimposed over the violence of *Vinyl* and her voice could be heard singing 'I'll Keep It with Mine', a Bob Dylan song. Nico on stage then picked up the refrain from Nico on the screen with the band joining in behind her.

Lou Reed and the band segued into 'Venus in Furs', which would become one of their major hits, and Gerard and Edie moved on stage doing a free form dance to the music.

To Edie, the *Up-Tight* show must have seemed the ultimate in the excitement that had surrounded her for the past year in Manhattan. Surely it made her forget for the moment that she was close to being phased out. *Lupe* was a kind of *tour de force*. She was doing on screen what she had come close to doing in life several times. It had impressed the audience, and now she was spinning around Gerard to the music before this capacity crowd. Her publicity had peaked that winter, and nearly everyone who read a New York daily or *Life* or *Vogue* magazines knew who she was. The entire theater vibrated and seemed to be exploding as they danced, with Andy's lights bouncing off them, the ceiling, and the walls.

When Lou Reed began singing 'Heroin', Gerard slowly unwound from one of his gyrations and settled on the stage floor. He then lit a candle and kneeling over it, undid his belt, pulled a spoon from his hip pocket, rolled up his sleeve, heated the spoon over the candle-flame, touched the spoon with a 'hypodermic needle' (really a pencil), and flexed his arm to the music in an up and down motion, pressing the 'needle' into his arm. With the music cueing him, he slowly arose and began whirling frantically around the stage. At the song's conclusion, Gerard lay stretched out on the stage staring up blankly at Lou.

If one theorized about what was going on or down, it was either a musical parable about the horrors of being a junkie or it was a hymn to the drug itself as an Aztec might dance into oblivion in the name of a fierce god.

The audience was forced into the act as well. Barbara Rubin, a noisy, boyish young woman, had her movie camera in her hand, and when she was not thrusting it towards the musical action or the audience, she was racing down the aisle with her sun-gun blinding one member of the audience after another and screaming, 'Is your penis big enough?' to the men and 'Does he eat you out?' to the women. This was no place for faint hearts.

By March, the combination of Andy Warhol and the Velvet Underground had evolved into a traveling extravaganza called the Exploding Plastic Inevitable. They did shows at college campuses with young Ronnie Cutrone, the art student and Warhol groupie who was a very good dancer, gyrating on one platform and Gerard Malanga, who was professionally at least into S and M, doing a whip dance, all with big metal flashes of the strobe lighting. Cutrone described some of this:

> 'We had about a hundred feet of this phosphorescent flexible lighting that we would wrap around our bodies . . . . It was a way to be involved with the art without actually touching it. There was music, film, dancing.'

Andy handled the lights, and Barbara Rubin was bouncing all over the place filming the audience as well as the performance. There was nothing more dizzying than watching a Barbara Rubin film with the camera bouncing up and down at such a multimedia event as one of these.

Andy always brought along several of his recent films to show on the two screens. At Rutgers University in New Jersey, he screened Edie playing the doomed Lupe Velez drowning herself in a toilet bowl. A contemporary account of the evening told of the Velvet Underground coming on stage:

> '. . . a four-member musical group whose most notable attribute is a repetitive howling lamentation which conjures up images of a schooner breaking up on the rocks. Their sound, punctuated with whatever screeches, whines, whistles and wails can be coaxed out of the amplifier, envelopes the audience with disploding decibels, a

sound two-and-a-half times as loud as anybody thought
they could stand.'

From New Jersey, they went to Ann Arbor, Michigan, where
Andy screened *Vinyl*, his version of *A Clockwork Orange*, in
which Edie Sedgwick tortures Gerard, who incidentally seemed
ideally cast as such a victim. (Originally, it was to have been
an all-male cast, but Andy had insisted on including Edie over
Gerard's protests.) Andy put a red gel over the projector lens,
making this excursion into S and M more lurid than ever.

Andy seemed to love this free-form entertainment he was
sponsoring and to which he was such a vital contributor. Occasionally, Edie would show up, but usually with one of her
boyfriends, Bobby Neuwirth more often than not. It was clear
to all involved that the year-long honeymoon between Andy and
Edie was over.

Nico had supplanted her and she seemed to accept it. But it
was a new experience for her. She had never been dumped
before by anyone. It is possible that Edie never completely
got over that. As for Nico, Gerard said that 'Andy got
the idea that maybe we should include her with the Velvet
Underground because the Velvets didn't really have any charisma. Andy and I felt that the Velvets would have something
to attract them further than with the loud music they were
playing.'

Andy loved the ambience of the rock disco, the rock shows. He
adored youth. He abhorred getting old. He always complained
about parties where the guests were his age or older. Now
he immersed himself in that young world and took over
the Dom, a huge Polish dance hall on St Mark's Place. He
said it was the biggest disco dance floor in Manhattan, and
perhaps it was. He took over the lease, and the next day
Morrissey and Andy and half a dozen other Factory people
were there painting the walls. They used lots of Stroblite's
Day-Glo paint. They brought in five movie projectors –
carrousel-type machines where the image changes every ten
seconds, and, in Andy's words, 'where, if you put two
images together, they bounce.' They brought in a revolving
mirrored ball like they used in the old marathon dance halls.

It was stored at the Factory, something Andy had picked up a long time ago. A light man came in from outside and put in spotlights and strobe lighting to highlight the Velvets and the people in the audience. They advertised the Dom in the *Village Voice*:

> Come Blow Your Mind
> the Silver Dream Factory presents the first
> ERUPTING PLASTIC INEVITABLE
> with
> Andy Warhol
> The Velvet Underground
> and
> Nico

The Velvets were staying with Stanley Amos at the time. The apartment was on West 3rd Street, and they could walk to work. Tom O'Horgan's things were still there – weird decor with a big black coffin as its motif, and a heating system that was a fifteen-foot gold dragon affixed to the ceiling and spitting flames from its mouth. In the back, Stanley had a jungle decor contrasted with Johnny Dodd's panel of 40,000 George Washington postage stamps, which he had acquired.

As in the very early days of the Factory, Andy's crowd began hanging out at Stanley's. Ingrid Superstar would lounge around there, often going to one of the two floor-to-ceiling mirrors to stare at herself and wail: 'I'm so ugly, so ugly.' Then whatever guys were there would take out their cocks and pretend they were Senor Wences of television fame with his hand puppet and have their cocks talk to her.★

They were nearly all on something, and Lou Reed and Ondine would quarrel over trading Desoxyn for Obetrols, the former being twice as expensive. Ondine's pal Rotten Rita would bring in his home-made speed, which nobody wanted but would take if there was nothing better around. The Turtle came around

---

★ Senor Wences was a puppeteer who used his bare hand to create a man-about-town forever in pursuit of young women or a good time. He appeared regularly on *Ed Sullivan's Toast of the Town* television show in the 1950s and 60s.

sometimes to deliver drugs – he lacked a bone in his spine where it connects to the head so he had no neck to speak of. His real job was at a hotel switchboard in the Village.

Ronnie Cutrone, who was still dancing along with Gerard to the Velvets' rock, was allowed to hang out at Stanley's, too. Soon, this good-looking kid whose ambition was to be an artist like Andy was there a good part of the time. The company of speed freaks there was on a slightly higher level than Cutrone's street friends like Jimmy Smith.

Andy, still high on Obetrols, stayed in this groove for nearly a year. After a night of running the gels on the lights for the show at the Dom, Andy would go partying with Lou and the others at the afterhours clubs.

In the midst of this non-stop 'grooving', Leo Castelli arranged for a new show of Andy's work. Andy had time to prepare for this, too. Castelli described the show as being

> 'extremely amusing and daring. I had two spaces at 4 East 77th. I had one big space where the *Flowers* had been and then this space in the back with a nice circular window, which was sort of like an office space or rather a place where one could sit down and talk things over. We papered this whole room with the cow wall paper from top to bottom. In the front room were the famous floating silver pillows. We had some trouble with our technician, who had been working on all kinds of projects in art and technology . . . . He had taken care of the technical problems with those pillows, making them helium-tight, not air-tight. But the problem wasn't solved. They didn't stay filled for a very long time. It was very amusing. They just would float around. They would float down the stairs and some of them even floated out to the street. We had the most trouble getting the wallpaper off of the wall. It took more than a week. We didn't salvage anything. It was all scraped off. There were two other occasions in which wallpaper was used – one with the cow image in a different color at the Whitney Museum, where the whole museum was papered with the cow image and then the paintings of the people were placed on the

wallpaper, so there was the comparison of the cows
and the people, no criticism intended.'
At the Castelli opening, Andy announced that he was giving up
painting to be a filmmaker. He did not mention his activity as
a rock promoter, so he must have considered that a sideline.
Castelli, of course, did not panic. He had a marvelously equable
temperament. This was all part of the new way of looking at
things, and he would try to see all of Andy's movies that he could
manage.

Everyone knew that Andy was behind the Dom, so it became
the place to go and be seen. Many of the kids never would get to
the Factory, but they could at least see the Man with the Silver
Wig and the dark glasses running the lights. One night, Andy
even dyed his wig a day-glo blue just to see how it would look.
He asked the day-glo tycoon, Ray Andersen, if that would make
his hair fall out. Andersen did not know he wore a wig and said
he didn't think so. If he had known it was a wig, he might have
said 'What does it matter?'

Paul Morrissey was made manager of the Exploding (changed
from Erupting) Plastic Inevitable tours. He lined up spots for
them around New York, and then he added tours across the
country at college campuses. They began to make some money.
Lou Reed and the Velvets even made some records with Nico
singing 'I'll Be Your Mirror', 'All Tomorrow's Parties' and
'Femme Fatale'.

Andy, Morrissey and the troupe spent all of May 1966 in
California, where they had been booked into the Trip, a nite
spot on the Sunset Strip in Hollywood. After about a week,
that collapsed when the Trip was closed down due to some
dispute between the owners. Irving Blum had a show opening
at the Ferus Gallery on La Cienega of Andy's helium pillows,
but they had trouble keeping them up halfway to the ceiling, and
some of them were leaking and falling down. Andy spent all one
afternoon pumping them up and arranging them.

Bill Graham had invited them to play at his Fillmore auditorium
in San Francisco. Morrissey and Graham had a run-in over drug
use. Nearly everyone on the bill was high, and Morrissey was
taunting Graham about it in a sarcastic way and boosting heroin
as a cure for the common cold. But Andy thought it was Paul's
dropping his tangerine peels on the backstage floor that was really

the last straw for Graham, who shouted: 'You disgusting germs from New York! Here we are, trying to clean up everything, and you come out here with your disgusting minds and *whips* – !'

Morrissey continued his jeremiad on drugs and hippies all the way back home:

> '. . . LA, I liked because the degenerates there all stay in their separate suburban houses, and that's wonderful because it's so much more modern – people isolated from each other . . . I don't know where the hippies are getting these ideas to "retribalize" in the middle of the twentieth century. I mean, in New York and LA people take drugs purely to *feel good* and they admit it. In San Francisco they turn it into "causes" and it's so tedious . . . .'

Jonas Mekas was concerned about this major distraction of Andy's and told Morrissey: 'What about some films now? Forget about the Velvet Underground.' Morrissey passed along Jonas' request:

> ' "You know Jonas would like to show something. What do we have . . . . That's sort of good where Eric talks to the camera . . . and those other things. Why don't we show them all on a double screen and give it a title to make it look like a collected thing?" Andy sort of flinched at that because he didn't like the title to have any logic.'

But when someone suggested *The Chelsea Girls*, Morrissey convinced him that it would work. Some of it – like the business with Eric – had been shot already, and what would emerge as the most popular of all the Warhol films would be as much a salvage job of old camera sessions as it would be a new production.

One thing can be said for the Obetrols. They allowed Andy to pursue three separate careers simultaneously – he was still turning out silkscreen paintings; he was shooting his films; and he was sponsor and producer of an extraordinary rock band and light show (*The Exploding Plastic Inevitable Presents the Velvet Underground*). His energy was boundless, and what was even more extraordinary was the durability of each of his separate interests.

His art would survive him; his films would survive him; and the Velvet Underground would go into the rock history books as one of the first bands to give the world the punk sound, which became the permanent delinquent side of rock.

There was a consistency to all of Andy's efforts. What he was producing was not pretty. There was nothing nice about it. When he told interviewers that he was from Cleveland or Philadelphia, perhaps he believed he was giving Pittsburgh a break. He was the bad boy of American culture, but in a decade when that was precisely what was called for, Andy and the sixties became one.

TWENTY-FIVE

The Chelsea Hotel near the corner of 7th Avenue and 23rd Street is something more than a landmark. It is a life raft thrown to drowning writers, artists and others striving to survive in one of the various modes of self-expression, where the American insistence on the nine-to-five work ethic simply does not apply. Although criminals and psychopaths have been known to have lived there (we will deal with one shortly), it is not disreputable. Playwright Arthur Miller kept a suite there until the end of 1966, and his daughter, an actress, has lived there. Miller liked it because it was close to the theater district, and he could run downstairs and through the lobby without putting on a jacket. Novelist William Burroughs maintained rooms there, where he wrote *The Naked Lunch*. Viva (Susan Hoffman), who came into Warhol's life as Edie moved out, lived there with her two daughters. In the nearly one hundred years of its history, Mark Twain, Sarah Bernhardt, O'Henry, Eugene O'Neill, Thomas Wolfe, Brendan Behan, Edgar Lee Masters, Dylan Thomas and Virgil Thomson have stayed there for weeks and, in many cases, for years.

It is an especially good place for someone established in the theater or the arts who is raising a family in Connecticut, upstate or on the Island to keep a Manhattan studio. A suite with kitchenette and even a spare room for storage or a guest is within the financial reach of most of those people.

Despite its bohemian and slightly raffish look, it is reasonably well maintained and the atmosphere is healthy enough for one of its long-term tenants to be, as of this writing, 112 years old.

The time had come for Andy to film the subterranean world surrounding him before it dissolved completely. Edie was fading, trailing her gauzy and fallen friends behind her; Freddy Herko had killed himself; everyone seemed to have dropped Eric Emerson but Eric himself, who now was lost in masturbatory fantasies. All during the summer of 1966, Andy was shooting *The Chelsea Girls*.

He had shot his earlier films in a variety of locations – the Factory, friends' apartments, the streets, Fire Island. Then it occurred to him that he might best pull together his outsider friends into one special place, where their kind was as tolerated as in his own studio – the Chelsea. He went to Stanley Bard, manager of the hotel, and asked him what he thought of the idea. Bard remembered that he was apprehensive. It was one thing to be tolerant; it was quite another to have your place of business described, in a movie that possibly could be a success and seen around the world, as a freaks' paradise.

'He approached me on it, and I relented after persuasion, and I took a lot of abuse on that film because it depicted the hotel as being a wild establishment. Some of my stockholders were a little upset. And Andy explained to me that it would be very good for the hotel. He said it is not a negative film. It is a very good movie. It is not a true kind of situation, and people will know that. He thought that it would bring much more beneficial publicity than negative publicity. We were always busy, and we were busy after the film. I don't think it mattered one way or another. A lot of people saw it and I really can't tell whether people thought it was a real-life situation or that it was a fantasy. It didn't matter. I liked Andy. I thought he was a talent. We always got along well. I did it for him. In retrospect, it never harmed the hotel . . . . They were shooting here for months, but they used the apartments of people that were there, living there. Nico, Viva, Ultra Violet, some of his people were living here, so he used them and their rooms.'

The film in its prime state ran three and a half hours, or seven hours of shooting time – it was always projected on a wide split screen with two images, one action on the left side of the screen, and quite another seen on the right. There were twelve reels, and

in each of them one of the Factory crowd is involved in the sort
of thing he or she has been doing regularly around the premises.
The opening shot, usually projected through a red filter, shows
Emerson, totally self-absorbed, slipping into an erotic situation
with himself, fooling with his blond curls, twisting a small mirror
in his hands. He sucks at his fingers. The colors change, from red
to blue. Eric begins to strip, doing his favorite routine from Max's
back room, dropping his pants. Then the left side of the screen
flashes on in black-and-white, where seated on a black-draped
couch is Ondine as the Pope. In Andy's mind, this was casting to
type. The Vatican Pope, as Andy thought of him in his Catholic
mind, knew everyone as God knew everyone, including the tiny
sparrow. Andy thought that Ondine knew everyone and kept
his eye on everyone. There was no one in that underworld of
druggies, transvestites, drug-dealers, bar and disco owners, petty
thieves and juvenile runaways whom Ondine did not know.

Ondine began shooting his 'Confessional' scene in a foul mood.
He was weary of improvising dialogue and said that he was
spouting 'drivel'.

> 'These scenes seem to be going nowhere, and it was
> very annoying, so I decided the afternoon that I was
> going to do the Pope, and I had done two episodes
> previous to this, and this was the longest-sustained
> character that I had in any of the movies, I decided
> that I was really going to do it up right, that I was
> not only going to get on the screen but I was going
> to shoot up so everyone could see that I was a drug
> addict, and openly playing that I was a homosexual . . .
> and that did happen. In that film, I show you that I'm
> shooting up and I show you that I'm a homosexual. My
> dialogue is fairly clever. A confession. Now at that point
> you know I'm really baring my soul. I'm being really
> very vulnerable. And the girl that came in, the girl that
> they used who was my co-star, took advantage of that
> scene. She took advantage of my vulnerability and tried
> to make me look like a fool on the screen. I mean the
> only way I could counter it was to slap her. Part of the
> thing about making those movies is to stay in a kind
> of character. You can't go around and say to a person

who's hearing your confession, least of all to the Pope,
"I think you're a phony." You just don't talk like that
to a Pope. When I see the film to this day I get angry at
her presumption. I get furious. Of course, I felt very bad
when I got finished whacking her, indulging in some
kind of violence, and I'm not happy with that. But there
was no other remedy. And, of course, what happened to
that sequence of film, it just blows it off the screen. The
whole film runs around that pivot. It's a dynamite piece
of work. And it's the first time that Warhol slips out of
his mildly joking, satirical, put-on joke like *Vinyl*, which
is *A Clockwork Orange* but pretending. This was the first
and only time that Warhol did not pretend anything.
This was really happening, and it's scary. It was scary
to me, too. Audiences even today, when they see this,
they gasp. Coming on reel eleven, after three and a
half hours, it becomes quite a monument. Of course,
I realized when I did it that it was *the* thing. I knew
after I'd done it that I was going to have a tough time
with the rest. How the hell do you top that one?'

Marie Menken, who had played Castro's sister for Andy, was
now cast as Gerard Malanga's mother in an episode where she
castigates him for claiming to have married Hanoi Hannah, who
as played by Mary Woronov huddles in a corner listening to the
harangue. Then the story swings in Hanoi Hannah's direction
with Woronov and three other Warhol women – International
Velvet, Angelina 'Pepper' Davis and Ingrid Superstar.
   There are the usual Warhol film quirks in the nearly four hours
of running time. Often the camera zooms in on something quite
irrelevant just as it passes over without stopping something that is.
But that seems to be Andy's purpose – to strip all of these random
scenes of any meaning. These are people off the track, so nothing
is meant to cohere. Gerard Malanga called it 'a power thing,
because it's like he can look down and watch it all happening,
like a chess game, he can move people around. And although
he's basically a voyeur and wants everybody to expose themselves
completely, he won't expose himself. He likes to keep a lot of
mystery.'
   Later, after *The Chelsea Girls* opened, even such bright minds as

Gore Vidal's and composer and diarist Ned Rorem's missed this essential point, this deliberate disassociation in perception, finding it boring.

The movie opened at the Cinemathèque on 15 September 1966, and was quickly moved to a 'mainstream' movie-house, the Regency on upper Broadway, where it ran for weeks. Before the uptown run, all references to specific hotel room numbers were eliminated after a threatened lawsuit by the Chelsea Hotel. Relations cooled between Stanley Bard and Andy and his film people in the final weeks of shooting, and before the last episodes were shot, they were thrown off the premises. No matter, friends' apartments were used and they seemed to be all part of the Chelsea.

The critics really took notice of this one. They picked on its honest vulgarity (Brigid on the phone: 'Listen, I can't talk now, I'm on the john') and its relevance to the chaotic sixties. Jack Kroll raved about it in *Newsweek*, and Bosley Crowther chided Andy in the *New York Times*:

> 'It has come time to wag a warning finger at Andy Warhol and his underground friends and tell them, politely but firmly, that they are pushing a reckless thing too far.'

Writing in the London-based *Arts and Artists* (edited by Andy's good friend and supporter Mario Amaya), Brian O'Doherty explained:

> 'It is a strange near-amalgam, somewhat as if *Last Exit to Brooklyn* had been crossed with *Grand Hotel*. The whole ambience tends, through a very carefully handled effect of boredom, to dissociate mind and body, and thus to become metaphysical. Warhol's world is as de-realizing as William Burroughs' and its surface is as narcotic and beautiful. The absence of narrative direction, the purposeless to and fro movement within which action merely emphasizes paralysis, and the random spasms of sensuality, are common to both . . . .
>
> 'The action, such as it is, is made up for the most part of the troughs between crises – deviants dallying, bitches

bitching, addicts mainlining, somnambulistic wanderings in which characters cross from room to room
(screen to screen), set pieces, improvizations, and of
course people doing – *nothing*, although nothing, like
boredom, depending on the frame of reference, becomes
a productive entity . . . .'

In that same magazine a year later (March 1968), William Wilson
wrote about the film:

'The people emerge not as sinners, but as repeaters, as
patient martyrs to repetition, trimming hair, washing
dishes, complaining, torturing, failing. Appropriately
enough the movie opens with a mock Holy Family
(mother, child, and a man who is too short to be the
husband, and who doesn't seem to be the father), and
closes with a mock confession to a Pope who says so
beautifully that it isn't easy being a Pope, but that it
isn't hard either, it's just something you are.'

John Gielgud summed up the typical viewer's reaction to *The
Chelsea Girls* as well as anyone. Morrissey happened to see him
as he emerged from the Regency Theatre on upper Broadway
after a screening. 'I'm curious,' Morrissey asked him. 'What did
you think of the movie, Mr Gielgud?' 'I don't know what it
was,' Gielgud replied, 'but once I started watching, I couldn't
stop watching the goddamn thing.'
  Morrissey thought that the film was

'very effective. It was the successful version of Andy's
idea of putting the emphasis on character and personality. He didn't verbalize what it was, but I understood
what was going on. Here was a film minus story, minus
direction, in which there was pure human character,
exaggerated, artificial, stylized, theatrical character. It
was all color. There were no camera stops, no cuts.
There was an attempt to build emphasis on some characters and make some stories. Some people I used over
and over again. Now they were with their mother, now
they were with their father, now they were with their

girlfriend. Now they were just talking to the camera. So there was a strand of repeated characters.'

Morrissey said that he enjoyed these 'film experiments' with Andy.

'Andy has been ridiculed and laughed at by people in film, but . . . I thought he had a genuine interest in human personality, which I felt we shared. I felt bad about rejecting some of Andy's [casting] suggestions. Sometimes I'd say: "Okay, let's do it" and they wouldn't work out. But Andy was no moron, and he noticed that, so it really required a funny kind of selecting, casting. Those films we did were very comparable to the epistolary novels that began the novel, in which letters written between people – they had no plot – in which in the letter a character became a character by being ridiculous, and the concept that you can apply to those early movies Andy was doing without realizing what he was doing. He took a camera and he pushed a button and they [the actors] would do something. He was that impressed. He had the innocence of people when they first saw a film [back in Edison's time]. So he maintained this simple innocence when he bought the Auricon [sound camera].

'He was not doing what Jonas Mekas wanted of him. He was not taking shots of this and shots of that and pasting them together and calling it poetry or metaphor. He was going into the simplest form of narrating before narrative got there, but there was always some story – Edie would say: "I've got to get off the phone."

'This to me was a very interesting thing and this is what I basically managed during this period – to find interesting people and make that worthwhile. He had the same kind of approach as Edison. That is a good comparison.

'We'd get the film back and say, "That's really great! That girl is great!", especially if it was funny. If she was serious, Andy would say: "Well, let's not do another reel."

'And in this way Andy's most famous film was put together.'

The concept of filming 'slices of Factory life' appealed to Andy as well as Morrissey, and throughout the rest of 1966 and well into 1967, they were filming and accumulating reels of episodes that eventually would be given the title *The 24 Hour Movie* (literally) or alternately **** (also known as *Four Stars*, although Morrissey said that Andy preferred the asterisks). According to underground filmmaker Jonas Mekas, it had only one screening and that was at the New Cinema Playhouse on West 41st Street in December 1967, where all twenty-four hours were shown. In the latter part of the sixties, the film was disassembled and today it can no longer be put together.

The most ambitious section of **** is an eight-hour curiosity called *Imitation of Christ*, starring Patrick Tilden Close, a former child actor, Brigid Polk, Nico, and Taylor Mead. Mekas is certain that this part is now lost. Among the Warhol Superstars making appearances in this most ambitious film was Tiger Morse, in one of her rare film appearances. Tiger was a designer for various boutiques who created a much publicized disposable paper dress. By the end of the sixties, she had her own salon, but not for long. She was a drug addict, and her models were often so stoned they fell over while modeling her fashions. She died of an overdose in the early seventies.

Morrissey said of the film:

'It happened in '67 or '68. I think we happened to bring the cameras to San Francisco and filmed the hippies sitting around, jibbering and jabbering. So I think it has a lot of feeling of the period. But, you know, people in New York were never hippies. The film was entirely made in New York. I think the contrast between the New York neurotic and the west coast aimless, mindless, blathering hippie is an element in this twenty-four hour thing. Whatever it is, it's a very interesting document.'

In November, Andy was finishing the episode of **** that featured Tiger Morse. Albert René Ricard was appearing with her, and he was high on Obetrol at the time of shooting. Much of his 'high' came through on camera, and Andy later told him: 'Oh, you're so good tonight; let's do that movie I've wanted you to do.' A bit earlier, Andy had proposed that Ricard do a movie with him playing Andy in *The Andy Warhol Story*. Even though Ricard said that he hated Andy at that point for his 'passive exploitation', he agreed, and they adjourned to Ricard's Fifth Avenue apartment to shoot it.

They filled the apartment with orchids of the best kind, and then Andy asked Ricard whom he wanted as co-star, and he surprised Andy by telling him 'I only want Edie Sedgwick. Who else is there in your life but Edie Sedgwick?' By that time, Andy was out of touch with Edie and he told Ricard he wasn't sure they could get her.

Telephone negotiations were begun and about three hours later, Edie showed up wearing a cheap dress and a dirty blond fall. Ricard said: 'She looked like hell! . . . She, too, hated Andy at that point: she had been eighty-sixed.' Ricard attributed her mood and appearance to the pills she was taking, saying that when she was with 'the fairies', she was high on speed, but when she was with the straights, like her boyfriend Bobby, she was on downs. 'Edie on downs was not pretty.'

They began shooting with Ricard and Edie both venting their hatred of Andy through their improvized dialogue, but Ricard insisted that what he said about Andy coming from the lips of the character of Andy Warhol was all true – about how he disposed of people. Morrissey was behind the camera and he turned white with rage as Ricard proceeded to say things like ' "Gerard, get me an egg." Do you want to know how I paint my pictures, you people out there? I'd crack the egg in a glass and then I'd say to Gerard: "Cook it!" That's how I paint my pictures.'

Andy was transfixed and loving every moment of it. He asked them to do another reel. Again, shooting began and Ricard as Andy was telling Edie: 'You're not dressed up enough for this movie. So do something. Take these flowers.' She took the orchids and crushed them, wrecked them and cried out: 'I hate them! I don't want to be beautiful!' Morrissey then reached out from behind the camera and ripped Ricard's clothes off his body, a new white silk shirt and a new pair of white linen pants. It was all caught on film.

Ricard was invited to see a rough cut of the film at the Factory, and Andy got his revenge. Edie's dialogue was perfectly audible, but when Ricard as Andy spoke, absolutely nothing could be heard. The young man given the chore of handling the sound had the improbable name of Rod La Rod. Andy may have made it up, since he had an interest in the boy beyond Rodney's questionable talents as a sound man. It should be mentioned that the (sound) equipment given him was not state-of-the-art, and there was considerable criticism of the quality of the sound track in Andy's early talkies. Still, Rod claimed heavy credentials. He said that he had been road manager for the soft rock group Tommy James and the Shondells.

Rod had very light blue eyes, and was possibly Irish, although his ungentle manner was more like a German menace from a World War II film. Several inches taller than Andy, very soon after coming into the Factory, he fell into an intimacy with the artist in which intimidation was a part of the game. Sado-masochism was very much 'in' during this period. It was visible at the Factory in the studded wide leather belts worn by some of the men, the leather jackets, the boots. Andy's 'banana boots' were so uncomfortable he could barely walk in them. With Rod and Ondine, and even his dachshund on one or two occasions, Andy enjoyed going to a heavy leather bar in the far West Village (near the Hudson River in fact) called the Anvil. Its patrons were mainly truckdrivers and bikers. Of course, Andy dressed for the evening, including a leather cap.

The back room at the Anvil was its main attraction, for there sexual activity took place, usually between strangers, in semi-darkness.* Andy was stimulated just watching, but back at the Factory, half a dozen witnesses have corroborated Rodney's 'punishment' of Andy. He would shake him and slap him; throw him onto a sofa or into a chair. Andy said of these episodes: '. . . it was so outrageous that I loved it, I thought it was really exciting to have him around, lots of action.' But on at least one occasion, Ronnie Cutrone happened to come around a corner of the studio and found Andy in tears trying to ward off Rodney's slaps.

Since outsiders were frequent drop-ins, Morrissey and Fred

* The Anvil was closed by the city authorities in the mid-1980s soon after AIDS had reached epidemic proportions.

Hughes decided that Rodney had to go. By that time, Andy and the boy were practically inseparable; Rodney even had accompanied them on several tours with the Velvets and had gone to Europe with Andy. It was made clear to Andy that such behavior around outsiders was bad for business. Andy quickly got the point, and Rod La Rod was fired and never turned up again.

When Andy and Morrissey were not busy filming, much of 1966 was consumed by the tours of the Exploding Plastic Inevitable. Ronnie Cutrone's family would not allow him to travel outside the New York area, so another dancer was found to balance the extraordinary whip dance by Gerard. Andy was now more concerned with stage lighting designs, supervising the choreography, and putting pressure on Morrissey to get them more performance bookings than he was in doing art.

During one of their periods off the road and back in the Factory, Andy was interviewed by a German reporter:

> *German reporter*: 'You know this is the second evening I am here and first you weren't here and now you are here, I finally got you. Und what I felt is a feeling of composition of many things which are seemingly disconnected, yet they make a whole, and is that what you want to do right here as we just talk about the discotheque, a match between the dance floor, the music, the film, etc.?'
>
> *Andy*: 'Different people getting together.'
>
> *German reporter*: 'Und to get these people who have a fund of sensual impulses from what they are getting here.'
>
> *Andy*: 'Yeah.'
>
> *German reporter*: 'How does that fit into the other work you are doing. Because, now you are called a pop artist, which I know means very little, because what does "pop" mean after all. It's something totally new and we can put anything into it that we want. How would you yourself put it – how would you define what you are and what you want to do?'
>
> *Andy*: 'It keeps me busy.'

German reporter: 'It keeps you busy, but you are working, you are a craftsman, an artist, and you have a
studio, you are making films. Now, for instance, let's
take filmmaking. You are making so-called "underground" films, also another word. But what does it
depict, and what do you want to depict in the films
you are making?'

Andy: 'I haven't thought about it yet.'

German reporter: 'You are a difficult subject to inter-
view . . .'

TWENTY-SIX

In the autumn of 1967, a college lecture bureau approached Andy about delivering a series of lectures and film screenings at various campuses about the country. Of course, Andy was too terrified of such situations to go all by himself, given that he always took his entourage with him even for a snack at Max's Kansas City a few blocks from the Factory. But he agreed to go, and he and Paul mulled over what films they should take.

The following month, Andy was booked into the University of Utah at Provo and the University at Eugene, Oregon, and Andy kept saying over and over that he just could not do it. So Alan Midgette, a dancer who had been in half a dozen Warhol films, including *Couch*, *Nude Restaurant* and *Lonesome Cowboys*, spoke up and said, 'Well, why don't I just go as you.' Midgette was as slight as Andy and his only drawback was that he was too good-looking. But with a Warhol wig, dark glasses and a makeup on his skin to give him a pallor, he could pass. Morrissey was to go along; they would screen a film and then talk about it. 'Andy' would refer all questions to Morrissey to answer.

They got by in Utah, Oregon and then Arizona. But by the time they got to the University of Florida in Gainesville, doubts were circulating on the college grapevine. Hiram Williams, a noted painter and then a full professor in the art department, recalled:

> 'There was a reception for Warhol. He was here at the screening of a film of his and Paul Morrissey was with him. Morrissey had a great mass of hair on top of his head, and Warhol wore his silver wig. But he never said anything that I can remember, and looking back on it

I wondered if it was really Warhol. I heard he used someone else sometimes.'

Morrissey confirmed that Midgette often went to these lectures as Andy. 'I was going on lecture tours with somebody who looked like Andy, and that was twelve or fifteen engagements at least, and then that became a bit of a stink . . . . ' In actual fact, Alan Midgette's 'Andy look' vanished one day as he and Morrissey were getting off a plane and a blast of wind blew all of the silver powder out of Midgette's wig. Morrissey remembered the lecture bureau telling them:

> ' "You know, you could get in trouble doing this." And we said, "We'll give you the money back," and then they said, "Listen, you don't have to give the money back. You just go to the colleges again with the real Andy."
>
> 'But Andy was really shy. He couldn't cope with having to answer things under pressure. When he was with people who he felt weren't hostile, he was very good at being very comical . . . . You see it in these documentaries . . . . When I answered for him after he would go ommm . . . and ahhh, they liked that because they said, "Andy is very inarticulate and cryptic." Then Andy said he would go if we would take Viva along, so we went to fifteen or twenty colleges. But it was tiring, getting on a plane and going to those cocktail parties. It really was a horror. I remember that at the University of Florida, we used the imposter. I remember it very well because we got off at Miami for the interconnecting . . . and when we got into the plane it was a Piper Cub, and I thought "Jesus!" I'd never been in a Piper Cub before.'

★★★

In late November, Truman Capote gave his Black and White Ball in the Grand Ballroom of the Plaza Hotel. It was an authentic masked ball, and it was, the invitations announced, in honor of Mrs Katherine Graham. Kay Graham owned the *Washington Post*. Although he did not know it then, Capote was to alienate much of New York's upper strata with his guest list. He restricted the list to five hundred, which meant he excluded many hundreds of his friends, including some members of his own small family, an aged aunt in particular resenting it bitterly. If he disliked a husband or a wife, he eliminated both of them. Single people could not bring a guest as company, but he supplied an attractive line-up of young men, many of them known to Andy, for the single women or men, if that was their inclination. He ordered a few key friends to throw pre-ball dinners and then he drew up their guest lists himself. He excluded President Johnson, but invited his daughter, Lynda Bird. He also invited Margaret Truman Daniel and her husband. Anita Loos and a dozen other octogenarians were invited, but the aging Tallulah Bankhead was not until she pleaded with Truman and he relented.

Andy *was* invited, not only as a personal friend but because he was by that time as recognizable and famous as anyone in New York. So was Henry Geldzahler, who was still a curator at the Metropolitan Museum. Andy and Henry decided to go together, although their friendship had been ruptured earlier that year when Henry was commissioned to organize the Venice Biennale, and he invited Roy Lichtenstein to contribute work but not Andy. This was not only incomprehensible to Andy but a betrayal of a friendship that went back half a dozen years. Not only that, but Henry had been a significant mentor, giving Andy emotional and artistic support and even suggesting the *Disaster* series.

Henry had come back from a trip to Brazil and he was two days back in New York when he was asked to be the Commissioner of the Biennale which was to open six months later. Rauschenberg had won the Grand Prize at the Biennale two years previous, and Andy coveted that distinction. As Henry recalled that occasion:

> 'What I wanted to do was to finish up that crowd of great American artists in their middle careers. I chose Jules Olitski, Helen Frankenthaler, Elsworth Kelly and Roy. What those four people have in common, when you think about it, was that they were of an age and they were all [working] in color. Andy at that point was very much a black-and-white artist. Roy balanced Elsworth Kelly beautifully. The other thing was that my curatorship at the Met was coming up [for review]. My boss was retiring, Robert Beverly Hale, and the trustees

were a little bit antsy about me because of articles in *Life* magazine, and so on. And if I took Andy over in June '66, the Velvet Underground with Andy's movie crowd would cause an incredible stir and get the trustees not to appoint me.'

A few months earlier, Andy had ignored a blackboard-chalked 'message' which Henry had scrawled before leaving the Factory for the last time: 'Andy Warhol doesn't paint any more, and he hasn't learned how to make movies yet.' But being passed over in favor of Lichtenstein and his other peers (Frankenthaler was born the same year Andy was) was too much. Even though Andy wrote that 'that year our friendship had really cooled out', it had cooled to the point where when someone asked if he had heard about the Biennale selections from Henry, Andy would say 'Henry who?' He had forgotten that he had made a public announcement that he was not going to paint anymore, but just make movies.

Henry had made the conciliatory gesture of coming by the Factory to pick Andy up. They were both in tuxedos, and Henry was wearing a mask of his own face. Andy had gone to some trouble to paint a day-glo black mask on his face that could only be seen in the dark. He had gone to the Stroblite Company, which was supplying him with day-glo paints, which he used liberally both in his art and now in his work with the Velvet Underground and the new disco he had opened. Ray Andersen, the proprietor of Stroblite, equipped Andy with a portable battery-pack to operate the black light necessary for the effect.

All of the equipment proved to be cumbersome to Andy, so at the last minute he put on his usual dark glasses and perched a big cow's head on his shoulders (a black-and-white Holstein cow's head, following the invitation's instructions).

The greatest concentration of celebrities 'in the history of the world' dazzled and intimidated Andy. 'We're the only nobodies here,' he told Henry.

TWENTY-SEVEN

Edie made a movie for another filmmaker, Robert Margouleff, in 1967, called *Ciao! Manhattan*. Its premise was to show a day in Edie's life as the girl of the year in Manhattan, but by the time this $350,000 film portrait was made, she was the girl of *last* year. Chuck Wein had exited with Edie, and he wrote the script for the movie. Allen Ginsberg and other counter-culture heroes were featured in it, and much of it was filmed in Fort Lee, New Jersey, where American filmmaking began. But for Edie, except for a brief interlude back with Andy and a sequence used in a future opera, this was where her filmmaking ended. Near the end of the shooting, she looked as marvelous as ever, but she was so disoriented by the variety of drugs she was taking, they had to shoot every scene so many times they lost count. One of those involved in its production, Bobby Andersen, recalled:

> 'She just had no concept of what she was doing. She held it up for hours and hours. She had to do her exercises, she had to do this, she had to do that. I just loved every minute, egging her on: "Don't pay any attention to them. You're having a good time, Edith. That's all that matters. It's about time you had a good time" – as if she'd never had one before! We danced most of the day and we disappeared in the castle attics for hours. With a photographer . . . .'

She somehow knew that she was not at her best, and it became an *idée fixe* that she was only good around Warhol. She phoned him and she went to see him. Andy, remarkably enough, showed some compassion for her and they talked for a long time. At her behest, he even shot a short film with her and Ondine. Ondine did not think

> 'it will ever be seen; it's in Warhol's closet. I was the one who asked her to do it, because I had the feeling that if Edie was going to make it, she really should make it with Warhol. But I didn't realize there was so much pressure and that so much had gone on between her and Warhol that it was no longer viable. Once Andy makes up his mind against you, you don't return in a Warhol film. But in this case he tried.'

Gregory Corso cornered Andy at Max's Kansas City and tore into him for making Edie into a Superstar and then dropping her. 'You pick these little birds out and . . . look what happened to Edie!' Allen Ginsberg tried to shut him up, saying: 'Gregory, you're laying too much weight on this man. It's really not his fault.'

After that aborted movie, Edie took off for California with a rock promoter. She spent a few nights in the Castle in Laurel Canyon, a run-down mansion that was now taken over by druggies. She kept looking for 'junk' (drugs) and she even went through a friend's room who had hid some and she found it, without making any mess. She had a nose for drugs like a police dog trained for the job.

The incredible thing was that people around her did not give up on her. In August 1967, she was asked to film some sequences as Lulu, for use in Alban Berg's opera of the same name (the story had been filmed with Louise Brooks years earlier). It was being done in Boston, and when she was flown in at the Boston Opera Company's expense, she was on a drug that gave her convulsions whenever she stopped using it, so everyone ran around town seeking supplies of it to get her through the shooting. The Boston audience was a little puzzled about the grisly business on the screens behind the opera action – Lulu is finally caught up with by the dreaded Jack the Ripper, who kills her and cuts her up into little pieces. On the screen, the audience saw Edie's distorted head wearing a red wig with a huge pool of blood spreading around it.

Her father, Fuzzy, turned against her, and would not come to the phone when she called home. She then went back to New York, but there was no going back to Andy. To him, she was a lost cause and, to be absolutely fair, he had gone farther out of his way to help her than any other known instance. Perhaps he toured with the Velvets, spent time at the disco, and began making movies away from his own studio to avoid her phone-calls. She finally stopped calling.

Rejected by her two fathers, Andy and Fuzzy, she retreated to her childhood and kept showing friends photos of those years and talking of the good times at the ranch in California. Then Fuzzy died, and her friends thought that this was an emotional weight off her that could only do her good. But she was barely pinned-together and she kept going in and out of hospitals for drug withdrawal and nervous disorders. She lived for a while with L. M. Kit Carson, a young filmmaker, at the Warwick Hotel.

After trying to get her off the drugs cold-turkey – she was crawling the walls – Kit saw it was hopeless and phoned her doctor. The doctor told him to clear out, but he did not want to leave her alone. He phoned Andy, who would not come, but who suggested Ondine. Ondine got on the phone with her and they began screaming at each other. Carson seemed a bit reassured. He said: 'She was finally being handled by somebody who knew exactly what she was up to.'

But Ondine did not go to the Warwick, perhaps on Andy's advice. He and Andy were working on a novel based on a day in Ondine's life, which was not a work of fiction at all but a series of taped recordings of a day in Ondine's life around Andy, Rotten Rita, the Turtle, the Duchess, and even Edie, who alone among the characters is given a fictional name – Taxine. All of this happened the first week of May. She was admitted to Bellevue and then quietly transferred by her family to Gracie Square Hospital. The gods were displeased that spring of 1968. Andy himself would be at death's door, gunned down by Valerie Solanis, exactly a month later.

The *New York Post* picked up on Edie's story and phoned Andy to see what he knew, and he went into one of his defensive and incredible positions of never having known her very well. That was the last word anyone got out of Andy about Edie until he wrote his book *Popism*, where he sensibly gave her more space than anyone except Paul Morrissey and Gerard Malanga.

During Henry Geldzahler's years at the Metropolitan Museum and since he had left them, he had been going to California once or twice a year to see what the artists were doing out there. 'Santa Barbara was a very natural place to go and visit,' he said. 'I went there to visit the museum, but the primary reason was to visit her.' Edie was then hospitalized at the Cottage Hospital in Santa Barbara. Henry took her out to lunch at a restaurant with an open patio, and described her as being 'heavy. She had a roundish face, poor thing. She looked like somebody who had been taking super tranquillizers. She was chatty, not depressed, but a little out of touch. One memorable thing was her wanting to stop by a photographer's.' She married another patient at Cottage Hospital. His name was Michael Post and he was trying to quit drugs. The wedding was held at the Sedgwick ranch, then they went back to their own apartment in Santa Barbara.

On the last day of her life, Edie attended a TV crew shooting at a fashion show in Santa Barbara. It was for an episode of the Public Television serial *An American Family*, on the Louds of Santa Barbara. She had befriended Lance Loud, the adolescent son in the family. Lance was gay, but she did not know that. She seemed to have turned her back deliberately on that world. She died of a sleeping pill overdose on 16 November 1971.

Brigid broke the news to Andy by phone. She thought that Edie had suffocated during her sleep, and Andy could not understand that. But he did remember Edie's origins and he wanted to know if her young husband would inherit the money. Brigid told him that Edie had no money, and then Andy changed the subject.

Edie had died among a commune of bikers, where she had lived with her husband. They were among the hold-outs after nearly half a decade of the hippie era.

The hippies and flower children were mostly gone from California by 1971, and the Diggers' Free Store in Haight-Ashbury was closed. The Haight, that center of hippiedom, had become an ordinary ghetto again, and as much as anything else, its collapse as a haven for runaway youth marked the end of an extraordinary decade.

Their influence, for most people, had been a positive one. They helped put the war in perspective and thus prepared America for a 'retreat with honor' from an impossible political and military

situation. Their music may have been a reflection of untold
numbers of acid trips, but it survived to mark a time of liberated morality, with such rock groups as the Grateful Dead,
Big Brother and the Holding Company, Jefferson Airplane (with
Grace Slick), the Cleveland Wrecking Company. First there were
'the gathering of the tribes' and Human Be-Ins in Golden Gate
Park and Central Park, leading to the climactic Woodstock Festival.

Andy followed all of this with fascination, and surely he felt at
least partially a caring older person in shepherding his little flock
of society dropouts at the Factory (although he only acknowledged that he was older to his Diary, begun in 1976). In Ondine,
who seemed to have dropped out almost totally (except for rare
recuperative visits back home to Queens), he could watch one
of these rebels as under a microscope. Ondine more charitably
chose not to see that while he was struggling to survive and
support his drug habit, Andy was slowly accumulating something
more than a nest egg. Better not to look too closely at Andy,
who poor-mouthed himself through much of his heyday of the
Factory.

Ondine was not a hippie. The difference, of course, between
Ondine and the Haight-Ashbury druggies was that he was a bit
older, so he bridged the time-gap between Andy and the hippies;
and he was gay, so that brought the whole scene home for Andy.
Gays would not rebel until 1969 at the Stonewall Inn in the
Village, a time when Andy would be 'in hibernation' (Gerard's
phrase), recovering from his wounds and moving in an entirely
different world.

Hippies aside, Andy was tapped into a much older tradition of
the Outsider, going back to Cocteau and Wilde. He rarely went
to 'drag' bars or hang-outs of transvestites, but he enjoyed having
them come around to the Factory. There were three who would
be filmed by him – Candy Darling, who, Andy insisted, looked
more like a girl than any girl, Holly Woodlawn, who would be
the most successful in films and far from beautiful, and Jackie
Curtis, who appeared briefly with the other two in *Flesh* (1968).

Ondine had met Jackie Curtis early in the sixties. He described
their meeting:

'I had a pair of shoes that really were hurting me because

they were too small. And I saw this rather good-looking young man cruising me from shop windows and he made it quite obvious that he was cruising so I went along with him and he said, "You're Ondine, right? I just saw *The Chelsea Girls*. Why don't you come up to my grandmother's place. She lives right on this street." His grandmother owned a bar called Slugger Ann's on Second Avenue. So I went up to this apartment and we had sex. Then I told him that I had to get a pack of cigarettes and asked could I please wear his shoes. Of course, I had no intention of returning. I just wanted to steal his shoes. As I was going out, his head popped over the banister, and he said, "Come back now, you know it's the second bell." And I said, "Yeah, I'll be back," and I fled. They were a nice white pair of loafers. They fit perfectly.

'And the next time I saw him was in 1968, and he was in drag and I didn't recognize him. We were doing something for Warhol. I don't know what it was [it was *Flesh*] and he took me aside, and he said, "Do you remember me?" and I said, "No, I'm sorry, I don't." He said, "The pair of white loafers?" I was really horrified.'

Jackie Curtis had 'gone all the way' by this time and was living full-time in drag. He moved into the Hotel Albert in the Village with Candy Darling, who had been living as a woman for more than a year. He told Andy that it was easier 'to be a weird girl than a weird guy'.

Andy was much taken with Candy Darling. Candy was a drag queen he was 'proud' to be around and there are numerous pictures of them together. They met in the summer of 1967, and did all he could to promote his/her career. He even got Candy a spread in *After Dark*, a monthly show business magazine. In the early seventies, Tennessee Williams would cast Candy in a small role as a woman in his off-Broadway play *Small Craft Warnings*. While Candy's lasting regret was that Fox studios did not cast her/him as Myra Breckenridge in their film version of Gore Vidal's fictional satire (they cast Raquel Welch as Myra; and Rex Reed as Myron), he/she had much the biggest success of any drag queen in New York, largely thanks to Andy. Candy died of cancer in 1973, said to have been brought on by hormone injections, and was buried in drag, following instructions left behind to the family.

1967 was a year of the most intense, almost feverish activity for Andy. He had stopped painting and was filming constantly. With the dropping of Edie, he was acquiring a whole new set of friends and Factory people. Ondine was drifting away from him, very sensitive to changes in the wind. Gerard had acquired a wealthy and beautiful girlfriend, Benedetta Barzini, the daughter of Luigi Barzini (author of *The Italians*). She was traveling with him as *The Exploding Plastic Inevitable* toured. Gerard seemed far more interested in dancing than he had ever been in helping Andy with his art. He had become extremely protective of his dancing role as they toured and he had already dispatched one strong letter of complaint to Andy when he believed that he had been upstaged. In Boston, during his finale, as he later wrote in *The Secret Diaries of Gerard Malanga*:

> 'I interpret an entire crucifixion scene with Rona (Page, who had been the actress in the scene with Pope Ondine in *The Chelsea Girls*) standing behind me, arms outstretched with two flashlights in each hand, aiming their beams through my outstretched arms, at the audience.'

Gerard also assumed a crucifixion pose in the film *Vinyl*, which was often shown at these performances.

When *The Chelsea Girls* was premiered in San Francisco in late August, 1967, Andy decided not to take Gerard. It might have been Benedetta's presence that nettled him. As a consequence, Gerard and Benedetta flew to Italy where Gerard had an invitation from the Bergamo International Film Festival to show his film, *In Search of the Miraculous*, which was about three generations in the Barzini family. Andy was upset by his departure and, as Gerard prepared to go to the airport, told him to forget what he had said about not going to San Francisco. But offense had already been taken and Gerard told him that it was too late. He left with a one way ticket, which was all he could afford. Andy told him that he would gladly send him his return fare, if he would just call him, but Gerard remained away for nearly a year, and he was replaced at the Factory. He was never to regain his former status there. By the end of that year, the only survivors from the old group were Paul Morrissey, Brigid, and latterly, Fred Hughes.

Fred was a Texan, whose father was a furniture sales representative in Houston when he was growing up. There, Fred had met the de Menil family, millionaire Texans who were beginning to be known in art circles for their American modern collection. In 1967, he was in New York for the de Menil Foundation working on a variety of projects, including a Merce Cunningham Dance Company benefit, where he met Andy. Fred had also worked for the Iolas Gallery in Paris and maintained a small apartment there.

Fred wore his hair long then and often was seen wearing a Marine Corp jacket, according to Jim Rosenquist. He was then in his early twenties but had not fallen into the grave maturity that would mark his managerial years with Andy. In the wee hours, he was occasionally seen spouting absurd verse from public fountains and even dropping his trousers and mooning the other party stragglers.

This year, too, marked Viva's advent on the scene. Viva, originally Susan Hoffman, lived at the Chelsea Hotel. When Andy saw her at designer Betsey Johnson's party, Viva asked him if she could be in his next movie. Within a week or so, he phoned to tell her that she could come around the next day and do a movie, but that she would have to show her breasts. When she arrived, she had small band-aids pasted over her nipples, and Andy was very amused by that.

The movie was *Bike Boy*, Andy's motorcycle epic. It was not much of a film, although Brigid was in it and looked almost beautiful in color. If we are to believe Viva's autobiographical novel, *Superstar*, Andy gave her the name Viva because Susan Hoffman sounded too Jewish. (In the novel she was Janet Lee Schumann.) Minor though the film was, Viva created some excitement. She was called Warhol's Garbo because of her gaunt face and the haunted look in her eyes.

Before the movie opened at the Hudson, Andy got another movie, which was shot just prior to *Bike Boy*, ready for a brief run. While Viva was waiting for her movie debut, Andy phoned her frequently and they began a strange but very close friendship. She complained about Andy to her friends, and he was very put off by her complaints about her life in general when they were together. It was a wry joke to Andy – his 'Garbo' never shut up, but the genuine Garbo reputedly never said anything.

The earlier movie came and went very quickly. It was originally Nico's idea. She wanted to make a film with Jim Morrison, lead singer with the Doors. Morrison had an austere, untouchable kind of beauty, the look of a marble angel guarding a tomb. The movie was called *I, a Man* and was intended as a parody of *I, a Woman*. Nico had fallen in love with Morrison, and he had agreed to do the film. But when Andy was ready to shoot, Nico turned up with another man, a Hollywood actor named Tom Baker, and he played the lead.

I, a Man was one of the least of Andy's efforts when it was made, but less than a year later it became notorious as the movie Andy made with Valerie Solanis, who was on the screen for less than five minutes (out of a hundred) and who, it must be said, was extremely good in her part. It also featured Ultra Violet, Ivy Nicholson and Ingrid Superstar.

Ondine had moved in with a lover, and was not around very much. In fact, the last movie he made for Andy was *The Loves of Ondine*, which was shot in October, and was in a way Andy's bid to keep Ondine in the fold. Of course, Ondine's loves were all male and there were numerous 'tricks' brought in and filmed who were never seen again. But one young Italian, whom Morrissey found, was so handsome and Adonis-like he became the most successful of the Warhol Superstars and was the most consistently employed of any, although he never became a gossip column darling as Viva and Ultra Violet did. His name was Joe Dallesandro, and he would be for Paul Morrissey what Dietrich was for Josef von Sternberg. The movie opened and closed very quickly at the theater in midtown that Andy was leasing, the Hudson.

But Viva was being groomed by Andy for 'bigger things'. He was to make only four more movies on his own before turning the filmmaking over to Paul Morrissey, and Viva was in all of them. There was *Bike Boy*, *Nude Restaurant*, *Lonesome Cowboys*, and *Blue Movie* (also known as *Fuck*). There is some dispute as to who really filmed *Blue Movie*, and Viva wrote after Andy's death that it was

'. . . entirely my idea, and enthusiastically seconded by

Andy; [it] was the occasion of so much embarrassment
to Paul Morrissey that he could not stay on the set and
watch the filming. In his book *Stargazer*, Stephen Koch
places *Blue Movie* under the heading *The Films of Paul
Morrissey*. From its inception, a year before Andy was
shot, to its actual filming in August of '68, Paul had no
say in the filming, never went near the cinema, did not
direct in any way.'

Since Andy was shot on 3 June, and the film began shooting in
August, it seems unlikely that he was physically able to film
Blue Movie unaided. Viva says it was made six months after the
shooting, but in fact it was less than three months afterward.

Nevertheless, with Viva the slate was wiped clean. She was
brighter than Edie. She saw beyond her own needs and hang-ups
to get at least a small purchase on what was happening to others.
She was almost but not quite anorexically thin, and the camera
loved her as much as it did Edie. In that winter of 1967–8, Viva
suddenly became very famous.

Viva had an enormous respect for Warhol, and as he saw her
aura growing, as it fed upon his own fame and her distinctive
appearance, that respect was returned. She evoked the Hollywood
of Dietrich and Garbo as well as the wiry sixties look. With
her first film, she moved into the number-one spot as Andy's
Superstar of the day. Following Warhol's death, she recalled what
it was like that first day:

'My role in *Bike Boy* was to seduce Joe Spencer. I was
given exactly three directions. The first was to change
my position, moving to Joe's other side, the second was
to remove my clothes, the third was to repeat a laugh
I'd just uttered. I repeated the laugh, the camera began
grinding again, and all of a sudden there wasn't any
more film. The scene was finished, as it always was
when the newsreel camera ran out of its 35-minute load
of film. It wasn't until five years later, upon seeing
the movie for perhaps the fifth time, that I realized
why Andy had asked me to repeat that laugh: Joe's
slack penis, prominent in the foreground but previously
unnoticed by me . . . .'

She described the Warhol-Morrissey scripts as being

> 'the common body of experience vibrating in the space
> between the actors. The success of the films was depend-
> ent on our ability to summon our lives' experiences to
> the front of our brains, the tips of our tongues, so tangi-
> ble as to be almost visible out in front of our craniums.
> The dialogue was already there, we had only to read it,
> basing our technique on an intuitive knowledge of what
> was vibrating in that space.'

Viva effortlessly stepped into Edie's shoes in Andy's social life,
but it was a far steadier companionship since, like Morrissey,
she was not on anything, nothing that was incapacitating. She
had a string of male admirers, but she did not allow them to
come between her and Warhol. If Andy needed her, she was
there.

She always had a problem managing her finances, but Andy
made certain that she always looked good when it counted. There
was a general consensus that the Warhol entourage was fairly
seedy, but for a time Viva helped to change that impression.

Diana Vreeland, who had been Andy's good friend from the
early fifties, and was then, in 1967, editing *Vogue*, thought that
Viva was one of the most exciting presences she had encountered in years. She planned an entire issue of new fashions for
her magazine featuring Viva with Richard Avedon handling the
photography.

Others were equally enthusiastic. At least on the surface, Viva
seemed quite unlike the other Warhol 'Superstars'. She seemed
to be in control of her own destiny. The television talk shows
wanted her – Merv Griffin, the *Tonight Show* – and the only
problem was that, quite unlike Andy's inarticulateness, it was
hard to shut her up once she got on camera.

Despite her obvious respect for him, Viva was not uncritical
of Andy. She told Barbara Goldsmith for an article in *New York*
magazine that 'He just gets you and you can't get away. Now I
can't make the simplest decision or go anywhere without asking
Andy.' What she probably meant was that she was on the phone
with Andy nearly every day when she was not accompanying him
to some function. And since Andy often invited her to go with

him and his entourage to some distant place for an art opening or whatever, she did have to check with him when she wanted to go some place on her own to make sure it did not conflict with his plans.

Diane Arbus was assigned to take the photographs of Viva to accompany the Goldsmith article, and Arbus, who liked to familiarize herself with all her subjects before photographing them, accompanied Viva to a number of her evening engagements, including a visit to the back room at Max's Kansas City where Arbus said that Viva sniffed methadrine (speed) from a spoon because she told them she was suffering menstrual cramps. On another evening, Arbus went with her to an actor's apartment where, in Viva's words, 'we all got stoned on hash, Diane, too, and we were all very comfortable and friendly together.' Later that evening, Arbus took some photographs of Viva having sex with the actor and his wife (the latter, unfortunately, was murdered in the apartment several months later by an intruder).

When Arbus returned the next morning to Viva's upper East Side apartment (she lived in the Chelsea Hotel irregularly until 1968, when she began living there most of the time), she planned to finish the last session of photos. Viva's recollection of that occasion is one of the few critical reactions to Diane Arbus, who was a disturbed but brilliant artist in her field, known for her photographs of twins, freaks and the desolate:

> 'Diane rang the doorbell. I'd been asleep on the couch. I was naked, so I wrapped a sheet around me and let Diane in and then I started putting mascara on. I was about to get into some clothes when Diane told me, "Don't bother – you seem more relaxed that way – anyway I'm just going to do a head shot." Asshole that I was, I believed her. She had me lie on the couch naked and roll my eyes up to the ceiling, which I did. Those photographs were totally faked. I looked stoned, but I *wasn't* stoned, I was cold sober. They were planned and manipulated. Diane Arbus lied, cheated, and victimized me. She *said* she was just going to take head shots. I trusted her because she acted like a martyr, a little saint, about the whole thing. Jesus! Underneath she was just as ambitious as we all were to make it – to get ahead.'

Viva phoned Richard Avedon and told him about the Arbus
pictures and he groaned and said 'Oh, my God, no! You shouldn't
have let her.' Andy was equally critical, although he had begun
to take an interest in Arbus's photographs and had gone to the
opening of her show at the Museum of Modern Art.

The photographs appeared and Arbus' biographer, Patricia
Bosworth, called them

> 'absolutely merciless . . . . In a jarring, grainy close-up
> Viva appeared dazed and drugged, eyes rolled back in
> her sockets. There is no suggestion here that life is
> still paradoxical and complicated; it is merely brutal
> . . . . In the other portrait Viva can be seen naked and
> roaring with laughter on a sheet-draped couch. There is
> a raunchy casualness about the pose; she appears pleased
> with herself right down to the soles of her dirty feet.'

When Diana Vreeland saw the pictures, allegedly she screamed
and canceled the rest of Viva's bookings for *Vogue*. There was
talk of advertisers pulling out of *New York* magazine because of
the notoriety that followed publication. Viva even threatened to
sue Arbus, but it was not pursued. A friend of Arbus', Tom
Morgan, said the pictures were of watershed importance. 'They
broke down barriers between public and private lives. They
were painful photographs – that's what made them significant.
You're repelled by Viva's campy self-image, but you're drawn to
it, too.'

The episode did not permanently damage Viva's reputation. It
might even have enhanced it. She left the Warhol film factory
soon after Andy's convalescence in late 1968, and spent the next
half-dozen years appearing in films for others (in 1971, she starred
in *Lion's Love* for the feminist filmmaker Agnes Varda). In 1970,
her autobiographical novel *Superstar* was published in New York,
and garnered mostly favorable reviews, Gore Vidal comparing it
favorably with Mary McCarthy's *Memories of a Catholic Girlhood*.
She was encouraged to continue writing, but her second novel,
Baby, was not a success. By then she had married the filmmaker
Michel Auder and had a baby daughter. They made their home
at the Chelsea Hotel and she took up painting when she had the
time – she was very involved with raising her child and shortly

had a second girl. While her marriage eventually fell apart, her life did not. She raised her girls herself and survived the Warhol years well.

Fred Hughes was the other 'new breeze' that would help sustain and augment Andy's growing reputation as the most popular artist of his time. Fred once said that he started out at the Factory with a broom in his hand, but this is probably a fanciful recollection borrowed from Bob Rauschenberg's experience with Eleanor Ward. Andy began to see that he could put the art business safely into Fred's hands, and the movie business just as safely into Morrissey's hands. The triumvirate was born and the Warhol empire began to grow.

They brought in a succession of secretaries and clerical assistants. Pat Hackett, who was to become Andy's Boswell and work with him on all the autobiographical works, was fairly typical. She came down to the Factory as an undergraduate at Barnard College 'to see if Andy Warhol needed a part-time typist . . . to inject some glamour into my college years . . . he suggested I work for him just whenever I could.' He never paid any of this help much, and even expected some of them to volunteer, as though helping an artist with such matters was charitable work. In 1958, besides Pat, there was Susan Pile, who was more or less full-time, with Brigid pitching in wherever she was needed. Brigid's past as 'the Duchess' became a myth that was hard to pin down. Some of those 'kids' who worked around her at the Factory knew nothing of that former life of hers, and when they would read about the Duchess in *Popism*, they would ask 'Who is she?'

Taylor Mead had come back from Europe after fleeing the Warhol film scene because he thought there was 'too much irresponsibility and incompetence'. Seeing *The Chelsea Girls* in a Paris theater, where the audience walked out in droves, had convinced him that Andy was a gifted filmmaker and that America, particularly Andy's America, was the place to be.

For the first time since the Factory concept was set in motion, Andy seemed to have pulled it all together. The craziness of the sixties seemed safely at an end. But then it was all shattered when one afternoon, a man burst into the Factory with a gun. Andy was to write:

'. . . The guy made us all sit together on a couch:
me, Taylor, Paul, Gerard, Patrick [Tilden Close, a former child actor then appearing in Warhol's *Imitation
of Christ*], Fred, Billy, Nico, Susan . . . . He started
screaming that some guy who owed him five hundred
dollars had told him to come to the Factory to collect
it from us. Then he pointed the gun at Paul's head and
pulled the trigger – and nothing happened . . . . Then
he pointed it to the ceiling and pulled it again, and this
time it went off. The shot seemed to surprise him, too
– he got all confused and handed the gun to Patrick
– and Patrick, like a good non-violent child, said, "I
don't want it, man," and handed it back to him. Then
the guy took a woman's plastic rain bonnet out of his
pocket and put it on my head . . . . Everybody just
sat there, too scared to say anything, except for Paul,
who told the guy that the police would be coming
any second because of the shot. But the guy said he
had to get his five hundred before he would leave –
and now he was demanding movie equipment and a
"hostage", too.'

At that point, Taylor, whose build was as slight as Andy's, leaped
onto the man's back, and the intruder opened up a folding knife.
Then Taylor leaped down and grabbing the rain-hat from Andy's
head, raced to the window, covered his fist with the hat and broke
the glass, screaming out 'Help! Help! Police!'
    The man panicked at that, ran down the stairs and jumped into
a waiting car.

Viva had a rival in Ultra Violet, who probably did meet Andy
earlier (in 1963 when Ultra was with Dali), but the record should
be set straight about Ultra's role as a Warhol Superstar. In Jonas
Mekas' filmography of Andy's work, Ultra only appears in the
cast of two films. Doubtless she made others that have not
survived or are moldering in film cans somewhere in storage.
What she did do incontrovertibly was attach herself to the Warhol
entourage. She went with Andy and the others to Los Angeles
early in 1967 to attend the opening of *The Chelsea Girls* there.

There are no photographs I have ever seen of Ultra with Andy taken prior to 1966.

In her memoir, *Famous for 15 Minutes*, written after Andy's death, she placed herself in the midst of his entire career and even claimed that it was she who suggested that he paint Campbell Soup cans. This is, of course, nonsense, as is her 'warning' to Andy on the day he was shot. The pity is that she did not reveal much of her interesting personal life in that memoir because her past was far more colorful than that of any other actress to get close to Andy. She had long affairs with artists John Graham, Dali, John Chamberlain, and Edward Ruscha. She had sexual alliances with millionaires who supplied her with a penthouse and limousines. But she barely mentioned these matters since, in the wake of Andy's death, she wanted to be the first to exploit the Warhol legend.

This came as no surprise to the Factory staff. Even Andy recalled that 'Ultra would do almost anything for publicity. She'd go on talk shows "representing the underground", and it was hilarious because she was as big a mystery to us as she was to everybody else.' She was mistress to some of the most important artists of our time, and it is to be hoped that if she ever writes another memoir, she will abandon her theories and embroideries of Factory shenanigans and concentrate on her own life, which would make an infinitely more fascinating book.

TWENTY-EIGHT

*L*onesome Cowboys was the first Warhol movie I ever saw. It was playing on a double bill with *Vinyl* at the Hudson Theater in Manhattan, and it topped the bill. As with nearly all 16 mm films projected in a large auditorium, there was a certain graininess to the image but that did not work against a general mood of befogged brains in shiftless cowboys, whose chief pursuit in life seems to be playing puerile sexual games with each other. A woman, Viva, is an intruder, so they move away from her. The parody of macho males begins early. Like most macho types whom they are counterfeiting, they are obsessed with their own cocks and what they can do with them – but only with each other. After the early encounter with Viva, who is cast here as a taunting provocateur whose male 'nurse' (played by Taylor Mead) is enraptured by the good-looking cowboys. Once they are out of town and into open country, the cowboys throw off their clothes and roll around with each other, stroking thighs and mildly petting, getting off on fleshly contact with each other.

Now there is a myth broadly circulated in gay circles but never voiced in western genre (fiction or film) that most cowboys are gay. It is this myth that Warhol has seized upon as the theme of *Lonesome Cowboys*. Whether it has any basis in truth or not is beside the point (if I were to accept the Marlboro man as typical of the cowboy, I certainly would believe it). These men play with the kind of innocent vacuity as those cherubs played in the caricature drawings Andy did back in the early fifties. He continues the cowboy as gay myth with the dialogue.

Then the cowboys begin drinking beer as they frolic and splash one another with it. We note that beer drips from their cocks, probably a fairly corny metaphor for semen. When Viva and her male nurse again intrude upon their pleasures, they are clothed again so, naturally, having made it very clear that they abhor any intimate contact with a woman, they 'rape' her, a peculiar rape indeed since no cowboy unzips his pants – not for a woman, even in violence.

In essence, that is the film. It is an old gay myth made visible and there is no point made beyond that. If there is any incongruity in the film, it is only the presence of Joe Dallesandro as one of the handsome cowboys. Except for hustling, he will not offer his body to any man again in a Warhol film.

The movie was shot in Arizona in January 1968. Most of the actors flew out, but Eric Emerson drove out with a new Warhol groupie named Vera Cruise, a small Puerto Rican girl from Brooklyn. Vera, Eric and John Chamberlain, the pop sculptor, who had joined Eric in getting a free ride out west, greeted them at the airport. Vera was driving an old bus that seated eighteen. They all got into it and she cut off the paved road into the desert, taking a short cut. Suddenly there was a great thud as something crashed into the windshield. It turned out to be an American bald eagle, the national symbol and protected by stringent laws. Vera took the dead bird into a taxidermist, who called the police. Vera was arrested and detained until she had established that the bird had been killed accidentally.

Rancho Linda Vista in the western town of Oracle had been the location previously for numerous traditional cowboy films. When the local citizens began to converge on the location 'movie shooting' going on, dialogue filled with 'cocksucker', 'fags', and 'motherfucker' soon had dumb-struck mothers herding their children away. Those locals, who were working as usual at their temporary movie jobs as electricians and grips, gradually became aware that this was no ordinary cowboy film. One of them called the Warhol group 'perverted easterners' and told them 'go back the hell where you came from.' Viva told the man to fuck off. A sheriff flew in by helicopter and then stood on top of a water tank and followed every move they made with binoculars. He had been alerted to the fact that men were getting naked in the sage and touching each other in front of the camera. Andy wrapped up the location shooting ahead of schedule and they left prematurely.

Someone, possibly that sheriff on the water tank, called in the FBI, alerting the Phoenix Field Office to the fact that these were

New Yorkers who were taking 'obscene' film out of the state and back to New York, which would have been a felony. An FBI investigation was launched into the filming on 1 February. Agents reviewed the guest registration cards at the Rancho Linda Vista; they showed photographs taken by Arizona newspaper photographers to 'witnesses' – the locals who had seen the Warhol company shooting the film; they showed them a photo of Viva and Andy that had appeared in the *Arizona Republic* in November, and identification was made. The FBI report further quoted Andy as saying in November that he liked the desert and was thinking about filming a movie there called 'The Unwanted Cowboy'. Viva told the reporter that she planned to ride bareback in the film. She did not say whether she or the horse would be bare. By late March, the investigation was still continuing out of the Phoenix office and the charge was 'Interstate Transportation of Obscene Matter'. They were looking into airplane departures and reservations for the night of 30 January, when Andy prematurely pulled his people out of the hostile town and flew back to New York with the film.

American Airlines appeared to be protective of their passengers' identities and as of September, the FBI still did not know who was on Flight 90 out of Phoenix for New York, nor did the agents have any luck extracting a print from Andy's Factory in New York. An FBI report of 3 September stated 'Editing of the film "Lonesome Cowboys" has not been completed by Andy Warhol Films, Inc.' Obviously, no violation of the law could be prosecuted when the government did not yet know what would be shown on the screen in the final print.

When Andy was shot in June, the FBI fed all of the news articles on the shooting into his FBI 'Lonesome Cowboys' file. It is doubtful that they would have pursued this matter with any vigor if Andy had died. He seemed to be the target more than the film. The government had looked on as traditional values and attitudes had been assailed throughout the sixties and only rarely could it get a grip on some offender. Now they believed they could nail one of the most famous.

An FBI report dated 16 January 1969 is fascinating:

'. . . The film, "Lonesome Cowboy" [sic] was shown 11/1/68 at San Francisco, California International Film

Festival. The film showed a male and female actor in the nude. The men sexually assaulted the female in the nude. Various sexual acts and implied sexual acts in the nude were shown. Obscene words, phrases and gestures, were used throughout the film. The female actress, VIVA, said "Now look – you have embarrassed those children." There were no children in the movie.'

Here, the agents overlooked the possibility that 'female actress' Viva was talking about the children who were watching the shooting of the film.

After the film's shooting in San Francisco, an agent was asked to 'review' the film and the proceedings that night at the Masonic Auditorium where the Film Festival was taking place. What is marvelous about his lengthy report is that it shows perfectly the government's Victorian sexual attitudes and what disturbs them. The agent prefaces his synopsis of the movie's action by noting the presence in the auditorium of some of the actors in the film. Taylor Mead was introduced, and the agent said that he 'spoke to the audience for a few minutes in a senseless monologue and said something about not knowing whether to put the beginning of the movie at the end or vice versa.'

'. . . The characters in the film were a woman, played by VIVA; her male nurse, played by TAYLOR MEAD, a sheriff who resided in a small Arizona town – population, three, and a group of about five cowboys with an additional new member called "Boy Julian". All of the males in the cast displayed homosexual tendencies and conducted themselves toward one another in an effeminate manner. Many of the cast portrayed their parts as if in a stupor from marijuana, drugs or alcohol.

'It appeared that there was no script for the film but rather the actors were given a basic idea for a plot and then instructed to act and speak as they felt.

'The movie opened with the woman and her male nurse on a street in the town. Five or six cowboys then entered the town and there was evidence of hostility between the two groups. One of the cowboys practised his ballet and a conversation ensued regarding the misuse of mascara by one of the other cowboys. At times it was difficult to understand the words being spoken, due to the poor audio of the film and the pronunciation by the actors. The film also skips from scene to scene without continuity.

'As the movie progressed, one of the actors ran down a hill. The next scene showed a man wearing only an unbuttoned silk cowboy shirt getting up from the ground. His privates are exposed and another cowboy was lying on the ground in a position with his head facing the genitals of the cowboy who had just stood up. A jealous argument ensued between the cowboy who was observed running down the hill and the one wearing the silk shirt. The man in the silk shirt was then seen urinating; however, his privates were not exposed due to the camera angle.

'Later in the movie the cowboys went out to the ranch owned by the woman. On their arrival, they took her from her horse, removed her clothes and sexually assaulted her. During this time her sexual parts were exposed to the audience. She was on her back with her clothes removed and an actor was on his knees near her shoulders with his face in the vicinity of her genitals, but a second actor with his back to the camera blocked the view. The position of the male and female suggested an act of cunnilingus; however, the act was not portrayed in full view of the camera . . . .

'There were other parts in the film in which the private parts of the woman were visible on the screen and there were also scenes in which men were revealed in total nudity. The sheriff in one scene was shown dressing in women's clothing and later being held on the lap of another cowboy. Also, the male nurse was pictured in the arms of the sheriff. In one scene where VIVA was attempting to persuade one of the cowboys to take off his clothes and join her in her nudity, the discussion was centered around the Catholic Church's liturgical songs. She finally persuaded him to remove all of his clothes and he then fondled her breasts and rolled on top of her naked body. There were movements and gyrations, however, at no time did the camera show penetration or a position for insertion.

'Another scene depicted a cowboy fondling the nipples of another cowboy.

'There were suggestive dances done by the male actors with each other. These dances were conducted while they were clothed and suggested love-making between two males.

'. . . Obscene words, phrases and gestures were used throughout the film.'

What the reader will observe at once is that the focus of interest on the part of this FBI agent is far more prurient than anything that has been touched upon in this volume up to now. If the angle is 'juicier' here, this is the government agent's preoccupation.

By the end of 1969, Federal attorneys in New York, Phoenix and Atlanta had declined to prosecute Andy Warhol's Film Company in the matter of *Lonesome Cowboys*. Officials in Atlanta seemed particularly keen to prosecute and must have been disappointed. Earlier, they had seized the print of the film during its local run, and now the Atlanta police were advised by the US government to return it to the plaintiff, Sherpix and Craddock Films, Atlanta-based companies authorized by Andy Warhol Films to show the film in Georgia. The reason given by Judge Albert J. Henderson, Jr, was that seizure of the film was unconstitutional.

Of all major American metropolises, Atlanta was surely the most schizophrenic in its patrolling of public decency. It was and is a peculiar amalgam of contemporary mores and Southern Baptist puritanism. Even in the middle 1980s, two consensual males were spied upon and arrested *on the premises of the consenting parties*, in the bedroom, to be precise, for sodomy. This was incredible, but it happened, and since no straight married couples were prosecuted under this very old and outmoded statute, the word was clear – homosexuality might well be the norm for certain 'sick' individuals (despite a 1974 declaration by the American Psychiatric Association that it was no longer to be considered an illness), but its practice would be prosecuted in the city of Atlanta.

During 1969, Andy and Morrissey made six cuts in the movie when it was released nationally. These excisions were sufficient to remove most of the previously objectionable material from *Lonesome Cowboys*. A Federal attorney in Phoenix, Lawrence Turoff, viewed the film in Scottsdale, Arizona, on 29 August and advised the Justice Department that

> '. . . The scenes that were allegedly being photographed during the filming of this picture were not shown in this movie. While in my opinion the movie had no redeeming value whatsoever, neither was it obscene within the definition of that word as defined by the Supreme Court of the United States.
> 'Because of the above reasons prosecution is hereby declined.'

★★★

In 1976, Andy would be invited by the Democratic National Committee to do a portrait of Jimmy Carter to be published in portfolios (fifty sets) signed by both Andy and the future President, the proceeds to be used as campaign funds for the Carter run for the presidency. Very soon after the Democratic convention, Andy and Fred Hughes flew down to Plains, Georgia, by way of the Atlanta airport, to photograph Jimmy Carter for both an ink drawing silkscreen print and two variations in color. At Jimmy Carter's suggestion, his mother, known as 'Miss Lillian', posed for Andy's polaroid. It was not yet known that she was a very strong and individual character, but it was Jimmy Carter's notion even then to make this fact known to the American public as part of his total image. In time, Andy's *Lillian Carter* became even more widely exhibited than his Jimmy Carter painting.

On 15 June 1977, a summary of the FBI investigation of Andy Warhol was sent to the Jimmy Carter White House. It may well have been a precaution on Carter's part since there was an informal gesture made to Andy around this time for him to be considered the 'official White House portraitist'. Carter was far more sophisticated than either his predecessor or his successor, particularly in cultural matters, an aspect of the Carter presidency not generally perceived.

Andy's world was not even grasped easily by the average, jaded New Yorker. Having followed Andy's career as closely as any outsider could, I hastened to have a look at what was advertised as his first novel. *a, a novel* is the only work of fiction I have failed to understand on some level, and what is maddening about it is that Andy assumed that one of his average days abroad in Manhattan with his cronies would be worthy of setting down in print, and that if he used verbatim their private language, an amalgam of gay argot, speed and street slang, the result would give the interested public a look into the Warholian experience. It started with Andy's fascination with Ondine and Andy's notion that a tape recorder could take the place of an author's mind.

Ondine spent one Sunday that summer with Andy that has been preserved in book form. It came about this way. They often spent Andy's days off together, just ambling about Manhattan, dishing what they did the night before and who was doing what. Ondine's friends like the Turtle and Rotten Rita amused Andy, and Andy's friends like the Duchess (Brigid) and Billy were Ondine's kind of folks. Oftentimes, Andy carried his Norelco tape recorder with him and he just left it on wherever they went. It was this Sunday-long recording that provided the basis for the 'novel' that appeared in 1968, some months after Andy was shot. The actual events recorded had taken place two years earlier.

At the time of the 'action' of the twenty-four-hour period covered by the book, the Duchess is in the hospital. She went to the dentist and when he was through working on her, he would not let her out of his office but sent her straight to the hospital for being 'bruised and demented'. There, she has stolen a blood pressure machine, three thousand uppers, and is working on getting a stethoscope and doctor's white jacket out of the hospital.

Andy is called Drella in the book, as he was by most of his intimates. Ondine has spent all of Saturday night in drag in a teenage whore house. They are walking around the upper east side looking for something to eat at bakeries and luncheonettes. It is supposed to be all true to the original recording, but there are clues here and there that it is adulterated. For example, Ondine describes Everhart's baths to Drella, giving rates and describing what goes on there – 'three floors y'know of complete utter gaiety' – and Andy knew Everhart's baths as well as any other gay male in Manhattan, even though he probably did not frequent them.

They discuss Rauschenberg, which is probably right off the tape, and Andy calls him 'the father of art' and he confesses that he, Andy, has a little 'of the natural Bodheim'* in himself, 'and I can't help it . . . I know it's tacky.'

They describe the Duchess as having been on drugs since she was twelve years old, and there is much talk about Taxine (Edie) and her 'deadly' childhood.

If the book has any merit, it is in giving us some taste of what Andy's life was like when he was away from the Factory and spending a day with his 'downtown' friends. The talk is fairly rough, with the variations of gay sex spelled out in some detail. It is the literary equivalent of the Factory films without the redeeming and wordless eye of the camera.

Grove Press published the book, but their editorial staff obviously did not know how to handle it. The misspellings by the transcript typist are all left intact, so that you comes out as 'youeu', and more often than not the speaker is not identified, so that you must puzzle out if it is Drella (Andy), Ondine, or Paul (Morrissey). If you know them from another context, then you realize that when 'P' is talking about a new way of making movies called 'Electronovision', it has to be Morrissey, but there are pages when talk goes back and forth between unidentified speakers, and it is all a great muddle. The critics unanimously panned it, and Ondine himself found it unreadable. 'It was given this horrible review by the *New York Times* who I think tried to read it all the way through, and it wasn't a readable thing.'

Ondine himself was soon to give up this entire scene and flee to Pittsburgh, where he would get a salaried job and try to live an ordinary life. Then, once back in New York or Queens in the early seventies, he turned to booze, but he believed that his addiction to alcohol saved his life:

> 'This is a terrible thing to say, but I believe alcohol saved me from AIDS. I spent the last – this is '88? – I spent the last fifteen years of my life drunk and unable to function sexually. And, boy, I couldn't be happier! Yes, I do have a bad liver, but yes, I can *live!*'

Billy Name (Linich) was already gone from the Factory when Ondine drifted away. He had spent the last two years of his time

---

* A reference to the murdered poet Maxwell Bodenheim.

there shut up in his darkroom, and no one ever saw him. It was no joke, and here was one instance where Andy should have put aside his aloof attitudes and intervened. Nearly everyone believed that Billy was waiting for Andy to give him the word to please come out. But the word never came, and Andy pretended to ignore the situation or to regard it as a tolerable eccentricity of Billy's.

Billy would sneak out at night for food at a nearby deli, but the lack of any light other than the red bulb of the darkroom had affected his skin and eyesight. His body was covered with scabs, including his scalp. His eyeballs turned yellow. Morrissey got concerned that he might die in there and Andy would be confronted with an unnecessary scandal when the tabloids published screaming headlines about 'Andy Warhol Locks Man in Closet for Two Years.'

But then one day, just before they left the East 47th Street Factory, when Andy arrived for work he found the darkroom door open and Billy gone:

> '. . . The room smelled horrible. There were literally thousands of cigarette butts in it and astrology-type charts all over the walls . . . . He'd tacked [a note] to the wall when he left that night. It read:
>
> *"Andy – I am not here anymore but I am fine*
> *Love, Billy"* '

PART SEVEN

SCANDAL
IN A
VACUUM

TWENTY-NINE

Andy got word in late 1967 that the Factory building on East 47th Street was coming down, so it was essential to find a new work-space quickly. Fred Hughes and Paul Morrissey could not agree on just what kind of place they wanted. Morrissey was looking for something antiseptic white with file cabinets and a receptionist – the headquarters of a successful movie company. But Fred insisted on another loft situation, which he considered the only possible place for an artist. He wanted Andy to combine his movie-making with his art. That was Andy's notion, too, so that was what they took at 33 Union Square West in February 1968.

It seemed to be working out well, although there was the same accessibility as in the old place. But the silver foil was gone, Billy was gone, Gerard was gone. Morrissey discouraged idlers, and only the old crowd that was closest to Andy – Ondine, Brigid, Candy – they could be counted on the fingers of one hand – were around now. But the new faces were – Jed and Jay, the Johnson twins, Vincent Fremont, who was helping Fred out, and of course, the Superstars: Viva, Ultra, Ingrid, Nico, Eric, Louis Waldon, Geraldine Smith, and half a dozen lesser luminaries. Henry Geldzahler almost never came around.

But they had been there only about seven months when tragedy struck, and Andy was shot by Valerie Solanis. With hindsight, it seemed an inevitable event – so many crazies cluttered Andy's past. The move downtown had not erased that recent history. Twice they had been invaded by a gun-totting eccentric, once at the firehouse, and then at the old Factory.

Andy was shot around four-thirty in the afternoon and reached the hospital approximately twenty minutes later. His friends were shocked but some of them were not surprised. His door had been open to too many people who did not quite fit into society. The Warholian world was not bohemian; it was the permissive place every truant youth was seeking, where nothing was frowned on.

Around seven-thirty that evening, Valerie Solanis, still wearing the raincoat over her dress and armed with two pistols, one emptied of bullets and recently fired, walked up to a policeman in Times Square and said 'They're looking for me.' She had left a paper bag behind in the Factory with a fresh Kotex with which she thoughtfully had supplied herself before going on her murderous journey.

Valerie was more thoroughly a misfit than anyone who had passed through the Factory before. Her small role in *I, a Man* was impressive, but it had not elevated her to the ranks of Superstardom. She did not have the blonde, society girl-gone-slumming aura of Baby Jane Holzer; she was not gauntly seductive like Viva; she did not have Edie Sedgwick's gamine and other-worldly charm, although Edie was now gone some months to fresher fields, where she would soon be buried. The Superstars had to look at home both at the Factory and at parties as a kind of appendage to Andy – a beautiful woman at his elbow completed the public's concept of Andy Warhol.

Born Valerie Solanas in Atlantic City, she changed the spelling of her last name after she arrived in Manhattan. She resisted all discipline as a girl, and her family gave up on her. Her first and only affair with a man was when she was fifteen. He was a sailor and her family broke it up. She moved out and her high school records show that she was living by herself when she graduated. A classmate recalled: 'She was the odd one, definitely. Such a loner . . . terribly bright, and she was always decent, though she kept her distance, except when provoked. Then she would flare up.' At the University of Maryland, she excelled in psychology and was given a job in the psychology department in the experimental animal lab. Her professor employer said he got the impression that 'she was licked around a little bit. She was older, more mature, and has seen the seamier side of life. Even then she knew all the four-letter words . . . .' She did not have that fresh-from-the-tub, hair-neatly-combed appearance, but she was reasonably well put-together. She went on to graduate school at the University of Minnesota, but dropped out in 1959, though she got mostly As.

In 1965, she turned up at the Chelsea Hotel, where she became a semi-permanent resident. Arthur Miller kept a studio there, and in 1966 he complained to the hotel manager about the mimeographed literature she was handing out in the lobby. There were vicious and generalized attacks on men, which she later particularized in her mimeographed SCUM Manifesto (from 'the Society for Cutting Up Men', of which she was founding president and, so far, the only member). Miller told the manager: 'She's dangerous. She's going to wind up killing somebody.' But Stanley Bard, the hotel manager, simply told her to move out, which she did.

Valerie Solanis had been radicalized before ever meeting Warhol. It is easy to see where she came from. Like many radical feminists in the late 1960s, she felt isolated. Even within the radical movement, women were not expected to lead. When they stood up for their rights, they might well be shouted down with boos and calls for them to come down from the platform and into the back alley 'for a fuck'. Valerie knew all of this, and there was only one group in New York where the renegade radical might fit, male or female, and on New York's lower East Side that was The Motherfuckers (Up Against the Wall, Motherfucker). It was from revolutionaries like this that the late Abbie Hoffman had risen.★ Hoffman was a radical who essentially ran by himself, the congenial 'floater' who dropped into this movement or that or spontaneously created a new movement of his own, which is what Valerie had done with SCUM. The Motherfuckers had indirect ties to the Yippies, who would win notoriety during the 1968 Chicago Democratic convention. They had in their number several individualist and anarchic men and women who did not conform enough to belong in the cadres of the radical left. When Valerie was arrested, the Motherfuckers performed a street-theater piece in her defense.

When she woke up on the day of the shooting, it was Valerie's intention to have a showdown with Maurice Girodias, publisher of Olympia Press, for whom she had agreed to write a pornographic novel. He had given her some money, but she claimed that he still owed her five hundred dollars and she had armed herself to force him to pay up. But Girodias happened to be out of town that day, so she shifted her ire to Andy.

The Warhol tribe gathered in the waiting-room at Columbus

★ Abbie Hoffman died, a suicide, in April 1989.

Hospital. The media – newspaper photographers, reporters, and TV crews – saw an opportunity for some dramatic and perhaps unusual coverage of a major event, and while they waited for Andy to die, when they expected some extraordinary weeping and wailing from this strange assortment of people, they interviewed Viva and Ultra Violet and half a dozen others.

Andy clinically died during the five-hour surgery to save his life. His heart stopped twice, but was started again. On the following day, he began coming out of the anesthesia – the surgery lasted until early that morning. He was in horrible pain, and deep scars criss-crossed his torso where the surgeons had to cut in to reach his pierced lungs, patch up his stomach and his liver.

Julia sat for a long time in the hospital waiting-room. Viva and Gerard, who had been the only ones to remember her after the shooting, tried to comfort her. Ultra Violet did her best when she was not being interviewed. Gerard and a few other loyal friends kept reporters away from Andy's mother, so there was a kind of human cordon around Julia, securing her from the press.

She alternately wailed that they had killed her Andy, while fingering her rosary and praying for a miracle. But then she was told that there would be no news for some time, so Gerard and Viva took her home in a taxi.

By the next morning, her other sons, John and Paul, were there, and they were a great comfort to her. When Andy came to and heard that his brothers were in town, he seemed relieved that John was there, but was suspicious of Paul's motives. There was some old and abiding resentment of Paul, his wife and even his children. This feeling was only made apparent to Paul after Andy's death when he was left off the board of trustees of the Warhol Foundation.

That night at midnight in California (three a.m. New York time), Bobby Kennedy was shot in Los Angeles. Andy fretted that all the media attention would shift away from him, and he was absolutely right. *Time* magazine prepared a cover story on Andy, but he later learned it was put on hold, waiting for his death. Anyone trying to find out how Andy Warhol was doing after his brush with death had difficulty finding any mention of him in newspapers that were filled from front page right through to the editorial page with the Kennedy assassination.

The Warhola stamina and toughness saw Andy through, and

after a week, it was evident that he was going to recover. He was not the same man, of course. He was now stitched up inside and out, and for a long time, he would have to wear a corset to hold his insides in place. But when he began asking questions about the shooting not of himself or anyone else but of the film *Midnight Cowboy*, Morrissey and Viva realized that he was beginning to seem like the old Andy. Morrissey was cast as an underground movie director in the film, and since Viva was playing the underground movie party hostess, he chose Ultra Violet to play his superstar. Andy resented John Schlesinger's Hollywood movie a little bit, even though he paid Andy the tribute of using his people in the 'underground' part of it. Andy felt that audiences would prefer to see the prettified version of sexual low-life rather than the raw, real thing as he and Morrissey were filming it.

That July, while Andy was still hospitalized, Morrissey began shooting *Flesh*, his own version of a hustler's story as played by the beautiful Joe Dallesandro. He was using Jed Johnson as his assistant. Jed was doing a variety of jobs around the Factory. When he had worked for Andy, they had got to be very close. Andy may have been a little jealous, since some sort of relationship began to develop between Andy and Jed during Jed's hospital visits, and when Andy was discharged on 28 July he and Jed began spending a lot of time together.

The other beneficiary of Andy's convalescence was Fred Hughes. When Andy seemed to have stopped breathing while they were waiting for the ambulance, Fred gave him mouth-to-mouth resuscitation. Andy could not forget that, and the result was that when he was back at the Factory for the first time, he put Fred in charge of all the art business, which was just giving him formal authority over something he was doing anyway, and Morrissey in charge of all the movie business. Vincent Fremont, one of the more attractive persons around the Factory, became Fred's assistant and office manager.

The shooting had sobered Fred considerably. Earlier, he had seemed to be as much of a party animal as Andy, but now he seemed to be all business. Perhaps his elevation had done it. A kind of transformation had taken place, and a new age had begun at the Factory.

Andy's tough Czech peasant roots brought about an incredibly speedy recovery from beyond the brink. Given less than no chance to live in the emergency room (one doctor was heard to say 'It's hopeless', and Mario Amaya on the next bed over, from a prone position, shouted: 'That man is a famous artist. He's got money. Lots of money. It *isn't* hopeless'), after less than eight weeks of recovery and convalescence he was going home.

He was never to be the same, of course. His brother John believed that the shooting might have contributed to his death, weakened him in some way. He delegated much of his authority. Fred Hughes was now head of everything except the movies, and even had some say in that. The Hughes imprint on the Warhol empire would in time turn out to be nearly as important as Andy's. Paul Morrissey would rapidly move from shooting Warhol movies to doing Paul Morrissey films 'presented by Andy Warhol'. Morrissey would write, direct and photograph all of them, and Andy would increase the budget. Both Morrissey and Andy believed that they could groom Joe Dallesandro into a major star. They had come close with the women they had turned into 'Superstars' – Edie and Viva in particular – but they were both more excited over Dallesandro than anyone except Edie during her first weeks at the Factory.

Morrissey had begun shooting *Flesh* while Andy was in the hospital. It had a cast of Factory people, including Geraldine Smith and Louis Waldon. One of the scenes had been shot in David Bourdon's apartment. Bourdon remembered that he was always encouraging Morrissey to go out on his own as a filmmaker:

> '. . . to do his own work and not get swamped by Andy because I had seen so many people get sucked into the Warhol vortex. I thought Paul was too good for that. He shot this one scene in my apartment. I'm not sure it was August. I think Paul had an assistant. It might have been Jed Johnson [it was – Jed Johnson is credited as being Associate Producer].'

The small contingent that descended on Bourdon included Morrissey, two actors, and Jed Johnson, who was associate producer on the film and later co-editor with Lana Jokel. It was September. Bourdon remembered the scene being shot on the bed 'with the two men [Joe Dallesandro and Louis Waldon] sitting on the bed next to the window, and the doorbell rang. It was Andy and Viva – I *think* it was Viva. So this was the first time I'd seen Andy after the shooting, and so I was very impressed and so happy to find he was able to walk and everything. Before we sat down, I said "Paul is shooting in the bedroom." I assumed that Andy had come there really not to see me but to help in the shooting and to see what Paul was doing. "Do you want to go in?" And he said, "No," and he sat down and he started thumbing through my magazines . . . . He just sat there. He made a point, I thought, but to this day I don't know what he meant by that behavior. He just sat in a chair skimming magazines. He never once got up to open the bedroom door to peek inside. I didn't know whether he was so confident in what Paul was doing that he didn't want to interfere or he was showing such supreme indifference to what Paul was doing that he didn't want to acknowledge that they were making a movie.'

Andy had abdicated as a filmmaker. He did lend his name to the productions, and often his presence, but usually in this disinterested way.

Taylor Mead would say that Andy 'died when Valerie Solanis shot him. He's just somebody to have at your dinner table now. Charming, but he's the ghost of a genius. Just a ghost, a walking ghost.' And Stephen Koch would write:

'. . . he had "died". This "death" has played a curiously important role in Warhol's private mythology ever since that time. He has often spoken about his Lazarus-like passage at Columbus Hospital, this Coming Back, addressing the subject with his strangely unexpected little-boy eloquence. "For days and days afterward, I wasn't sure if I was back. I felt dead. I kept thinking, 'this is what it's like to be dead . . . .' Being that close to death is like being that close to life, because they're both nothing . . . I wasn't afraid before, and having been dead once, I shouldn't feel fear. But I am afraid. I don't understand why." '

There is no reason to doubt any of this, and, like Lazarus, he had a second life after he was shot. It differed markedly from his earlier one. The crazies were gone forever. He was no longer a filmmaker. He no longer worried so much about how he looked, although in some ways he began to look better – he remained permanently slender; that look of over-eagerness to be admired or accepted was gone. As he regained his strength, he gradually became what he always had professed he was but wasn't quite – a man who was in the business of making art.

But the strength to do art did not come right away. Around this time, a portfolio called *Flash* was done. In fourteen silkscreens, it covered the entire Kennedy assassination week. What is troubling about *Flash* is that some critics have found it too close to the original front pages which supply its basis. After its inclusion in the huge Warhol retrospective at the Museum of Modern Art in 1989, Adam Gopnick wrote in the *New Yorker*:

> 'The images that Warhol made of the Kennedy assas-
> sination . . . are completely flat, the most mundane
> journalism he ever did . . . . The assassination makes
> an absolute rupture in Warhol's work, as it did in the
> world at large.'

While Gopnick makes the erroneous assumption that *Flash* was done in the wake of the assassination and not in 1968, as in fact it was, a colloquy on camera between de Antonio and Andy and Brigid suggests very strongly that his 'hands off' art was literally that for a period during the closing months of 1968. And so it seems likely that this work had been signed by Andy for more than one reason. It would not be worth very much without his signature, and he wanted to demonstrate that he could indeed inspire a work to be entirely done by a colleague as part of his theory of the artist as a machine.

Less than two years after *Flash* was produced, Andy was inter-viewed by de Antonio for the documentary film *Painters Painting* (1970). On camera, Andy said: 'Brigid does all my paintings, but she doesn't know anything about them.'

de then asked: 'What do you mean, Brigid does all your painting?'

'Well, Brigid has been doing my paintings for the last three years.'

This could only be a typical Warhol exaggeration, since this would have meant Brigid doing his art work before he was shot in 1968. However, it is probably based on truth, and it makes sense to have someone who has been closely following Andy's art process begin to turn out the art again when he was still too weak to do it himself. Brigid, too, was being filmed, and she explained:

> 'I just call Mr Goldman, and I just tell him the colors. Or I go down there, and I just choose them from anything that's lying around – a Stella poster, you know – and I just pull off a piece, and say, "That color and that color." I take polaroids of the four flowers [Andy's *Flowers*, 1964], and I switch the colors around and superimpose four cut-outs one on top of the other. Take a picture and have Mr Goldman do it . . . . Andy does all his own ideas though. That's his art.'

★★★

It has become traditional in writing of Warhol to make a division between his own films and the later ones, post-Solanis, made by Paul Morrissey and only 'presented' by Andy. To give Morrissey his due, they *are* totally his creations, but they use Warhol people and the story ideas are Warholian. Morrissey was given the means to become a filmmaker through his association with Andy, not only the means but the people, as well as the peculiar homoerotic obsessions of the big man himself. We will never know if these were also Morrissey people and Morrissey obsessions.

Flesh is the most intense love-letter to a male body ever composed. Morrissey's camera explores every permissible angle of Joe Dallesandro. But the film, when one overlooks its primitive aspect (it is again shot in 16 mm with only one camera set up at a time, so there is an annoying jump from cut to cut), is wryly funny on its own terms. Joe is a straight street hustler. He most enjoys making it with his wife (Geraldine Smith), but she is a layabout who spends most of her time in bed with her pregnant girlfriend (Patti D'Arbanville). If she likes anything about Joe it is his cock, and she even ties a pretty bow around it. He then spends twenty-four hours on Manhattan's streets, trying to hustle $200 from a series of tricks, to pay for an abortion for the girlfriend. Not all of his customers are pick-ups (he phones a few of them from his little black book) and not all of them male (one very foolish young woman obsessed with the size of her breasts – she thinks they are too small and she is anything but flat-chested – pays Joe to let her blow him, while two drag queens look on). Such is the plot and it is in one bedroom and out the other as the camera tails after Joe, who is undeniably beautiful. It would be sordid, but Joe looks so innocent, like a drop-out choir boy on a typical weekday of work.

Flesh was not meant to be an underground movie, but a low-budget sex comedy. It had a long run in New York and in other major cities, and then became a smash in West Germany, which Morrissey and Joe visited on a personal appearance tour.

Trash was filmed the year after *Flesh*. Once again Morrissey's camera jealously covets Dallesandro's face and body. He is almost never out of camera range, but the film is heisted easily by Holly Woodlawn, the Factory's wittiest drag queen, who plays Joe's live-in lover, who pretends pregnancy in an attempt to get on welfare in an hilarious, ludicrous confrontation with a welfare case-worker. The title is ironic; the central figures not only paw through garbage (Holly is supposed to be a good 'trasher' and furnishes their hovel with furniture off the street), but they have sunk as low as humanity can sink. Joe has been on dope so long he is impotent and yet trying to hustle, and even if he could get it up, he tells us that it wasn't all that great. Geri Miller asks him: 'Didn't sex get you high when you'd come?' And Joe answers: 'No, it was over.'

Sometime over Christmas 1968, Valerie Solanis phoned the Factory and asked to speak to Andy. Paul Morrissey answered and was shocked to hear her voice. They had assumed that she was in jail. Morrissey told her that Andy was not there and told her not to call there anymore, but she was insistent and threatening. She wanted $20,000 for the 'losses' she had incurred in her writing, and insisted that all criminal charges be dropped or she would do it again. Morrissey, a bit unnerved by the call, said, 'I'm going to hang up now.'

Andy was trembling visibly when he asked Morrissey: 'Was that Valerie?'

According to Ultra Violet, who appeared with Solanis in *I, a Man*, she was out on bail of only $10,000. Ultra Violet

Henry Geldzhaler and his cigar. The costume suggests that he always tried to fit in with the 'Factory kids' (© Archives Malanga)

Andy's confidante and Factory veteran Brigid (Polk) Berlin daughter of Hearst Corp. former Chairman, Richard Berlin (© Archives Malanga)

Andy Warhol with Paul Morrissey and Viva visiting his exhibition at the Museum of Modern Art, Stockholm, 1968. (© Nils Göran Hökby)

Edie Sedgwick observing Gerald Malanga lifting dumbells in the opening scene from *Vinyl* (Ondine is in the background wearing glasses), 1965 (© Archives Malanga)

Tom Hompertz and Louis Waldon in *Lonesome Cowboys*, 1968 (© Archives Malanga)

Lou Reed, lead singer with The Velvet Underground, the rock group Andy sponsored and toured with. Still taken from *Screen Tests*, a film by Andy Warhol and Gerard Malanga (© Archives Malanga)

Marie Menken (scowling in the centre) in the title role in *The Life of Juanita Castro*, 1965 (Marina Ospina is on the left) (© Archives Malanga)

Andy and his long-term companion Jed Johnson, 1970 (© Archives Malanga)

Ronnie Cutrone, Andy's art
assistant 1972-80, shown
with his own work (Ronnie
Cutrone, photo by
Wolfgang Wesenor)

Rupert Jason Smith, Andy's silk-screen
technician for the last ten years of his life
(Dorothy Benson Blau)

A Swedish cow confronts
Andy's wallpaper at the
Moderna Museet,
Stockholm, 1986.
Photographer Peter Gullers
led her in (Photo courtesy
Peter Gullers)

Andy with his cousins in front of Diamond Dust Shoes (1980) (Christine Soley)

Andy with his cousin Christine on Park Avenue, 1980 (Christine Soley)

Andy with Stuart Pivar at a Manhattan flea market, 1986 (Stuart Pivar)

Andy's home on East 66th Street. His aunt, Olga Zavasky and his cousin, Christine Soley are seated on the steps (Amy Passarelli)

Andy's waterfront home in Montauk on Long Island (Tina Fredericks)

Designer Billy Boy in Paris, 1988 – friend to Andy and Fred Hughes and an American original (Billy Boy)

Andy with choreographer Martha Graham at the unveilling of his portrait of Miss Graham in 1986 (Popperfoto)

Andy presents his sketch of St Michael's Church in Hamburg on a visit to West Germany in 1980 (Popperfoto)

Andy's good friend Liza Minelli with his brother John Warhola at the memorial service for Andy, held at St Patrick's Cathedral, 1 April (Christine Soley)

Andy's burial in Pittsburgh at the foot of his parent's grave. Paige Powell and Andy's cousins, Amy Passareli and Christine Soley are in the background (Christine Soley)

A memorial billboard in Pittsburgh, 1987 (Christine Soley)

Andy at the opening of an exhibition of his self-portraits at the Anthony d'Offay Gallery, London in 1986 (Popperfoto)

said that when Solanis' trial took place, Maurice Girodias, her publisher, arranged for two lawyers to represent her, but she sent them to hell and would not even accept a court-appointed counsel. Then she was committed to Elmhurst General Hospital in Queens. When she was declared incompetent to stand trial, she was sentenced to three years for first-degree assault and served her time in Bedford Hills and then at Mattewan Prison. Once free, she again went on the warpath, this time sending threatening letters to Barney Rosset of the Grove Press, publisher of Andy's novel, Howard Hughes, and Robert Sarnoff, head of NBC. Fortunately, she seemed to have lost interest in Andy. In these letters, she told them: 'I have a licence to kill.' For the next six years, she was in and out of mental hospitals. Then in Ultra Violet's memoirs of those years, it is recorded: 'Valerie Solanas [sic], crazed would-be assassin, died on April 26, 1988.'

Taylor Mead threw a party-wake at the Café Bizarre, but even that did not settle the matter. He knew only that was the word that was circulating, and it gave him an excuse to party. He told a reporter that he bore no malice for Solanis' memory, and said that Andy was playing so many 'head games, if Valerie hadn't shot him, I might have done it myself.' Later, he said that he 'might have been misquoted'. Taylor Mead could be a very vague man when he wanted to be.

THIRTY

Andy Warhol was a very visible member of an oppressed minority, the gay population of America. Just after midnight on 28 June 1969, the gay liberation movement took off, launched by a police raid on the Stonewall Inn at Sheridan Square in the Village. The police claimed that the Stonewall was selling liquor without a license, but that seemed to be a pretext for homosexual harassment, and the patrons took it as such. Three police cars and a paddywagon were filled with patrons, as the atmosphere became increasingly tense. An attempt was made to push the paddywagon over, which would have been something new in homosexual behavior in New York, but the paddywagon somehow roared away to the Precinct House. The inspector in charge called to the drivers to 'hurry back'.

Then tempers erupted, and the gays began throwing coins at the police, then bottles. The inspector ordered his men inside: 'Lock ourselves inside. It's safer.' They bolted the door. The front windows were covered with plywood inside but were glass outside. The sound of smashing glass was heard and what sounded like bricks pounding on the locked door. The police became uneasy. Then the door crashed open and beer cans and bottles hurtled inside. One cop got hit under the eye; he screamed and his hand that flew to his face was covered with blood. Then the police rushed outside and grabbed a token gay and yanked him inside, slamming the door again. They began beating him to near the point of unconsciousness. His name was Dave Von Ronk. He was the first casualty of what went into history as the Stonewall Riot.

An uprooted parking meter was used as a battering ram to smash the door open again. One policeman attempted to turn a firehose on them, but the stream of water was weak and all it did was make the floor so slippery the police could not keep their footing. Reinforcements then arrived; the riot was over.

The next morning, a graffiti message scrawled on the wall of the Stonewall Inn read: 'Insp. Smyth looted our: jukebox, cig. mach, telephones, safe, cash register and the boys tips.' Also: 'They invaded our rights'; 'Support Gay Power'; and 'We are open'; and that night they were. That Saturday, 28 June, became the first Gay Liberation Day, and marches and celebrations were held on every anniversary up to and including the present year – all over the world.

Perceptions about gay persons changed everywhere. This was no longer a quiet minority; it was a militant group that would force media people, writers, artists, everyone in show business, to pay heed. Gays were not to be insulted or patronized. Scripts were changed on TV shows, and an entertainer had to be as popular as Eddie Murphy to get away with 'fag' jokes.

Then on 15 October 1969, the first great Vietnam Moratorium Day took place across the nation. It was a clear signal that millions of Americans were united against the war's continuance. The largest gathering was on Boston Common, where more than 100,000 assembled. 30,000 people marched past the White House, and in North Newton, Kansas, students at Bethel College began tolling an old church bell once every four seconds for every American soldier killed in Vietnam. They rang the bell for four days. Afterward, even President Richard Nixon was convinced that 'after all the protests and the Moratorium, American public opinion would be seriously divided by any military escalation of the war.'

Andy was not unaware. He kept up with the news, although it is in character that there were no wars used as inspiration for his Disaster series, and the only riot he took note of as a painter was the Birmingham race riot. As for Gay Liberation, he had made his statement in *Blow Job* and *Lonesome Cowboys*, and so that year of tumult was spent exploring the museum cellars for *Raid the Icebox*, another operation in March to alleviate some internal pain from his earlier surgery, a journey to Hollywood, and the launching of his very own movie magazine.

Andy's life began to sort itself out in early 1969. Fred Hughes seemed the ideal partner – shrewd in many ways, knowledgeable about art, an amusing companion. He had secured for Andy a firm connection in the art world beyond Leo Castelli and the others, the de Menils of Texas. In 1970, Dominique de Menil was Director of the Institute for the Arts at Rice University in Austin. The Dia Foundation in New York, founded by her sister Philippa, had become a gallery of distinction and a source of funds to artists.

In early 1969, John de Menil, their brother, visited the Museum of Art at the Rhode Island School of Design. He was much impressed with what he saw displayed, and then they went to storage, where the bulk of the Museum's holdings were 'hung floor to ceiling on racks', as Daniel Robbins, the Museum Director, pointed out. They were inaccessible to be seen by John de Menil or anyone else, including art students or scholars with a particular interest.

'What would happen,' John wondered, 'if some important contemporary artist were to choose an exhibition from your reserve?' The organizing principle was to be whether or not he liked whatever he saw. Would the artist impose his personality on such a show? If he were famous enough, would the public be persuaded to come and look? Naturally, John de Menil had Andy in mind, and naturally Andy accepted.

Andy made six visits to the museum storage cellars, provoking the Museum Director to say: 'The true cataloguing curator of the nineteenth century is Andy Warhol!'

Not surprisingly, the first antique articles he sought were shoes. He did not examine each pair or select anything in particular; he ordered the whole cabinet of shoes to be included in the exhibition. He also chose bandboxes (for hats) but not the hats themselves, he chose parasols. Interestingly, he focused on what protected the nineteenth-century woman (her feet and herself from the elements) and not what she wore, passing by dresses and jewelry. Ignoring laces and exotic textiles of the past, he zeroed in on American Indian blankets. He picked an entire row of early Windsor chairs, which had been put back for use as spare parts in the museum's collection of antiques. He also picked out a trove of Indian baskets. He noticed his own silkscreen painting *Race Riot* (1964), but passed it by, muttering 'It stands up.'

The resultant show, called appropriately *Raid the Icebox*, opened at the Institute for the Arts at Rice University in late October 1969. It then moved for a month in New Orleans at the Isaac

Delgado Museum and came to rest for its final months back at the Museum of Art at the Rhode Island School of Design. So in the show, the bandboxes were stacked as they might be found in any attic, the shoes in three tiers of the cabinet in which he had first seen them, the three Windsor chairs on bare planks to support them, the old paintings in stacks of three or four so that only the front one was visible. It was the first strong hint to the public that Andy Warhol was fascinated by the 'attic principle', the idea that valuables, like armies, are strongest when flanked together in their numbers.

In February 1969, Andy was deeply involved in his art again. Since Fred Hughes had taken over managing the art side of his career, commissions were beginning to come in. One of the early ones came from the Los Angeles County Museum of Art. Maurice Tuchman, its Curator of Art and Technology, wanted Andy to experiment with holograms (three-dimensional pictures). Andy flew out with some of his staff. Tuchman discussed creating such art through the use of lasers to make the 3-D images. Tuchman and Andy went to see some hologram art done by artist Bruce Nauman at the Nicholas Wilder Gallery. Andy was excited by what he saw there.

When he returned east, Andy built some small structures that might contain three-dimensional images. The most interesting of these was a 'rain machine' created by a simple pump recirculating water through apertures in a horizontal pipe at the top of a box-like structure. By late June, a designer for Cowles Communications, Allen F. Hurlburt, was contracted to work with Andy on a hologram art work to be exhibited at the Osaka (Japan) Expo 70. Within a couple of months, he told Tuchman he was concerned about costs. Andy kept rejecting designs, but he finally settled on a color photograph of four daisies, which was repeated serially over a large area in the typical Warhol manner. He told Tuchman finally: 'You know, this 3-D process isn't all that glamorous or new or exciting.' Eventually, the work made its appearance in the US Pavilion at the Osaka Expo signed by Andy Warhol, but really built from his sketches by Maurice Tuchman and his Expo Design Team members. One of those involved commented: 'Of course Andy's forcing everyone into the act.' The 'rain' from the horizontal pipe flowed continually over the series of colored daisies with the rain illuminated from the top.

What they all must have learned from this episode was that any involvement with Andy Warhol was one with collaborators as well, theirs or his.

THIRTY-ONE

In the spring of 1969, a film producer named John Hollowell approached Andy about the possibility of working with him and Morrissey on a Hollywood-produced movie. The title of this movie was *The Truth Game* and it featured an attractive girl reporter on *Life* magazine, to be played by Andy's favorite drag queen, Candy Darling, interviewing Hollywood stars in the film colony. Andy's adrenalin shot up when the prospect of a Hollywood movie made in a major studio presented itself. He abandoned his preoccupation with painting. Very quickly, he got Rita Hayworth and Natalie Wood to agree to cameo appearances as interviewees. Then he got Troy Donahue.

Andy had always been generous with his time and contacts in trying to promote those he liked. It was his belief that Candy Darling could become the first major transvestite movie star, and here was the magic moment he had been waiting for.

Somehow Leslie Caron's husband, Michael Loughlin, got involved in the project's financing and distribution. Then Andy cast about for some wedge into a major studio. Without much hesitation, he thought of Gerald Ayres.

Ayres was an old San Remo acquaintance of Andy's who had gone out to Hollywood with his wife where they found work at Columbia Studios writing synopses of available properties. Ayres soon became right-hand man to studio head Mike Frankovich, and when Frankovich left to become an independent producer, Ayres still remained at the studio, being elevated to Vice President of Creative Affairs. A transitional studio head named Bob Weitman came on the scene. The studio management was looking for a powerhouse head, like their Harry Cohn and Frankovich, but Weitman was there when Ayres first heard from Andy about *The Truth Game*.

Ayres had kept in loose touch with Andy's activities, and they had mutual friends in filmmakers Agnes Varda and Jacques Demy (Varda was then planning her film starring Viva, *Lion's Love*). Weitman was a veteran of the big band era, and was manager of the New York Paramount Theater when Benny Goodman, Tommy Dorsey, Woody Herman *et al.* were starring in their stage shows. He followed the adage of never booking any act blindly. He had to see it for himself. The package was attractive; Loughlin had budgeted the whole production at a million dollars or less, but as Ayres remembered it:

> 'He [Weitman] wanted to see what these people looked like so I said to Paul: "They want to meet Andy." So out they came and we put them up at the Beverly Wilshire Hotel. Everybody came. Joe Dallesandro came; Jackie Curtis; and some others. So they all arrived and so we gave them a sort of reception party at the Factory [a modish oversized restaurant probably named after Andy's establishment in New York, but located in a former factory].
>
> 'I had gone over to the hotel to see how they were doing and they were having a great time. They were charging everything to room service, and they were having their hair done down at the beauty parlor. So they were having a great old time . . . . After they had been there a few days, they had this meeting with Bob Weitman, so I walked in this big Hollywood front office and there was Paul and Joe and Jackie and this guy Hollowell and Andy. Andy sat over in the corner, white-haired and dark glasses, and Paul conducted most of the meeting in that adenoidal way that he speaks . . . . And sure enough, Bob Weitman lit up his pipe and started talking about the old days of Woody Herman and Frank Sinatra at the Paramount. Paul, being a very resourceful man, encouraged him to talk along, and they had a good meeting with Weitman. When they had gone out the door, Weitman said to me: "I like that Warhol fellow, but who was that little jerk with the white hair?"

Then, mostly for budgetary reasons, Columbia Pictures wanted Andy and Morrissey to submit an outline of the number of days they would be shooting and of what. By this time, the studio knew that it was something to be shot 'on the fly' with nothing much on paper, but they seemed to have bought that concept, since Andy's filmmaking methods had been widely broadcast on both coasts. Andy and Morrissey did this, but they 'got carried away', according to Ayres:

> 'Andy included scenes in which they visited Pat Rocco,
> who makes boy pictures, porno movies of naked boys on
> pogo sticks, and some sort of scene of the boys involving
> a boxer dog, and a few other things.'

This went, without Ayres' knowledge, to the budget supervisor's office, and the next day Ayres found a memo on his desk from Weitman saying, 'Let's forget all about this Andy Warhol thing.'

The Hollywood episode was Andy's only flirtation with the American movie establishment, but it distracted him sufficiently from his art so that he kept thinking about Hollywood and its undeniable glamor almost constantly upon his return to New York. The farce at Columbia served to reignite an old passion of his to get into the magazine business.

Andy had wanted a movie magazine all his own for a very long time. In late 1969, soon after his return from Europe, his friend John Wilcock came to him with a concept for a magazine that would combine show business and art world gossip with articles on current cultural matters. Andy was always quick to pick up on a good idea. Within days, he, Morrissey, Wilcock and Gerard had laid out the entire magazine, which was to be called *Inter-View* (later *Interview*). It was to be published out of the Factory at 33 Union Square West.

In some ways, it was a promotional thing, since many of the stories and much of the gossip focused on Factory people – the Superstars and their Manhattan prowls with their friends, most of whom were in show business or fashion. But there was a strong emphasis on nostalgia, as Joan Crawford, Marion Davies, Garbo, Bette Davis, Marilyn, and all the Hollywood legends were given their due. Glenn O'Brien was an early editor and still was writing a column for the magazine in 1989. Gerard, who was back helping Andy at the Factory in early 1969, now was asked to help out with the magazine. Andy said later that he had founded *Inter-View* to give Gerard something to do.

But like so much that Andy touched, the magazine turned into something of growing value. With his uncanny timing, he had come in with it just when nostalgia was about to peak. But that was not the sum of its appeal. It survived by turning into a slick fashion-entertainment-gossip monthly and soon began to turn a profit for Andy Warhol Enterprises.

The New York humorist Fran Leibowitz joined the staff with a monthly page called *I Cover the Waterfront*. Capote began contributing stories and non-fiction. Somehow the more serious side of John Wilcock's concept was lost as the magazine began to take on an identity, but Andy was enormously proud of it, and throughout the rest of his life always made it a point to take fifty or more copies of each issue and personally carry them onto the street, where he would give them away to passers-by, often autographing them.

It was another instance of Andy helping to shape current culture. In the wake of *Inter-View*'s success, a venerable American monthly, *Vanity Fair*, was revived, and its contents were only a little broader than *Inter-View*'s.

Commissions for paintings, many of them arranged by Fred, built Andy's considerable fortune, beginning in the early seventies. Leo Castelli sold and resold particular silkscreen paintings, but he believed that Andy's millions were amassed through Fred setting up portrait sittings and then selling them to the sitters for a great deal of money. For instance, Castelli believed that in the mid-seventies, Fred and Andy flew to West Germany with a list of approximately fifty prospective clients, and during a forty-five-day period, Andy executed more than fifty portraits, which were completed back in the United States. The going rate for a single portrait was $25,000, and for a double image $40,000. In many cases, six slightly differing silkscreen images were paired for the sitter and most were so intimidated by Andy's reputation that they took all of them, which brought in $120,000 per sitter. Thus, during a six-week period, Andy earned possibly in excess of four million dollars.

The serious commission work was well under way by late 1969 and Andy had lots of money to spend. He and Fred went to Paris late that year, accompanied by Peter M. Brant and his wife. Brant was Andy's publisher at Castelli Graphics and would become the heaviest investor in *Inter-View* magazine.★ They were all seeking Art Deco pieces. Andy's greatest collecting joy was when they visited the old Puiforcat emporium where they saw an old showcase containing the work of Jean E. Puiforcat, whom Fred described as

> 'the most famous silversmith of the twenties and thirties. We asked the incredulous assistants if any of these objects (which to them were totally outmoded) were for sale and consequently bought almost every item for little more than scrap value.'

Wholesale quantities of this exquisite Art Deco silver would be sold in small lots (usually a set at a time) during the mammoth Warhol Auction at Sotheby's, fourteen months after his death.

★ In 1989, Peter M. Brandt purchased *Interview* magazine from Andy Warhol Enterprises.

THIRTY-TWO

By 1971, Andy had reached his optimum recovery. Lidija Cengic, a physical fitness trainer, came by once a day to see him through his exercises. He worked out with weights and his back muscles became incredibly strong. It does seem unlikely that his general physical condition was better after he was shot, but some friends insist that it was so. He had massages several times a week, and his masseur advocated eating several cloves of raw garlic every day. This was something that Eleanor Roosevelt had done for many years, and since both Mrs Roosevelt and Andy were very social creatures, the garlic fumes posed a problem for those around them. The solution in Andy's case was heavy doses of perfume, Andy generally preferring Chanel No. 5, Guerlain scents, and others he had made up for himself. He was sensitive about the deep scars on his torso, but he allowed photographer Richard Avedon to photograph them and the painter Alice Neel to paint him with his scars exposed. For a long time he hated to take showers. 'It's so scary. I close my eyes. But it doesn't look so bad. The scars are really beautiful; they look pretty in a funny way.' Throughout the second half of 1968 and all through 1970, friends were on a *qui vive* for a collapse, but it never happened.

This could have been a time when Julia might have been most helpful to him. Instead, Andy was in frequent conference with Fred and others about what to do with her, because of her failing health and occasional lapses into senility.

Despite the abysmal reviews accorded *a, a novel*, Andy still was attempting to write, and he had written a play consisting of twenty-nine acts. Around this time, he publicly announced that he wanted to be a 'Leonardo da Vinci' type, and there is no doubt that he meant to suggest that his ambition was to be an all-around genius. It was possibly with this ambition in mind that he later invented 'the Andymat', a fast-food operation that never got off the ground. What is interesting is that in making such comparisons of himself with Leonardo, he invariably skipped over Jean Cocteau, whose self-promotion nearly obscured his great talent, a parallel to Andy's own situation he doubtless would rather not dwell on.

Andy loved the theater almost as much as film. He was constantly attending opening nights on and off Broadway, and Ronnie Tavel, who had written his early film scripts, was now working with Charles Ludlam and his Theater of the Ridiculous, which throughout the 1970s enjoyed an enormous success. Tavel's stage works retained their screen origins in a 'performing-for-the-camera' structure, with scripts that were partially written and then extended on stage by the actor's improvizations drawn from his own fantasies, according to Simon Fuld. Mario Montez, who played *Hedy, the Shoplifter* (based on Hedy Lamarr's day of embarrassment) for Andy's camera, was one of the Ludlam players. One critic wrote: 'The actors are merely doing in public what they had been doing in private just a few minutes before.'

Inexplicably, *Pork*, as Andy's play was called, was cut to less than half an hour when it was done on a program of experimental works in London, in 1971, with characters based on his Superstars. There was a transvestite parody of Viva in a character called 'Vulva', with a shock of wiry hair, a scarf about a scrawny neck, and 'spoiled child' lips. Other targets in this abbreviated work were Joe Dallesandro, Brigid Polk (Berlin), Jane Forth, Gerard Malanga, and Paul Morrissey.

The play opened around the time of an Andy Warhol show at the Tate Gallery (18 February–27 March), which concentrated on five major series of images: Brillo boxes, Campbell Soup cans, Disasters, Flowers, and Portraits.

Andy was going abroad more frequently now, and Fred Hughes kept his apartment in Paris, which Andy always used. The two men traveled to West Germany, where Andy's reputation was high and growing, with much credit going to Hans Mayer, his Düsseldorf dealer. In actual fact, in the early seventies Andy was more highly regarded abroad than in his own country. For one thing, he began to be faulted for his omissions. Gregory Battcock, who once had been filmed by Andy wearing a sailor suit and was an esteemed

critic of American cultural matters, wrote in the February 1971
issue of *Art and Artists* (edited by Mario Amaya, Andy's friend
who was wounded by Valerie Solanis in the Factory)★:

> '. . . Blacks and the poor do not like Warhol's art or mov-
> ies. Documents that are mainly intended as deliberate
> references to a predominant white culture cannot incite
> the imaginations of those who don't give a fuck for that
> culture in the first place, even if they did understand what
> it was all about. This inability of Warhol to reach blacks
> and the poor represents the weakest aspect of his art.'

The point was well taken, of course. There were no black
Superstars. The closest Andy would come to depicting a black
was in his 'Mammy' in the ten *American Legends* (a negress
with a bandana on her head and scarcely calculated to endear
him to the rising black activists in America), his portraits of
singer-model-actress Grace Jones, whom he had befriended, and
the mutual portraits done by Andy and his protégé, Jean-Michel
Basquiat, in the 1980s. There was never any overt prejudice in
Andy, however, and the oversight seemed to be a cultural one.
He was depicting the world in which he grew up, a world where
the black man figured as a servant, an entertainer, or an artist, but
not as Everyman, who was his real target as well as audience.

The last of the 'trilogy' Morrissey made starring Dallesandro
was the slickest and had the greatest success. *Heat* is generally
believed to be a parody of Billy Wilder's *Sunset Boulevard*,
but Morrissey had an entirely different film in mind as his
inspiration. He drew his parody from seeing *The Blue Angel*,
and he made Sylvia Miles his bourgeois, obsessed lover of a
heartless beauty (Joe Dallesandro). Despite making Sylvia play
an unsuccessful screen actress who never made it to the top,
memories of Norma Desmond were too strong in filmgoers'
minds. When they saw that Sylvia as Sally Todd lives in a decaying
Hollywood mansion and moves in aggressively on the beautiful
Joey, nearly everyone thought of Billy Wilder's masterpiece.

Heat does not go very deep; it is as shallow as life in the

★ Battcock was slain in Greenwich village within the decade; Mario Amaya
died of AIDS in the mid-1980s.

lane the Factory crowd was traveling. Joe Dallesandro is a far
cry from William Holden and has, from the camera's point of
view, a much less interesting face to look at. But his body is
something else, and we again see a great deal of male flesh,
nearly all of it belonging to Joe. Not once during this entire film
is a woman's body seen to any advantage. They are frumpish,
fat, aging, or scarred by cigarette burns. That is Morrissey's
gift to the gay world. Perhaps even more than Dallesandro,
what *Heat* has going for it is the presence of Sylvia Miles, the
Oscar-nominated, genuine film star. Obviously, Miles did not
come cheap, but Andy put up the financing, and it included her fee.
In place of a decent salary, they gave Joe Dallesandro equal billing
with Miles. The others in the cast toiled for token payments.

Once again, Dallesandro plays a stud, not as obviously playing
Sally for a fool as Dietrich was Emil Jannings, and in this film
he is not on the street, hustling. Instead, he hustles in a motel
as an out-of-work and obviously washed-up child actor now
pushing twenty. Women, of course, can't keep their hands off
him, and he quickly succeeds in bedding the grossly fat motel
operator (Pat Ast) for a 'discount' on his room. Andrea Feldman,
the exhibitionist of Max's Kansas City, and a disturbing screen
presence (one can see her precarious mental state privately even
as she performs), plays Jessica, the lesbian mother of an infant,
whom the child abuse authorities have not yet caught up with.
She leaves the baby with her suicidal girlfriend, Bonnie, who
shares her motel suite, and attempts to seduce Joe, probably
because she is afraid of Bonnie, who has violent tendencies. Joe
sees her craziness as quickly as we do, and will have nothing to
do with her although he does not fight her off when she grabs
him from time to time. (He will be more generous with her
later when he becomes part of her mother's household.) The
girl's mother is the Jannings character, a washed-up secondary
leading lady who five years earlier did a long-running television
series with Joe as a boy actor called *The Big Ranch*. When she
runs into him as she is visiting her daughter and the baby,
she is overwhelmed by his beauty as an adult. Later, when
her daughter drops by her house to get some money to pay
her motel rent, she takes Joe with her, and Joe is obviously
impressed with the mother's mansion, which is only slightly
run-down. It has a dozen or more bedrooms and no servants.

Sally falls for Joe and invites him to stay with her, which he does. Jessica has to leave suddenly when Bonnie phones to inform her she is about to kill herself.

There is one recurring Warhol hold-over in this Paul Morrissey film and that is Eric Emerson, playing a moronic young man who runs around in a shortie flannel night-gown masturbating constantly. He is rarely seen without his hand on his cock, and it is in frequent erection, shrouded by the flannel.

In her bed, Sally implores Joe to tell her that her breasts are still attractive, and he grudgingly says they're 'okay'. But doubts begin to arise about Joe's fidelity. She takes him with her to settle something financial with her ex-husband, who is living with an aging gay queen (Harold Stevenson). The queen puts the make on Joe and begins to blow him just as Sally comes out from her conference. She blames the boyfriend and not Joe. Then she visits Joe at the motel, where he is keeping his room just in case things don't work out with Sally, and the fat motel manager tells her that she 'has had him'. This stuns Sally. She can't believe that Joe would have sex with this mountain of a woman, but the woman nastily asserts that it is true and she gave him a discount for it.

Joe wearies of the lovemaking, which seems to be non-stop at Sally's and involves Jessica as well, since she, too, can't seem to keep her hands off him and she has moved back in with her mother. Fed up, he tells Sally he is leaving and not coming back. She races after him down a staircase that is almost identical to the one Norma Desmond uses in *Sunset Boulevard*, but he is quickly gone. Then she gets her gun and follows him to the motel. She finds Joe at the motel flirting with a new girl and she aims her revolver at him, but it fails to fire – click, click, click. Sally is so disgusted she throws the weapon into the motel pool. Joe registers some faint shock – it is very hard for any emotion to come into that kept-boy face.

Jed Johnson was credited as co-editor of the film, which was released in 1972. Andy was making certain that Jed had a significant role in everything that mattered to him. Jed and Andy were living together at the Warhol house. This had begun after the shooting. Jed was as handsome as his brother Jay was beautiful, and the twins made an interesting contrast. The men Andy and Jed customarily socialized with were often trying to make time with him. David Bourdon recalled that he found Jed very attractive and

> 'I was always trying to steal him away from Andy, if only for an hour or so, and Jed would never do it. He was always very loyal to Andy, so I assumed that there had to be some bond between them.'

Jed and Andy's close relationship survived into the 1980s, when Jed moved out of the Warhol townhouse, so the two men were together fairly constantly for a period of more than ten years.

Miles came into the movie with a nomination for an Academy Award for her brief role as an upper East Side patroness of hustler Joe Buck's (Jon Voigt). Andy had been a fan of hers and she remembered him coming

> 'to see me in a lot of off-Broadway plays when I was the "queen of off-Broadway". When I did *Midnight Cowboy*, which I shot in 1968, I met Andy then because the Factory group were in that party scene, which I wasn't in, but I met him during that period. At the beginning of 1970, I began to get friendly socially with Andy . . . we were both celebrities and famous at the same time. The movie was a tremendous hit and that sort of catapulted me . . . that turned me into a bona-fide star. I became friendly with Andy and Paul . . . we were in the same scene; we were the beautiful people at the time. Paul had the idea that he wanted to use me in a film since I had done *The Kitchen*, the Arnold Wesker play in '66 when I first saw *Chelsea Girls* . . . . I thought it would be wonderful to work with somebody like that but with professional actors. Paul proposed the idea of me playing in *Heat*, which was an updated version of *Sunset Boulevard* with me playing the film star. I was certainly a film star in terms of the legitimate ones that they used and the biggest one. I've never regretted that decision because I had a wonderful association with them . . . . When I saw *Trash*, I was very impressed with Joe's screen persona and I thought we would be very good together. I sort of stood next to him [Joe] whenever

we were out in order to impress in their minds that we
looked good together . . . .'

The movie was shot in Los Angeles over the Fourth of July
weekend and the days following. The locales were the Tropicana
Motel and then a mansion that was across the street from a Frank
Lloyd Wright house that had become a landmark. The mansion
allegedly had been owned by the former lover of James Dean,
during his abbreviated career in Hollywood before his premature
death. There was a hippie cult living in the mansion at the time,
so they could not shoot the bedroom scenes there, but had to wait
until the end of summer, when they shot them back east in Andy's
rented house in East Hampton.

Miles had lost weight during the summer, 'so you will notice
that at the end of *Heat*, I look pretty good.'

Andy promoted the movie all over the world, wherever he could
drum up any excitement. Miles, Joe, Morrissey and Jed Johnson,
accompanied Andy on these excursions, Morrissey doing a lot
of the leg work necessary to publicize it.

It was shown at the New York Film Festival in 1972, and
prior to that it was seen at the Cannes Festival. Miles said that
they were

'lionized by everyone there, by the international film
community . . . . Then we went to Colombia to the Film
Festival in Cartagena. That was kind of fantastic. That
was in November 1971. You know how it is in most of
those South American countries. The Press is always on
top of you . . . .'

Honored guests at the Cartagena film festival were, besides Andy,
the novelist Joan Didion and the rugged western actor George
Montgomery.

Andy and his movie company were like gypsies flying wherever
there might be some interest in their show or some possibility of
promoting something. Miles recalled going to London in 1974
with Andy and the others, and

'prior to that we went all over Germany and Austria.
It was a tremendous hit. I was the queen of all the

film festivals, and I got quite a number of best actress awards. Andy was wonderful. I always found him a pleasure to be with. He was quite talkative . . . . He was always trying to introduce me to rich people and marry me off. Then I remained quite close through the time I was nominated for *Farewell, My Lovely* in '76. We were very close. We all went out together, met on foreign shores, and things like that. I began to withdraw from the crowd when I began to be thought of as a Warhol actress when all I had ever done was *Heat* . . . . I went to England and I was there all through '78 doing *Vieux Carré*, Tennessee Williams' play, in Nottingham and then in London . . . . I drew away professionally . . . . So I would say we were very friendly from '69 through '76.'

In 1971, before Andy went west to do *Heat* as Morrissey's producer (and to give the film the Warhol imprimatur, which would guarantee advance interest in it), David Bailey, the English photographer who had made his name in the London fashion world, came from London to make a documentary on him for British television audiences. Bailey had prepared for this film by having a researcher, Mary Herron, contact nearly everyone who had known Andy and been connected with the Factory in any important capacity. The public view of Warhol, especially in England, was of an eccentric and unique painter who had run this wildly permissive atelier where finally he was nearly killed. Carnaby Street was still setting the trendy styles, and hippies strolled through Chelsea and even in the West End. Warhol 'types' were often seen in these places, and visiting Hampstead Heath. There was a common perception that he was gay, but then there were all those women surrounding him – Viva, Ultra Violet and Ingrid Superstar.

'The cast' of Bailey's documentary was impressive. He filmed Andy, of course, both standing in his studio and in bed with Bailey. Then there were Leo Castelli, Jane Holzer, Brigid Polk (Berlin), Henry Geldzahler, Paul Morrissey with Candy Darling, Roy Lichtenstein, Fred Hughes, Philip Johnson, Pat Ast and Jane Forth. He wanted to interview Julia Warhola, but she had deteriorated physically a great deal since the shooting. According to Andy, Bailey then hired an actress named Lil Piccard who is billed as 'Mrs Warhol'. Since Julia herself was suffering from heart disease and slipping in and out of senility, it did seem insensitive of Bailey to have an actress as 'Mrs Warhol' saying during one take: 'I don't think he should get married if he doesn't want to,' and on a later take coming out with the astonishing comment: 'I was only thinking about my son Andy when he gets all these visitors and all these beautiful people coming in the house, all these boys. I wouldn't mind if he would really get engaged and marry one of the boys . . . . I mean maybe he would get a little baby, I mean a little Andy . . . . It's really lonely this way . . . he has so much fun I would have all these little Andys, you know, Andys, Andys, Andys, etc.' Impudence does not go much farther than this if what Andy said is true and an actress impersonated his mother. Of course, one can imagine him being asked and, of course, he would have said 'yes'. Nor would he have objected if Bailey had indeed filmed his senile mother and she had made these same observations.

Sadly for Julia, whether it was an actress playing her in the documentary or herself, the result was traumatic. Word was discreetly circulated that Andy's mother had become 'unpredictable' and was causing him concern.

In November 1971, within weeks after Bailey returned to England with the documentary footage, Julia was taken to Pittsburgh to the Wightman Nursing Home in the Squirrel Hill section. Her other sons, John and Paul, then took over in looking in on her, while Andy, it is said, phoned her every day and once or twice visited her without telling anyone, according to brother John. If his visits to his own mother had to be kept secret from his staff, then there must have been some showdown over her continued presence in New York.

Julia Warhola died in the nursing home exactly a year later in November 1972.

Andy did not go to his mother's funeral. There is no point in analyzing his motives; his quotient of sentiment had not risen because of all those years he had felt a very real devotion to her.

He got on with his life. Nena and Aurora, the Filipino sisters who looked after him, continued as before. His boxes of collectibles, including jewelry, Art Deco, fiesta ware and silver, were stored in the upper rooms. He was being squeezed from his attic down to the parlor floor and the English basement beneath it, which opened to the street from under the steps going up from the sidewalk – his mother's old quarters that were now being swamped by possessions like the rest of the house.

THIRTY-THREE

In the summer of 1972 Andy joined Morrissey, Jed Johnson and the others in the Warhol-Morrissey movie company at the villa they had rented on the Via Appia Antica, which is in the southernmost quadrant of Rome. Morrissey had done his successful *Andy Warhol's Frankenstein*, and now he was sending up the vampire legend in *The Blood of Dracula*. The shooting had finished and it was then being edited by Jed Johnson and Morrissey.

Andy discovered that Anita Loos and Paulette Goddard were in Italy, where Anita regularly took the waters at the Montecatini spa. When he contacted Paulette to photograph her for a magazine series (his first attempt had not worked out back in New York), she told him she would be accompanied by Anita.

The ladies arrived at the villa promptly (Anita was the most punctual writer who ever lived). Paulette asked to use the bathroom, went upstairs, and found Jed's twin brother, Jay, inside touching up his make-up. Paulette fled back downstairs and said: 'I'm sick. I've just seen a Botticelli fallen angel *for real*.'

If we are to believe Andy, Susan Johnson, the twins' younger sister, only discovered Jay's weakness for lipstick and mascara at that moment and came running down the stairs sobbing: 'My brother is a transvestite.' Guests were streaming in by this time, and the ladies seemed disconcerted by the commotion, especially Paulette, Anita being the unflappable original flapper. Paulette jumped to her feet and screamed, 'Get me out of here!' Andy did not get his picture, and in moments they were gone.

Anita, who wrote on something every day of her life, set down the experience with relish. She was then collaborating with Paulette on the latter's memoirs, to be called *The Perils of Paulette*. Back in New York, Paulette confided to Andy and

Bob Colacello, his friend and editor of *Inter-View* at the time, that she was unhappy with what Anita was doing with her life story. She thought there was too much of Anita's point of view in it. Andy said: 'Gee, maybe we could do it because we could just tape-record and it would be you telling your life.'

For the next two years, in their mutual spare time, Andy and Paulette were taping away at expensive restaurants, Halston fashion shows, in Monte Carlo, Paris, before or after Broadway openings. But once again, Andy was defeated as a writer. Paulette was even more unhappy with Andy than she had been with Anita. They abandoned the project in mutual relief.

By 1972, Ronnie Cutrone, the surviving 'youngest' member of the speed freak crowd at the old Factory, had gone clean. He had straightened up so much that it was possible for him to come onto the premises of the second Factory on Union Square and impress Andy with his poise, maturity and squeaky cleanliness.

Andy was looking for an art assistant, someone to pull the silkscreens, someone with a strong back who could shove the squee-gee with real force. He offered Cutrone the job, and this was 'toward the end of '72' . . .

> 'So that's when the next ten years started, you know, working on the arts projects. Now it was just me and him making all the art, and he never really had all that many people working. . . . People used to think that he had this army of people working, but one crazy fact is that in ten years he and I worked in a space that was six feet by six feet. It was absurd. Can you imagine ten years of Warhol art being produced by only two people in two feet of space? . . . . We had to roll up paintings and paint them a little at a time because he collected so much.'

While Cutrone doubtless exaggerated the smallness of the work-space, Andy was storing things from his auction and shopping trips in the Factory as well as his home. 'He needed a back room to store things . . . and he needed a big lunch room to appear fancy so we had just this tiny space and we were always tripping over each other.'

With the move to 860 Broadway in 1973 they had some extra space for a brief time, and a lunch room was installed with kitchen facilities. Friends would drop in for lunch, although as Brigid recalled:

> '. . . a lot of times we'd just order up box lunches from Brownies, the health-food store downstairs, like we did at Union Square. Also, McDonald's was just getting to be big, and Andy would sit on the windowsill eating his hamburger. He'd sit there folding up the little tissue the hamburger came in and save it. He just wouldn't throw anything out. All of this began to go in the boxes – you know, the things we called his time capsules.'

Some of Andy's eccentric garbage obsession spilled over into Morrissey's project, appropriately called *Trash*. The difference between Holly Woodlawn's trashing and Andy's was that Andy could not bear to throw *anything* away. Empty coffee cans, used napkins, absolutely nothing was thrown out around him. Brigid used to sneak in early to put worthless trash into garbage bags, but he became suspicious when he found empty cans missing and when he discovered that Brigid had cleaned out some desk drawers that had roaches mixed up with paper clips, he began yelling at her: 'I know you're an heiress, but who do you think you are, throwing perfectly good paper clips out!'

The seventies were not innovative years for Andy; they were years when he felt no need to stretch himself. They were relaxed years in the workplace where for the first time since coming to New York, he concentrated exclusively on executing one portrait after another, some of them icons, like his *Mao*, first done in 1973 – an immense silkscreen painting done from the official photo. In 1972, as his contribution in behalf of McGovern for President, he did a poster showing an unattractive Nixon. His portrait of his mother, done in 1974, is one of his most successful studies since it shows us a warm, very human person, quite unlike the cool Warholian look of nearly all the other portraits. His silkscreen on paper of Mick Jagger became a series (1975) that captured that rock star's sullen sensuality perfectly. Ten different poses were published in a portfolio signed by Jagger and Andy. It was published in London and was a great success. He did many other entertainers of the day, including Liza Minelli, which became famous for its painterly look, removing itself completely from its polaroid origins. His most celebrated portraits of fellow artists certainly were his *Roy Lichtenstein* (1976) and *Man Ray* (1974).

It had been a long time since one of the best-known painters of the day was also becoming famous for depicting the celebrated among his countrymen. Suddenly it became a great honor for a legendary entertainer or a president of the country or presidential contender (Edward Kennedy) to have Andy Warhol do a portrait of them. Significantly, they were done almost without the touch of the artist's hand – polaroids were taken, the artist selected his choice, the silkscreens were made, touches of color were added and, *voilà*, the portraits were finished. No tedious sittings. No interpretation. What you were is what you got. It was simply an extension of the technique Andy employed in doing Ethel Scull, the art patroness, from a series of fotomat machine pictures of the lady.

For anyone willing to look, Andy's vision of the world was the artist's equivalent of the front page of the daily paper, the one-minute 'news break' on television, Charlie Chaplin's cane and derby. The Pop look in Andy's hands had become serious art, serious enough for museums around the world to realize that they had to have a Warhol or several Warhols if they intended to have significant contemporary collections.

In Ronnie Cutrone, Andy had very nearly the equivalent of his great assistant/collaborator Gerard Malanga. Cutrone was young, handsome, of Italian descent, and straight. Andy preferred that the faces around him during his long work days be pleasing to look at, but they were not to be boyfriends. Cutrone said that their relationship was 'a think tank one' . . .

> 'Andy would bounce ideas off me. Like he went to Italy [in 1976] and he noticed that all the graffiti was hammers and sickles . . . so recognizing an icon as he had the ability to do, when he came back he said "Why don't we do hammers and sickles?" So I spent the next

three weeks in communist book stores, and I got really
paranoid because I thought if these places are watched
[by the FBI], I'm going to be on every video tape, and
I got really nervous . . . I never found one that was
really adequate because Andy would use shadows. . . .
So I went to Canal Street and I bought a real hammer
and a real sickle, and I did all these photographs. And
he chose some, and he made them [the silk screens of
Hammer and Sickle]. . . .

'Same thing with the skulls. He came back from Paris
and he had bought a real skull, and he just handed it to
me and said, "I'd like to do some skulls," and I said,
"That's brilliant! That's really great!" '

The skulls did not sell easily, according to Castelli, but there
were museum acquisitions, and Andy liked the idea so much
that in 1978 he combined the familiar Warhol skull image with
a self-portrait that bore a a startling resemblance to his mother,
Julia. While there is little point in looking for a motive in
Warhol beyond the concept, he may well have unconsciously
paired the images to evoke Julia's memory because he genuinely
missed her.

Andy always seemed to know what he wanted on the silkscreen,
but he liked to have that concept confirmed by someone else.
When he would ask a person, Cutrone, for example, for an
idea, he really was hoping for a kind of telepathic signal to be
transmitted from them to himself. He was trying to function like
a highly sophisticated machine.

And so it was with the skull image. He wanted the skull to
throw a shadow that would flash to the viewer exactly what a
human skull really represents.

Cutrone said that of the many photographs taken of the skull

'. . . the one he finally used has a shadow that is like a
small child's head, so it's almost like a birth and death
combination. You see, Andy didn't really think like me,
but we worked well together. I would think of how to
make it tricky and clever, and Andy would think in
much simpler terms, but then we'd agree on something
and I'd point it out and he'd say, "Oh, great! Let's do

that one". He was real easy that way. We'd never fight
or anything.'

The most abstract work Andy ever attempted was his silkscreen
painting called *Shadows* (1979). It was unusual for a Warhol image,
but it came after a heated exchange with Fred Hughes when one
day Andy proposed that he abandon obvious imagery and do
abstractions for several years. Fred told him that he was very
unsure about such a move, that he did not know if the work
would still sell when an artist changed his direction so dramati-
cally. When Andy saw the flow of money possibly drying up, he
was frustrated but conceded the point. That was when Cutrone
proposed he try doing 'something that is a real thing yet it is also
abstract, like a shadow'. 'Oh, yeah!' Andy exclaimed, relieved,
and they set to work.

PART EIGHT

LONER
AT THE
BALL

THIRTY-FOUR

For Andy, the seventies were a time of exchanges. It was as though this were the Monday after Christmas and he was at the exchange desk at Bloomingdale's telling them everything he got was just a little bit tacky and he was trading up.

In 1973, he had exchanged his loft at 33 Union Square West for antiseptic offices at 860 Broadway. They did have some character: Andy's personal office had a round window that looked down on the street, and some wood paneling. There was a receptionist's desk out front, and behind it several offices where good-looking young men in suits and ties looked as though they knew precisely what they were doing.

Within a year he would move out of his not-so-elegant town-house on upper Lexington into a posh brick mansion on East 66th Street. The rooms would all be 'done' by his housemate Jed Johnson, who was now more into interior design than films. Jed created a hushed, elegant, traditional look for the rooms. No Warhol was allowed to be hung – Andy's orders. The furniture was mainly from the Federal period with Art Deco flourishes. Jed experimented with stenciled designs on the walls and put up a frieze of Directoire wallpaper in Andy's bedroom. The bed was a Sheraton four-poster, and Andy added a crucifix to the room's furnishings. Fred Hughes was given the use of the old place on upper Lexington.

Gerard was no longer a 'contributing editor' to *Inter-View* maga-zine after the autumn of 1969 because of a falling out he had had with Paul Morrissey and Pat Hackett, who were, in Gerard's words, 'undermining my position with the magazine behind my back'. He stayed on helping Andy out for another year and then, as he puts it, 'my association with the Factory ceased to exist in

Fall, 1970.' Gerard's photography was now nearly as important
to him as his poetry and he was getting some recognition for it.
Viva had disappeared from Andy's life. Ultra Violet was gone to
fresher pastures.

Socially, Andy was now moving with two distinct groups –
the 'uptown' set, comprising designer Halston, actress and model
Marisa Berenson, editor Diana Vreeland (of *Vogue* and *Harper's
Bazaar*), Liza Minelli, young Cornelia Guest, and the de Menils.
With them, possibly excluding Diana, he went every night to
Studio 54, the huge disco which was the greatest attraction at the
time. Andy became one of its greatest assets. One of the owners,
Steve Rubell, suddenly was one of Andy's closest cronies. He
would arrive at Studio 54 with a crowd of people from whatever
private dinner he had attended last. Andy would say of it:

> 'Studio 54 is a way of life. People live there. They dance
> there. They drink there. They make friends there. They
> make love there. They break up there. They become
> stars there. They do business there. They sleep there.
> Sometimes, when it's really fun, I can't help but think
> somebody will be murdered there. We've never had an
> earthquake in New York, but if we did, it would be at
> Studio 54.'

Andy's aura brightened Studio 54 as it had his earlier Factories.
It was a good exchange, less expensive and a lot less dangerous.
At the disco, he developed his late strong regard for Truman
Capote and Bianca Jagger, who often stayed at Halston's. From
there one night, he coerced out of Rudolf Nureyev permission to
come watch him rehearse, and when he did so the next day, with
his cheap polaroid, and began snapping pictures of the great one
in 'imperfect' poses, the dancer was enraged, grabbed the pictures
from Andy's hand and tore them up. When Andy attempted to
pick up the pieces as they fluttered to the floor, Nureyev stepped
on his hand.

But no matter, Andy was now in an altogether different sphere.
It was a world where Fred Hughes fitted in perfectly. Fred could
not help being something of a snob and Andy could pretend to
be the opposite. Fred's pretensions had not mattered in the sixties.
Now they were very useful. Fred put Andy in touch with

potential portrait clients and collectors in the upper social strata of the de Menils, his aristocratic friends in London and on the continent, their friends and friends of friends. He did all this so efficiently, soon it was obvious that the Leo Castelli Gallery had been superseded by Andy Warhol Enterprises. Fred also sterilized the workplace and cleaned out the 'walk-ins'.

Andy had known a number of artists very well. He had come to know some of New York society through Fred Hughes, Jane Holzer, and Bob Colacello. But in the seventies there was a stepping up of his social life among other artists and the upper strata of society in America and Europe. These two groups had meshed in the sixties when the art market began booming and the struggling artist of the nineteenth century had been replaced by the affluent artist of the twentieth who worked out of a loft in downtown New York, often owning the building, and played or worked at his place in the Hamptons.

There was a sense among those who knew Andy best that he could not stand being alone. He seemed a man without the inner resources to bear his own company.

He often had lost his temper in the past with Gerard or Brigid or Fred, but with his ascension to the status of social desirable, the one guest no smart New York hostess could exclude, there came an assertion of power around the Factory. He chewed his own people out with more frequency. Unless there was someone living with him in his house, he found the place nearly intolerable. When Jed moved out in December 1980, he tried desperately to persuade another boyfriend, Jon Gould, to move in, but he failed. If he was alone in the house, he relied on the television, the phone or sleep to keep the chief bogeyman of his life, himself, his own person, Andy Warhol, out of his thoughts.

When he stepped out the door of his house to begin his day, other people were there at once. Someone always accompanied him to the Factory, someone went out the Factory door with him at night. He never arrived at a party or dinner unaccompanied. There would be anywhere from one companion to a dozen or more in his entourage. There was Halston's circle of friends, and Halston saw to it that they became Andy's friends as well. There was the group around *Inter-View* editor Bob Colacello, who had come from an upper middle-class family but had made it his business to move up into Manhattan's upper strata. Young

Christopher Makos, the 'cute' photographer from the Village, and his lover, Peter Wise, became yet another 'downtown' connection.

Truman got much closer to Andy in those years. He always had seemed to have liked himself enough to spend long periods alone with his work on Long Island or in Manhattan or California, but the aging process or some other demon of equal force had made him more and more reliant upon alcohol and prescription drugs to get through the days and nights. He was like the town belle who had lost her looks and was thus lost herself. He had begun a major work that never would be finished. He began working for Andy's *Inter-View* doing 'thought pieces' and stories. One of his best late works, *Handcarved Coffins*, first appeared there. As the crowd of Andy's friends grew, Truman's own circle diminished. He had struck back at the fates by striking out at his friends. He wrote about them 'honestly' and possibly thought he was doing no more than Thomas Wolfe had done in *Look Homeward, Angel*, but he was not writing about his own family; he was writing about other people and their friends and families and he aired all their dirty linen as publicly as he could in the name of art.★

Some of Halston's closest friends, like his frequent live-in companion Victor Hugo, felt Andy's inner turmoil more than others. Even at the most crowded affairs, Andy seemed to be alone. He observed but did not connect. His chief social interaction was in having an eager ear for gossip. He loved it and he spread it. The intrigues and affairs of his friends became the core of his life. It was all too ironic. He had lived through the fifties living vicariously through his friends, Ted Carey and all the others, hoping that he might begin his own life and enjoy all these ups and downs he was taking in second-hand. But it never happened, a.1d now he was in the seventies and many of the people in his life were more important or better-known than any of those he knew two decades earlier; but it made no difference.

The hustling after portrait commissions never stopped. Oddly, it seemed more pronounced in him than in his lieutenants, who were more subtle in their pursuit than he was. If his life made any

★ Andy chose to do the same thing only when he was safely dead. *The Andy Warhol Diaries* (1989) are more outrageous than any 'fiction' Truman Capote ever wrote. No doubt he thought to do a mischief, but the book went much further than that.

sense, it was in his work, in executing the silkscreens.

Cornelia Guest was very much an 'uptown' girl. Her father, Winston, was 'old money', and her mother, CZ, had once been a showgirl and even an artist's model (for Diego Rivera). Cornelia got to know Andy really well as a teenager in 1976. She first had met him when she was around five years old at a party given by her parents in New York. She found that his way of getting to know someone was to show them all of his recent paintings and the things he had collected. He seemed to be saying: 'What I paint and what I collect are who I am.' They became very close friends at once, and it was not at all unusual for Andy to fly to, say, Palm Beach, where Cornelia was attending some polo matches. Her mother, CZ, had been a close friend of Truman Capote and when he was in disgrace, following publication of parts of *Answered Prayers*, she and Winston remained loyal, and none of that was lost on Andy.

Cornelia was aware that Andy would

> 'mix incredible people together . . . other artists. I met Halston through Andy. He loved young people. He was a wonderful teacher and he would spend a lot of time with you to show you different things. He was one of my dearest friends, and a very intelligent man. He was an extremely inquisitive person, like a sponge that absorbed knowledge. That knowledge was his greatest asset, and he used to hand it to people. He would tell people about what he knew and what he saw.'

Around her,

> 'he was very talkative. He would be at dinner and people would come up and talk to him, and he would sign an autograph, but he was very shy. He did not speak as freely with people he did not know.'

If in the seventies Fred Hughes had introduced Andy to a new lifestyle, it was Halston who ensured that he would stay there until he died. Halston was an international pace-setter and a fashion designer of the first rank.

Halston's real name was Roy Halston Frowick, and he had been born in Des Moines, Iowa, that metaphorical capital of mid-western bliss. When he first met Andy, the Factory crowd, although carefully stripped of the crazies, was still moving with Andy everywhere he went. Halston was a famous party-giver and he said

> 'I would invite Andy to the parties and he would bring this enormous entourage of people. He was always surrounded with a cast of maybe twenty people. It got to be sort of difficult because you'd want to see Andy and you didn't necessarily want to see all the surround– all the drag queens and Superstars. You didn't have enough plates to accommodate everyone if you wanted to give a dinner or something. Little by little, Andy and I became friendly, and I think we really opened up a whole facet of society to Andy that he hadn't been in before. I mean, he was more of a downtown boy and I was an uptown boy and I introduced him to so many uptown people. That really did help. You know, he was quite lonely, and I think that's the reason he surrounded himself with people, but finally I'd have him always for Thanksgiving and Christmas and things like that. I think really through that experience and having a lot of star-type friends and social friends, he learned to give presents [Halston is speaking here of costly presents and not the roses, Easter eggs and kittens of the fifties]. Never before did he do that. It gave him an opportunity to do something at Christmastime for everyone. I'd do his birthday for him and he'd be here on the major holidays . . . . We were very close, and we would see each other as many as three or four times a week. He met Liza [Minelli] through me. I gave Liza her first Andy Warhol pictures. I bought them for her as a wedding present, and a birthday present and stuff, and I talked Liza into having her portrait done. Liza commissioned him to do it at my suggestion.'

With a handful of exceptions, Halston's circle of friends was dominated by powerful women, most of them famous in show business. He dressed them and he dined them, and some of them, like Bianca Jagger, would even come to live in his Manhattan townhouse when they needed a place to stay (Bianca came when she left her husband, Mick). The Berenson sisters, Marisa and Berry (who would become Mrs Tony Perkins), were often around. Elizabeth Taylor never visited or stayed in New York without seeing Halston frequently, so Bianca, Liza and Elizabeth all became close to Andy.

Andy's entourage was cut down at a suggestion from Halston. One birthday, Halston told him: 'Andy, let's not have such a big party because the parties are getting out of hand . . . . Let's give a small little birthday party with maybe twelve or fifteen people so it's more intimate.' Andy especially loved Halston's birthday parties for him because they were, as Halston described them, 'like a children's party', with favors and funny hats and lots of ice cream and cake. Halston said: 'Why don't you pick out eight people that you want? And then I'll get you Liza and you know that sort of stuff there.'

Rather surprisingly, Andy said, 'Well, I don't want anyone from the Factory.' He told Halston that he did not want any of the people with whom he worked, so Halston said that was just fine, but he had not counted on the hard feelings that were to follow: 'They all held it against me and I never saw Fred [Hughes] much after that because he thought it was a personal affront to him. He's very sensitive.'

Halston described Andy as 'mad' in an endearing way:

> 'He was such an interesting character. In those days, he'd always have his camera and a tape recorder. We'd perform for Andy. You know in that book [*Andy Warhol's Exposures*], many of the pictures are in my house or out in front of my house or something. Getting into a car, he shows Bianca Jagger shaving her armpits, which she wasn't really doing. It happened to be a mad picture that he liked. And there's a funny picture of me with some lips and some nipples, I believe. Elizabeth Taylor holding up the nipples and the lips. And there's a picture of Elizabeth Taylor . . . . I happened to have some elephant masks from some Republican window I did or

something like that in my store, and she put the elephant mask on after a fund-raiser for her husband, John Warner [a Senator from Virginia to whom she was married at the time]. Elizabeth and Andy came over here afterward . . . . And so he would do all those pictures here. We never knew what he would do with them. Andy seemed to be harmless, but every time they turned up in a publication some place. I think Andy is the great record-keeper of the times, set aside being the great artist that he is. He wanted everything he did to be recorded. He was a packrat and he saved everything, every ticket for every show. We would all sign everything and he would pack it away in boxes in his Time Capsules . . . . In the beginning, I thought it was a mad idea, but it was a wonderful record. He would put them in this box and put a date on it and when it was filled up, he would close it and do another one. So he was a great record-keeper of the times and his life in those times. His life crossed many different levels of society.'

Andy always kept Jed moving upward in his role at the Factory. After an apprenticeship as editor and associate producer of *Heat*, and even more important work on the horror send-ups filmed in Italy, Andy decided in 1976 that he was capable of directing *Andy Warhol's Bad*, which was shot in 35 mm with a union crew and a big budget and which starred Carroll Baker and Perry King, the latter a major TV leading man, along with Factory regulars like Geraldine Smith. The film got mixed notices, but Vincent Canby in the *New York Times* wrote that it was 'more aware of what it's up to than any Warhol film . . . to date.' Pat Hackett, who had begun taking down Andy's Diary over the phone that year, wrote the screenplay.

Jed was not convinced that his future resided in the movies and soon afterwards became affiliated with a major interior decorating firm before branching out on his own.

Despite all this, there may have been some old and chronic contention between Jed and Andy over Andy's increasing closeness to Halston, Victor Hugo and their circle as the seventies advanced, and it was full-blown by the eighties. It did not appear to be jealousy, but it would seem evident that whenever Jed stepped out on his own, Andy countered with an evening crowded with parties that often wound up at Halston's house. It had become a pattern in their lives. With Jed gone and out of the house, this only became a problem if they were invited to the same affair.

Predictably, Andy measured up to the demands of the sharper and more intellectual crowd in which he was now moving. When he sat down at a formal dinner he no longer relied on schoolboy exclamations to punctuate the monologue of his dinner partner; he spoke eloquently on various matters. Stephen Koch, a novelist and critic, was shocked to find that Andy had read one of his novels. He even discussed its content with insight, and this was no ordinary fiction, but the kind of thing Iris Murdoch was doing in England – a fictional satire set in a very special world.

It was not at all unusual for anyone meeting Andy for the first time to be apprehensive, to be intimidated by his celebrity, by his strangeness ('this Martian come to dwell among us'). Koch, before meeting Andy at a dinner party, was even fearful.

> 'He exerted an aura of domination of the room through his passivity and shyness, rather than the opposite, which was quite remarkable, and inescapably, totally, one of the most dominating personal presences I have ever seen. He would walk into a room and everything would change . . . Diane Kelder [their mutual friend] had set me beside Andy at this dinner, and I thought, Oh God, I'm just going to squirm through this meal. He won't say anything and I'll say nothing but the wrong thing, and it will be really lousy. On the contrary, what happened was that his charm, which could be very considerable, just flowed very naturally. At a certain point, I looked up . . . everyone had left the room and I had not even noticed, and Andy and I were simply locked into this conversation.'

That was the way the seventies unfolded as Andy began his odyssey in New York society, as different from the Factory and that subterranean world as could be imagined.

THIRTY-FIVE

In the sixties when Andy wanted to get away for a weekend, it was usually to Fire Island or Connecticut. Now, in the general move upward he rented a carriage house in Southhampton. On one rainy weekend, he was out there with Jed, Morrissey, Fred, Vincent (Fremont) and a couple of other men, and suddenly Andy decided he wanted to look at property. He knew that Tina Fredericks was now one of the leading real estate agents in the Hamptons, so he phoned her. She was delighted to hear from Andy. She was not in close touch with him. They had no friends in common any more except for de Antonio.

'We went out in the car, and we drove along the oceanside because he definitely wanted oceanfront, knowing that was the best investment. He had a polaroid and kept taking pictures and handing them around.

'When we got out to Montauk, he seemed to perk up. We went to see this house, which had just been sold to somebody else, but he liked it so much, he bid a little more and got it . . . Andy and Morrissey shared ownership. They had about twenty-four acres, of which few of them are actually building sites because there are a lot of ground water problems in Montauk. It is worth five, six or seven million today [1988].'

His nearest neighbors were photographer Peter Beard and the TV host Dick Cavett and his actress wife, Carrie Nye.

Andy did try coming to Montauk for weekends, but out there on the end of Long Island it is windy most of the time, and gusts would keep blowing his wig off whenever he went down to the water, which was right next to the complex of houses. It consisted of one main house and two guest houses, one of them very large, plus a small house for the servants. A caretaker named Winters went with the place. Winters was impressed by the amount of candy Andy consumed. Once he found a family of ants under Andy's bed and he had to disinfect the room. Very soon afterward, Andy gave up trying to go out there at all and began renting it, nearly always to celebrities. He was his own guest on occasion when he would be invited by the resident tenant, but 'Actually,' he said, 'I hope I'm never invited. I dread going there. I hate the sun. I hate the sea. I hate slipping between those damp wet sticky sheets.'

His first tenant was Lee Radziwill, Jackie Onassis's sister. Lee's little dog got into a fight with Dick Cavett's big poodle and had to have stitches at the vet. Then Mick and Bianca Jagger with their daughter and nanny took it for the season, putting Montauk on the map, according to Andy, since the motels filled up with Rolling Stones groupies.

One summer it did not rent, and Andy felt compelled to spend some time there because of his huge property investment. A friend, Maxime de la Falaise, came out and cooked for him, trying out medieval dishes on Andy and his crowd since she was writing a cookbook based on the recipes of the Middle Ages, things like sixteenth-century Russian borscht. Sometimes when the gas ran out, she would run around screaming for Mr Winters to restart the stove since her soufflé was falling.

Elizabeth Taylor came out one weekend. She came as Halston's guest, since the designer had no guest accommodations, while Andy's complex could handle several guests at a time. So Elizabeth slept at Andy's and spent the rest of her time with her old friend Halston. She was then between marriages. She had divorced Richard Burton and not yet married Senator John Warner. Halston came by from his neighboring house, a renovated old mill he had redecorated and then leased from photographer Peter Beard, and picked up Elizabeth to go sailing out to Block Island, but there was no wind that day so, as Andy put it: 'they just floated around in the ocean like a rubber duck'.

Andy said that Elizabeth was so relaxed that weekend, she even hitch-hiked into town, and the 'hippies' who picked her up failed to recognize her in her Botswana teeshirt, kerchief and jeans. At the end of that summer, the Beard house burned down.

In 1978, Andy had begun a close association with Catherine Guinness (of the British brewing family) and she was around the Factory a great deal, often on salary. She had fallen in love with Tom Sullivan, a rock singer and composer, and, according to Andy, a drug-dealer. Sullivan went into partnership with filmmaker Ulli Lommel to star in and produce the film *Cocaine Cowboys*, which was about a rock star and his band who become drug-dealers in order to back their music ventures. Sullivan had rented the Montauk place from Andy for the summer, but he and his rock band were riding horseback over the premises and neighboring property and driving Andy's caretaker, Mr Winters, crazy.

Shooting began on the movie, using Andy's complex as its principal setting. The horse shit, drug-taking and general pandemonium made Mr Winters ill and he died soon afterward of heart disease. Sullivan rather easily persuaded Andy to appear in the movie, and he was, in fact, co-starred with Sullivan and veteran film actor Jack Palance. But *Cocaine Cowboys* has none of the ingredients of a good movie. The story is impossibly insular in its point of view. It is Tom Sullivan's own tawdry life story, and in this film the rock star gets involved with a drug-smuggling operation that goes bad when a male secretary to the rock group attempts to steal the cocaine, after it is dropped in the marshes near the beachhouse. Jack Palance is a villain, although the rest of the cast is so thoroughly rotten it is a little hard to keep track of the 'good guys' and the 'bad guys'. Andy plays himself, and he is the one who is constantly photographing everything going on, so naturally he takes a picture of the secretary fishing the bag of cocaine out of the marshes after it is dropped by a plane. There is a fairly sustained view of Andy as the camera follows him around his own house. His is the only credible dialogue in the film. He asks obvious questions of the rock singer: 'Aren't you afraid of getting busted?' The rock star/smugglers ride horseback over the sand dunes around the Montauk complex. It is all very strange, but seeing Andy 'acting' himself is almost worth the admission price. A few years after it opened and lost its investment, Sullivan died of an overdose.

Halston rented Andy's place after the Beard house burned, and used it for ten successive summers. Andy would come out for the occasional weekend with his friend and tenant. Halston recalled one of '*those* weekends':

> 'There was a bunch of people there and they were all down at the beach, and I was in the kitchen making pancakes, and Andy was sitting there reading a book and talking to me. He was saying, "Oh, gee whiz! I don't have any ideas, and you have so many ideas. I don't know what's new. What should I do?" I said, "Well, Andy, I wanted Elsa Peretti to do some solid gold plates for caviar, so why don't you do pancakes? [Halston laughs.] He was so vulnerable. He went down to the Factory, and for one week he made pancakes down there. He made plaster pancakes; he made pancake paintings, all of which I'm sure were thrown away. But Brigid Berlin told me later that he did all this for a week and they wanted to know who in the hell told him to do pancakes.'

That Christmas, Halston came up with a more practical suggestion and proposed that Andy do silkscreen paintings of the Studio 54 drink tickets. The disco was then at its peak.* Andy gave them to Liza, Halston, Truman, Victor Hugo and his other close friends as Christmas presents. He would do other commonplace 'souvenirs': double frames from his old movies (*Kiss* and *The Chelsea Girls*; *Watercolor Paint Kit*). It would seem he chose to screenprint whatever his eye chanced to see, but there was something selective about the banalities he would record. The Watercolor Paint Kit was lively and in a high key, with vivid pads of color. The movie frames were either in black and white (the first ones) or brilliantly colored (the later ones). If there was any rule of thumb, it was the simplicity of the thing silkscreened and whether or not it would lend itself to color variations. Portraits were something else again. The various near-replications of the original were arbitrarily colored – the women in complementary shades; the men often in clashing or strongly opposite colors.

* It folded when Andy's friend, Steve Rubell, and his partner Ian Shrager, were sent to prison for 'skimming' profits from the business. Andy, Halston, Liza Minelli and many others remained loyal friends to Rubell until his release.

Victor Hugo's silkscreen portrait (1978) was done from a deliberately campy pose by Hugo, but the campiness is subdued
by cropping the original polaroid so that just his face, neck,
one shoulder, armpit and one upraised upper arm (cradling his
head as a beauty contestant might) are seen on the canvas. The
colors are complementary, as in the case of the women and
other handsome men (*Joe Macdonald, Irving Blum, Jamie Wyeth*
and *Halston*). Hugo, a fashion illustrator, was a good-looking,
well-built young Venezuelan whose family had given him the
air fare to New York to make his fortune in the fashion world.
He was often in Halston's company, and the two of them partied
with Andy. There was something of the tease in him and Halston
said that 'Victor Hugo could talk Andy into doing anything . . .
Andy was just like a big kid, he was just so innocent.'

While this may be hard to accept – that a close friend of Andy's
would look upon him as an innocent – consider the evidence.
Surrounded by drug-users, he was never 'busted' by the police
throughout a decade of being the host of one of the druggiest
scenes in New York. His earliest compadre in Manhattan, Philip
Pearlstein, thought he had an angelic quality. His classmates in
Pittsburgh looked upon him as an endearing soul, a naif, a person
who needed help that was gladly given. We are, after all, what
we are perceived to be. There is no use in looking into the fires
within, especially when those fires were banked so very long ago.

Rupert Smith was a Florida boy who had gone to New York
to attend Pratt Institute, then had specialized in print-making. By
chance, perhaps, he first met Andy when he had been in New
York from a Florida 'cow-town' just a month. In the autumn
of 1969, they met in the Electric Circus on St Marks Place. The
disco had formerly been under Andy's control as the Dom, the
launching place of the Velvets and Lou Reed. Andy was with
Ultra Violet that night and she was arranging an impromptu
seance. Rupert found it all very strange and exciting. 'It was all
very psychedelic with pink cubicles and crazy lights. It was very
different from Florida.'

A few years later, Rupert was working for a silkscreen studio
just a few blocks from Andy's Factory at 860 Broadway. He was
able to follow Andy's work by way of a friend of his, Charlie
Yoder, who worked for Castelli Graphics. Castelli had published

the hand-colored *Flower* series, and Andy had just finished the *Mick Jagger* series and there was some problem with it. It turned out that Andy wound up paying for the printing costs, and he told Rupert that

> 'it cost $50,000, and in 1974 that was a lot of money to him. So he was determined that on the next press series, he'd hand-color everything. But with the idea of hand-coloring Andy got a little disillusioned, I think, because he had three or four thousand prints to hand-color. Castelli Graphics was involved. They were concerned about production time and also curating. Charlie Yoder of Castelli Grahics brought me in and I helped him. Andy would come in and do some, and Ronnie Cutrone was Andy's man at the time. That's how it started.'

In the middle of June 1977, Andy underwent minor surgery to remove a lump from his upper back, just below the neck. The operation was done at Sloan-Kettering, the leading cancer hospital in America. While he waited for the results, he discussed with Victor Hugo the notion of having a joint exhibit in Victor's new loft of Victor's *Come* paintings and Andy's *Piss* paintings. He had done a series of so-called *Oxydations*, paintings in which the pattern was random and, in fact, created not by hand but by the way human urine was either painted, poured on or splashed over the canvas and its copper-painted background. The combination of copper and urine created the oxydized result. He had had Ronnie bring in his urine, since it was stronger and brighter in color than Andy's own. Andy was seeing Victor nearly every day, and was now calling him 'my new Ondine'.

Ronnie had insisted that Rupert was straight, but then one day Rupert walked in wearing a lady's jumpsuit, so Andy asked him, 'What are you wearing *that* for? Are you a fairy?' and Rupert said, 'Yes, I am.' That was probably not the main reason, but after that, Andy began calling in Rupert to proof things, and finally he quit his former silkscreen studio (Heinrici) and began sending everything to Rupert. It was the beginning of a beautiful collaboration. As Andy saw there seemed to be no limit to what Rupert could achieve with a silkscreen, he became bolder and bolder. Some critics have called this phase of Warhol's work 'an awakening', but it was more complex than that; it was the product of two creative minds focusing on the same image, one with the concept and the other the execution.

For the first time since the fifties, Andy returned to the nude male and produced *Sex Parts* (1977), a graphic view of a male rear end with the cheeks parted, and *Torso*.★ The series had been suggested by Victor, and it became a year-long obsession of Andy's. Throughout 1977, he worked on these homoerotic silkscreen paintings of male nudes, culminating in 1978 in the bold view of oral intercourse called unequivocally *Fellatio*. In the score of years between these works and his naive drawings of boys kissing that had been rejected by the Tanager coop artist members, Andy had become his own man, with a strong sense of gay identity. He was no longer in the thrall of straight society's dictates, let alone disapproval.

But despite this seeming boldness, his mind was a repository of old ideas, collected like his hoardings in storage, which he would trot out from time to time in new trappings. In 1980, he decided to go back to shoes for a new series of screen-prints.

By chance, Rupert was then living on Duane Street, which was the old Jewish wholesale shoe district. Andy asked Rupert to buy him large quantities of shoes there, and Rupert took him at his word:

> 'They often had sidewalk sales . . . and one time I bought two thousand pairs of shoes for Andy; they were all really odd, either four quadruple A, petite little Cinderella feet, or they were Drag Queen shoes, size 13 quadruple D like Divine boats! Andy's big concern was that I make sure I get all the boxes and keep all the wrapping. I just kept bringing shopping bags with the shoes . . . it was like buying a whole museum.
>
> '. . . When the shoe paintings were finished and Halston saw and loved them, I had to do a whole new batch with Halston shoes to make sure Halston's name showed up.

Andy was relieved to get the report that his lump was not

★ In early 1980, the *Torsos* were visible in the background of the finale of the Richard Gere movie *American Gigolo*. Gere had become a friend of Andy's.

malignant, but his peace of mind was disturbed around this time when he heard that Valerie Solanis was back in the Village. When he and Victor or Rupert were walking around down there, his eye was looking out for a sudden ambush.

Andy and Rupert often partied together, and Rupert got to know him well. They looked good together, and they had similar, slight builds. Rupert was cute rather than handsome, with strawberry-blond hair and a fresh-scrubbed boyish look. Even though Andy was more than twenty years older, Rupert did not look at Andy as a father figure the way Ronnie Cutrone did. Nor did Andy's extraordinary fame bother him unduly. He saw the insecurities in Andy when they would go out together, and also his disinterest in his own celebrity in the art world. Andy's status as a media celebrity of the first rank was something else, and he knew that Andy was interested in seeing his name on the gossip pages or in any other place that seemed glamorous. The movie world still dazzled him, and Rupert recalled that:

'He always wanted to be known as a producer or a director of film. He thought it was a little more glamorous. He was always in awe of celebrities . . . . Like a little boy when he walked in the room and there were some really famous people like Liz Taylor and his knees would just melt. Liza Minelli became a pretty good friend. All these friendships originated through Halston. Halston was Andy's real friend and so Halston had these soirees at night, and he'd band everybody together the nights that Liza was going to perform. Halston also supported Martha Graham both financially through his company and personally. He got Andy doing an art project called the *Martha Graham Series*. He always was a friend of mine and acknowledged me when I was thought of as a boy doing work for Andy . . . . Andy and Martha Graham had dinner a lot, and I think she was a little skeptical about the worth of the art he gave her, but then he died and those [silkscreen] prints are worth a fortune. She must have made about a millon dollars, and that's a nice gift from anybody . . . .

'The first couple of years, that's what we did [went out together]. I was young and energetic, and Andy was

going through a kind of a break-up with his boyfriend
Jed Johnson.'*

During the Christmas holidays in 1980, Andy and Jed Johnson,
who had been quarreling for months, broke up and Jed moved
out of Andy's house, taking his own apartment, settling finally in
a spacious duplex across the hall from Andy's friend, Stuart Pivar,
who had told him of the vacancy. It was the longest emotional
involvement of Andy's life, and the breakup left him despondent.
He told his Diary:

> '. . . now I'm living alone and in a way I'm relieved,
> but then I don't want to be by myself in this big house.
> I've got these desperate feelings that nothing means
> anything. And then I decide that I should try to fall in
> love, and that's what I'm doing now with Jon Gould [a
> Paramount film VP], but then it's just too hard. I mean,
> you think about a person constantly and it's just fantasy,
> it's not real, and then it gets so involved, you have to
> see them all the time and then it winds up that it's just
> a job like everything else, so I don't know.'

The affair with Gould turned out to be as difficult as Andy suspected it would be. Within a year, Andy persuaded Gould to move
into the East 66th Street house with him, but Gould kept his apartment and maintained a life apart from Andy that would result in
a rupture in their relationship before Gould died in 1986, probably
of AIDS.

Rupert saw that Andy was on his own a great deal, so very
soon he was spending all of his free time with Andy. He said:

> '. . . I was very enthusiastic with Andy. It was kind of
> like a honeymoon. His assistants would never get the
> work done during the week. They wouldn't have the
> photographs ready, so I would come in the afternoon
> around four o'clock and line Andy up and we'd work
> for three or four hours. Then we'd go out for dinner

---

* Andy and Jed had acquired the dachshunds, Amos and Archie, together.
When Jed moved out, it was arranged for the dogs to spend weekends with
Jed. He took the dogs full-time on the weekend of Andy's death.

and go to a party. And a lot of times, I'd go back then
to my studio. I had a night crew. I went out with Andy
from about '78 to about '81. Then I sort of got tired
of the scene and I think he did, too. We did a lot of
the current restaurants, openings, screenings, the Studio
54 or whatever the current discotheque was . . . . Andy
always was home by two [a.m.] He knew Steve Rubell
[co-owner of Studio 54] pretty well, but Steve needed
Andy more than Andy needed Steve. Andy and Truman
were always bringing people, ten or fifteen people. We
hung around with Debbie Harry for awhile. There were
no crazies anywhere near Andy then. If anyone looked
a little odd, he got rid of them. I'd say this was the
post-shooting period. Still a little fearful. I would spend
anywhere from four to eight hours a day with Andy,
sometimes even longer. Saturdays and Sundays, we used
to work by ourselves. I kind of got trapped, so by the
mid-80s, I bought a house in New Hope. Andy was a
little pissed off, but I felt I had to get away. Andy was
a very hard worker and very committed even though
people think that he delegated everything out. He put in
time, he really did. I used to discount him sometimes,
but when I look back upon it, I see he really put the
time in.'

Once this team was fully in harness, a great quantity of work
flowed out of Andy's studio. Essentially it did not stop until
he suddenly died in 1987, and so the two men collaborated
on the art for more than a dozen years. Once they mutually
agreed to abandon their more intimate relationship, Rupert did
the actual printing in his own studio, a large establishment, since
he continued to do work for several other artists as well.

'But Andy was my primary client and he really held
reign over me, and it was very fun. It was a real collaboration, and Andy gave me a lot of freedom because
he wasn't there. In my studio, I had to make artistic
decisions, never so it would not be like Andy, but
we [his staff and himself] made technical and aesthetic
decisions. Andy was a-scared of fire. He didn't want

any solvents in the house. I had this big print studio, and he would give me a photograph that pertained to the silkscreen, and we added . . . color, various colors.'

It was during the years of their close collaboration, lasting more than eight years, that Andy began to excite the critics with his color. Scarlet, plum, brilliant blues and greens, various gradations of brown, orange, yellow – from a sunlight shade to gold. In a work like *Siberian Tiger* (1983), all of these colors were combined in a remarkable tiger's head. *A Pine-Barren Tree Frog* (1983) literally glows with color.

Rupert remembered when Andy was invited to visit Plains, Georgia, during the Carter presidency:

'Andy and Fred went down to Plains, and he photo-graphed Miss Lillian [the President's mother] and he came back, and the polaroid was blown up to the exact size of the silkscreen. Then he did a drawing which was in black for that work, and that was converted and done in the same registration [as the photograph], and then the undercolors were like a flesh, and pink, and, I think, there is some yellow in that print, too. The areas are sometimes cut by a ruby [for the colors to be applied], then you print a half-tone photograph, and then the line. It's a very simple process. You generally alternate flat and glossy inks to give them some surface, and sometimes you use diamond dust to give the print a kind of richness. I did the bulk of Andy's prints from the mid-seventies on. I would say about three or four hundred.'

As the seventies waned, Andy's reputation was in semi-eclipse. He began doing other things as well as art, just as he had in the early sixties when Castelli failed to take him on right away. This time, he turned to TV rather than film.

He thought it would be fun to do his own situation-comedy rather like *The Bickersons*, a quarrelsome couple in the mid-fifties that had a run of about two years on the radio and, more briefly, on television, starring Don Ameche and Frances Langford. He asked Charles Rydell to come out of his semi-retirement in the

Hamptons, where he had retreated following the death from cancer of his lover Jerome Hill. He knew that Charles was always in some sort of dispute with Brigid Polk (Berlin), and he also knew that Charles was one of the mainstays in her life, keeping her afloat in difficult times. Andy saw their relationship as akin to that of the Bickersons.

He put Vincent Fremont in charge of pulling it all together, and Ronnie Cutrone was asked to help out as well. Cutrone had missed out on the Bickersons because of his youth, but he remembered Jackie Gleason's *The Honeymooners*, in which the couple fights all the time, so he could relate to what they were doing. As Cutrone remembered it:

> 'Brigid and Charles were roommates and both of them were trying to diet, but neither of them could, and they were both cheating [on their diets], and they would fight and torture each other, about dieting primarily, but then from that they would get into other areas, you know, politics, whatever the situation called for. And every time Charles would get totally furious with her, instead of going like, "Alice, POW to the moon!", he would grab this thing that was called the bull-worker, which was an exercise tool.'

Charles recalled that the weapon was something like a baseball bat:

> 'I was in therapy at the time, and I was supposed to take this thing and whenever I got really angry, I would vent my anger on the mattress of the bed, pounding the shit out of it. Just total hostility . . . getting it out of my system.'

They shot the series in various apartments, and there would be the people residing there drawn into the action, so the plot was very loose.

The series did not sell to any TV station or network, but Andy followed its production closely. It wound down when the art work picked up again.

More successful was *Andy Warhol Television*, a series of television portraits, each fifteen minutes long, of celebrated persons Andy knew, like David Hockney, Diana Vreeland and others, shown on cable television in 1982. A second series, aptly called *Andy Warhol Fifteen Minutes* after his most famous utterance when he told an interviewer that in the future everyone would be famous for fifteen minutes, was done in 1986.

Television was far more important to Andy personally than it ever could be professionally. It was his surrogate best friend. He watched two color sets at the same time, which he said doubled his pleasure

> '. . . always in bed, usually while I'm talking on the phone to somebody who's watching the same thing. Sometimes I switch from color to black and white for a few seconds. That's very nice.
> '. . . it's fascinating to study people getting old on up-to-the-minute TV. I have watched Barbara Walters get older and, do you know, she has another crow's foot. I've been counting . . .
> '. . . commercials are pick-me-ups; programming becomes too intense if there aren't enough commercials in between. Whenever I watch a show "without commercial interruption" I get itchy.'

His favorite shows in the seventies were the morning movies shown at ten a.m., *I Love Lucy*, a faith healer named Kathryn Kuhlman, *Star Trek*, *Rhoda*, *All in the Family* and *Sanford and Son*. Except for *Star Trek*, these were all working-class, family-oriented situation comedies. *Rhoda* was a 'spin-off' from the *Mary Tyler Moore Show* (spin-offs being series with the central character taken from previous, popular shows). If the television set was his best friend, the people on the screen were his surrogate family. He identified with Rhoda because she had been a windowdresser in Minneapolis before coming to do window design in New York. And certainly Andy was not alone in preferring the company of these television characters, with their problems, to most everyone he knew in real life.

His TV-viewing began early in the morning, was interrupted by his work at the Factory and his partying in the evening, and then resumed after midnight with the *Tonight Show*. He preferred

Johnny Carson to Dick Cavett because with Carson he never got involved; he just watched. 'Johnny doesn't care about "issues" – he wants to make things easy but entertaining. . . .'

Around the time Rupert Smith bought his house in New Hope and dropped away from his daily routine of work and partying with Andy, Andy was weekending at his own house, which Halston had leased, and grousing about having to do everything alone. Being alone was something he could not tolerate for long.

That was when Benjamin Liu took up the post of Andy's elbow companion. It almost seemed foreordained; Liu just happened to be out there visiting Halston that Labor Day weekend.

Liu, from San Francisco, was a delicately beautiful drag queen. When he was with Andy, sometimes he would be in drag. In Andy's world, it didn't seem to matter. Halston affectionately dubbed him 'Ming Vauz'. Liu had a fabulous collection of feathers and expensive and vividly colored fabrics.

Liu brightened Andy's life perceptibly. He was witty and engaging, and he had known Halston and Victor Hugo for several years. At one time, Liu had worked for Victor Hugo. When Andy, bereft of Rupert's constant company, asked Liu to come work for him, Liu thought that Andy might be kidding.

> 'He had an understated manner . . . I didn't know whether it was for real or not, so I just kept saying, "No. No. You're kidding." But about the third time, and this was about two months later, well, maybe I'll just say "Yes." I'll give him a price and I'll just go, and that's what I did.'

What Andy really needed was just someone to be around, and Liu believed that *he* seemed desirable because Andy envied his friendship with Halston and Victor Hugo, and 'he thought it would be great to have somebody like that. . . . Sometimes he would call me his bodyguard, but I never carried a pistol, nor do I know karate.'

Beyond being within hailing distance of Andy from morning until around two a.m., he had some specific chores. He helped Andy with his Photo Book, that vast collection of polaroids from his social engagements. Liu curated the photos and placed them into the current book (where they reposed forever, most of them, although sometimes they would go into *Interview* or some other periodical). Then, just as Rupert had done, they would go to dinner either at a restaurant or to a dinner party, followed by a series of openings or parties, whatever had been stapled that day to Andy's calendar. Liu conceded that there were a great many parties, but

> 'He knows when to make an appearance, and when to leave. He never really lingers on that much . . . . in essence, he spends just the right amount of time. . . . He knows his timing. He never gets off work until after seven when the traffic has thinned out . . . . He'd been doing this for at least twenty years. I mean, he's always been going out, ever since he landed in New York.'

Like many of those who were close to Andy, Liu unconsciously slipped into the present tense when talking about him. Liu knew a lot of the people who invited Andy, so it was comfortable being with him socially. It was not like he was 'just tagging along'. Liu became a confidante. He was always the first to see Andy, except his maids.

> 'He might go to his nutritionist. We went to auctions together. He might go for coffee with a close friend of his. Basically, it's a good way to go to work. It clears out all the crap from the night before . . . . At night, there might be a drop-off at twelve or two or two-thirty.'

Again, Liu was asked to hang around on Saturday when the Factory was officially closed, but he realized that this was just to be a companion, so he gradually begged off, just as Rupert had done to keep his weekends free.

Liu left in 1985 because he thought he would never be on his own. 'So I sort of made a three-year pact with myself.' But he remained a friend and Andy occasionally would call him to go out for dinner or just to chat. During his years of employment with Andy, he was in essence a salaried friend and the sort of companion Andy preferred.* Liu's departure coincided with the time when Paige Powell stopped seeing much of the painter Jean Michael Basquiat, so Paige very easily slipped into the role of constant companion, and, mornings, Stuart Pivar often picked Andy up at his house and they would shop together for a couple of hours before his day at the Factory began. It all worked out just fine.

Yet for all of this, Andy struck Halston and Victor Hugo and Rupert as someone who was totally alone, no matter who was with him, Halston calling him 'the loneliest person I ever met'. If one seeks a metaphor, he was like that small kid lost at Harrods or Bloomingdale's waiting for his mother to show up and fascinating everyone while he waits, and, of course, she never shows up.

---

* By the last decade of his life, Andy had fallen into the same pattern as his favorite icon, Marilyn Monroe. Throughout the ten years of her intense fame, she chose as confidantes and constant companions those few who were on her payroll. In truth, she only trusted those who were in her employ.

THIRTY-SIX

Andy became not only fashionable as a portraitist, but slipped into a vacant spot in art of the twentieth century. There were no internationally known portrait painters working anywhere in the world. His old friend Richard Banks was painting the Newport and Palm Beach *grandes dames* and an occasional theatrical celebrity. But his formal portraits were traditional, with very strong links to British portraiture.

By the end of the seventies, Andy had amassed several dozen portraits of sufficient distinction to make a successful show at the Whitney – *Portraits of the Seventies*. In reviewing the work for the catalog introduction, art historian Robert Rosenblum compared them favorably with the work of the French impressionist Edouard Manet, who painted demi-mondaines in real settings the way Andy had filmed them with his movie camera, and then did portrait masterpieces of Clemenceau, the poet Mallarmé, and the novelist George Moore, among others. In our times, Rosenblum found only the British Graham Sutherland as a predecessor. Sutherland did not turn out numerous portraits the way Andy did, and never approached the huge body of figurative paintings of Manet, but he gave the world insightful and brilliant portraits of Somerset Maugham and Winston Churchill, among others, although the Churchill allegedly was destroyed by Clementine Churchill after her husband's death because it was 'his wish', since he hated it so. It showed a half-scowling, ravaged Churchill looking out at the viewer in a challenging way. After it was presented to him on his eightieth birthday in Parliament, he went into a fury. It was painted in tones of brown except for his wrinkled flesh, his white shirt and blue bow-tie.

Almost exclusively, Andy did portraits in this period of men and women of money and distinction, with the occasional show business figure. Included were *Giovanni Agnelli* and his wife *Marella* (both 1972), *Marion Block* (1975), gallery dealers *Irving Blum* (1970), *Alexandre Iolas* (1971), *Leo Castelli* (1975), *Ileana Sonnabend* (1973), and *Ivan Karp* (1974), *Marilynn Karp* (1975), novelist *Truman Capote* (1979) – at a moment Capote agreed to after having lost a number of pounds and having a facelift – *Carolina Herrera* (1979), painter *David Hockney* (1974), former Warhol superstar *Jane Holzer* (1975), screen actor *Dennis Hopper* (1970), *Brooke Hayward* (Hopper) (1973), painter *Roy Lichtenstein* (1976), *Dorothy Lichtenstein* (1974), *Daryl Lillie* (1979), *Joe Macdonald* (1975), *Golda Meir* (1975) – whom he would do a second time in the 1980s, *Liza Minelli* (1978), painter *Jamie Wyeth* (1976), *John Richardson* (1974), designers *Halston* (1974) and *Yves St Laurent* (1974), *Sao Schlumberger* (1976), *Michael Heizer* and *Barbara Heizer* (both 1978), *Sofu Teshigahara* (1976), *Frederick Weisman* (1974), *Marcia Weisman* (1975), *Diane von Furstenberg* (1974), old friend *Henry Geldzahler* (1979), *Helene Rochas* (1975), and *Norman Fisher* (1978).

Nearly all of them were commissioned by someone, quite often the subject. Andy and Fred Hughes were very clear in dealing with everyone that it was a business transaction as well as an artistic one. If a work turned out especially well, as in the case of the two *Weismans*, Andy entered into an agreement with the subject to knock off his own versions for his private collection. He also did this with the *Liza Minelli* work, which Halston had persuaded her to commission. As we will see, it became a model for Andy's future women portraits.

Leo Castelli remarked on Andy not being concerned with flattering the men. This was true of older men, but did not apply when the man was relatively youthful and handsome. In the case of Joe Macdonald, who obviously had beautiful blue eyes, Andy blotted out the photographed eyes and painted in the eyes in a bright blue. He did the same with one version of *Halston*. Jamie Wyeth, who had a Byronic look, has not one line on his flesh, not even around the ears.

One of his most successful portraits of women is that of *Janet Villella* (1979). Here he used something of the *Minelli* technique but allowed a subtle line of her small, slender oriental nose to be visible. Her dark hair and eyes dominate the portrait so that the backgrounds could be infinitely varied and look right. Likewise,

Helene Rochas, (1975) has a design created by the lady's elbow and arm, on which she is resting, and the angle of her upper body, which seems to be horizontal. Here, like the *Joe Macdonald* work, the eyes have been omitted from the polaroid emulsion and painted in.

Perhaps his most successful male portrait is that of *Mick Jagger* (1975–6). He did ten silkscreen prints of Jagger for a portfolio in 1975 in which most of the face and shoulders is hand-drawn. Andy had begun using abstract blocks of color – in this case black, tan, gray and a sand tone. He then would draw in the features beneath the color (or perhaps the drawing preceded the blocking out). Then in 1976 Andy did a more conventional silkscreen painting of Jagger, using the *Joe Macdonald* technique, although Jagger's features were more interesting than handsome.

With *Paloma Picasso* (1975), he covered one eye, much of her forehead and all of the top of her head with four swatches of flat color. He did something not quite as obliterating with his own pulls of the two *Weismans* (1975), but the blocks of color have been superimposed over the image beneath.

There is an oriental look to his *Merce Cunningham* (1974), which has the full figure of Cunningham, the dancer, printed on Japanese gift wrapping paper with a brown background. One pull is extremely dark, creating a 'black-on-brown' abstraction. It is Andy's only full-figure portrait in the seventies.

With the *Geldzahler* and with *Paul Jenkins* (1979), Andy has taken a brush full of paint and swabbed the print with it in a random fashion. It gave the portraits a painterly look. Likewise with his friend *Victor Hugo* (1978), he has painted out the top of his head with purple paint in one pull. The *Hugo* is fascinating in other ways – he has not eliminated the lines of the young man's face, and he even allows us to see the hair of his armpit (the arm is upraised, campily pillowing the head).

Of course, the most familiar portrait of the seventies was Andy's *Mao Tse-Tung* (1972). Using the portrait from the posters in China as well as the frontispiece of *The Little Red Book*, he did countless pulls. Some were very large, and the technique resembled that of the *Marilyn* painting. The color on the lips was smudged, the flesh area of the face varied from dark blue to green (liberties he did not even take with Marilyn). Here we see Andy's intention plain. He took the totem of a billion people and treated it with the same casual disregard as he did with his *Marilyn*, the icon of the western world.

In the eighties, with the assistance and probably the actual artistic collaboration of Rupert Jasen Smith, the portraits became more inventive and moved farther away from their polaroid origins. *Speed Skater* (1983) is full-figure, like the *Merce Cunningham* of the seventies, but it is an action painting, with the skater almost thrusting himself off the surface. The figure holds up in almost any size and it could become a beautiful postage stamp or a huge poster and be equally effective as either. The hockey player *Wayne Gretzky* (1984) becomes a delicately drawn head and upper body with the head and shoulders highlighted within a white rectangle. Three separate photographs were the foundations for three studies of *Ingrid Bergman* (1983), and the most conventional one (called *Herself*) shows us how sophisticated Andy had become in adapting a photo into a silkscreen painting. In the Bergman portrait *With Hat*, he has substituted each photographic area with a color field, completely eliminating the photograph underlying the work. It would be wrong to assume that he already had done this with the Minelli portrait, because Liza's heavily mascaraed eyes and eyelids have been left relatively untouched.

Finally, there was his mother, *Julia Warhola* (1974). Here he has taken no liberties. Her open regard as she looks into the camera lens is left untouched. He simply toned the silkscreen painting in various colors. A ragged blaze of halo outlines one side of her head. It is touching and reverent, and in its pristine way quite unlike any of the others.

Perhaps his mother's portrait, which Andy did two years after her death, is the affirmative side of his *Norman Fisher* portrait, in which the recently dead subject is seen in a negative reversal as a ghostly outline. There is a ghostly tenderness to *Julia* but he has not surrendered her to the other world.

Perhaps it is too early to discuss the value of the many commissioned portraits Andy undertook from the late seventies until his death. There were several hundred of them, and each is slightly different, although they tend to fall into patterns. Many of the female portraits follow the *Liza* model. In that one, the polaroid photo is not visible in any way, and the pinkish-white paste used on the face has allowed Andy to create a poster-like flat flesh tone that shapes the head and shoulders. In one version, a red background serves to fill in the spaces necessary to model the head, neck and shoulders. A black cap of bobbed hair has been superimposed over a purple rendering of the hair. A black line creates her chin-line, and red lips have been painted over the photographed mouth with acrylic; likewise, a light blue acrylic follows the pattern of the original eye shadow, with the eyes themselves outlined (the eyelashes) in black. It is, in essence, a poster portrait, in which Andy has taken more liberties creatively than he took with any of the *Marilyns*.

So that is the well-traveled course Andy followed when a typical client sat for him one day in 1984. Beverly Chalfen was a businesswoman from Minneapolis. She said that she wanted to have her portrait done by Warhol because

> 'I thought he was the supreme portrait artist of our cen-
> tury . . . . I talked to Dorothy [Blau] about it and she
> in turn talked to him, and I flew into New York . . . .
> He made me feel so comfortable with this posing
> . . . . First we had lunch and we had a lovely time. He was
> extremely shy, of course, I really didn't understand that
> about him . . . . He took about fifty photos of me with
> his polaroid . . . he was so concentrated and intense
> about it. He had a lady there who put some clown
> make-up on me from my forehead to my chest. He
> didn't change me at all. I put a little more mascara than
> usual, and Andy loved my lipstick . . . . Fred Hughes
> was wandering around. Brigid was there. Everyone
> came in to see how it was coming along. Rupert Smith
> was there, of course, and people were wandering in and
> out . . . very informal.'

Beverly Chalfen's polaroid photo chosen by Andy was given the *Liza* treatment, and in the end she purchased six panels. That is what Andy had made up, and she did not want to offend by refusing any of them.

But despite the success of this kind of portraiture, it did not advance Andy's career as an artist by much, since it was just a refinement of a statement he had made in the sixties. There was a sense, which pervaded the Factory as well as the art world, that Andy was passé.

★★★

Three people were involved intimately in Andy's renaissance. It
happened in 1980, soon after Jay Shriver became Andy's painting
assistant. One of the three, Rupert Smith, was already in the
picture, but he was to become increasingly important. The second
was Dorothy Berenson Blau, a dealer in Florida who in that time
of doubt and reappraisal stayed with her conviction that Andy was
the greatest living painter of the age. For Dorothy Blau, to spend
a day at the Factory was like being in the lap of the gods. She
always brought Andy 'goodies', usually candy of some sort, not
because she was courting his favor but because she very simply
adored the man. She respected Rupert's work, too, and thought
they were both geniuses.

The third of Andy's trio of admirers who helped bring him
back to the prominence of the sixties was a gallery dealer, Ronald
Feldman, who shared Dorothy Blau's conviction about Andy's
place as an artist.

Feldman, a former lawyer, had taken over the old Stable Gallery
space on East 74th Street and opened his own gallery in the early
seventies. One of his earliest shows was devoted to the work
of Marcel Duchamp. Andy came around twice because of his
admiration for Duchamp and his sense of identification with
him. Also, he told Feldman, he had come back 'to haunt his
old gallery'. During the Duchamp show, Andy suggested that
Feldman have his portrait done. Andy often did this, but Feldman
told him he did not want one. Andy persevered since this was
just after he had gotten into the swim again with his art. Despite
Feldman's objections, he came in one day and took polaroids of
the dealer. He followed Feldman around all day, snapping photos
of him in the course of his gallery work. Finally, he paused in his
picture-taking and said: 'I don't like the shirt you're wearing. It's
too complicated. Take off your shirt.' So Feldman spent part of
the day in just his teeshirt. Then Andy went away, and about a
month later Ronnie Cutrone came by and said 'Oh God! You
should see the great portraits of you!'

Andy then brought by three portraits of Feldman in his teeshirt
holding a telephone next to his ear. This was Andy's impression
of him, in communication with the world. They were in the same
style as his later *Lillian Carter*.

When Feldman, who was not a wealthy man at the time,

told Andy that he did not know how he was going to pay
for them, Andy said 'No problem'. It turned out that Andy
coveted the Duchamp 'readymade' *Fountain*, which was part of
the recent show. Feldman's portrait was an expediency to acquire
the Duchamp work. Andy was so eager to conclude the deal that
he said: 'Do you want more portraits? You can have five, six,
as many as you want . . . . *And* I'll make you wallpaper of this
portrait, and you can hang it up.'

Feldman was dumbfounded, and told him the wallpaper was
not a good idea, that he was a father of little children and he
did not want them walking into the dining-room and seeing
their father's image plastered all over the wall. Andy was quite
surprised by his reaction, but Feldman settled for three silkscreen
paintings and the trade was made.

It was a learning experience for Feldman. He found that Andy
was 'very purposeful in his actions. He was determined, manipulative, and he was funny. And he was very passionate. He *wanted*
that Duchamp. It was later sold at the auction.'

From that bartering came a relationship that would last to the
end of Andy's life. It was casual at first. Andy would drop by
the gallery and chat. Feldman realized that when they spoke of
Duchamp and de Chirico and other masters, Andy was very
bright. He knew a great many things about art history. Feldman
found these ideas always

> 'came from left field. It was always a surprise. So I was
> very surprised by his take on some of these very famous
> artists . . . . After that, Andy continually asked me for
> ideas. He would come in and say, "Is there anything
> you want me to do? What do you want me to do?"
> I threw out two or three ideas which he immediately
> dismissed . . . .
>
> 'You had to know how to read Andy, the inflection
> of "Oh, gee! Gosh!" meant different things.'

Almost always, when Andy showed up at the Feldman Gallery,
he carried his little dachshund Archie under his arm. He had a
partner for Archie back at his house, Amos, but Archie was now
his constant companion.

An Israeli artist, who had got out of the Soviet Union, by the

name of Sacha Herari, became part of the New York art scene and
befriended Feldman. He told Feldman that he had seen a silkscreen
painting by Andy of Golda Meir that he admired very much. It
was then the eighties, and Andy just had finished a *Muhammad Ali*
portfolio, and he had begun portfolios where the images changed
– you had Ali's fist, his elbow, etc. From that, Feldman got the
idea to have Andy make a portfolio that was ten different images.
He conferred with Sacha, who was helping Feldman at the time,
and they agreed that Andy should do a portfolio of *Ten Jews of
the Twentieth Century*. Feldman said that he called the Factory and
got Fred:

> 'Fred liked the idea, and he yelled across to Andy . . .
> and Andy said, "Great! Gosh! Gee!" And that was it.
> Then he said, "Let's do it." Andy made a list of people
> he thought should be in it. I made a list. Sacha made
> a list. We started to compare these . . . Andy always
> called this portfolio *The Jewish Geniuses*. He wanted to
> do portraits of people who were deceased. He wasn't
> being commissioned by anyone to do these by someone
> because they were alive. That was important to him.'

Feldman published the portfolio in 1980, and it met with some
criticism before it was even completed. Henry Geldzahler never
liked the concept because it was just pandering to a group for
commercial reasons, that group being the Jewish art collectors
who constituted Andy's largest body of patrons. And there were
others beyond Geldzahler who disliked the portfolio almost out of
hand. Feldman was surprised by the reaction and said:

> 'There were people who didn't like Andy in general and
> thought that he was a chic society artist. It was about
> the same time that Truman Capote was thought of the
> same way . . . . I also got criticism from some in my
> profession who said, "Why do you want to get involved
> with Warhol? That's all over with." I felt that Andy had
> a long way to go . . . . Andy was a very good receiver of
> ideas.'

Despite mixed critical reaction to the published work (it was

not included in the major retrospective of Andy's work at the
Museum of Modern Art in 1989, possibly because of Geldzahler's
negative reaction to it, although the selection was not his to make),
Andy had faith in the idea, and eventually it turned out well for
both himself and Feldman. The Jews selected by Andy, Feldman
and Sacha Herari were catholic in range, no pun intended. Included
were Franz Kafka, Gertrude Stein, George Gershwin, the Marx
Brothers, Martin Buber, Albert Einstein, Louis Brandeis, Golda
Meir, Sarah Bernhardt, and Sigmund Freud. From this group of
artists, Andy would segue into another series of ten prints, *Endangered Species*. His critics failed to note the connection.

What is truly marvelous about the Ten Portraits, making them
a great leap forward for Andy, is the color spectrum. Kafka is
in shades of blue; Stein's likeness becomes a drawing with blocks
of blue and a light brick shade dividing her Roman senator
head, with a shaft of what is obviously sunlight striking her
ear; Gershwin is unevenly quartered in tones of brown, deep
green and red; the desert sun strikes Golda Meir on her cheek
and chin – a truly extraordinary portrait of the lady; Einstein is
seen in tones of gray and black – gray matter?

The portfolios were published, the first printing numbering
fifty, but they were not selling. This fact, confirmed by Feldman
the publisher, should refute for all time that this was designed to
be sold to Jewish patrons. They were out there and they all knew
about the project, but few were buying. Andy's reputation was
at a low point at the time and it appeared that *Ten Jews of the
Twentieth Century* might not restore it. Feldman was worried:

> 'If this doesn't turn out well, that isn't Andy's problem.
> It's your problem. You've invested all this money in
> advance. Andy doesn't give you these prints with his
> signature on them until you finish paying him. When I
> realized that this was the way this was going to work, I
> also decided that Andy was going to have to work very
> hard at this project because basically I'm a perfectionist.
> I realized that Andy was a workaholic and it was all right
> to drive him crazy. That he respected it. And Andy did
> work very hard on these projects, and I enjoyed that
> part . . . I was very supportive of him and he never
> did forget that we established a market for his work at

a time when it was waning and that we did it seriously and we did it first-class.'

Feldman had run his gallery to show important contemporary art but not necessarily commercially successful art. It had not been a big money-maker for him and now that he was so heavily involved in this first major portfolio, somehow it had to work out for him.

'So I got this idea of pre-selling some of this work in advance to people, sight-unseen, just on the description that there would be an Andy Warhol portrait of Einstein, of Martin Buber and the Marx Brothers and so on. I had made the acquaintance of, but did not know that well, Dorothy Blau. I had met her when she had her own gallery in Florida and she was now running the Hokin Gallery, and I told her what this was. She had been a long-standing fan of Andy's. A professional groupie on the highest level. She just adored him. She said to me, "I love this idea. I think this is incredible . . . ." I said to her, "Dorothy, can you sell these sight-unseen, because I have nothing to show. I have to collect the money in advance." I knew there was no market for this now. You could buy the *Marilyns*, the *Flowers* and the *Electric Chairs* for not much money. Here I was having to pay Andy a good deal of money to do these and wondering how I was going to get the prices of the art work up so I would make this pay. And Dorothy said that she would try. Then she would call me every few days and she would say [he laughs as he speaks] . . . now Sacha Herari was out there and supposed to be selling a lot of these sets, and he did sell some but not many. Dorothy would report in every few days, "I sold five more. I sold six more." Finally, I had to say to her, "Dorothy stop!" I think from my point of view in reality Dorothy Blau really made the Warhol market. She started the comeback, making this economically successful.'

Yet there were the bogeymen from the past to imperil the

series. When the finished portraits were being hung at the Jewish Museum by Andy, Feldman and Andy's friend David Whitney, Hilton Kramer, who was still at the *Times*, phoned and asked to see the show. Andy and David groaned, and Feldman exclaimed: 'Oh God! Not him!' So Feldman attempted to keep Kramer at bay until the show opened, but Kramer would have no part of that. He wanted to review the show in time for the Jewish holidays, and Feldman just knew that Kramer was going to trash the show. Andy knew Kramer as an old enemy and said, 'Oh, why him? He's just going to say nasty things about me.' But the museum felt that it had to let Kramer in to get an advance look at the show, and he came and he trashed it, as predicted.

Andy took it in his stride, but Feldman was upset since this meant so much to him. There was one consoling call from artist Jim Rosenquist, who phoned to say, 'I just want you to know that I have seen Hilton Kramer's art work. It's third-rate Reginald Marsh.' Rosenquist had reason to be peeved at Kramer since he had been trashed at a crucial moment in his life when his first show opened after a terrible car accident that had nearly killed him and his wife. For most artists, Kramer was their equivalent of the actors' John Simon.

Dorothy Blau was not daunted by the bad notice, and went on selling the work. She was not even stopped by the Robert Hughes attack in the *New York Review of Books*. If anything, the Hughes review was more blistering than Kramer's (and Hughes was to write one of the few bad notices of the huge posthumous Museum of Modern Art retrospective).

To Andy, all of this was an enormous game. He had powerful enemies, and in a strange way he drew strength from their animosity. It was a little like his reaction to bad reviews of his films, grinning and saying 'Oh, they hate it! They really hate it!'

Of course, his enemies knew that Andy had a great deal of power himself, and it must have been very annoying to them when he made his 'comeback' in the eighties after they had assumed that he was thoroughly squelched.

Andy helped to promote the portfolios and the sale of the silkscreens that 'spun off' them. In 1981, when he did the *Myths* series, he 'went on the road' to promote the project. The *Myths* were ten traditional American images, and it is perhaps significant that he included himself, 'disguised' as the enormously popular

radio voice 'The Shadow' ('The Shadow knows . . .'). There was
no false modesty in Andy. He knew that the media had recognized
him as the most famous American artist of his time, and this may
have been a gesture of contempt for his enemies, who would
try to deny him what was already his. Other *Myths* were *The
Star* (Garbo as 'Mata Hari'), *Uncle Sam, Howdy Doody, Dracula,
Mickey Mouse, Santa Claus, The Witch* (from *The Wizard of Oz*),
Mammy, and *Superman*. Andy's critics certainly could have made
as much fuss about *Mammy* as they had about the *Jews*. But they
would have been crying into the wind: Andy was delineating on
silkscreen canvas the images of our culture, and *Mammy* certainly
was one of them, whether she was Scarlett O'Hara's beloved
companion or simply the face on a box of Aunt Jemima Pancake
Flour.

The collaboration with Rupert in achieving absolutely exquisite
colors in screen-prints was even more ravishing in this portfolio.

On one of their promotional junkets, Feldman and Andy were
on their way to the show's opening at Weinstock's in Sacramento.
Feldman said that they drove up from San Francisco in a lim-
ousine:

> '. . . and all of a sudden the roof of the limo started
> to leak, and Andy held a cup catching the water all
> the way to Sacramento, while we were talking about
> politics. Bob Colacello was in the car. His was sort of
> a conservative Republican point of view, and Andy was
> listening to Bob and then turned to me and said: "That
> sounds right." '

And, of course, it was. They arrived at a newly renovated inn,
and Andy and his party were to be the first guests, although he
was unaware of it. Andy wiped the fog off the windows and
looked out at the landmark building and said: 'What's this?'

Bob and Fred (Hughes) looked as aghast as Andy. They went
inside and it was beautifully set up for their arrival with a
luncheon buffet laid out for them. Andy and the others went
upstairs and shortly came down and Andy told Feldman: 'We
don't want to stay here.'

Feldman knew that Weinstock's had gone to some trouble to
arrange their accommodation, and he wanted to know what

was wrong. Andy said they had no privacy, that it was 'not anonymous enough'. This seemed like a flimsy excuse to Feldman for leaving what were obviously luxurious rooms, and then he managed to dig out the truth from Andy. There were no television sets in the rooms. So he phoned Weinstock's and they quickly told him, 'It's no problem.' While they ate their lunch, all of their rooms were equipped with brand-new televisions.

The opening at Weinstock's was a turning-point for Andy as a television guest or interviewee. Before, he usually had someone else answer questions for him, but at Weinstock's Department Store, the television stations had worked it out with the store to have an individual interview with Andy in each of several decorator rooms in the furniture department, and each room had a different Warhol on the wall behind him. Suddenly he began answering questions on his own, and for the first time felt at ease staring into a TV camera.

That night, Andy wanted to party, and they had heard about a place outside of town. They piled into a couple of limos and drove about fifteen minutes until they reached what looked like a truck stop. Feldman described it as

'quite large, and inside there was the whole front of a truck, the cab of a big interstate truck, and it was turned into a disco. It was packed and it was a gay disco. I sort of hugged the wall, and it was the most amazing phenomenon because as I walked around I heard comments like "Andy's here!" Not "Andy Warhol's here", but "Andy's here!" It was as if they knew from PR that Andy was in town and it seemed so natural that Andy would arrive in a scene like this . . . . The pace of the dancing picked up and it was like an incredibly lively electric party, an enormous amount of fun. It was with great respect and love that they spoke Andy's name. I realized that Andy meant a tremendous amount to all those people in the room . . . . He never spoke directly about his sexuality or anything like that . . . but at the same time, it was clear that Andy wasn't afraid to identify with gays. We left with an enormous number of people and we went back to the Inn, and I was sure that this old house was going to fall apart with the number

of people we brought back there. It turned out that
these two wonderful women who ran it had closed all
the shades; they had made food for everybody. I went
to bed at I don't know what hour, and Andy was very
happy that we were staying in that inn.'

Ronald Feldman knew that Andy and Fred Hughes had now
taken their art business away from the Castelli Gallery and he
had no intention of 'stepping on Leo's toes. I satisfied myself that
Andy was a free agent, and that this was not a problem.'

As for Castelli, there seems little doubt that Andy was 'a special
case'. He had made his art a business, and he was running
it without any consultation with Leo Castelli. There was no
animosity between them. It was simply understood. And later,
when a series seemed truly exciting to Leo, he would sit down
with Andy and discuss the possibility of a show (*Camouflages*,
although their discussion came too late and the show would not
open until after Andy's death).

For Rupert Smith, the collaboration with Andy on the successive series was the culmination of his lifelong ambition to leave
something behind that would have his mark on it. The bolder
colors, the dark outlines, the diamond dust, all of those things
had come from long sessions of working things out with Andy.
Andy's new look in the eighties was engineered by Rupert.

The third series portfolio, *The Endangered Species*, was perhaps
the most successful one of all. Here in dazzling, brilliant colors were *Grevy's Zebra*, the *Giant Panda*, an *African Elephant*,
a *Pine Barrens Tree Frog* of incredible beauty, a *San Francisco
Silverspot* (butterfly), the American *Bald Eagle*, a *Black Rhinoceros*,
the *Siberian Tiger*, the *Bighorn Ram*, and the *Orangutan*. It seems
to me that the *Jews* led the way to this mature, breathtakingly
beautiful work.

The fourth series was closer in spirit to Andy's early work and
possibly closer to his heart as well, but less exciting in concept
than the two earlier portfolios. This was *Ads* (1985), and Andy
had done his own versions of famous magazine advertisements,
including one featuring his old friend, the late Judy Garland, in
a Blackgama mink, which is a bit wry, since Andy's immediate
previous work was *Endangered Species*, a series that was a boon
to animal rights activists; but now he had glorified a mink coat

ad.* Still, this only underscored one obvious fact about Andy: he
seemed to be totally unaware of 'causes'.

When Andy died, he was in the midst of creating a series of
TV Legends, with Lucy, the Honeymooners, and other significant
television landmarks. One that was finished was his version of
the greatest live TV coverage in our time, *Moonwalk*, showing an
astronaut on the moon. It is bold, the colors brilliant, the figure
taking a dramatic step forward. Andy and Rupert had found a
new path, but this has become known as Andy's last art work and
it was tragic that it had to end there at the start of their journey
into a new way of looking at the very familiar.

They also were only part of the way into a major commissioned
series to be called *Cars*. Andy's friend and dealer in Düsseldorf,
Hans Mayer, had interested the Daimler-Benz Company in having Andy do a series of silkscreen paintings of their famous cars.
In 1986 Mayer had come across a Mercedes ad commemorating
the first hundred years of the invention of the automobile. The
advertisement was captioned 'bow to the engineering genius'
and there were seventeen different vehicles from various manu-
facturers displayed – the Benz Patent Motorcar of 1886, the
Daimler Motor Carriage of the same year, the 1889 Panhard
two-seater, the Ford Model T of 1917, a 1910 Rolls Royce Silver
Ghost, a 1935 Bugati, a 1935 Opel Olympia, a 1931 DKW, the
1938 Volkswagen Bug, a Mercedes-Benz truck of 1931, a 1935
Studebaker, the Glas Goggomobil of 1957, a 1954 Citroen CV,
a 1956 Citroen DS, the Apollo-15 moon vehicle of 1971, a 1967
NSU Ro 80 and a 1984 Mercedes-Benz sedan. The idea was for
Andy to do a series of silkscreen paintings and serigraph portfolios
of the cars in the ad.

Mayer was so taken with the project, he ordered four paintings
from Andy before anything was finalized with Daimler-Benz.
Andy chose to do one not in the ad – the sleek 300 SL coupé,

---

* By the end of the eighties, Halston and other designers would be forced
to come down on one side or the other on the issue of wearing furs. In
England, Andy's long-time friend, photographer and documentarian David
Bailey, was one of the leaders against the use of furs. He created a brilliant
TV 'commercial' depicting a fashion show runway down into a crowd of
fashion-conscious spectators into whose midst a number of beautiful models
in furs parade. When they are all lined up and preening in their minks and
sables, there is a flood of very red 'blood' that begins gushing from the coats,
covering them, the runway and splashing the spectators with gore.

a sports car noted for its upward-swinging gullwing doors, produced in 1952 by Daimler-Benz, a design Roland Barthes in
Mythologies described as 'the inception of a new phenomenology
of juxtaposed elements that cohere solely by reason of their superb
form.' Andy completed four panels of the 300 SL coupé in May
1986. The Mercedes people were delighted with the works, and
that September a contract was signed for the series. Ever the
corporate friend, Andy proposed that the series be limited to
one hundred years of Mercedes cars exclusively. He planned
to do twenty different models. The contract would give forty
separate paintings to Daimler-Benz with another forty reserved
for the artist.

Design material on eight cars was furnished to Andy by the
company in 1986, and he and Rupert immediately began working
on them, work that was done in tandem with the *TV Legends*,
which was already laid out. Andy was supposed to fly to Stuttgart
in February or March of 1987 to pick out design material on
twelve additional cars. He completed the first eight cars, totaling
thirty-two images, in early January 1987.

It was an ambitious undertaking, but Andy was notably self-
confident in the last years of his life. He had no qualms about
anything that he undertook because he knew that he could not
only do it but turn it into something of permanent value. The
Cars series showed how Andy moved back and forth in style from
the brilliant colors of his work in the eighties to the half-drawn
silkscreens of the mid-seventies (*Mick Jagger*, the *Flowers*, *Black
and White*, etc.). The resultant large format silkscreens suggest
Dufy, and the selective omissions in the all-sketched version of
Karl Benz and Josef Brecht in the Benz Patent Motorcar (1886),
a horseless carriage, resembles Edouard Manet's oil sketch of
novelist George Moore (1879) right down to the derby hat.

In the catalogue for the show, art historian Werner Spies
comments on Warhol's repetitive imagery, which 'revealed the
difference between Warhol and the other artists of the Pop scene
with whom he is generally lumped . . . let us inquire into the
message hidden behind so much emphasis on surface. Though
apparently this message consists largely in absurd gestures meant
to underline an inability to explain, we find indications enough
that Warhol's indifference is an assumed role. Particularly his
central motif, repetition, is expressive of a fear of life. There

are many statements to corroborate this, usually couched in whimsical form: "I really do live for the future, because when I'm eating a box of candy, I can't wait to taste the last piece. I don't even taste any of the other pieces, I just want to finish and throw the box away and not have to have it on my mind anymore." '

THIRTY-SEVEN

Andy made several new and en-
during friendships in the eighties. In New York, there was Paige
Powell, who had just begun her job at *Interview*. There were
others met abroad. He was traveling to Europe often, usually
on the Concorde and in the company of Fred and a young
photographer he had met some years earlier, Christopher Makos.
In 1983, in Paris he met one of Fred's 'protégés', an expatriate
American who called himself Billy Boy. Billy Boy was a very
young jewelry designer who had amassed a fortune before his
twenty-fifth birthday. While he had done all of this in Paris,
he and the Parisians still thought of him as an American. Like
Andy, he seemed to be turning his life into a myth so that
the facts of his life as set down by him cannot be considered as anything but apocryphal. But he said that he was an
orphan:

> 'I was adopted and I disowned my family, so I have
> no family except my friends. I really had a very, very
> private relationship with Andy, and he treated me really
> well . . . . He respected me. He was very conservative,
> you know. He'd go to church. He was very charitable
> . . . . He would tease me about things, but it was always
> in a very friendly, sweet way.'

Billy Boy had created his own niche in Parisian *haute couture*
circles. He was respected and admired because he had become
an authority on the subject of high fashion, and spent much of
his money collecting *haute couture* of the past. He had hundreds of
gowns from past decades, and when museums wanted to have a
show of such artifacts, they always contacted Billy Boy. He also

collected jewelry, so he had that in common with Andy, and they
would shop together.

They made an extraordinary appearance walking down the
street together – Andy in his silver wig and Billy Boy, with his
dark hair hanging down one side of his face, black fingernail polish, his fingers encrusted with over-sized rings, and both visages
as pale as the moon.

Billy Boy also collected Barbie dolls, and had over 10,000
stacked in his quarters, each one catalogued and reposing in a
little coffin of cardboard. In honour of their friendship, Andy
would do a painting of *Barbie*. Later, Billy Boy would write the
definitive 'biography' of Barbie, which met with some success.
He also began writing his memoirs, though he was not yet thirty.
He seemed to be an eccentric combination of Andy Warhol and
Truman Capote, although Truman had been very ordinary in
his clothing and hairstyles, while Billy Boy had created his own
unique image.

In polar contrast to Billy Boy was Andy's friendship with the
young graffiti artist Jean-Michel Basquiat. In the eighties, there
was a movement in the arts away from the by now expected
modes of Pop and the minimalists. Color was in vogue again
and feeling. Cy Twombly, in the seventies and even earlier,
had made the graffiti scrawl an acceptable art form. Now in the
eighties, Basquiat and Keith Haring had taken their graffiti from
the walls of old buildings and subway stops into the galleries.
Andy was interested, and befriended both of them, but Basquiat
took special pains to cultivate Andy. He was then broke and
selling postcard-sized graffiti art on the street and in restaurants
in the Soho area, where he had confined his outdoor work with
the Magic Marker. He needed money for drugs primarily, since
he then had no home of his own but 'crashed' the apartments of
friends.

Basquiat was a handsome black youth in his early twenties.
He came from a middle-class Brooklyn home (Boerum Hill,
which was just a step down from posh Brooklyn Heights),
his father being a Haitian-born accountant who owned his own
brownstone.

Andy may have been in a repentant mood when they met since
he became a father-figure in Basquiat's life, determined to get him
clean of drugs. He supplied Basquiat with paints and canvas and,

within a couple of years, loaned him the use of a loft on Great Jones Street that he owned. Basquiat was wild and in constant motion. He danced with Andy's crowd, he ate and drank with them, and then went back to his loft to paint and do drugs. He was on cocaine, heroin and pot. Andy was particularly disturbed about the heroin and was determined to get him off it.

There were other would-be saviors in Basquiat's life. One of them, Vreg Baghoomian, was a dealer who opened a new gallery in Soho primarily to promote Basquiat's work. And there were several girlfriends, the last being Kelly Inman, a beautiful girl who took her own apartment in the Great Jones Street building Andy owned after finding it impossible to live with the young painter. A gallery dealer, Annina Nosei, gave him a place to work in ahead of Andy in the basement of her gallery, and it was there that he created the first bold Basquiat images, the bright colored and black-outlined canvases with primitive figures and graffiti legends. Words were as important to him in his paintings as the images themselves.

Sometimes, Andy invited Basquiat to the Factory and they collaborated on a canvas. This was extraordinary, of course, since Andy had not painted on a canvas surface with acrylics, oils or anything else for more than twenty years.

Their collaborations were exhibited, but the critics were more excited by Basquiat's solo work. Andy was gracious about this and encouraged his friends to buy them, and he acquired a number of them himself.

One of Basquiat's earliest boosters was Henry Geldzahler. He 'overpaid' Basquiat for a painting, giving him $2,000 for it instead of $1,000, but within a short time Basquiat had moved into a larger gallery, Mary Boone's, and his work was selling for $20,000 to $35,000. He was winning acceptance in Europe through a dealer in Switzerland. Still, the drug-taking escalated. He perforated his septum snorting coke. He tried to quit, even taking 'cold turkey cures' by withdrawing to a remote Hawaiian island, but he was too far gone into the habit.

Andy edged away from him a little bit, although the cooling off may have been mutual since Basquiat felt that he was getting a reputation as a Warhol protégé, a label that he resented fiercely. When Andy died suddenly in 1987, he was overwhelmed by a sense of guilt, and the drugs took an even tighter hold on him.

In the middle of August 1988, a year and a half after Andy's death, Kelly Inman found him lying on the floor of his apartment in his own vomit. He was dead at twenty-seven.

Andy had introduced Basquiat to an attractive young woman who worked for him, Paige Powell, and she was known as one of the young artist's several girlfriends. Andy and Paige became close, and she frequently accompanied him to parties, openings and other social events. She was pushed along by Andy and, through her own talents, very soon became Advertising Director of *Interview* magazine. She had come to the Factory in 1980, and had moved rapidly up through the ranks at *Interview*. Andy always kept a close eye on how much ad space was being sold. He believed implicitly in the connection between a magazine's success and its advertising. Paige often invited him to a luncheon to clinch a deal and used him in that sense, but, after all was said and done, it was *his* magazine and he was the one who was obsessed with ad space.

Despite Andy's occasional gestures towards liberal views (the McGovern for President poster, the Mao silkscreen paintings, which had made the founder of the People's Republic of China as much of an icon in the western world as in his own country), he held mostly conservative political views. There was nothing paradoxical in this. Perhaps he knew as well as anyone how anti-liberal the leftist regimes everywhere were in dealing with sexual matters.

In the summer of 1981, President and Nancy Reagan's new daughter-in-law Doria had become a contributing editor to *Interview* magazine. Through her good offices, an interview with the First Lady was set up for 14 October.

Andy arrived at the White House with his editor, Bob Colacello, and Doria (Mrs Ronald Reagan, Jr)★. They immediately adjourned to the library, where Nancy Reagan, wearing a black-and-white Adolfo suit and black pumps, awaited them.

The First Lady lightened the mood immediately by telling them that she was giving secret Tupperware parties upstairs in the White House, which prefaced her handing Doria a piece of Tupperware 'for her collection'. Rather surprisingly, Andy told

★ Doria Palmieri married Ron Reagan, seven years her junior, soon after the Reagans moved into the White House.

her 'I don't think I've ever actually seen a piece of Tupperware.'

Then Andy volunteered the thought that 'they should have a lottery where they invite one family to dinner every night [at the White House] because it's so exciting to be here.'

Soon, Nancy was telling them how unique Bess Truman was, which Colacello countered with: 'My mother used to tell me that Bess Truman wore her corsages upside down, and that it was an embarrassment to the United States. But my mother's a fanatic Republican.' Nancy ignored this and went on to Eleanor Roosevelt, followed by a long monologue about drug abuse and how parents should deal with it.

Like a skooter-car in an amusement park, the conversation bounced off that one and into another sure short-run with a colloquy on television news. Andy said, 'Sometimes the Press makes crime seem so glamorous.' Nancy quickly agreed and spoke of the medals 'we gave to some young people who performed great, heroic deeds . . . an eleven-year-old boy who crawled on his stomach over thin ice to a schoolmate who had fallen through.' She uniformly used 'we' to mean the President, so clearly the Reagan presidency was a collaboration at least as far as awards were concerned.

Young Ron Reagan had helped brief Andy and Colacello on what areas were 'good things' to talk about with his mother. Now Andy complimented Ron by saying to Nancy: 'Ron seems so close to you and his father.' Nancy quickly agreed. '. . . You know, we were in a business which always meant a public life. To some extent it was difficult because of that, but we always did try to stay close to the children, sometimes maybe closer than they would have liked.'

To this, Andy commented: 'Well, movie people are kind of weird . . . .' A mistress of composure, Nancy laughed indulgently and said: 'Andy, I have to tell you that you're losing me.'

Then Nancy revealed that her godmother was Alla Nazimova. This should have interested Andy, since Nazimova's previously banned silent movie based on Oscar Wilde's *Salome* had done very well in an uptown revival in Manhattan, chiefly among gay audiences. But he let this pass without any comment except 'Really? Great.'

She spoke at length about her actress mother (Edith Luckett), and then said that she herself was on Broadway with Mary Martin in *Lute Song*, in which she doubtless played an oriental, and she added that Mary had lunched at the White House 'the other day'. Andy thought that Mary still looked 'great, probably because she went to Janet Sartin.'★

Inevitably, they got around to discussing the grand old days at Metro-Goldwyn-Mayer, 'the last days of the contract system', as Nancy described them, and she confided that she was so unsure of herself as a movie actress, she kept her New York apartment. Then for the second time, Andy brought up the movie of Cristina Crawford's book, *Mommie Dearest*, and said: 'There's one scene where LB fires her, where you really feel sorry for Joan Crawford, where she really is a person. It's a very strange movie though.' And Nancy responded: 'I just don't think you write a book like that about your mother.' (Within less than five years, her own daughter, Patti Davis, had written a less than flattering account of parents very like her own in a novel called *Home Front*.) The interview remained comfortably on that track, Nancy concluding with: '. . . We've been talking about Ron and Doria and Patti. I'm very lucky. I love them all very much. I'm very lucky to have them.'

Less than two months later, Nancy Reagan made the cover of *Interview*'s Christmas issue, wearing one of her red dresses against a green and white starry background.

Andy was modeling for the Zoli and the Ford agencies. Years before, he was flattered to be asked to pose. He knew that his was a famous image the ad people coveted. But then it got to be a frequent affair, and he saw no reason why he should not be paid, so he alternated between the two modeling agencies. Andy's look was unusual; he had made it so, and it turned out to be valuable. The old hustle was still there, and he felt no shame about it. In fact, he took a certain pride in being a sought-after model. As Chris Makos described his look: 'When he was younger, he played with the idea of looking older, and when he was older, with that of looking younger.' Only in the privacy of his home did he put that image aside. There, he was a Warhola again, the boy whom the lost Julia spent more than

★ Janet Sartin ran a chain of skin-care centers.

half her life looking after. Paige sometimes was allowed to see that self:

> 'He came from the eastern European mentality of being traditional and conservative. He loved waking up early in the morning, watching the news, making his little breakfast – he ate seven different grains. Then he had his carrot juice, but then he had his sweet tooth.'

Towards the end, he was in such discomfort from his gallbladder he had cut out chocolates altogether, a great sacrifice. He would have chicken soup, tea and other bland food. For his gallbladder problem, in addition to the practical measures of diet and doctoring, he also wore a huge crystal around his neck that was supposed to have healing properties. He wore another one at his waist to zero in on the gallbladder. Sometimes, the crystals had to be recharged and he would take them to his crystal person, Ernestine, where they were laid up for a day or so while their magic was restored. He was half-ashamed to be involved with such voodoo, and he was greatly disappointed when they failed to do what they were supposed to. On the practical side, he went to Dr Karen Burke for collagen treatments which erased the wrinkles from his face but were extremely painful at the time. Then he went regularly to a nutritionist, Dr Linda Li.

When one considers the time Andy spent keeping himself in shape, and the hours consumed by partying and other social functions, here was a person in nearly constant motion nearly all his waking hours. He truly never allowed himself to catch up with himself.

The wonder is how he made it to all the parties he did. If the invitation or mention did not go onto his daily calendar pad, he might well forget to go. Andy was perhaps the most disorganized person his friends and staff ever had encountered. He sometimes forgot appointments or he would get there late. He was forever jotting down phone numbers on scraps of paper and then losing them. A rollidex would have been unthinkable to him because then he would have the people in his life in some kind of order and accessibility and he did not want that. It was as though if he kept the phone numbers of those people who meant something to him memorized and not on a printed card, they were somehow always there, available to him. But sometimes he would lose a scrap of paper or a matchbook with a phone number of someone recently met who had struck him as being attractive and he would get very angry with himself.

THIRTY-EIGHT

At the end of August 1984, Truman Capote died in California of arrhythmia (an erratic heart beat leading to failure) that was probably brought on by a drug overload.

Of course, Andy was more concerned about gossip around what Truman had left than about his loss. He thought that Truman's old boyfriend Jack Dunphy had got $600,000.

Andy then had a girl on his Factory staff whom he thought to be Truman's niece, Kate Harrington. But when talking over Truman's passing at work, Brigid figured out that Kate Harrington was really Kate O'Shea, the daughter of one of Truman's married boyfriends, John O'Shea.

It was 'Truman week' around the Factory because *New York* magazine had commissioned Andy to paint a cover portrait of Truman for their next issue.

So his old idol was dead and, of course, his feet had turned to clay a long time ago. But they had many long sessions together reminiscing as only aging queens can do. And certainly the irony was not lost on either of them that in the end, the ardent worshiper was helping to keep the idol's food and drink on the table.

Andy thought, too, of Truman's possessions. There would be no sale of his furnishings. Better call the Salvation Army. His sofa and chairs in his posh United States Plaza apartment were torn beyond repair by his bulldogs. There were other valuables, however, and Andy must have wondered if there would be a sale.

Andy had always been a collector and now it became a passion. With Stuart Pivar, a businessman whom he met in the seventies through a personal friend, Todd Brasner, Andy would go foraging every day. Pivar was now successful enough with his business interests to turn over the work to his staff and spend the day shopping. But first they would talk on the phone. Andy would discuss for a couple of hours with Pivar what happened last night, and then around eleven or twelve o'clock Pivar and his driver would go by Andy's house and pick him up. Pivar and Andy loved to shop in quantity and made no apologies for buying 'lots of everything'. Pivar tried to explain:

> 'Most real collectors have loads and loads of things. Very few people who own art are really art collectors. People who are furnishing their houses with an impressionist painting – most so-called art collectors are like that – they pay attention to one kind of thing and that's what they buy. They don't look at anything else. These people are not really art collectors. People who are connoisseurs of art buy art of every single period. They buy art from every single period and go into galleries and look at every single sale that there is and go in and buy the things. Andy was like that and so are a lot of other people . . . . Criticism of Andy [after his death and the sale of his things] revealed their fundamental inadequacy in understanding collectors. What he did was normal.'

They went to flea markets uptown and downtown. It became a ritual for them to go to the flea market every Sunday. For Andy, whatever else he might have planned, it was always mass at St Vincent's and then the flea market with Pivar.

Pivar explained something of Andy's catholic taste:

> 'He collected things from classical antiquities to the present. Paintings, decorative objects. I can't think of any area he did not . . . . He used to artificially draw lines and try not to look at certain things because everything was just so overwhelming as he would discover category after category . . . . "Oh, my god! Another category!" he would say. For example, we didn't get interested in oriental art. We tried to draw the line. But still, we'd go to look at it. One of his very big interests was folk art, but he stopped being interested in folk art

a long time ago for a very interesting reason. The only
other institution he had anything to do with besides the
Academy [American Academy of Fine Art] was the Folk
Art Museum, but he said they threw him off the board
and he was very offended by that. I guess he didn't
come to some meetings. He was permanently insulted
to the point that there was something about folk art that
irritated him and he wouldn't look at it again.'

Whatever Pivar has said about Andy's collections, it is fairly
obvious that Andy was a shopper of the first order. Shoppers
differ slightly from collectors in that they usually buy *everything*.
He would buy everything that was available, if he liked what he
saw, meaning if there were one hundred cookie jars in the shape of
a black mammy, he bought the entire lot. Such purchases became
part of his hoardings and usually never were seen again. In this, he
was like William Randolph Hearst, another shopper, who bought
wholesale quantities of antiquities which remained in crates in
warehouses in the Bronx and in California until he died, with the
exception of a forced sale of part of it when he got into financial
trouble.

Andy loved the things he bought. All the Art Deco he acquired
was the very best that survived the Deco years, which began in
the 1880s and lasted until 1960. Deco works were created after
that year (for example, Elsa Peretti silver), but the heyday of the
style was in that eighty-year time-span.

Both Andy and Hearst enjoyed the possession of things they
would never see again. There was something in Andy that drew
cheer from just knowing that he owned something precious. If he
enjoyed a party and made a photo record of it, the chances were
good that the photos would go into storage, either a photo storage
case or a Time Capsule, and sealed from his sight forevermore.

The auction houses knew him well, and he was in Sotheby's
the week before he died. Knowing his fondness for the place,
it was Fred Hughes's decision to have them handle the sale of
what became known as the Andy Warhol Collection. When the
contents were revealed and everyone knew that he had watches
by the hundreds, cookie jars by the gross, and enough silver
to keep Tiffany's stocked for several months, most everyone
wondered why he bought so much and why his estate seemed

to be unloading everything he had ever touched. It became a media field-day, and editorial artists even drew cartoons showing the auctioneer selling off Andy's corpse.

But it was all part of his strategy to acquire what pieces of life he could put his hands on – things that were beautiful or functional or both that had meant something to other people. It was of a piece with his party-going, which was incessant and beyond anything the average person could keep up with. His Diary is filled with such events and with the names of the people there, but there is real desperation in those pages and in his acquisitions. Ordinary life seemed to be eluding him always because he was different, and he was always in pursuit of it. He was also an inveterate fan of the celebrated. He asked them for autographs almost up to the end of his life, and many a famous person wondered why Andy Warhol, who they thought was more famous than they were, wanted their signature on a scrap of paper.

In 1981, Jon Gould had introduced Andy to Aspen, Colorado, and they had spent their first Christmas holiday together there. Andy even tried to ski on the baby slope. It became a tradition and they went there for four successive Christmases. But by 1985, their affair had cooled to the point where Andy spent the holiday at the Church of the Heavenly Rest in their soup kitchen doling out food to the needy and homeless. Paige went with him and was distressed by the quality of the food. She had been spoiled by too many years of the best restaurants and catered dinners.

It had been a bad year in other respects. Two of his *Interview* editors had died of AIDS. In the autumn, his distinguished book of photos and text called *America* was published by Harper and Row. The book was in part an album of photos of his friends, from sexy John Sex and his python to Bob Rauschenberg, whom he snapped as he peed in a toilet (discreetly shot from the back). But he also had a shot of himself in drag under a harsh light, children, a homeless woman, a variety of dogs, celebrities, anonymous young men working out, and spreads on his favorite places from Montauk to California. He did not get along with his editor, but he had to tour the bookstores with him. And then at Rizzoli's Book Shop on Fifth Avenue, some young woman was in line in front of the table where he was signing books, and when she handed him her book, she reached across and snatched his wig off his head. Then she threw it over the balcony to a male confederate, who ran out of the store with it. Andy was wearing a Calvin Klein coat with a hood so he instinctively pulled the hood up over his head and continued signing. But the incident offended him profoundly and for days he could not shake his anger and sense of humiliation.

THIRTY-NINE

In late summer 1986, John Warhola's son, Donald, arrived in Manhattan seeking a job with his Uncle Andy. A recent graduate of the University of Pittsburgh, he had majored in computer science, and he proposed setting up a computer system at the Factory, including the *Interview* office. He came with a friend, and the idea was that Donald would handle the software and his friend would purchase and maintain the equipment. Andy said, 'He's cute and smart. If he works for us, he'll have to change his name to Warhol – I couldn't take a "Warhola" running around the office.'

Meanwhile, Basquiat had changed galleries so frequently, by this time he had run out of them. He spoke to Andy of wanting to go with Castelli, but Andy knew how seldom Leo took anyone new on.

Benjamin Liu had dropped by the Factory one day and picked Andy up to go out on the town. That greatly cheered Andy, who had fond memories of Benjamin's years of elbow companionship. They saw each other frequently the rest of the year, and Andy was excited about the delicate jewelry Benjamin was creating as well as the personal fashions, including one dress made entirely of sleeves and another entirely of pockets.

When Jon Gould died on 18 September at the age of thirty-three, Andy could not bear to talk about it. When he died, he was down to seventy pounds and had gone blind, but he denied right up to the end that it was AIDS. This was Andy's last real commitment to anyone and even though it had not worked out, he obviously cared deeply, which probably surprised even him. It must have frightened him, too, since the disease had taken off so many of his friends, seeming to move closer and closer to him. At first, he had succumbed to the hysteria that had gripped many of the uninformed and was even leery of eating food that might have been touched by an afflicted person, but then sometimes other gay men would kiss him when he knew they had the disease, or their lovers did, and he had to handle that. He always told his Diary but he never complained to anyone else.

He spent his last Thanksgiving Day and Christmas at the Church of the Heavenly Rest feeding the poor. He took a friend each time but they were not as committed to their task as Andy was.

On 22 January 1987, Andy's variations on da Vinci's *The Last Supper* were unveiled at the Alexandre Iolas/Creditor Valtellinese Gallery in Milan. With Andy were Fred Hughes, photographer Christopher Makos and the Italian journalist Daniela Morera. The work itself was not-so-typical late Warhol. He had taken photo reproductions of Leonardo's work and made a very formal composition of them, several of them upside down.

Guests at the opening were invited to visit the refectory of the Church of Santa Maria delle Grazie, right across the Corso Magenta from the Iolas Gallery, where the original fresco of the work might be seen, although only partially restored (the refectory was closed to the public soon afterwards to complete the restoration, a project that would become so controversial, in early February a petition – which Andy signed – went into circulation to stop the restorers, who were applying new layers of paint rather than attempting to salvage the original). The Iolas show attracted a crowd of nearly 3,000 people and became a media event, with the gallery (another converted refectory) overwhelmed by television crews and equipment.

Afterwards, Andy was the honored guest at a dinner party in the Via Matteotti Gallery run by the antiques dealer Dino Franzin, an old friend of Andy's. Before midnight, Andy was back in his hotel, the Principe e Savoia, and while passing through the lobby, a stranger came over to him to express admiration for his *Disaster* paintings of the 1960s. 'Oh, thank you,' Andy said, pleased. 'That's very nice.' He had exactly one month to live.

Fred and Chris Makos flew back with him. Makos had become the kind of young friend Andy preferred. He had a mission in life other than being a companion, and when Andy planned it so that Chris's work turned out to be, often as not, taking shots of Andy, at the Great Wall in China, or in Paris or London, that was fine.

Andy always picked up the tab and got some great pictures.

Paige described their own deepening relationship as 'like a marriage, but nothing sexual.' They were together nearly every evening.

> 'One really sweet thing that he did was on his last birthday and we were having dinner with some people and he gave me two paintings on *his* birthday. It was August 6th, his 58th birthday. He was very witty, and very reliable.'

He had a tuxedo and black tie, but it was not unusual, according to Paige, for him 'to paint his tennis shoes black because we were supposed to be formal.' He was no longer recording every conversation when he was out for a social evening, but once in those last months, he pulled out the tape recorder when they were with Holly Woodlawn because he wanted to record Holly.

On Sunday night, 16 February, Andy dropped by Serendipity with with his friend the novelist Tama Janowitz. He had entered into an agreement with her agent to buy the film rights to her new novel, *Slaves of New York*, which was to be filmed by James Ivory. He was not up to much that evening and he had to forego his usual chocolate-covered sundae, but he said hello to Stephen Bruce.

Monday was a holiday, Lincoln's and Washington's birthdays combined in that convenient way of the American government. Paige recalled that the staff had the day off:

> 'Then on Tuesday, Andy was modeling for this fashion show for a Japanese designer at the Tunnel. I met him there and he was modeling with Miles Davis. . . . He had lace coming down his sleeves, and I asked, "Why are you wearing this outfit, Andy? I don't like that look on you." . . . I had to go to another appointment, and he called me that evening and said he wasn't feeling well. Then on Wednesday, I was to lunch at the office, and Andy didn't show up, and I felt a loss of dialogue going on . . . I phoned Dr Cox [Andy's personal physician]

to see if he wanted to come to dinner and he wasn't
there. So then I called his nurse up and asked "Is Andy
there?" '

Paige was frightened. She thought she was not being told everything. The nurse told her 'He was here, but he's left.' Then she
called Andy's house and spoke with the Korean sisters who ran
the household. Neither knew anything was wrong. That night on
the phone with her, Andy was breathing very hard as he spoke.

Paige did not know that Andy's gallbladder surgery was long
overdue, that Dr Denton Cox had wanted it removed years
earlier, but Andy was afraid to enter a hospital again. He told
Beauregard Houston-Montgomery: 'If I get into a hospital again,
I won't come out. I won't survive another operation.' Stuart
Pivar recalled that whenever they would go to Sotheby's auctions,
they had to take a circuitous route to avoid passing New York
Hospital, which was Sotheby's neighbor.

Although the weekend is a very poor time to have an operation
done, Andy's doctors considered the situation critical enough for
him to undergo surgery on Saturday midday to have his gallbladder
removed.

That evening, he was alert, and Nurse Chou, a private nurse,
considered his condition stable enough though intravenous flu-
ids were flowing into his body. What happened next remains
a mystery. Sometime during the night, Nurse Chou was distracted from her patient. Some say she fell asleep; others that
she stepped out for a while. In any case, at 5:30 Sunday morning she found that he had turned blue and was unresponsive.
There seems to be some evidence that she found him dead.
New York Hospital doctors and nurses flew into the room
and could do nothing. Andy had gone, just as he knew he
would.

He was taken home to Pittsburgh for burial next to his mother
and father, taken back to a city he had left forever nearly forty
years earlier.
Andy was buried at Bethel Park, a Catholic cemetery, in the
Warhola family plot at the foot of the graves of his mother and
father. This was not his expressed wish, if we are to believe

The Philosophy, a book filled with half-stifled yearnings, random thoughts which he snatched on the wing and recorded during his usually hectic days, or which floated across his ceiling like revelations during a sleepless night:

> 'at the end of my time, when I die, I don't want to leave any leftovers. And I don't want to be a leftover. i was watching TV this week and I saw a lady go into a ray machine and disappear. That was wonderful, because matter is energy and she just disappeared. That could be a really American invention, the best American invention – to be able to disappear. I mean, that way they couldn't say you died, they couldn't say you were murdered, they couldn't say you committed suicide over somebody.
>
> 'The worst thing that could happen to you after the end of your time would be to be embalmed and laid up in a pyramid . . . .'

Andy was to get the last part of his wish. As is often the case, for a number of days he had no tombstone. His burialplace had a simple marker in the shadow of the tall black tombstone of the elder Warholas. Someone, not in jest but in reverence, placed a Campbell Soup can atop the marker, where it remained for a day or two.

In mid-February 1989, Rupert Smith died after a long and game battle against AIDS. And so there was that reunion on the other side. In fact, there was a sizeable crowd over there of people who had been close to Andy, which is reassuring to know because he did need people just as he needed his distance from them.

Among those he left behind – Jed Johnson, Gerard Malanga, Leo Castelli, Paul Morrissey, Brigid Berlin, Fred Hughes, Paige Powell, Heather Watts, Dorothy Blau, Stuart Pivar, Liza Minelli, Tama Janowitz, Vincent Fremont, Henry Geldzahler, David Bourdon, and that interesting family of Warholas – not to forget the earlier ones: Ondine, Billy Linich, Stanley Amos – there is a remarkable sense that Andy has not gone very far away. Scott Burton, a friend, said: 'That Day-Glo moonlight has gone out', but many of the others are not at all sure that it has. Even among persons he knew only in passing, his passage through this life left an indelible line. A New York cabbie wrote a letter to the *Daily News*:

> '. . . to cabbies, like me, Andy Warhol was a hero. Once, in my cab, he praised my Irish pug nose. I hold my head higher now so people can see my fine Celtic nostrils. He was always surrounded by beautiful women in silk, sequins and feather boas. He was as visible on the New York streets as the traffic signals. May the lights always stay green for Andy.'

Amen.

BIBLIOGRAPHY

BOOKS ON ANDY WARHOL AND THE FACTORY:

Bailey, David, *Andy Warhol: Transcript of David Bailey's ATV Documentary*, published jointly by Bailey Litchfield/Mathews Miller Dunbar Ltd., London, 1972.

Billeter, Erika (ed.) *Andy Warhol: Ein Buch zur Ausstellung im Kunsthaus Zürich*, Kunsthaus, Zürich, 1978.

Brown, Andreas, *Andy Warhol: His Early Works, 1947–1959*, Gotham Book Mart Gallery, New York, 1971.

Coplans, John, *Andy Warhol*, New York Graphic Society, New York, 1970.

Crone, Rainer, *Andy Warhol*, Frederick Praeger, New York, 1970.

Crone, Rainier, *Andy Warhol: A Picture Show by the Artist, The Early Work 1942–62*, Rizzoli International Publications, New York, 1988.

Feldman, Frayda and Jörg Schellmann (eds.) *Andy Warhol Prints: A Catalogue Raisonné*, Ronald Feldman Fine Arts, Inc., Abbeville Press, New York, 1985. Also Editions Schellmann, Munich.

Gidal, Peter, *Andy Warhol: Films and Paintings*, Studio Vista, New York, 1971.

Hanhardt, John G. and Gartenberg, Jon, *The Films of Andy Warhol: An Introduction*, Whitney Museum of American Art, New York, 1988.

Koch, Stephen, *Stargazer: Andy Warhol's World and His Films*, Marion Boyars Publishers, New York, 1974.

Kornbluth, Jesse, *Pre-Pop Warhol*, Panache Press at Random House, New York, 1988.

Kramer, Marcia, *Andy Warhol et Al.: The FBI File on Andy Warhol*, UnSub Press, New York, 1988.

Makos, Christopher, *Warhol: A personal photographic memoir*, W. H. Allen, London, 1988.

Pasolini, Pier Paolo, *Warhol*, Luciano Anselmino, Milan, 1976.

Ratcliff, Carter, *Andy Warhol*, Modern Masters Series, Abbeville Press, New York, 1983.

Salzano, Giancarlo, *Andy Warhol*, Magna, Rome, 1976.

Salzmann, Siegfried, *Kultstar – Warhol – Starkult*, Horst E. Visser Verlag, Duisburg, 1972.

Smith, Patrick S., *Andy Warhol's Art and Films*, UMI Research Press, Ann Arbor, 1986.

Spies, Werner, *Andy Warhol Cars,*

Solomon R. Guggenheim Museum, New York, 1988, and Kunsthalle, Tubingen, 1988.

Stein, Jean and Plimpton, George (eds.), *Edie: An American Biography*, Alfred A. Knopf, New York, 1982.

Ultra Violet (Isabelle Collin Dufresne), *Famous for 15 Minutes: My Years with Andy Warhol*, Harcourt Brace Jovanovich, New York, 1988.

Vester, Karl-Egon (ed.), *Andy Warhol*, Verlag Michael Kellner, Hamburg, 1988.

Viva, *Superstar*, G. P. Putnam's Sons, New York, 1970.

Warhol, Andy, *a: a novel*, Grove Press, New York, 1968.

Warhol, Andy, *America*, Harper & Row, New York, 1985.

Warhol, Andy, *Blue Movie: A Film*, Grove Press, New York, 1970.

Warhol, Andy, *The Philosophy of Andy Warhol (From A to B and Back Again)*, Harcourt Brace Jovanovich, New York, 1975.

Warhol, Andy with Colacello, Bob, *Andy Warhol's Exposures*, Andy Warhol/Grosset & Dunlap, New York.

Warhol, Andy with Hackett, Pat, *The Andy Warhol Diaries*, Warner Books, New York, 1989.

Warhol, Andy with Hackett, Pat, *Andy Warhol's Party Book*, Crown, New York, 1988.

Warhol, Andy with Hackett, Pat, *Popism: the Warhol '60s*, Harcourt Brace Jovanovich, New York, 1980; Harper Colophone Edition, New York, 1983.

Warhol, Andy with Malanga, Gerard, *Screen Tests: A Diary*, Kulchur Press, New York, 1967.

Warhol, Andy with Paul, David and

Shore, Stephen, *Andy Warhol's Index Book*, Random House, New York, 1967.

Whitney, David, *Andy Warhol: Portraits of the Seventies*, Whitney Museum of American Art/Random House, New York, 1979.

Wilcock, John, *The Autobiography & Sex Life of Andy Warhol*, Other Scenes, New York, 1971.

SELECTED WARHOL MUSEUM CATALOGUES:

Andy Warhol: A Retrospective, The Museum of Modern Art/Bullfinch Press, Little, Brown, Boston, New York, 1989.

Andy Warhol, Moderna Museet in Stockholm, February–March, 1968, Worldwide Books, New York, 1968.

Andy Warhol, Galerie Ileana Sonnabend, Paris, 1965.

Andy Warhol, Musée d'Art Moderne de la Ville de Paris, Paris, 1971.

Andy Warhol, in *Warhol*, Tate Gallery, London, 1971.

The Andy Warhol Collection, Sotheby's, New York, 1988.

Andy Warhol: Das graphische Werk, 1962–80.

Andy Warhol: Death and Disasters, Menil Collection and Houston Fine Arts Press, Houston, 1988.

Andy Warhol's 'Folk and Funk', Museum of American Folk Art, New York, 1977.

Andy Warhol: Ladies and Gentlemen, Mazzotta, Milan, 1975.

Andy Warhol: A Memorial, Dia Art Foundation, New York, 1987.

Andy Warhol: Portrait Screenprints, 1965–80, Arts Council of Great Britain, London, 1981.

Andy Warhol: Schweizer Portraits,
    Kunstsammlung der Stadt Thun,
    Thun, 1982.
*Andy Warhol: Ten Portraits of Jews of
    the Twentieth Century,* Lowe Art
    Museum, University of Miami,
    Miami, 1980.
*Collaborations. Andy Warhol, Jean-
    Michel Basquiat,* 21 November
    1988–21 January 1989, The
    Mayor Rowan Gallery, London.
Raid the Icebox I with Andy Warhol,
    Museum of Art, Rhode Island
    School of Design, Providence,
    1969.
*Remembering Andy: Warhol's Recent
    Works,* Galerie Watari, Tokyo,
    1987.
*'Success is a job in New York . . .':
    The Early Art and Business of
    Andy Warhol,* Grey Art Gallery
    and Study Center at New York
    University and the Carnegie
    Museum of Art, New York
    and Pittsburgh, 1989.
Warhol '80: Serie Reversal, Museum
    moderner Kunst, Museum des
    20. Jahrhunderts, 1981.
Warhol/Beuys/Polke, Milwaukee Art
    Museum, Milwaukee, 1987.
Warhol Shadows, Menil Foundation,
    Houston, 1981.

PROMOTIONAL BOOKS PUBLISHED BY WARHOL:

A Is an Alphabet, with Ralph T.
    'Corkie' Ward, 1953
Love Is a Pink Cake, with Ralph
    T. 'Corkie' Ward, 1953
25 Cats Name Sam and One Blue Pussy,
    with Charles Lisanby, 1954
A la Recherche du Shoe Perdu, with
    Ralph Pomeroy, 1955
In the Bottom of My Garden, 1955

A Gold Book by Andy Warhol, 1957
Wild Raspberries, with Suzie Frank-
    furt, 1959
All of the above promotional books
were printed in New York, most of
them by printer Seymour Berlin.

BOOK BY JULIA WARHOLA:

Holy Cats by Andy Warhol's Mother,
    Andy Warhol, New York, 1956

LITERARY QUARTERLY BY WARHOL:

*Intransit: The Andy Warhol–Gerard
    Malanga Monster Issue,* Toad
    Press, Eugene (Oregon), 1968.

BOOKS RELATED TO WARHOL AND HIS LIFE AND TIMES:

Alloway, Lawrence, *American Pop
    Art.* Collier Books, New York,
    1974.
Alloway, Lawrence, *Lichtenstein,*
    Abbeville Press in Modern
    Masters Series, New York,
    1983.
Amaya, Mario, *Pop Art . . . and
    After,* Viking Press, New York,
    1966.
Antonio, Emile de and Tuchman,
    Mitch, *Painters Painting: A Candid
    History of the Modern Art Scene,
    1940–70,* Abbeville Press, New
    York, 1984.
Bockris, Victor and Malanga, Gerard,
    *Uptight: The Velvet Underground
    Story,* Quill Press, New York,
    1983.
Bosworth, Patricia, *Diane Arbus,*
    Alfred A. Knopf, New York,
    1984.

Canaday, John, *Embattled Critic: Views on Modern Art*, Farrar, Straus & Cudahy, New York, 1962.

Clarke, Gerald, *Capote*, Simon & Schuster, New York, 1988.

Cooper, Douglas, *The Work of Graham Sutherland*, David McKay Company, Inc., New York, 1962.

Crichton, Michael, *Jasper Johns*, Harry N. Abrams, Inc., in association with the Whitney Museum of American Art, New York, 1977.

d'Harnoncourt, Anne and McShine, Kynaston L. (eds.), *Marcel Duchamp*, The Museum of Modern Art, New York, 1973.

D'Oench, Ellen G. and Feinberg, Jean (eds.), *Jim Dine Prints: 1977–85*, Icon Editions, Harper & Row, New York, 1986.

Ellman, Richard, *Oscar Wilde*, Hamish Hamilton, London, 1987.

Federal Bureau of Investigation, *Andy Warhol: File* 145–4011 (Freedom of Information/Privacy Acts Release), Washington D.C., 1989.

Finch, Christopher, *Pop Art: Objects and Image*, Dutton, New York, 1968.

Geldzahler, Henry, *Pop Art, 1955–70*, International Cultural Corporation of Australia Ltd., Sydney, 1985.

Gerdts, William H., *The Great American Nude*, Praeger, New York, 1974.

Gitlin, Todd, *The Sixties: Years of Hope, Days of Rage*, Bantam Books, New York, 1987.

Goldman, Judith, *James Rosenquist*, Viking/Penguin, New York, 1985.

Gruen, John, *The New Bohemia*, Grosset & Dunlap, New York, 1967.

Harrison, Helen A., *Larry Rivers*, An Artnews Book, Harper & Row, New York, 1987.

Haskell, Barbara, *Blam! The Explosion of Pop, Minimalism, and Performance, 1958–64*, Whitney Museum of American Art in association with W. W. Norton, New York, 1984.

Kitaj, *Kitaj: Paintings, Drawings, Pastels*, Thames & Hudson, London, 1983.

Kligman, Ruth, *Love Affair*, Morrow, New York, 1974.

Kramer, Hilton, *The Revenge of the Philistines: Art and Culture 1972–84*, Secker & Warburg, London, 1986.

Leymarie, Jean, *Balthus*, Skira/Rizzoli International, Geneva and New York, 1982.

Lippard, Lucy, R. (ed.), *Pop Art*, Thames & Hudson, London, 1967.

Magocsi, Paul Robert, *Our People: Carpatho-Rusyns and Their Descendants in North America*, Multicultural History Society of Ontario, Toronto, 1984.

Oldenburg, Claes, *Claes Oldenburg: Drawings and Prints*, Chelsea House, New York, 1969.

Oldenburg, Claes with Williams, Emmett, *Store Days: Documents from The Store (1961) and Ray Gun Theater (1962)*, Something Else Press, New York, 1967.

Pierre, José, *Pop Art: An Illustrated Dictionary*, Methuen, London, 1977.

Raphaell, Katrina, *Crystal Enlightenment: The Transforming Properties of Crystals and Healing Stones*,

Aurora Press, Santa Fe, 1985.

Rorem, Ned, *The Final Diary*, Holt, Rinehart & Winston, New York, 1974.

Rose, Barbara, *American Painting: The Twentieth Century*, Skira, Geneva, 1969.

Rose, Barbara, *Claes Oldenburg*, The Museum of Modern Art, New York, 1970.

Rosenberg, Bernard and Fliegel, Norris, *The Vanguard Artist: Portrait and Self-Portrait*, Quadrangle Books, Chicago, 1965.

Rublowsky, John, *Pop Art*, Basic Books, New York, 1965.

Russell, John and Gablik, Suzi, *Pop Art Redefined*, Praeger, New York, 1969.

Sandler, Irving, *American Art of the 1960s*, Harper & Row, New York, 1988.

Sandler, Irving, *The New York School: The Painters and Sculptors of the Fifties*, Harper & Row, New York, 1979.

Scheugl, Hans, *Sexualität und Neurose im Film: Die Kinomythen von Griffith bis Warhol*, W. Heyne Verlag, Munich, 1978.

Shapiro, David, *Jim Dine*, Harry N. Abrams, New York, 1981.

Stealingworth, *Tom Wesselmann*, Abbeville Press, New York, 1980.

Steegmuller, Francis, *Cocteau: A Biography*, Constable, 1986.

Teal, Donn, *The Gay Militants*, Stein & Day, New York, 1971.

Tomkins, Calvin, *Off the Wall: Robert Rauschenberg and the Art World of Our Time*, Doubleday, Garden City, 1980.

Tomkins, Calvin, *The Scene: Reports on Post-Modern Art*, The Viking Press, New York, 1976.

Tuchman, Maurice, *A Report on the Art and Technology Program of the Los Angeles County Museum of Art 1967–71*, Los Angeles County Museum of Art, Los Angeles, 1971.

Vickers, Hugo, *Cecil Beaton: The Authorized Biography*, Weidenfeld & Nicolson, London, 1985.

Viola, Jerome, *The Painting and Teaching of Philip Pearlstein*, Watson-Guptill, New York, 1983.

von Hoffman, Nicholas, *Citizen Cohn: The Life and Times of Roy Cohn*, Doubleday, New York, 1988.

Walker, Alexander, *Garbo: A Portrait*, Weidenfeld & Nicolson, London, 1980.

Williams, Hiram, *Notes for a Young Painter*, Prentice-Hall, Englewood Cliffs, 1984.

Wilson, Colin, *The Outsider*, Pan Books, London, 1978.

INDEX